NO GO THE BOGEYMAN

NO GO THE BOGEYMAN

Scaring, Lulling, and Making Mock

Marina Warner

Chatto & Windus
LONDON

Published in 1998

2 4 6 8 10 9 7 5 3 1

This edition published in Great Britain in 1998 by
Chatto & Windus
Random House, 20 Vauxhall Bridge Road,
London SW1V 2SA

Random House Australia (Pty) Limited
20 Alfred Street, Milsons Point, Sydney,
New South Wales 2061, Australia

Random House New Zealand Limited
18 Poland Road, Glenfield,
Auckland 10, New Zealand

Random House South Africa (Pty) Limited
Endulini, 5A Jubilee Road, Parktown 2193, South Africa

Random House UK Limited Reg. No. 954009

A CIP catalogue record for this book
is available from the British Library

ISBN 0 7011 6593 6

Designed by Margaret Sadler
Index by Vicky Robinson

Papers used by Random House UK Limited are natural,
recyclable products made from wood grown in sustainable forests.
The manufacturing processes conform to the environmental
regulations of the country of origin.

Typeset by SX Composing DTP, Rayleigh, Essex
Printed and bound in Great Britain by
Butler & Tanner Limited, Frome, Somerset

*Frontispiece: Photo by Cristina García Rodero, Spain, 1980
(see note on p.423)*

Futile—the Winds—
To a Heart in port—
Done with the Compass—
Done with the Chart—

Emily Dickinson

As rational metaphysics teaches that man becomes all things by understanding them (*homo intelligentia fit omnia*), this imaginative metaphysics shows that man becomes all things by not understanding them (*homo non intelligendo fit omnia*). Perhaps the latter proposition is truer than the former, for when man understands he extends his mind and comprehends all things, but when he does not understand he makes things out of himself and becomes them by transforming himself into them.

Giambattista Vico, *Principles of New Science*

When children, frightened of the wolf at the window, were asked what did it want to do, the little boy replied, 'Gobble me up.' The little girl said, 'Let's ask it.'

Darrian Leader,
*Why Do Women Write More
Letters Than They Post?*

CONTENTS

PREFACE

This book began with the problem of men. After *From the Beast to the Blonde* was published, many people asked me why had I concentrated so much on women and on the female cast of fairy tales; they wanted to know about the male characters, too. I began to explore stories in this light and was led to the theme of ogres, since princes were on the whole too insipid. But the frighteners of fairy tales and related popular fiction and artefacts are not exclusively male, nor always specially masculine in character, so I found that *No Go the Bogeyman* took another direction, away from the historical study of gender towards a cultural exploration of fear, its vehicles, and its ambiguous charge of pleasure and pain.

The book's title comes from Louis MacNeice's poem, 'Bagpipe Music', which contains a famous verse beginning, 'It's no go the Yogi-man'. I thought he was playing with an existing nursery rhyme, but I have not been able to find it: the bogeyman has remained a ghost behind the lines.

The subject is a huge one, and I have concentrated only on some aspects that struck me as neglected and set aside several important figures who have contributed to the theme: Dracula and Hitchcock, to name but two. Vampires, *film noir* and Hitchcockian suspense have been dealt with admirably by other writers. Nor have I grappled directly with the philosophical problem of evil, which lurks behind the looming spectre of the bogey and which is increasingly attracting writers' and thinkers' attention. I hope that my arguments convey my belief that there are particular acts of wrongdoing, but no force of evil itself.

Friends and colleagues have helped me beyond any words of acknowledgement I could write here; I have profited from conversations, perceptions, references, reading, and guidance of all sorts from Mary Douglas, Rudolf Dekker, David Scrase, Anne Barton, Wendy Doniger O'Flaherty, Bob Davis, Mariët Westermann, Edmund White, John Woolrich, Mark Dorrian, Malcolm Jones, Peter Dronke, John Forrester, Peter Wiseman, Estela Welldon, Lisa Appignanesi, Helen Langdon, Jacqueline Burckhardt, Clio Whitaker, Jacqueline Simpson, Christopher Gill, Sarah Lawson Lucas, Anne Kearney, Roy Foster, Marcia Reed, Jeremy Barlow, Anthony Barnett, Maya Slater, Gillian Avery, Ruth Bottigheimer, Jack Zipes, Louise Neri and Margaret Anne Doody. William Christian, Jr., who suggested the Patum of Berga as a relevant theme, has helped me unstintingly with wise

counsel and reading. To them all, much thanks, and hopes that the resulting book will give them pleasure. At the Warburg Institute, London, several people have been unfailingly generous with their suggestions, but I'm
grateful above all to Paul Taylor and Elizabeth McGrath. Antony Griffiths
of the British Museum led me through many wonders in the Print Room.
John Rawlins and Robert Davidson of the Carnegie Museum of Natural
History, Pittsburgh, conducted me through their wondrous archives of
insects. Eleni Vassilika and Penny Wilson of the Fitzwilliam Museum
guided me to magic amulets; at the BBC, Beaty Rubens traced dozens of
recordings of lullabies from all over the world. I am very grateful to Dña
Rocio Arnaez for giving me access to the Goya drawings in the Prado,
Madrid, and to Isabel Fernandez for her help in Spain. Nigel Glendinning
has been exceptionally generous in reading and commenting on my pas-
sages about Goya. I am very grateful indeed to him. The artists Janine
Antoni and Bobby Baker most kindly supplied images from their work; as
did the photographer Cristina García Rodero.

I have been richly helped by Clive Hurst and the staff of the John Johnson and Opie collections at the Bodleian Library, Oxford; by Leslie
McGrath at the Osborne Collection, Toronto; by Andrea Immel at the
Cotsen Collection, Princeton, and by Richard Crangle of the Bill Douglas
Centre, Exeter University. Rosemary Hall did some most helpful early
footwork on bibliographies. The London Library is as ever a treasure
house. The British Library staff, put upon by fate and by policy, were inde-
fatigably patient and knowledgeable. The notes attempt to chart the
research that informs this book, and give leads to interested readers; a full
bibliography would have become unwieldy in a book that seeks to suggest
lines of inquiry.

Mary-Kay Wilmers persuaded me, firmly and perceptively, to confront
themes I was avoiding; Carmen Callil supported the idea of the book from
the start, with verve and a true friend's warmth. I have been extremely for-
tunate in my publishers. Like many children today, I have more than one
family; they have truly helped me thrive: Alison Samuel at Chatto & Windus read the drafts with energy and care; I have benefited very much from
her criticisms. Elisabeth Sifton, of Farrar, Straus, and Giroux, groomed my
text so finely that I felt like a racehorse. I'm very grateful, too, to Philippa
Lewis for her help with picture research, and to Catherine Newell; as well
as to Beth Humphries for her careful copyediting. Peggy Sadler, who
designed the book, worked patiently and scrupulously throughout. My
agents Gill Coleridge in London and Amanda Urban in New York gave me
spirited support from the start. I hope that my efforts repay their confi-

dence and all their kindnesses.

I gave several talks while the book was in progress and such deadlines galvanize one's thoughts, so I am most grateful to Hermione Lee, who asked me to give the Patrides Lecture at York, and inspired me with questions, responses and suggestions throughout, to Michael Wood, who invited me to Princeton; to Edward Said, who asked me to talk at his seminar at Columbia; to Warren Chernaik, who invited me to give the John Coffin lecture at University College, London, and to Jacqueline Rose who chaired it; to Piero Boitani, who organized the *Ulisse* conference in Rome in May, 1996; to Colin MacCabe, at whose seminar in Pittsburgh I spoke; to Peter Hulme, who convened a symposium at Essex University on cannibalism; to the British Council; and to Andrew Norris, who looked after a lecture tour in the Caribbean where I was able to research the banana theme; to Catherine and Richard Thomas in Barbados; to Rachel Jones who invited me to the Centre for Classical Studies, University of Warwick; to the *Confraternitas Historica* of Sidney Sussex College, Cambridge; to Elaine Showalter and English Showalter, for their symposium on fatherhood at the Institut Français, London, to Richard Poirier and Suzanne Hymans for publishing work in progress in *Raritan*; to Cáit ni Cheallacháin, of the Kate O'Brien Society, Limerick; to Carmel Roulston and the University of Ulster where I taught in 1994; to Lissa Paul, who invited me to the MLA in Toronto, 1997. My thanks, too, to Ann Sutherland Harris, who invited me to the University of Pittsburgh, where I wrote much of the first draft of the book; to Medha Patel, my research assistant there, and to Matthew Roper, who was unfailingly helpful with illustration material from the art history department's slide library. Trinity College, Cambridge, which invited me as a Visiting Fellow Commoner for 1998, generously created time for me to buff and shine the final draft.

Helena Ivins has given me wise counsel, as well as patiently hunting for references lost and found; she has been altogether necessary to the making of the book.

Without Nick Groom, this book would be thin gruel. I thank him from my heart.

Marina Warner
Kentish Town, Spring 1998

PROLOGUE

Think of a time near the beginning: not at the start of history, but beyond it, in that outer circle of retrospection where dates turn into foam towers of bubble-like zeros. Imagine one of those divine children who found civilizations, start religions, provide origins in our stories. A baby. A boy. He sees shadows move around him: tall figures with deathly pale faces are approaching; they loom over his cot, giant faces, coming closer. Their intense pallor magnifies their hands and faces and attenuates their dark, swathed bodies, but they are offering playthings and sweeties with their big white fingers; they are wheedling and clucking from their whitened lips, which open onto the dark gaping void of their mouths, from which rise their voices, falsely high-pitched.

The baby does not know that the giants' pallor is faked, a daubing of gypsum over their usual earthen complexion, assumed perhaps to make them resemble him, to look like one of his kind. Or did they want to reveal themselves as spectres from another world where light does not reach, as in the mulch where mushrooms grow, where all is blanched and blind, like vine weevils? In either case, he recoils from their strangeness, though he cannot know they are beings risen from the magma, the hot core of ore and rock where they live. But their proffered gifts entice him: a doll with limbs that bend at clever joints, a pinecone, a rattle, shiny golden apples, a mirror, a set of knuckle bones, a soft wad from a fleece.

The toys delight the baby. But he recognizes that if he takes their gifts he will somehow pass into their power; though he is an infant, he is a wise child. He knows he should not take anything from strangers, and certainly not eat anything they press on him. But he begins to play with the mirror they hold out to him, and, fascinated by the distorted image of himself that appears in its curved surface, he drops his guard, and finds himself in their grip. They assault him with a knife forged in Tartarus, the underworld. He begins to twist and turn to escape. In their grasp he shape-shifts through a marvellous sequence of all the creatures and forms he has ever known; they struggle to hold him as he sloughs one body and then another, changing from a lion to a horse to a dragon to a tiger to a bull. But in this last shape the baby becomes less slippery, less lithe; the giants seize him by his horns and hooves and tear him apart. They toss his dismembered body into a pot and stew him, then they ladle out the pieces and skewer them, setting them to roast on a spit. When the meats are ready, they set to feasting on the baby.

The gruesome banquet is interrupted, too late, by a woman, who takes an interest in the child, as his great-aunt, sister to his grandmother. She disturbs the feast after the giants have demolished the small body. Only the heart remains, still beating; and they have also tossed aside his bones. Athena—for the belated good fairy is she, goddess of wisdom—takes the infant's pulsing heart and enshrines it in a clay figure she fashions from the same white gypsum that the giants used for their masquerade; it stands in well for the human flesh of the baby. Athena then breathes on her creation; the statue with the living heart in it quickens. It moves, it breathes.

This Orphic myth of the birth of Dionysus, god of wine and pleasure and excess, appears in different variations. In another story, Athena infuses the still-beating heart into a foetus, the child whom the mortal beauty Semele has conceived by Zeus. Semele is one of the numerous women who inspire the ever vigorous attentions of the father of the gods, but she makes the fatal—hubristic—mistake of asking to see him in his full divine glory. Zeus warns her the sight will overwhelm her, but she insists. He shows himself to her; the dazzle and thunder of his godhead blast her and consume her till nothing is left but ashes and the infant among them. Zeus then rescues the baby and sews him into his thigh. This will be another miraculous paternal parturition: Athena was born from his head after he swallowed Metis, goddess of cunning intelligence; Dionysus emerges from his father's leg a few months later.

Before he is reborn in the shape of Dionysus, the baby whom the Titans eat is called Zagreus; his mother is Persephone. The Titans' lures belong both in her cult and in Dionysus', where they have a ritual function: mirrors and puppets are common instruments of magic, and the pinecone was sacred to Persephone. Probably a very ancient myth, and Eastern in origin, the story of Zagreus' death and resurrection is connected to the Orphic mystery religion whose rites focused on a ritual meal. It has, however, come down only in tiny fragments of classical texts or in late, Hellenistic sources—through the historian Diodorus Siculus, writing in Sicily in the first century A.D., and in the Dionysiaca *of Nonnos of Panopolis in the fifth, who was disseminating classical myths so late that he also managed a Greek paraphrase of St. John's gospel.*

Persephone conceived Zagreus by Zeus, who visited her in the form of a snake, bequeathing serpentine powers of metamorphosis to the infant. This union took place before she descended into the underworld to become its queen, and though mythological chronology is always confused, overlapping and contradictory, maybe her abduction by Hades, lord of the underworld, took place soon after Zagreus' birth, hence her disastrous absence at the time of the giants' sinister visit. It is difficult to be sure, since Persephone was also Kore the Maiden, when she was raped in the spring meadow where she was picking flowers.

Whatever his mother the goddess was doing or suffering, the father of Zagreus–Dionysus remains consistent throughout the permutations of the story. When Dionysus bursts from Zeus' thigh, he is twice born of his own father. The myth serves to magnify Zeus and corroborates his cult. Another chapter in the history of Zeus' emergence as the pre-eminent, generative power among the gods, it pictures him triumphing ingeniously over his predecessors, the giants and the Titans; it relates to the struggles for authority between the old and the young that are woven into the fabric of ogre stories.

For the final outcome of the story is this: Zeus is so angry with his brothers, the giants, for their savage assault on his son that he hurls his thunderbolts against them and burns them to ashes. So the Titans, who ruled first in Olympus, are overthrown. From their cinder dust, according to one story, the race of humans then arises. Plato remarks that our wickedness was inherited from our 'Titan nature'. The word titanos, *in Greek, means 'quicklime'—the white powder obtained from firing lime and marble has such a devastating effect on flesh, burning it up on contact, that it is used in burial pits. Being also white and chalky in appearance, it is often confused with gypsum. Those spooky giants who loomed over the baby in his cradle were covered in the very matter that would become human flesh: they embody the contradiction of symbols in that they mimic death, they bring death, but the result of their intervention is new life. The giants and cannibals are deposed, the rightful father established pre-eminently, mothers are sidelined, even combusted. The defeat of bogeys provides a charter myth to justify heroes and their societies, to identify the place of safety from them, as in the game of He, where you can hide from the pursuer in a designated safe haven, or home. After their disappearance, human society, culture, and law begin.*

INTRODUCTION

Reading and sometimes tempting Nurse to tell
Of witches, pirates, angels, devils even. . .
Comfort and Fear—these two alone made Life.
But while the Fear too often stood alone. . .
The Comfort always had been mixed with Fear.

Graham Greene, 'Sad Cure'

 No Go the Bogeyman is about fear; it faces one of the most everyday yet least examined of human feelings, and it describes three of the principal methods of coping with anxieties grounded in common experience, as well as the nameless terrors that come in the dark and assail the mind. It is also a collection of stories about the bogeys who materialize fear in some kind of living shape, about their character and their ways; it traces themes and metaphors that refract kaleidoscopically throughout the material of terror.

Scariness has gained ground as a pleasure: it is perhaps a modern affect, a symptom of the late twentieth century, of the mixed feelings we suffer when new beginnings and new endings collide at the end of the millennium. So this book also explores the paradox that the imagination often stirs up dread on purpose for its own sake, as well as for the mind's stimulation. Attitudes to scariness change over time: the special flavour of scary things—funny peculiar and funny ha-ha all at once—already crepitates like a dried snakeskin in the traditional nursery tale, but it has swelled into a contemporary, loving obsession with monsters and other horrors. Fear has probably always played some part in amusement, but its peculiar pleasures have increasingly become an end in themselves; it is the defining flavour of the modern sensibility, which first surfaced in the perverse and ironical fantasies of fairy tale at the end of the seventeenth century, where dread was cultivated as an aesthetic thrill. Charles Perrault's version of 'Little Red Riding Hood' has survived sturdily alongside 'improvements', and many children and adults sigh with satisfaction at its grim and succinct conclusion, when the wolf simply succeeds in gobbling up the heroine. Needless to say, not everyone enjoys being scared. But the ambiguous satisfactions of scariness have been cultivated more intensely during this century than ever before. Many films today, with their brilliant use of new technologies—of animatronics and computer-enhanced imaging—are able

Der Kinderfresser or Child-Guzzler *(a popular figure on Carnival broadsheets)
snatches young victims, who react with graphic physical terror. Hans Weiditz,
woodcut, early sixteenth century.*

to conjure the terrors of bogeys to the life: from the devils in *The Omen* and other horror movies to the fearsome swarms in *Starship Trooper* and the giant cockroach ('the Bug') in *Men in Black*. *No Go the Bogeyman* draws from this repertory of images as well as from more mandarin literature and art.

Uttering the fear, describing the phantom, generally scaring oneself and the audience constitutes one way of dealing with the feelings that giants, ogres, child-guzzlers, ghouls, vampires, cannibals, and all their kind inspire. Dreaming of their horrors and desires and crimes, exaggerating them, reinforcing them, repeating them over and over again, works to squeeze pleasure out of the confrontation. Aristotle commented on this contradiction between direct experience and the aesthetics of representation: 'Inborn in all of us is the instinct to enjoy works of imitation. What happens in actual experience is evidence of this; for we enjoy looking at the most accurate representations of things which in themselves we find painful to see, such as the forms of the lowest animals and of corpses.'

But the scared response is not identical with this brand of horror. Being scared by a story or an image—scared witless, scared to death—can deliver ecstatic relief from the terror that the thing itself would inspire if it were to appear for real. That children's word 'scary' covers responses ranging from pure terror to sheer delight, and the condition of being scared is becoming increasingly sought after not only as a source of pleasure but as a means of strengthening the sense of being alive, of having a command over self. Hellish themes—infanticide, damnation—seep into the most light-hearted songs and stories for the nursery current by the end of the eighteenth century and then spread into Gothic entertainment in various genres. Both children and adults, hearing the tales, playing the games, contemplating the images and even learning the songs, find their double in the mirror that these fragments hold up to them: they are made to stare at the possibility of their non-being, at death itself, but they then discover that they are still alive, outside the tale. Thus, the state of pleasurable fear has emerged, in our own times, as a common response to philosophy's old command, 'Know thyself'; the changing features of the bogeyman mirror the insecurities and aggression of those who see him.

The taste for fear has spawned a profusion of terrifying yet seductive beasts, from Maurice Sendak's wondrous 'Wild Things' to the vampires of popular macabre horror to stalkers who come after you for their own lethal ends in murder mysteries and slasher films. Gruesome and violent tales range in their effect from awe to laughter, from terror to pleasure, but for the moment there is nothing like a flesh-eating giant coming for his prey to make a child thrill and giggle, while the adult recounting the episode feels delight in taking the child to the edge. But the bogeymen (and -women) whom the stories and images evoke cast their shadows across not only infantile material; adult myths, legends and writings of many varied types are vividly preoccupied with ogres and their appetites, from the *Odyssey*, where so many of these cannibals make a dramatic—and tragic—appearance, as we shall see, to Jonathan Swift's 'A Modest Proposal', in which he notoriously satirizes British policy towards famine in Ireland by suggesting with impassive rationalism the simple economic solution that the Irish eat their babies.

❖   ❖   ❖

The states of mind or feelings that art can excite have been helpfully distinguished in Sanskrit aesthetics, where they are called *rasas*, from a word meaning 'juice' or 'essence'. A fully achieved work of art should flow with all nine of them: their names might be transposed into English as wonder, joy, sexual pleasure, pity, anguish, anger, terror, disgust and laughter. Few artefacts or texts express them all, and the harmonious ideal of blending different juices does not flow strongly through Western cultural aspirations. But the *rasas* do offer a ready analytic tool for different registers of artistic expression, and in some cases they stimulate particular parts of the brain. For example, disgust, which is excited by a threat of contamination, sparks a different brain circuitry from fear, which is excited by a threat to survival. The two may combine into a reaction of horror, as in the response to assault, to plague, to decay, but they are distinguished in the brain in the same way as savoury and sour are sifted by the taste buds on the tongue. The tendency to grotesque imagery, to thrills and spills, in contemporary culture has introduced a new hedonistic twist to this emotional complex.

The history of some words connected to fear casts an ambiguous light: the Latin verbs, *terrere*, to terrify or frighten, and *tremere*, to tremble or quake, are still yielding epithets, in Romance languages, for the most common emotional responses, frequently with positive or intensive meaning: so-and-so or such-and-such is *terrific*, *tremendous*, or simply *terribly* nice. The variations of meaning in these derivations present tricky territory for a non-native speaker, for they slide inconsistently between positive and negative: 'tremendous', in English-English and in American-English delivers high praise, unequivocally; in Italian, by contrast, *tremendo* is currently the most popular of all dismissive adjectives, still close to Latin *tremendus*. In French, 'Ce n'est pas terrible' means something's not up to much; however, in the same language, to be *terrible* does not quite mean the opposite;

The tyrant Lycaon killed a man and cooked him; for this cannibal crime, Zeus turned him into the first werewolf. The illustrator of La Bible des poètes, *Paris, 1493, set the scene in a medieval kitchen.*

by contrast, in Italy, *terribile*, though not very commonly used, resembles English, being a derogatory term.

'Tremendous' as an English term of praise entered spoken usage in the nineteenth century, a late development of meaning that interestingly coincides with the nursery domestication of 'bogeyman' as a term. The ninth edition of Bailey's *Dictionary* (1740) still gave 'that is much to be feared, dreaded'. The change in desired response denoted by the word from 'astonishingly terrible', as in Dr. Johnson's *Dictionary*, depends on the acquired taste for the sublime and the related pleasures of the Gothic. The designation 'terrible', on the other hand, retains its pejorative character through the same period, and since then this meaning has thickened and hardened: 'A terrible beauty is born' reverberates with the aesthetic of the sublime, but W.B. Yeats is purposefully striking out for lofty effect through the intended 'sublime' anachronism. 'Awful', by contrast, has moved in the opposite direction: that which once inspired awe (a positive state of religious feeling) now merely meets with dismissal. Interestingly, 'awesome', a comparatively recent term of approval among the young, annexes another archaism to fill the gap left by the loss of 'awful'.

Edmund Burke, in his essay of 1757 on the Sublime, singles out spectacle and the sense of sight when defining this aesthetic of fear: 'No passion so effectually robs the mind of all its powers of acting and reasoning as fear; for fear being an apprehension of pain or death, it operates in a manner that resembles actual pain. Whatever is terrible, therefore, with regard to sight, is sublime, too.' The bogey's spectral character induces this response, which gained social and cultural approval around the same time as the publication of frightening fairy tales and verses for children began to be widespread.

The body tremulous, trembling, quaking: the language of sensation draws on these somatic symptoms of disarray, from Hellenistic romances like the *Aethiopica* of Heliodorus of Emesa in the third century AD through to the eighteenth-century moment of *sensibilité*. The affected organs vary in the passionate body—the liver was demoted by the heart—but empiricism does not consistently generate separate lexicons for the passions of love and terror. Emotions that thrill and pierce and shake or otherwise affect the body return presence and being to the person, recall us to our physical existence; this variety of pain does not obliterate the sense of self, but enhances it. 'Thrill' comes from 'drill', and means to pierce; so it is perhaps worth anticipating, in our confused times, that by analogy with 'tremendous' and 'thrilling' a similar shift may overtake other negative epithets. Lovers also turn pale and wan, but so far 'aghast' and 'appalling' and 'excruciating' and 'horrible' and 'dreadful' do not characterize the sublime or describe feelings of pleasure in the same way as 'thrilling' or 'stunning'. Of these, 'horrible' is possibly moving fastest towards approval, even enthusiasm, as in 'It's *horribly* good'.

The Orphic myth of Zagreus strikingly illuminates the character of fantastic terrors and dramatizes the different stratagems to allay, banish or defeat them. Magnifying menace of all kinds through the telling of tales has become one of the most frequently adopted measures of diminishing terror and substituting pleasure. To court fear and dread, to dwell on their catalysts with greedy intensity, represents a quest for catharsis through sensation, through the rush and high produced by an aesthetic of fear. Part One of *No Go the Bogeyman* consequently takes up the theme of the invented and imagined predator or ogre himself, from his ancient manifestations in the Titans who assault the baby Zagreus, to Kronos (or Saturn), the cannibal patriarch of the Olympians, to modern fairy-story giants who slaver after human babies or young flesh, or to dinosaurs in a feeding frenzy in horror films made for children today, like *Jurassic Park: The Lost World*. Appetite defines bogeys, and many myths explore obsessively a deep and insistent fear: that the thing that comes in the dark wants to gobble you up. Much of this lurid cannibalistic material acts as metaphorical disguise for issues of authority, procreation, and intergenerational rivalry: it relates ways of confronting the foundations of the sense of identity and the self and of the self's historical and social place. The changing character

In a comfortable Dutch bourgeois drawing-room (Engraving, Amsterdam, 1714), a child runs from his father playing monsters; and OPPOSITE *in a wilderness surveyed by a monkey, the symbol of canny laughter and art's tricks . . .*

of such diabolical or monstrous beings as infanticides reveals ideas about authority in the family and beyond it; fatherhood, its limits and its obligations are called into question above all in these grisly tales of cannibal banquets.

Bogey figures sometimes tear their victims limb from limb in their raw state, devouring them alive—or as carrion, as in the case of Grendel, the fiend in the Anglo-Saxon epic *Beowulf*. Bogeys can be black dogs, like the Padfoot feared in the North Country or the Skriker of Yorkshire and Lancashire. All of them death portents, they often specifically pursue children, like the Tankerabogus of Devon and Somerset, or Black Annis, feared in

. . . a small human flees furry beasts. (George Dance, pen and ink, c. 1790).

Leicestershire for her devouring of young lambs as well as babies, or Tom Dockin, 'a bogey with iron teeth who devours bad children', or Raw-Head-and-Bloody-Bones, a.k.a. Tommy Rawhead. He was 'a widely distributed nursery goblin, who dragged children down into marlpits or lurked in dark cupboards', Katharine Briggs writes in her valuable glossary of fairies and other goblins.

Monsters, ogres, and beasts who kill and eat human flesh dramatize the complexity of the issue: they variously represent abominations against society, civilization and family, yet are vehicles for expressing ideas of proper behaviour and due order. Female bogeys are equally hungry and

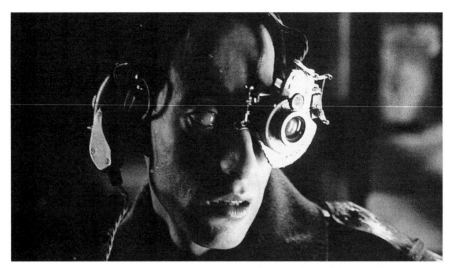

In The City of Lost Children, *1995, a Jeunet & Caro film, a band of Cyclopes, robotic descendants of the giants of antiquity, raid earth to steal children.*

thirsty, but they frequently tend to preside over kitchens: their outrages take place in domestic settings, by the hearth or the oven. Any hard-and-fast distinction between witches and ogres ultimately fails, however: Grendel's mother also seizes her living prey to feast on it almost instantly, while Lycaon, the sacrilegious host in Ovid's *Metamorphoses*, turns his victims into pies as domestically as the unlikely hero of a Stephen Sondheim musical, the demon barber of Victorian London, Sweeney Todd. Moreover, many victims of the witch-hunts were men, though this fact is often overlooked. However, female witches have been researched, analysed and debated with far more perception and intensity than ogres, and misogyny explored more richly than the fear of men, or its expression the male villains of popular storytelling, as killers, as predators, as abductors.

Cannibals magnify the normal hyperbolically, as if in a fairground hall of mirrors, and the issue of survival through eating spreads across this dark and bewildering place. At certain intervals throughout, this book offers a 'reflection', for example on Goya's terrifying painting known as *Saturn Devouring His Child*. It is as if, in the mirror with which the baby Zagreus is tempted, a single image, or connected group of images, lies waiting to be lingered over in close-up, intensifying the focus on the meaning of the material surrounding it.

The question 'Who eats and who gets eaten?' reverberates in the material of bogeydom. How cannibalistic impulses beat in the cultural imaginary and what significance they carry can still be heard in the tread

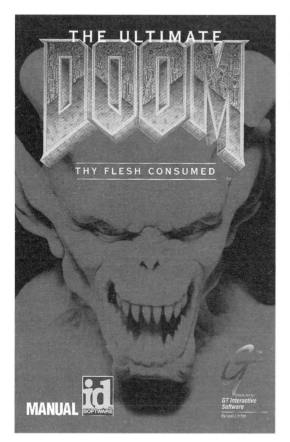

'Doom: Thy Flesh Consumed': the apocalyptic motif that colours legends about ogres, cannibals and hell lives on in this highly popular 1990s video game.

of the flesh-eating ogre and his progeny, whether he rattles his bones, strides in seven-league boots or comes whiffling through the tulgey wood. Control of food lies at the heart of the first werewolf story, the transformation of Lycaon, of famous fairy tales like 'Hansel and Gretel' and less familiar ones that feature ogres and ogresses like Baba Yaga. Vampires and the undead progeny of Bram Stoker's *Dracula* (1897), who walk abroad in the shadows of our culture, form part of the larger family of fatal monsters who cannibalize humans. Food—procuring it, preparing it, cooking it, eating it—dominates the material as the overriding image of survival; consuming it offers contradictory metaphors of life and civilization as well as barbarity and extinction.

Further chapters of *No Go the Bogeyman* look at classical fantasies, and at divine gorging on children and adults; Christian transmutations of the theme then follow. Metaphors bequeathed by classical and Christian nightmares of obliteration, including the cannibal Cyclops, the marine hybrid Scylla, and the ever-engulfing mouth of hell, inform contemporary terrors in a variety of ways, and their *Doppelgänger* and descendants are raised in order to contain and control them. The intertwined imagery of communion and cannibalism is discussed in Chapters 4 and 5. Sinners turn on spits roasted by devils in the fires of hell, while the sacrament of communion, partaking of the body of Christ in the Eucharist, places symbolic flesh-eating at the heart of the faith. The feast of Corpus Christi, or the Body of Christ, which recalls a famous medieval miracle in which a consecrated host bled, is celebrated in Berga, Catalonia with a wild festival conjuring the pit of hell itself and the defeat of the devils.

In that opening story of Zagreus the baby, his attackers and his defender reach for a rich range of mimetic devices—the gypsum masks, the toys, and above all the mirror, with its powers of reflection and self-reflection. Finally, an effigy is made from the heart of the victim. All these means survive in various forms, as part of the panoply of weapons we use both to instil and to withstand fear. The myth summons spectres from the shadows and enfleshes them; it conjures the bogeymen, spotlights their horror and their power, and then, in order to cope with their ability to imitate and entice, arrays against them more devices created by make-believe and art. The polymorphousness of Zagreus' attempts to escape the Titans' cannibal assault on him in his cradle offers a mythological precedent for shape-shifting in both art and life. In the struggle between the giants' appetite and the baby's attempts to escape and ward off danger, the story sets in motion the devices and ruses of art in its widest sense of fabrication and performance.

Zagreus' rejection of the Titans' blandishments enfolds a prime function of the ceremonies and artefacts that confront bogeymen and that are still applied today: to name dangers and to draw distinctions and boundaries between them and us. The second and third stratagems—to assume protean identities and outer forms, and then reincarnate by means of a copy or simulacrum—recur in living tradition, in that zone of the arts that cannot be contained within the category of the aesthetic. They belong neither in literary nor visual manifestations of art but in that indeterminate, elusive, itself protean, territory that has been called (since 1848, when the word was coined) folklore. Festivals, carnival, secular rituals and ceremonies, popular magical and superstitious practices involving parades and processions, dances and masks and puppet shows, and the stories, beliefs and images they represent and draw on, populate this territory.

Although much of the material that echoes to the bogeyman's tread is ancient, such as the mystery plays, the insistence on monsters in children's lives presents a new development in their entertainment: their affinity with

Like Hell's Mouth on the rampage, Grendel's mother on the loose, or Freud's worst nightmares made flesh: this colossal 'Squig' exercises customer appeal from the cover of a 1997 catalogue of figures for role-playing fantasy games.

monsters has grown with the stresses modern childhood puts on parents. Death the bugbear carried off infants in the not so distant past—and continues to do so; but the bogeyman has persisted, proliferating in number and species, and has even swollen in stature since infant mortality mercifully declined. The emphasis has shifted: from a threat to the child from outside forces to the threatened and threatening quality of child-rearing and the conflicts between parents and children. The question is not only 'Who eats and who gets eaten?' but 'Who consumes and who is consumed?'—taken with a new metaphorical rather than literal value in relation to survival. The cluster of meanings around the idea of consumption (devouring, swallowing, wolfing down, bloodsucking, to name but a few) communicates struggles about separate identity, filiation, and personal autonomy, as discussed in Chapter 6. Chapter 7 then looks in particular at the vision of the child as a monster, even an ogre.

Monsters have become children's best friends, *alter egos*, inner selves. While the monster mania of the last few years has obviously been fostered by commercial interests, it has also diagnosed an identification that children themselves willingly and enthusiastically accept. Witches and warlocks, orcs, trolls, dwarfs, giants, gremlins, goblins, dinosaurs, and a host of mythological and legendary characters populate comics and fantasy games for older children and youths, some of them sprung from recent classics like J.R.R. Tolkien's *Lord of the Rings*, others from the pool of ancient stories fished with an all-purpose net. Trolls with pink or green hair, squidgy, hybrid faces and enormous feet count among the most treasured possessions of primary schoolchildren; soft toys have expanded their range far beyond Pooh bear, to include crocodiles, velociraptors, tyrannosauri and snakes; cereal packets' give-away cards now detail venomous insects and reptiles when they used to itemize cars and film stars; Disney-style lovable dwarfs have enrolled into their ranks the Hunchback of Notre Dame (a self-declared monster in the book and the film). Family chain stores have developed lines in children's toiletries (to encourage them to wash!): bath 'goo' with sharks swimming in the murky bottle and 'Beast-lies', where purity meets danger—the 'pure vegetable glycerine soap' encloses in its translucent tablet a giant fly, roach or arthropod. As the Dutch historian Rudolf Dekker points out, play has its history and has been encouraged as an essential part of growing up only for the last two hundred years. The toys, films, and storybooks of today's children's culture reflect like two-way mirrors our expectations of children and our images of ourselves, *in potentia*. In the late twentieth century they are populating children's lives—and those of adults, too—with monstrous *alter egos*. Part One concludes with speculation about insects which provide an ever more effective visual lexicon of monstrousness. (The word 'bug' itself is related to bogey, and used to mean 'devil'.) Insect mimicry reveals that to copy an aggressor in looks and even behaviour has proved a well-tried device in natural selection. It is possible that scaring ourselves to death, by investing ourselves with the face and features of the bogeyman, by pretending to extremes of violence and aggression, may have become the most favoured way of confronting fear in times of anxiety and disarray.

Part Two examines lullabies, or cradle songs, that have traditionally been sung to overcome infants' fear of the dark, and still are, more commonly than expected, as I discovered when collecting examples from friends and family for this book. The songs deal with fear by confronting its possibilities, and these include the unknown destiny that lies ahead for the baby. Lullabies weave a protective web of words and sounds against raiders who come with the night, against marauders real and fantastic, and against the future and the dangers it holds. The singer keeps vigil at the same time as hushing the baby to sleep.

Athena's revival of the murdered baby through the creation of an effigy goes to the heart of such entertainments. Lullabies belong in the same domain as Athena's work of restoration: through art and music they perform domestic magic to preserve life. Verbal and visual representations in fairy tales assume the performative force of words: words make things real, words make things happen. This is an aspect of secular magic that is spreading through contemporary culture. It is not, however, so pagan or primitive as it may seem, for its basic principles are infused with Christian (Catholic) ideas about words and images and their realizing powers. Overcoming the objects of fear by naming them, picturing them, endowing them with vivid life, and then annihilating them corresponds to the mythic dynamic of contest and victory seen in the legend of Zeus' eventual victory over the Titans. Still, these dread figures often make their first appearance in a child's imagination in lullabies that conjure them up at the very moment of placating them. Lullabies are mysterious and paradoxical, charged with 'maternal ambivalence'; they convey aggression and conflict as well as peace. Surprising as it may seem, they are also deeply fascinated with death and they embody the special place of women's voices in the history of mourning. So here I also look at the history of the nightingale as a symbol of women's expressivity in song. In the classical myth about the bird, she is Philomel, who mourns her fate and a dead child. Only later, when sentimentality has overtaken the experience of mothering or child-raising, does her song become 'such an ecstasy' of joy. Nor is lulling the only effect of the songs, which function also to develop the baby's fundamental powers of expression, and in this are indeed like the nightingale. Lullabies, like other genres of 'Baby Talk' or babble, communicate the first sounds of native language and present the infant with its earliest images and ideas of identity of self and strangers.

The response, 'It's scary', often includes laughter: the third way of confronting fear examined in this book. Part Three of *No Go the Bogeyman* looks at comedy as a defensive tactic against fear of the bogeyman. Fairy-tale figures of terror are no longer so starkly terrifying as Kronos, who swallows his own children or the witch in 'Hansel and Gretel', and the responses at which horror material aims range from screams and squeals to sympathy and merriment. I have heard a theatre full of six-year-olds shriek with delighted terror when Gretel pushed the witch into the oven and she kept coming back to grab the little girl with her long nails and yellow fangs. Eventually, even after Gretel had managed to slam the oven door on her, the witch still emerged from under the floorboards, waving one clawed hand as in a horror film—to the ever more excited peals and squeals of the audience. But the thrills induced by creepy-crawlies, that special state of heebie-jeebies, the response of mixed joy and terror that produces laughter have been identified as peculiarly childish and are constantly being provoked and reinforced in children themselves.

It is worth recalling that the tale of Zagreus and the Titans offers an explanation for the origin of Dionysus, the god who presided—presides— over pleasure and intemperateness, sexual licence and social disorder, feasting and drunkenness, riot and debauch. (In Milton's variation on the theme, he becomes the lover of Circe and the father of Comus, lord of revels.) The story's gruesomeness gives it a grotesque flavour, and this taste continues in the celebrations that commemorate the god and in the representations associated with his sphere of influence: these used to be feasts like the Saturnalia and the Hilaria, and they survive as Carnival in many parts of the world. But celebrations that quarry the grotesque for their peculiar atmosphere and pleasure have grown in scope, and they now include films, comics and objects, including toys and video games: 'Making Mock' looks at the role that comedy plays in easing the fear of things that go bump in the night and, even more seriously, in quelling the anxieties that strangers provoke. Comedy not only makes one laugh but includes the monstrous and the grotesque, the low and the ignoble, the clownish and the foolish. The endlessly inventive fantasy that brings more and more bogeys to life in representations mines the seam of horror, but laughter, mixed in with the horror, produces the particular millennial flavour of the late grotesque.

Following a reflection on the Chimera, the monstrous embodiment of illusion itself, I discuss the development of the grotesque as a mode, and its paradoxical uses in exorcizing forebodings and fear, with special emphasis on Goya's mordant visions of human folly. 'Making Mock' continues with an account of the figure of Circe, the enchantress who turned men into beasts. Circe inspired one or two of the Greek heroes to remain with her, in the shape of beasts, and to embrace the animal life of instinct, pleasure, and play: she is a mistress of metamorphosis, a profound threat to the integrity of the self, who does indeed play havoc with bodies, mocking their original natures. But such metamorphoses can also provide release from self: they are a form of joking, of storytelling, and they offer supple resources for transforming anxiety into pleasure.

Circe's defiant, epicurean tradition includes a story about a certain Gryllus, whose name means pig in Greek but cricket in Latin. The cricket

OPPOSITE 'A Horribly Hair-Raising Experience', publicity leaflet for Museum of the Moving Image, London, 1998.

is the idle songster of fable, and his spirit animates the tradition of tales, rhymes, nonsense and fun—for adults as well as children. Metamorphic humour, which seizes the objects of fear, like beasts, and turns them into something different, something reassuring and even desirable, has been the most widely and successfully adopted stratagem in the confrontation of fear. Original and zestful interpreters of ogre material, like Giambattista Basile in Naples in the early seventeenth century and William Godwin in eighteenth-century London, made light of imagined threats and sought to overturn conventional attitudes to ugliness, to strangers.

But jokers are not always wise enough to play the fool, to show tolerance or scepticism, and the last chapters of 'Making Mock' concentrate on a strand of jokes that attempt to deal with fear of the Other. They examine old ideas about the black bogeyman who is coming to eat you, through an overview of bananas and the banana-skin gag. This fruit offers a micro-history of a symbol in its social function, for it first represented, to the Old World, the natural bounty of the New, and its gradual decline into a trigger of spontaneous laughter can be mapped onto changing attitudes to phantasmatic male power, to phallic aggression and desire, and, within that, to the spectral and threatening Other.

No Go the Bogeyman travels from ogres to lullabies to bananas; this eclecticism reflects the surprising variety and ingenuity of the methods used to deal with fear. The stories, the songs, and the jokes recounted here express fascination with the unknown and terror of what it brings; they are ways of confronting its compelling power as well as of resisting its most disabling effects.

PART ONE

SCARING

all I am saying is that the dread of death is in the faces

we love, the dread of our dying, or theirs. . .

Derek Walcott, *The Bounty*

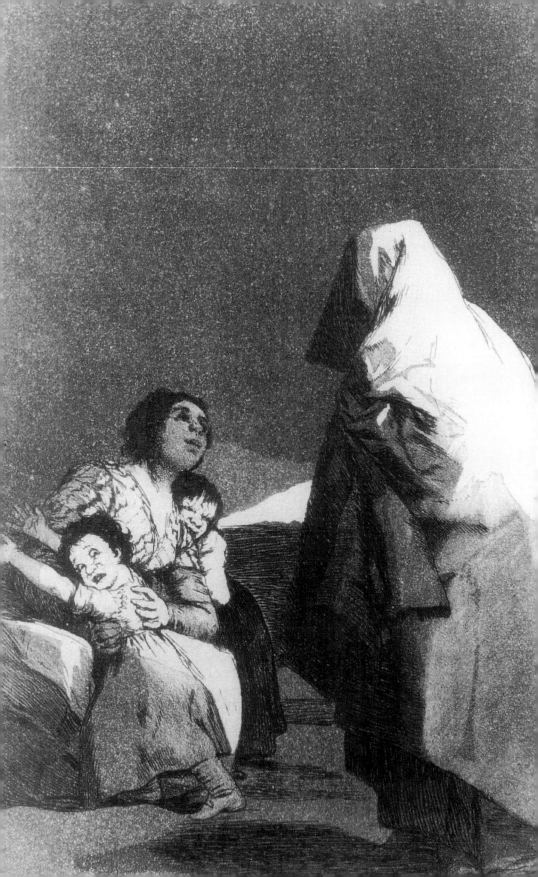

I

'HERE COMES THE BOGEYMAN!'

In a poem written in Germany in 1782, the poet Goethe evoked the Erlking, or the King of the Alders, wooing a boy who is riding with his father through the dark forest: 'You sweet child, come, come with me!' he calls out, 'we shall play lovely games together, there are flowers of many colours by the water's edge, my mother has many garments of gold.' The child immediately recognizes the danger as the Erlking himself, and cries out. But his father reassures him, 'In dürren Blättern säuselt der Wind.' ('It's the wind rustling in the dry leaves'.) Again the Erlking entices the boy:

'Meine Töchter sollen dich warten schön;
Meine Töchter führen den nächtlichen Reihn,
Und wiegen und tanzen und singen dich ein.'

('My daughters shall be your lovely attendants: every night my daughters dance a round dance, they will rock you and dance you and sing you to sleep.')

With the chanting refrain of a ballad, the boy remonstrates again, but again in vain, as his father once more dismisses his fears of what he sees: 'Es scheinen die alten Weiden so grau.' ('It's the old willow-trees looking so grey.') But each time, his words deepen the wraith-like horror of the child's assailant.

The Erlking loses patience. He desires the child for his own, the internal rhymes pointing up his ineluctable resolve:

'Que viene el Coco' (Here comes the Bogeyman) wrote Goya on this print, quoting words parents used to terrify children. Los Caprichos, 1793–8.

'Ich liebe dich, mich reizt deine schöne Gestalt;
Und bist du nicht willig, so brauch' ich Gewalt.'

('I love you, I am charmed by your beautiful shape; and if you
are not willing, I will use force.')

He seizes the boy, who cries out again; the father shudders, spurring on
their horse to reach home faster. But when he arrives:

'In seinen Armen das Kind war tot.' ('In his arms the child lay dead.')

Goethe's poem, in the spirit of Romanticism and German literary
nationalism, uses a simple, often monosyllabic vernacular vocabulary and
the rocking stresses of the ballad form to create a haunting epitome of a
recurring nightmare.

'The Erlking' was written when Goethe was still a young poet, in the
period when the scholarly circle of Clemens Brentano and Bettina von
Arnim was forming, the milieu that would produce Achim von Arnim and
Brentano's *Des Knaben Wunderhorn* (*The Boy's Magic Horn*, 1806), the
founding anthology of German songs, and would also nurture the young
Grimm Brothers' enthusiasm for fairy tales. Interestingly, it was a mis-
translation of a Danish legend that inspired the figure of the Erlking.
Johann Gottfried Herder misunderstood the Danish for 'king of the elves',
but his was one of those momentous, wondrous, mythopoeic errors that
enriches culture, for a 'King of the Alders' belonged by nature to the damp,
dark, spooky forests of Germany and to its native folklore. A slip of the ear
or of the pen shifted the whole uncanny underworld of the fairies into the
deep native woodland above ground, where it threatened more closely,
more thrillingly.

'The Erlking' is a song and a poem at once, expressing a timeless fear
and at the same time producing a recognizable contemporary Gothic
frisson. It personifies death as a danger above all to the young, who are
credited with a more intense perception of the other world in the first
place; this intimacy with the supernatural makes them vulnerable to its
charms and its desires. Fear is the child's bedfellow. 'The Erlking' makes a
characteristic Romantic move when it dramatizes the father's tragic
dismissal of the threat; the poem leaves its subjects nameless, thus bidding
for universality and widening the reach of the menace. The late eighteenth
century saw a decisive change in attitudes to children, and the poem
reflects it: the thoughts and apprehensions of children should not be dismissed, for they can be privy to some things we should know and should
fear ourselves.

The Erlking tale still circulates locally in different communities, as part of their contemporary 'urban legends'. On Dartmoor, in Devon, for instance, the story is still told of the demon huntsman Dewer who comes riding by Hameldown Tor, his black dogs with their flaming eyes streaking ahead of him and his hunting horn sounding. One day, as he passes, a man making his way home asks him what sport he has enjoyed that day. With a laugh, Dewer throws down a sack into his hands. When the man reaches his kitchen and opens it, expecting some tasty fowl or other piece of game, he discovers instead the body of his own child.

Where one century perceives the stalker as Death, another sees him as Eros: Angela Carter, in her consummate collection of fairy tales, *The Bloody Chamber* (1975), included a version, which, like Goethe's poem, angles the terror through the fascinated eyes of the Erlking's prey. She is a Carter heroine, in thrall despite herself to the woodland spirit's feral, eldritch charms: 'He is the tender butcher who showed me how the price of flesh is love; skin the rabbit, he says! Off come all my clothes.'

Child-stealers, night-raiders, cradle-snatchers: they inspired a rich and sinister body of tales that had every appearance of medieval and superstitious primitiveness, but continued to be retold at the height of the Enlightenment. Spirit assassins come in all shapes and sizes, as goblins, as little people and even as *belles dames sans merci*. The unfamiliar in every aspect moulds the phantom, and so, like witches, bogeys are crooked or moley or warty, or they limp or suffer from other unusual physical traits—fairies are often marked out, in the British tradition, by their red hair. Female demons predominate in earlier mythologies, but by the early-modern period male predators are increasing in numbers and prominence. Racial differences contribute, too: the *coco* in Spain is imagined as a black devil, as he is in Italy, where he is simply called *l'omo nero*. This tradition has survived in those countries longer than in England, where 'black-man' is no longer an alternative phrase for a bogey or hobgoblin, as it was in Middle English.

. Roman comedy featured a masked monster called Manducus ('Jaws') with clattering teeth and another, Dossenus, ever chomping. In northern Europe, trolls haunted the forests. These supernatural, underground creatures of Scandinavian folk tales come in varying sizes, from elf to giant, and are known by grandiose names, like Borbytingarna. They used to be terrifying until their recent domestication as sweet furry dorks. In Russian legends, the *bannik* and his wife, the *bannikha*, among many malign goblins, would suffocate or flay their victims in the night if they showed disrespect. The predatory witch Baba Yaga, who has a special liking for children, has developed into a far more definite, even individual, figure, with her woodland cottage that runs about on chicken legs, and her unusual mode of flight: she ferries through the air in a pestle and mortar, sweeping her tracks with a besom as she goes. Baba Yaga, Old Hag Yaga, like many other crones in fairy stories, fences her domain in the forest with the bones and skulls of her victims, whose eyes glow by moonlight. She sets snapping teeth on her door for a lock, with hands to bolt it and human limbs to support it; the tiles are made of pancakes and the walls of pies; a big oven blazes in the hearth where Baba Yaga sleeps at night: she is a close

'I love you, I love you,' cries the Erlking in Goethe's ballad, as he tries to snatch the boy from the safety of his father's arms. Engraving by Bernhard Neher, 1846.

cousin of the witch in the gingerbread house from 'Hansel and Gretel', and clever children can trick her into doing herself a great mischief. The derivation of 'Yaga' is disputed, but could be related to Slavic words for 'grudge' or 'brawl', or, perhaps more illuminatingly, to a Russian word for eating. For Baba Yaga is by no means always malignant; she is a cunning woman, in control of natural and supernatural magic and, above all, of food supplies. But she dispenses her hospitality capriciously. Baba Yaga has witchy traits, and the witch in nursery lore often stands in for the female ogre, sharing some of her characteristics, though she is seldom built on the ogress' Brobdingnagian scale. Instead she can take the shape of a bird or a cat or a simple old woman, like the jealous queen in 'Snow White'.

Nightmare visitors are not usually imagined as beating their prey, like Mr. Punch, in his delirium of baby-battering in the puppet play Punch and Judy. Raiders from other worlds want children for themselves. They are covetous, and the implication is that they have lost a baby or cannot have one and feel the lack. So they can be 'boo-baggers', who carry bags in which they stow babies and their other victims, principally children. Sometimes they are night-riders, like witches in the fears of the witchfinders, who described Sabbath orgies at which babies were sacrificed to the devil in a sacrilegious imitation of the Eucharist. Agostino Veneziano in the early sixteenth century made a terrifying engraving—'Lo Stregozzo', (The Carcass)—showing a witch's grand nocturnal parade in her high chariot of bones, hauled by naked and muscly slaves who have grabbed naked babies and carried them off; she sits high up on the coachman's box, urging them on, with more infants whom she has snatched for her purposes stowed around her. The fears here concentrate on the fate of miscarried, still-born and hence unbaptized babies, who, according to orthodox Christian belief, died in a state of original sin and therefore could not go to heaven. This issue is extremely complex, and inspired much debate as well as anguish. Eventually, the state of limbo, neither paradise nor hell but a condition of painless suspension, was devised to assuage the distress that parents—and others—felt at the fate of such innocents. Before the establishment of limbo in popular belief (it was never formally approved), numerous manœuvres and devices were adopted in order to prevent the damnation of infants. Joan of Arc, for example, was credited with resurrecting a baby for long enough for it to receive the sacrament and save its soul before it died.

Records of babies rallying in this way, to give the breathing space for baptism, recur in Protestant as well as Catholic communities, showing that the loss and the terror lie deeper than theological definitions of salvation and that different ideas of divine providence do not mitigate the parental pain of bereavement. The loss of infants may have been expected in times of high mortality, but it was not a matter of indifference. The stories communicate fatalism, but this is not identical with resignation. Rather they offer explanations, from the irrational store of the imaginary, in order to rationalize loss. In Ireland, the Tuatha Dé Danann traditionally left changelings behind in the cradle. In Scottish ballads, a demon with the misleading name of Lammikin nips and stabs infants until their mother is woken; then Long Lankin, as he is also known, proposes to drain the mother's blood into a basin. In Jewish folkore, Lilith, Adam's unruly first wife who was repudiated for her rebelliousness, roams at night looking for babies, to suck their blood or otherwise destroy them. Even the Snow

Queen, in Hans Christian Andersen's famous and beautiful fairy tale, retains traces of this terror, for she abducts her child victims, like the boy Kai, to her palace in the far north where she freezes them into statues of blue ice. The ogresses' Greek precursor, Lamia, can give a clue to the animus that is ascribed, in fantasy, to female child-stealers: for like her Jewish counterpart Lilith, Lamia began to prey on babies after she suffered ostracism and after her own children, yet more offspring of Zeus' philandering, had been killed by his jealous wife, Hera. The coral branch that Jesus wears in many paintings of the Madonna and Child is a survival of pre-Christian Middle Eastern magic against these raiders of the nursery. Recently, a remarkable, uncanny children's book by Valerie Dayre, *L'Ogresse en pleurs* (The Ogress in Tears), infused the old myths with contemporary fears: the malign protagonist wanders the world, searching for her prey, and, after several frustrated assaults, finds a delicious boy baby whom she instantly gobbles. Dayre's book, powerfully illustrated by Wolf Erlbruch, vividly expresses contemporary maternal fears when it closes with the ogress weeping, for it is her own child, whom she has (inadvertently) eaten, all other children failing to satisfy her appetite. This glassy-eyed, ravening and ancient hag embodies contemporary anguish about infertility and violence towards children in the same way as fairy tales like 'Donkeyskin' tell of father–daughter incest, concealed under the deep disguise of 'Once upon a time'.

Bogeymen and women are frequently imagined as single, anomalous outsiders—the Cyclops in his cave, the witch in her gingerbread house. This is not invariably the case, however: ogres are often king of the castle in a domestic setting—consider the giant at the top of the beanstalk. When the witch in her lonely cottage on the edge of the forest and the ogre in his remote castle prey on the young, their malignant envy of others who have and can bear children may appear to be their underlying motive for raiding cradles and devouring infants. Or, to reverse the point of view, those who are blessed with offspring fear that their good fortune may inspire destructive envy. The Egyptians even devised a deity with special powers in this area: the popular dwarf god Bes, whose squat, grinning figure has been excavated from birth niches, appeased forces that might harm mothers and children; he was set to watch in lying-in rooms and night nurseries, to protect against the jealousy of childless women.

Such stories, it has been argued, also provide a consoling explanation for mysterious cot deaths, or even, as suggested by Judith Devlin in *The Superstitious Mind*, a justification for neglecting babies with birth defects or other problems. A changeling could be discreetly made to disappear, as an evil gift of the fairies, or even of the devil; to dispose of a human child on the other hand, however unwanted or damaged at birth, lay beyond the frontiers of acceptable conduct. Doris Lessing in her dystopic fable, *The Fifth Child* (1988), chillingly reworked the theme. Infanticide, in cases where there was nothing untoward, could thus be concealed—blamed on 'the fairies'. Although perpetrators were sought out, and blamed, with anger equal to the feelings that raged in the case of Matthew Eappen's death and Louise Woodward's trial in Massachusetts in 1997, their crimes were attributed to witchcraft and possession, not to personal malevolence.

As in many cases of witchcraft accusations, guilt and fear underlie the famous story of the Pied Piper of Hamelin in Westphalia, which was suffering from a plague of rats. A mysterious minstrel appeared; he was dressed in motley and played a pipe, with which he charmed all the rats to follow him out of the town. But when he came back for the fee he had been promised, the good burghers of Hamelin refused to pay him. So he played his pipe again, and this time all the children danced in his wake until he led

The night-hag of Renaissance legend roams the dark in her chariot of bones gathering children for her sacrifices. Agostino Veneziano, Lo Stregozzo *(The Carcass, detail), sixteenth century.*

them into a mountain, which closed over them. Only two were left to report what had taken place: one boy who was blind and another, who was lame. They had not been able to keep up with the merry throng.

In 1842 Robert Browning turned the tale into a bouncy ballad, and children perform the drama today for summer crowds in the town square at Hamelin: a cautionary tale about unfair dealing that the prosperous mercantile town tells itself. More recently, the composer Thomas Adès responded more sensitively to the sinister, even supernatural, quality of the legend, with *Under Hamelin Hill*, an eerie piece that captures on a chamber organ the seduction of the Pied Piper's irresistible music.

For the legend also warns, as so many tales of fairy folk do, that the fey and the pied, the eldritch and the elf are dangerous to humans in their capriciousness: they personify the unpredictable mischief-making of fate. The Pied Piper story is dated to 1240, when Hamelin is known to have suffered a similar plague, and in several ways its hero prefigures many spectres who come to haunt Germany. Though not dwarfish or otherwise monstrous, the Piper appears in the motley

A merrily painted fountain, sculpted in the form of a monstrous Mr. Punch, shows a baker's dozen of children disappearing under his belt, into his maw, into his bags. Berne, sixteenth century.

sometimes worn by the devil, and even more often by the fool who mocks truth, while the mountain, which uncannily opens when he plays in order to swallow the children, is the familiar habitat of elves and dwarfs and giants and other messengers from the dark side.

After the invention of print, goblins known as 'child-guzzlers' (*Kinderfresser*) and 'child-frighteners' (*Kinderschrecker*) were disseminated in Germany and its neighbours through grotesque broadsheets. These are often associated with Carnival. Yet one such alarming dwarf makes an early appearance in the margin of a lavish private book of hours of 1533 belonging to the Duke of Lorraine, so the theme was not confined to popular or even secular settings. This dwarf is grabbing at naked putti no smaller than he is, and he bears a pannier on his back to which he has strapped children he has already stolen. In Berne, Switzerland, there is a statue on which a sixteenth-century polychrome sculpture of a kind of Mr. Punch stands, children slung about him from his belt, in his pouches, on his back and under his arm, while one dangles from his jaws, like a fish in a pelican's beak: it is called the *Kindlifresserbrunnen*, or Childguzzler Fountain. Jolly dancing and musical bears are carved around the pedestal and the bobble on the ogre's cap was regilded when the statue was restored in the 1920s; it is a great favourite with schoolchildren in the town.

In the mid-seventeenth century, Constantijn Huygens, secretary to the Prince of Orange and a committed, kindly and enlightened father, kept a pioneering journal about his children's progress; there he noted how he threatened his daughter when she was naughty with a hooded doll in a black cape called Lijs Huyck. In 1695, around fifty years later, Isabella de Moerloose of Ghent, one of the earliest women autobiographers, recorded in her memoirs how bugbears or bogeys were invoked during her childhood. One was called the *bullebak*, a typical comical giant name, and yet another was a more sinister, sexual, beastlike figure.

Moerloose's book appeared two years before 'Barbe bleue' ('Bluebeard'), 'Le petit Poucet' ('Tom Thumb') by Charles Perrault and other menacing tales by Marie-Jeanne L'Héritier and Marie-Catherine d'Aulnoy, and the spectres the stories conjure cohere with many of the imagined threats. Isabella describes 'the man with the long coat, of whom it was said that he looked for firstborn children in order to kill them, and that he put a ball in their mouths so they would choke'. She added, however, that she and her friends thought that this was a story her parents had made up in order to keep them from coming in late. Most interestingly of all, she records testing the truth of it several times by putting a ball in her mouth; she then discovered that she could still breathe and so discounted her parents' warnings. The overtones of the threat are clear and reveal that fears about children's safety three hundred years ago sometimes included fear of sexual violation and abduction.

Bluebeards, ogres and child-snatchers are close cousins to other wandering and hungry spirits that nurses—and mothers and fathers—have invoked to scare, cajole or bully children into obedience and quiet. If the death of a child was feared, the fear was also used as a weapon. The most notorious of night visitors, the Sandman, comes through the window and throws sand in wakeful children's eyes.

Today, his horrific nineteenth-century shape has been largely set aside, and he survives as a friendly and even whimsical helper, like Wee Willie Winkie. The nursery rhyme goes:

> The Sandman comes on tiptoe,
> Will through the window peep,
> And look at the little children
> Who ought to be asleep.
> And when a sleepless child he spies,
> Throws sand into its eyes.
> Lullaby, lullaby, O sleep, my darling child.

But in E.T.A. Hoffmann's eponymous fairy tale (1817), the old nurse explains, 'Oh! he's a wicked man who comes to little children when they won't go to bed and throws handfuls of sand in their eyes, so that they jump out of their heads all bloody; and he puts them into a bag and takes them to the half-moon as food for his little ones; and they sit there in the nest and have hooked beaks like owls, and they pick naughty little boys' and girls' eyes out with them.' The Sandman here has borrowed witch's clothes: witches were accused in the Inquisitor's manual, the *Malleus Maleficarum*, of stealing men's penises and storing them in nests up trees.

There is an echo of this horrific fantasy in an anonymous German lullaby of peculiar shivery menace. Bird feathers appear, logically connected at first to the baby's eiderdown or duvet, but they slip into metaphor and evoke the child as a nestling in danger of being blinded:

> Close your little eyes, my child,
> For outside blows a terrible wind,
> If the child won't sleep at all
> Blow it will right into his bed,
> Blow everyone of the feathers out
> And end by blowing his eyes out!

Freud, much affected by Hoffmann's 'The Sandman', explored the symbolic substitution of eyes and genitals and used it to refine his theory of the castration complex in his famous essay on the Uncanny. As a result, Hoffmann's spook haunts adult nightmares: in David Lynch's Gothic-erotic cinematic horror tale *Blue Velvet*, Roy Orbison's soupy rendering of the harmless hit song 'In Dreams' turns nasty when it is sung over the prowling of the child kidnapper and sex killer played with unfettered menace by Dennis Hopper.

Hoffmann gives the figure sinister intensity, but the Sandman has his counterparts all over the world. Wee Willie Winkie, the wolf at the door, the little people, the Tuatha Dé Danann, those 'good people' or fairy folk who may come in the night, and even the Man in the Moon have all played their part, with varying degrees of menace, in frightening children into submission. The spectres of the flesh-eating ogre and of death itself are not always invoked in order to be dispelled: threats are interwoven into the games and songs and stories of the nursery itself, the aggression expressed towards the child:

> Ninne ninne sause,
> der Tod steckt hinterm Hause.
> Er hat ein kleines Korbelein,
> da steckt er die bösen Kinder 'nein.
> Die guten lasst er sitzen
> und kauft ihn rote Mützen.

> (*Ninne ninne sause*, Mr. Death is hiding behind the house. He has a little basket to put naughty children in. He doesn't take the ones who are good, but buys them red caps.)

In an English chapbook translation of Perrault's 'The Sleeping Beauty in the Wood' (1750), the author adds a helpful footnote to explain the feminine of the word ogre: 'An Ogree [*sic*] is a Giant with long teeth and claws, with a raw head and bloody bones, who runs away with naughty Boys and Girls and eats them all up.' The Victorian artist Richard Doyle, a comic and whimsical fairy painter, drew a frighteningly long- and spindle-legged bogeyman with his haul of bad boys and girls. So do mythologies' cannibal giants with their complex significance turn into crude nursery bogeys, one of the large family of macabre terrorizers that includes Le Grand Lustucru, an ogre who in a still current French bedtime song threatens restless little girls and boys that he will come with his big sack and carry them off. Similarly, Père Fouettard (Father Flog) and M. and Mme. Croquemitaine in France, with their darkly comic surname—*croquer* meaning 'to crunch', echoing *croque-mort* (undertaker) and, more jocularly, the popular cheese-and-ham sandwich called *croque-monsieur*—took to 'the rat-cellar children who would not say their prayers'. They were much reproduced in nineteenth-century juvenile literature.

Dr. Heinrich Hoffmann's *Struwwelpeter*, published in 1845, began as a parody of such bogeys, but his creations, like the Tailor with his long scissors and Tall Agrippa, soon joined their predecessors as instruments of terror. Even Father Christmas was cast as one of these disciplinarians: in Italy, France, Germany, Holland and Belgium, children put out their shoes on the vigil of December 6, the feast day of St. Nicholas or Santa Claus, hoping he would bring them gifts. They would be left marzipan and gingerbread if they had been good, but coal if they had been bad.

The lullaby 'Le P'tit Quinquin' still widely sung in northern France, introduces this capricious bogeyman who so closely reflects adults' methods of raising children, dispensing rewards and punishments alike from the bag on his back:

> 'Next month, it'll be Santa Claus's day,
> And in the evening he's sure to come and see you,
> He'll give you a sermon
> And let you put a big basket under his knapsack
> He'll fill it if you behave with things that'll make you happy,
> If not, his donkey will send you a big whip. . .'

In Holland and Germany, Saint Nicholas was attended by 'Black Peter', who carried a bag in which to stuff naughty children to take them back to his native Spain. In Jan Steen's rambunctious evocation of such a seventeenth-century Dutch family scene, one big boy is bawling over his coal-filled clogs while his sister clutches a brand-new doll. But fashions in child-rearing change, and no parent or teacher now would suggest openly that Father Christmas might come with a big whip instead of bringing toys and gingerbread.

Though bogeymen are usually shadows that hug the shadows, they materialize intermittently as historical characters. The Breton nobleman Gilles de Rais, marshal of France and companion of Joan of Arc, was hanged after an Inquisition trial for sorcery and the murder of several hundred children in 1440. Georges Bataille edited the transcripts of his trial and took Gilles de Rais' spectacular confessions at face value. He did not consider the problem of evidence in witchcraft trials (Joan of Arc's had taken place only a decade earlier), nor the match between Gilles' crimes and the phantasmagorias of satanism, in which child-snatching played such a spectacular part. The infamy of Gilles de Rais lives on, entangled with a different kind of murderer, the legendary Bluebeard, and immortalized by J.K. Huysmans in his novel *Là-bas* (1891). Michel Tournier's *Le Roi des aulnes* (1970), a compelling variation on the Erlking legend, revisits his crimes in a wartime German setting: Gilles de Rais has become the

Even cheerful 'Dicky' Doyle, a much-loved Victorian fairy painter, steers close to horror with his vision of a rag-and-bone collector of hapless victims. The Bogeyman, *pen and brown ink, c. 1890.*

precursor of twentieth-century serial killers and a founding father of their modern cult.

The most terrifying of such night visitors are not always anthropomorphic nor consistently gargantuan in size. But the metaphor of devouring greed expresses their relationship to death. For although bugbears are not Death's twins or his messengers, though they come in shifting shapes, they resemble Death in matters of appetite and movement: both can come suddenly, and both are hungry for human lives. The most terrifying of bogeys may not always be men (or women), but their connection with food remains constant: they are ravenous, and ravenous for the wrong food. The nursery ogre of the stories, like Lewis Carroll's Jabberwock, snaps his jaws around the child in more ways than one. When it comes to ogres in fantasy, the fundamental principle behind ideas of pollution can be applied with a difference—not dirt in the wrong place, but the wrong food on the table dished up in the wrong way.

The opening tale of Ovid's *Metamorphoses* features Lycaon, the first werewolf; he is a pioneer cannibal chef, one of the earliest protagonists to serve up his acquaintance in a pie. An illumination in *La Bible des poètes,* or *Ovide Moralisé*, printed in Paris in 1493, gives coolly observed details of medieval kitchenware and cutlery as it pictures Lycaon's grim work of butchery. It is a story about hospitality and about trespass against the sanctity of guests, one of the most terrible crimes in epic morality. The age of iron has plunged humanity into greed and violence; Zeus takes human form to go about the world to see for himself the decadence of the 'children of blood'. He calls on Lycaon, 'the Arcadian tyrant'. When the Arcadian people recognize Zeus as a god, Lycaon scoffs at their awe and mockingly boasts that he will test Zeus' divine powers by offering him human flesh to eat. Lycaon then proceeds to make this blasphemous, inverted sacrifice. In Ted Hughes' version:

> Among his prisoners, as a hostage,
> Was a Molossian. Lycaon picked this man,
> Cut his throat, bled him, butchered him
> And while the joints still twitched
> Put some to bob in a stew, the rest to roast.

Zeus does not sup on this victim, unlike many others in analogous cannibal tales; in his godhead, he can tell straight away the difference between animal and human flesh. The myth relates the dangers of hubris, for Zeus razes Lycaon's house with one of his thunderbolts and then turns him into a werewolf, the beast who comes to haunt Gothic lore and children's tales. Interestingly, the anthropophage who cooks is condemned to sink one degree lower on the scale of bestiality and become an omophage, one who eats only his own kind, either raw or as carrion. Gods can pass the test of knowing what they are eating; humans pay extreme penalties when they make a category mistake.

An almost identical story lies behind the punishment of Tantalus in the

Underworld: he similarly dares to challenge the gods' wisdom by serving a cannibal feast; for this crime, he is sentenced to perpetual hunger and thirst, as Lycaon is condemned to be a werewolf and lust insatiably after blood.

By the seventeenth century, there is no suggestion that the most notorious mythic wolf of all—Little Red Riding Hood's 'grandmother'—was once human and punished by a bestial transformation; but oral versions of 'Red Riding Hood', collected after Perrault though probably in circulation before, do include gory episodes that echo with the dark merriment of cannibal jokes, for they involve the heroine in eating her own granny. One version goes like this:

> 'Hello Grandmother; I'm bringing you a hot loaf and a bottle of milk.'
>
> 'Put them in the pantry. You eat the meat that's in it and drink a bottle of wine that is on the shelf.'
>
> As she ate there was a little cat that said: 'A slut is she who eats the flesh and drinks the blood of her grandmother!'
>
> 'Undress, my child,' said the *bzou* [wolf] 'and come and sleep beside me.'

In several oral variants, the little girl does not exclaim at the size of the wolf's teeth, eliciting the famous reply, 'Big enough to eat you with!' Instead, she inquires after the teeth of the grandmother which have remained behind in the cottage, uneaten. In the Tyrol in northern Italy, the wolf then explains that they are rice grains; in the Abruzzi farther south, that they are beans.

Wolves haunt children's rhymes and tales; they are the most familiar predators, an actual danger in times of famine (wolves entering cities in winter are chronicled in the miracles of St. Francis, for example, and in the diary of the Bourgeois de Paris in the early fifteenth century), but straddling the realms of reality and faery. As the threat fades from Europe, it is those who are 'hairy on the inside', in Angela Carter's tremendous phrase, who terrify and thrill. Already, in the tongue-in-cheek moral Charles Perrault attached to his version of 'Red Riding Hood', the wolf had become a seducer, a stalker of young girls, a metaphorical consumer of virgin flesh. In Angela Carter's translation:

> Children, especially pretty, nicely brought-up young ladies, ought never to talk to strangers; if they are foolish enough to do so, they should not be surprised if some greedy wolf consumes

them, elegant red riding hoods and all.

Now there are real wolves, with hairy pelts and enormous teeth; but also wolves who seem perfectly charming, sweet-natured and obliging, who pursue young girls in the street and pay them the most flattering attentions.

Unfortunately, these smooth-tongued, smooth-pelted wolves are the most dangerous of all.

The sexual innuendo of the predatory bogeyman has become far more insistent since Perrault deftly introduced it into 'Red Riding Hood', and this change of meaning colours the whole range of images in stories about eating and being eaten. Cannibals like Polyphemus, who appear sexually indifferent to their prey, have mutated into figures of lechery. In the case of a late twentieth-century ogre like Hannibal Lecter in *The Silence of the Lambs*, for example, devouring of meat figures erotic appetite, which threatens to fascinate and overwhelm even his cool-headed adversary, Officer Sparrow.

The rising survival rate of children has not diminished the theme's interest; rather, the threat of the bogeyman lends itself to further interpretations, beyond the instrumental use for intimidation. Rematerializing in the figure of the child abuser and the paedophile, he condenses widespread fears in society that focus today on sexual, rather than mortal, danger—though one can follow the other. He also acts as a metaphor for internal states and private knowledge—indeed, Goethe's poem implies a reproof to those who do not take a child's fantasies seriously.

❖   ❖   ❖

'Que viene el Coco' ('Here comes the bogeyman'), wrote Goya under one of the first images of *Los Caprichos*, the series of acid satires on human folly he engraved around 1793–98. Using strong contrast and a stark light source from outside the frame, he captured the terror of the children shrinking from the apparition that looms, voluminously swathed and hooded, in front of them. The bogey's face is hidden from us, but he is clearly visible to the nearest child, who is screaming, and to the other child, who huddles into the body of the woman—their mother?—holding them both. Her own expression is enigmatic, much less fearful, even raptly ador-ing, and she may even have staged the scene with the children's father—or her lover—in order to bring them to order. Certainly Goya often attacks the ignorance and brutality shown to children. But in the setting of this sequence of prints, with their furious ambivalence about the supernatural and its powers, the image captures the nameless terrors of children far more frighteningly than it satirizes the manipulative devices of adults. The caption quotes a lullaby, still sung in Spain:

> Duérmete lucero
> que viene el coco
> y se lleva a los niños
> que duermen poco.

> (Go to sleep, evening star, for here comes the bogeyman, and he steals away children who don't go to sleep).

A later etching, from the even darker *Disparate* series made in the last years of his life, conjured another bogeyman-ogre, the *bobalicón* ('silly idiot' in Spanish). Close to an English 'booby', this giant is conjured as an even larger, more clownish figure, with a colossal round head. Lit from below, he clicks castanets with a lewd and terrifying grin, baring his big teeth, as a scrawny, pin-headed figure holds up a young woman to show him; in a preparatory drawing and in an earlier state of the print he is dressed as a friar, and she may be a religious effigy. Certainly, her offered body continues to appear puppet-like in its stiff fright. Meanwhile, gigantic ghouls' heads loom behind the rollicking dancer—haggard in contrast to his bulbous and beaming countenance, but also toothy; they are drawn more sketchily, as if not quite so corporeal as the giant, and are screaming and leering from under each of his jutting elbows. Goya also conveys his loathing for those who maltreat children in drawings observed from life, but even his skill does not always keep his scepticism firmly in place: 'Dream of a Good Witch', a sketch of 1801–3, with merciless irony gives the child-snatching nightmare a benevolent and even sportive air, as the putti-like victims ride on the old woman's back, one dangling naked from a stick, while she looks merely stoical and dedicated. Goya can strike a note of black comedy, for some viewers, with the hair-raising horror of 'Here comes the bogeyman', but what status does the make-believe he represents have for him? What kind of reality does such a game possess?

In the same spirit of grim humour, the artist's notebooks captured nightmare crones, such as a giant ogress at a fiesta pursuing her dwarfed victims. With such images, Goya was mocking the credulous—the faithful, the accusers of witches, the witches themselves and the Inquisition, who conducted the trials. At the beginning of the seventeenth century, in the Basque town of Logroño, a terrible eruption of popular panic about witch-craft took place. The confessions of the accused witches were read out in public in the course of protracted, solemn *auto da fé*, during which they were paraded in the Inquisition's garb of shame—the tall cap and tabard inscribed with diabolical symbols. In some cases they were conducted to the stake, in others they were imprisoned. Many confessed to horrendous crimes, to butchering babies in order to render down their fat to make the ointment they needed for flying to the Sabbath on their broomsticks, or of snatching them to offer them to Satan in a travesty of the Mass. In the case of a drawing inscribed *'Mala muger'* ('Wicked woman'), showing its haggard subject grimacing over a struggling baby in her arms, the artist may have been inspired by the confession of two sisters: they had poisoned their own children, they said, in sacrifice to the devil. The Inquisitors obtained the confessions, sometimes under torture, but not always; one of the most bewildering aspects of such witch-hunting panics is the willingness of some victims to collude with their accusers' fantasies. In these drawings and elsewhere, repeatedly, Goya attacked belief in witchcraft for its folly and cruelty: a ferocious disgust suffuses drawings of the executors and victims of its processes.

Yet Goya's own position remains enigmatic, in spite of the furious, impatient captions he scrawled on the drawings; and in this Goya is the forerunner of twentieth-century instabilities about the sovereignty of reason. His own latent longing for common humanity, reasonable and moderate relations and tranquil dreams thrashes about only to meet frustration and doubts at every turn. Does the condensed outrage of his art evince an instability in his own scepticism? The insistent return in his imagery to the Inquisition and its preoccupation with the diabolical certainly points to his troubled state over such questions. A sketch of 1818–24, showing a heretic, mitred and gowned for public exposure, bears the caption 'For having been born in other parts'; another, even more eloquent of Goya's distress, says 'They put a gag on her because she talked. . . [and hit her about the head . . . because she knew how to make mice].' Yet these drawings, as well as the *Caprichos* and paintings, evoke scenes of witchcraft with such virulence that it is hard not to feel the pressure of real fear.

When Goya drew the *coco* and the terrifying booby, possibly observed from his own everyday world, he disclosed something of his future method, which would dissolve the distinction between observed material and dream work, and would stage the reality of nightmares, and of other, allegorical and mythic ogres and giants—the Colossus of war and the infanticidal Saturn. His invisible *coco*, all-too-invasive *bobalicón* and snarling witches are cousins to the horrors streaming from the head of the dreamer in his famous print, *The Sleep of Reason Produces Monsters*: they communicate the power of such fantasies, even while Goya's sense of folly ridicules them. His monsters convince: they open the question of rationality's limits, and fear comes in through that door.

It is often difficult to date the material in which this or that figure of terror appears: even when the work belongs to a specific period, as does Goya's, the themes slip through time. In the case of fairy tales, antiquarian editors, scholars of folklore, collectors and writers began working with the material in the eighteenth and nineteenth centuries, and the great group of stories of fright and terror appear scattered through these early ballad collections and fairy-tale anthologies—French, German, Irish, English, Scandinavian. The narratives are ancient in their structure and the *rasas*

A looming, grinning giant capers, his castanets clicking, at the sight of a woman offered to him, while ghouls scream at his elbows. Goya, El Bobalicón, Las Disparates, *c. 1819.*

they excite, but it was only at this comparatively late date in the history of the stories' circulation that they achieved a literary form. This in turn fixed their protagonists' features more firmly than previous oral transmission: thus the jack-o'-lantern, which lures wayfarers to their death, may well be timelessly traditional in one sense, but has acquired its familiar pumpkin face through the media of modernity—print, graphic reproduction, and now, of course, television. The media have deepened the reach of these images. The same can be said of vampires, ghosts, loreleis, sirens and other fatal attractions of folklore. The familiar representations are not necessarily faithful to past belief, even when they wish to be so: myths, legends and folk stories are always changing, and they engage with their own times, with their own contemporaries' pleasures and fears.

❖   ❖   ❖

The original meaning and development of the word 'bogy' and all its related words, names, nicknames and associations remain obscure. There is no entry for 'bogeyman' as such in the *OED*, though, bizarrely, it quotes under 'bogey' a music-hall song of 1890 about the 'Bogey Man', and cites a sporting anecdote of 1908 about 'one of the most feared opponents on a golf course.' In this regard, Katharine Briggs remarks drily, 'The respectable and mediocre Colonel Bogey, whose golf score is always dead average, seems to have no right to his name.' The word 'bogy' [*sic*] was used as a proper name for the devil according to another entry, as in Thackeray's 'The people are all naughty and Bogey carries them off'. The dictionary then gives, as the word's second meaning: 'A bogle or goblin; a person much dreaded', thus introducing the concept of dread as defining the term. In both cases, it cites nursery usage only as recent as 1825. It goes on to offer 'bull-beggar' as a related word, first found, in written form, in Reginald Scot's *Discoverie of Witchcraft* (1584). The anthropologist John Widdowson, in a pioneering study, remarks that boo/bogeyman 'forms part of an extensive cluster of terms in the Indo-European languages which are related semantically, if not etymologically'. The predominant b-stem in the semantic family of words that evoke fear could be related to the Indo-European stem that gives 'big', (titanic), on the one hand, and on the other, produces many words for older, authority figures (Indian *babu*, Russian *baba*) as well as pet words for father (Italian *babbo*). Like 'mamma', the sound is one of the earliest to be pronounced by babies, but it also inspires Greek *barbaros*, savage, on account of the perceived gobbledegook of non-Greek, outlandish speech (hence 'barbarian' in English, *barbare* in French, and many related words in other European languages). Thus the b-sound that dominates the expression of bogeyman terrors is associated in English and in the Indo-European group with relations between children and their elders. It is also phonetically related to exclamations from the territory of night terrors, to the nonsense rhyme 'Fee Fie Fo Fum' and, in several languages, to the group in which 'Puck' belongs, that merry wanderer of the night, he who frights the maidens with his devilry. But more interestingly, Widdowson proposes a possible connection to Sanskrit *bhu*, the imperative command of generation, as in Latin '*fiat*'. As the linguist J. R. Firth wittily puts it: 'God created the world by saying *bhu*.'

Raymond Briggs, writing and illustrating his scatological classic for children *Fungus the Bogeyman* (1977), did his homework on the term, and glosses the Scottish divine Robert Baillie's passing comment on superstitions current in 1646: 'The Devils are nothing but only Boggles in the Night to terrifie Men.' In Dr. Johnson's *Dictionary*, 'to boggle' is defined as 'to start, to fly back, to fear to come forward'. This prime—and old—meaning of 'boggle' illuminates bogeys' intrinsically spectral character, as both Goethe and Goya capture so alarmingly. Bogeys come to our consciousness through visualization above all: one's inward eye sees them, but so vividly that they appear before the eyes of the body, too, as in phantasms. And because sight is the principal instrument of verification and guarantor of knowledge, these visions affirm the reality of the fear.

But the sound of the second letter of the alphabet also serves to defend against the terrors with which it resonates, and it gives rise to many a swearword, cry and jest. In one mood, we boo in disapproval, in another, we play peekaboo with children and cry 'Boo!' to give someone a fright—behaving in mock like a bogey or boogie, bugaboo, buggle-boo or bogle-bo or, indeed, bugbear. 'Boo' is attested in English as early as 1420 but the bilabial plosive, as the sound is known in phonetics, has been heard in children's games in places as different as the Middle East and North America. The words for *coco* revolve this sound: in northern England, boggart and barguest; in Scotland, booman, bauchan, bocan, beithir, bodach; bugaboo in the Isle of Man; bucca in Cornwall, buggane in Wales; similarly in Russian, *buca*; boogerman in the southern United States; in Newfoundland, boo-bagger and bully-boo. Hobyahs, originally Scottish cradle-snatchers, travelled to Australia with nineteenth-century reading primers; there they met and mingled with bunyips, the giant swamp monsters of the Aboriginal Dreamtime that drag wayfarers under with them. Alfred Jarry's *Père Ubu and Mère Ubu* (1896) massacring all opponents in a joyous delirium of beatings and murders, embody the parental ogre's spirit at its most ecstatically ferocious and extreme.

'The Jabberwock, with eyes of flame, / Came whiffling through the tulgey wood'—John Tenniel's pterodactyl-cum-velociraptor meeting his doom. Through the Looking Glass, *1871.*

The related word 'bug' originally referred specifically to devils and phantoms of the dark. The Coverdale translation of the Bible, made for

Henry VIII and published in 1535, is known as the Bug Bible, from its translation of Psalm 91:5: 'Thou shalt not nede to be afrayed of eny bugges by night.' Some Bibles repeated this wording, but the Authorized Version substituted 'terror' for 'bugges', while the Jerusalem Bible renders the vivid verse, 'You need not fear the terrors of night . . . the plague that stalks in the dark. . .' These perils may include Beelzebub, the devil who, in Jerome's Vulgate translation of the Bible, is 'Lord of the Flies' (Kings II, 1:2). Some of the force of the original charm against evil may have been lost in the common bedtime rhyme: 'Good night sleep tight / Don't let the bugs bite/ If they bite squeeze them tight / And they won't bite another night.'

The word 'bugge' or 'bug' was already used to mean 'insect' in the seventeenth century and was thence transposed to their stare ('bug-eyed'); by association, in contemporary American slang, it means 'to annoy', as in 'Don't bug me'. (The etymology of 'bugger' has been much discussed, but the word is thought to diverge from other bug-words, being derived perhaps from *bougre* or Bulgar.) It is worth noting here that aliens, currently the most disseminated and talked-about monsters of all—feared for their clandestine and often obstetrical operations—are ascribed the hugely magnified gaze of 'bugs', of flies and wasps, created by their pupil-less compound eyes. Startling a potential predator, as in the game of Boo!, is one of the most effective protective devices evolved in nature.

The b- and boo-sounds reverberate in dozens of later coinages, in English and in other languages: in the Brobdingnagian giants from *Gulliver's Travels*, and in more obscure corners of nonsense verse. This one makes his début in a book called *Blabberhead, Bobble Bud & Soade*:

> The Brobinyak has Dragon Eyes,
> And teeth about banana size.

Even Babar the Elephant, with his pet name from baby babble, retains the family association of giant size, but of course tames it into domestic harmony by sweetness of character. But the most dazzling performance of terror, in jest and in earnest, takes place in the joyous inventive nonsense of Lewis Carroll's celebrated 'Jabberwocky', and the monsters it invokes:

> 'Beware the Jabberwock, my son!
>   The jaws that bite, the claws that catch!
> Beware the Jubjub bird, and shun
>   The frumious Bandersnatch!'

In Carroll's later epic nonsense poem 'The Hunting of the Snark: An Agony in Eight Fits', one of the comic effects consists of an obsessive play on the letter *b*. Every member of the crew on the ship that will only sail backwards begins with a *b*—the Bellman, the Boots, a Bonnet-maker, a Barrister, a Broker, a Billiard-marker and a Banker, a Beaver and a Butcher. Moreover, the whole poem started, Carroll famously recalled, with a single line that came into his head: 'For the Snark *was* a Boojum, you see.' The line is not altogether nonsense, though, for with this riddling resolution of his comic quest epic Carroll resoundingly parodies the very phonemes and lexicon of bogeydom.

Bogey lore draws on conventional cathartic principles: Carroll's tremendous poem rises to its climax with the hero's great victory:

> 'And hast thou slain the Jabberwock?
>   Come to my arms, my beamish boy!
> O frabjous day! Calloo! Callay!'
>   He chortled in his joy.

Earlier giant-killer stories, the kind Carroll is lampooning so blithely, which range from Odysseus' exploits with the Cyclops and Arthurian legend to 'Jack and the Beanstalk', produce their effects of relief and delight with the undoing of the death threat. The nursery ogre is summoned only to meet defeat; many versions of 'Red Riding Hood' portray her escaping the wolf's clutches and dispatching the wolf, his guts slit open to release Granny and child. Indeed, if children are old enough to understand the words or grasp the sentiment of the stories they hear, if they remember them when they wake up, then every time they survive the night they have cheated the stalker who menaces them in the dark. This small, routine success, repeated daily, expands in nursery tales and songs and games to envisage and chronicle the full, crushing annihilation of the bogeyman. If he lives in the imagination, he dies the death in the late seventeenth-century and eighteenth-century fairy tale. The haven offered by such material— such perversely wakeful bedtime tales and songs—is the safety of the place where the child is held and wakes up to a new day, a place that is underlined as definitely not the same place as the lair of ogres, wolves, goblins and their like. It is worth bearing in mind the surprising lateness of the word 'bogeyman' as a term in widespread use: the bogeyman as a prime

OPPOSITE *Hannibal Lecter's appetite curbed (but not for long).* The Silence of the Lambs, *1991.*

figure of terror, both for the pleasurable thrills he can inspire and for the distress he excites, has been naturalized comparatively recently in the woodlands of modern childhood and, subsequently and interdependently, in adult culture as well.

Bogeymen reflect in one aspect intergenerational fears: and the link between ogres and fathers, between parents and children, between rulers and subjects, and between authority figures and subordinates, twists through the material, as we shall see in the myth of Kronos and later, in the Grimms' fairy tale 'The Juniper Tree'.

REFLECTION

GOYA: SATURN DEVOURING HIS CHILD

*Saturn is stark naked, bent at the knees, bestial in his vora-
ciousness. Daubed against a black background, towering in
the void with only the mangled and bleeding body of his prey
to give a sense of human scale, the god rolls his eyes till the
whites show almost all round the demented irises; his unkempt hair looks
like falling ashes and his mouth is so stretched in its frenzy that he appears
to be simultaneously screaming and devouring. Streaks of scarlet paint,
applied with the same jagged attack as the greys and bistres of his loose
flesh, ooze from under his hands where he is gripping the naked body by
the waist. More red pigment outlines, with coarse impatience, the victim's
one remaining forearm and the line where the head has been ripped from
the torso. The artist has confronted the scene head-on: we are in the front
row, within range of the blood and spittle.*

*Goya cannot keep his hands steady as he conjures the tale of intergener-
ational cannibalism, the incestuous version of the child sacrifices and
snatchings he depicted in his images of sorcery. His painting's sublime
ferocity struggles to communicate the extreme, crazed aberration of such a
crime as the murder of one's own child. It acknowledges the allegorical
tradition: both Father Time and Melancholy, devouring the life of mortal
beings, haunt his god. He is possessed, too, by the ghost of Hunger, the
starveling hag personified by Ovid. But Goya's Saturn (Pl. 1) touches
greater depths of rage.*

*Goya painted the cannibal god in 1821–23, when he was in his
seventies, after illness had left him totally deaf. Saturn is one of the figures
in the sequence of 'Black Paintings' he worked in oil straight on to the plaster of the walls of the Quinta del Sordo, the farmhouse where he had
secluded himself. The cycle includes several scenes which imply other cruel
and perverse feasts: a* Witches' Sabbath, *showing the women's faces lit as if
by firelight, also staring till the whites of their eyes gleam as they worship
the goat devil, here an open-mouthed silhouette;* Two Old People *hunched
over a table, one of them leering as he (or she) stirs something in a bowl;
and a* Judith, *the biblical heroine who dined luxuriously with Holofernes
before cutting off his head. With saturnine humour, the paintings may have
been intended as ornaments for Goya's dining room.*

Two of Goya's Black Paintings, Saturn Devouring His Child *and* Judith, *killing Holofernes, may have hung as a pair—in the artist's dining room.*

In The Colossus *(c.1808–12), Goya had earlier created a huge and terrible giant, a towering man-cloud, fists up, striding across the war-torn land beneath him, where men, women, children, baggage trains, horses and livestock are fleeing in all directions. His series of prints* The Disasters of War *drew on the atrocities he had himself witnessed or heard reported during the Peninsular War. His* Saturn *is consequently imbued with his own experiences of horror: the crazed infanticidal father develops the artist's preoccupation with human rage and greed, cruelty and folly. Already, in a drawing made in 1797–98, Goya had shown Saturn with the crafty, vulpine features of one of the artist's dangerous idiots; the aged god is smiling horribly as the leg of one of his children disappears down his gullet. He has another of his offspring (a daughter?) in his other hand and is looking out cannily as he munches, at the viewer—at the artist and at us. Though the drawing is almost gently executed, with lightly scored pencil marks, the effect is chilly, and anticipates Goya's later excruciating anguish and rage. The* Black Painting *made in the farmhouse more than twenty years later far surpasses even the ferocity of this sketch.*

The staring-eyed, ravenous, naked figure appears in the arrangement of the room as a pendant to Goya's Judith *(Pl. 2). The pairing can yield insights into a latent meaning of his image.* Judith, *in one of the chief exemplary episodes of Christian soteriology, defeats a tyrant: she kills Holofernes, synonymous with dissipation and luxury—an Oriental—in bed in his sumptuous campaign tent. In Goya's painting, Judith raises her knife while her maid crouches at her side. Goya has not followed Renaissance precedent here, but has transformed the maid into a witch-like crone, hunkered down in the shadows, a mass of thick black daubings swathing her head, while under her hand a light glows, turning her hand to shadow. This ominous attendant echoes the imagery of procuring, witchcraft and murder insistent in Goya's work.* Judith *is not overtly shown to be about to cook and eat Holofernes' head, but we can catch the reverberations leaping back and forth between Goya's obsessions.*

By juxtaposing the Judith *and the* Saturn, *a second aspect of the ogre's act becomes clear: look carefully at the headless figure whose left arm the murderous father is chewing, and the body appears not to be a child's at all, but a youth's. In this it follows the earlier drawing, where the struggling naked figures in the ogre's grasp are fully grown. Saturn's victim here has rounded, almost voluptuously painted buttocks, so rounded that Goya could be depicting one of the god's daughters, not sons, no longer an infant, but a nubile young woman. Kronos has possibly been imagined and shown devouring Hestia or Hera or Demeter head first. If this is so, the usual title ascribed to the painting—Saturn Devouring His Son—would be mistaken.*

The change in perception of the painting's content would then deepen, for photographs taken before the restoration of 1874–78 may show Kronos with a partially engorged and erect penis. Goya's Black Paintings were being transferred at that time from wall to canvas for exhibition in Paris in 1878, and clumsily restored: a flaccid and ill-assorted member hanging from around the god's navel was added. The original state cannot be established with any certainty, however, and it is possible that the wretched overpainting by the restorer, Salvador Martinez Cubells, is also responsible for the exaggerated curves of the child victim's body.

If Saturn was depicted as aroused, then Goya's choice of Judith *as a pendant would cohere with his despairing bitterness about sexual violence, evident in some of the* Caprichos, Disparates *and* Disasters of War. Judith *is a story about sexual excess, in which the heroine's behaviour is so ambiguous that the Book of Judith was excluded from the Protestant Bible. In the Vulgate, St. Jerome even added an anxious gloss to reassure* readers that the bedecked widow had not cynically seduced Holofernes in his tent before she murdered him. Despite Judith's canonical status as a Christian heroine, one of the Worthies—even a precursor of the Virgin Mary—she was seen as an anomalous woman: in the famous discussion about the placing of Michelangelo's David in Florence, one citizen wanted David to replace Donatello's Judith outside the Signoria as the symbol of the city's freedom because 'it is not right that a woman should kill a man'. With Judith and Holofernes, the sexes reverse their genders: he is soft, luxurious, sensual; she hard, warrior-like, virile.

The artist perhaps intuited that Saturn's famished assault on the body of one of his children would have excited him. Or, he may be showing that his sexual appetite stimulated his murderous violence. In either case, the ogre's drive to incorporate has erotic force for him. Goya's savage god is a forerunner of the Bluebeards of fairy tale, whose appetite to consume expresses metaphorically within the texts the sexual dangers, for women in particular, in the cycle from union to gestation and giving birth. If his greed claims his daughter as its particular prey, Goya's Saturn becomes a man defying the limits of maleness as well as time, frenziedly seeking to incorporate a female body, to possess it in ways twice forbidden to him— by the prohibition on incest and on cannibalism. In this he shadows his counterpart in Greek mythology, the ancestor god Kronos, and personifies aberrant rage against the laws of nature, death, and gender.

Uranos, the father of the gods, is castrated by his son Kronos and gives birth to Aphrodite (left); in this illustration to Ovid's Metamorphoses, *he is conflated with Kronos who ate his children and then regurgitated them, and with Saturn or Father Time whose scythe he holds.* La Bible des poètes, *Paris, 1507 edition.*

II

'MY FATHER HE ATE ME...'

"Oh yes,' the BFG said. 'A dream where you is seeing little chiddlers being eaten is about the most frightsome troggle-humping dream you can get. It's a kicksy bogthumper. It's a whoppsy grobswitcher. It is all of them riddled into one. . .'

Roald Dahl, The BFG

 The unholy combination of infanticide and cannibalism is a divine patriarchal prerogative, it could be said, part of the founding myth of the Greek divine pantheon itself, as told by Hesiod in the *Theogony*, his long poem that recounts the origins and genealogy of the Olympian deities. Kronos, chief of the gods in the second generation, is told that one of his children will supplant him, so he devours them one by one. But Zeus survives because his mother Rhea foils his father's plan. When it comes to his turn to be eaten, as all his elder brothers and sisters have been before him, Rhea:

> handed, solemnly,
> All wrapped in swaddling-clothes, a giant stone.

Kronos, the precursor of many duped ogres of fairy tale, 'seized it in his hands and thrust it down 'Into his belly, fool!'

The motif of cannibalism, in its earliest mythological expression, enfolds a threat to children above all, and appears to dramatize the struggle for survival within the family—mother, father and infant. The famous Olympians, male and female—Hera, Demeter, Hades, Hestia, Poseidon—are devoured every one in this way at birth in the Hesiod foundation myth. In Roman mythology, the same story becomes attached to Jupiter, the Roman Zeus, and his father Saturn, the Roman Kronos.

Hesiod, clearly aiming to sing of the glory of Zeus and his coming to power, then describes how, when Zeus grows up, his mother, Rhea, conspires with him to overthrow his father. Hesiod is unclear how much Rhea accomplished by herself and what exactly Zeus did, but a later writer like Apollodorus in his account of the gods' origins, *The Library*, clarifies Zeus' actions: he tricks Kronos into taking a purgative which makes him vomit, and one by one the gods are reborn whole from their father's belly.

Images of Kronos or Saturn devouring his children are extremely rare before the fifteenth century. The iconography that develops later, during the Renaissance, shows Kronos grasping his live children by a limb— sometimes upside down by one leg, in the same fashion as the babies in the Massacre of the Innocents or the Judgment of Solomon. The pose replicates, through a visual pun, the inverted ethics of the carnage. Sometimes the god grasps his offspring with one huge hand around its middle and prepares to wolf the infant whole, sometimes tearing at the chest, sometimes stuffing the head into his mouth; in other images, having chewed off a leg and a forearm, he is shown attacking another part with bared teeth.

A discrepancy thus exists between image and story: the logic of the Hesiodic narrative implies that, if Kronos could be tricked by a stone wrapped in swaddling bands, which he swallows as if it were simply a large pill of some kind, then he is not likely to have torn his other children naked limb from limb, piece by piece, gnawing and biting and chewing their undraped and vulnerable flesh as depicted with such appalled fascination by artists like Rubens in his savage painting *Saturn Devouring His Children* of 1636 in the Prado, which Goya was knowingly recasting in his fresco.

Such representations of Kronos were perhaps influenced by the much more famous cannibal ogre, Polyphemus the Cyclops, who devours Odysseus' companions. Renaissance artists did know classical interpretations of this scene, showing the Cyclops dragging one of Odysseus' men by the arm to the pot. But the deeper reasons for the myth's reappearance in this savage cannibal mood, in expressions ranging from macabre fairy tales to Goya's tragic *Black Paintings*, have to be looked for elsewhere, since desire, not practical intelligence, governs incident in stories of this kind.

The magical, implausible reprieve of the devoured offspring catches at the deeper meaning of the myth. It casts Kronos as a surrogate mother, giving birth from his mouth to the gods and goddesses as the issue of his body. Kronos' act of devouring his brood forms a prelude to birth; being eaten equals incorporation, and this in turn stands for a surrogate though unwitting pregnancy—of the male. In this way, his progeny re-enter the world, twice born of their father, begotten and brought forth. But this anomalous

Goya drops the trappings of classical myth to create a stark image of human madness and violence. Saturn Devouring His Children, *red chalk, 1797–8.*

behaviour implies the difficulty of male identity in the ordinary course of nature when it comes to parturition—later Zeus, Kronos' son, will give birth to Athena from his head in order to claim her as his true daughter, and, as we have seen, Dionysus also issues from his body. One of the strangest recurrences of the motif confirms this latent meaning of the story: in an illustrated alchemical fable called 'Lambspring', printed in Germany in 1625, a king pines for his absent son; when the son returns at last from his journey, his father embraces him so rapturously that he literally engulfs him. The engraving shows the bearded monarch, enthroned, his mouth open wide, clasping his offspring. Having accidentally swallowed him, the king in a fever then takes to his bed—a curtained four-poster in the next vignette, with his slippers neatly set beside it, the bed-curtains twined round the posts, and a chamber pot stowed beneath it. He is shown propped up on pillows, praying to be delivered of his son. His prayer is granted, and at the end of this symbolic lying-in, the boy is reborn, to be enthroned at his father's side on a nicely plump cushion with a sceptre in his hand, looking altogether very perky again.

It is significant that in Greek myth, women never appear to commit the outrage of devouring their children. Philomela and her sister Procne kill Itys, Procne's son, and serve him up to his father, Tereus, in revenge for his rape and mutilation of Philomela; Medea cuts up her brother's body and scatters it; she later murders her own children. But they do not eat their own offspring on purpose, nor are they duped into feasting off their own children. This can hardly be because they are soft-

In an alchemical fable, a king, having accidentally swallowed his son, takes to his bed, waiting to give birth. Lambspring, Germany, 1625.

hearted, given the extreme mayhem they perpetrate. Mothers in classical myth are infanticidal, but not incestuously cannibalistic, because the stories deal with the question of parental relations to nature and to generation. The act of eating represents an inverted birthing: biological ownership through incorporation. The idea lingers in modern fairy tales about giants and cannibal fathers.

By contrast, the mother who is shown deciding to kill her baby and cook it during the siege of Jerusalem is portrayed acting from merely practical, callous motives: she decides not to starve. Her act nullifies the meaning of maternity, rather than attempting to supplant the mother's role, and Josephus, who gives this episode in his history of the Jewish war against the Romans, portrays it as the ultimate horror that hardened Caesar against the besieged: 'He would bury this abomination of infanticide and cannibalism under the ruins of their country . . . It was even more revolting for mothers to eat such food than for fathers . . .' (Accusations of such crimes will haunt the propaganda of racism and anti-Semitism.)

The unnatural mother of this kind returns in the Renaissance with a vengeance, in Shakespeare's *Titus Andronicus*, in *The Bloody Banquet* by Thomas Dekker and Thomas Middleton, and in printed witch lore and fairy tales. Queens like Tamora in *Titus Andronicus* are represented as the heads of their lineage, and so attacking them through their children corresponds to the implicit genealogical structure of Greek and Latin myths, where lines of descent are established legally through fathers who then struggle to establish patrimony with paternity.

The myth of Kronos, as it grapples with the question about children's origin, passes through two phases before it interestingly suggests an answer: first, Rhea recognizes the authority of Kronos' paternity by allowing him to eat his children and make them part of his flesh; secondly, Kronos reaffirms his biological paternity when he vomits them out of his mouth. But Kronos' story—and indeed the outlandish births of Athena and Dionysus—admits that the riddle cannot be solved except by prodigious, unnatural procedures, and this implies an unspoken admission of the limits of paternal reach. The ogre, in the midst of asserting his absolute rights to incorporate, to make the child one with him, to take it into his body as if it were his own, has to accept defeat. The motif of the transgressive cannibal parent, as excess, as outrage, serves to define the limits on a father's power.

Kronos' devouring his children follows his own act of parricide against his abusive father Ouranos, or Heaven. Kronos' own mother—Gaia, or Earth—had hidden her offspring from Ouranos' jealousy, and then set them on to kill their father. Only Kronos agreed; Hesiod gives the celebrated episode in *Theogony*:

> Great Heaven came, and with him brought the night,
> Longing for love, he lay around the Earth,
> Spreading out fully. But the hidden boy
> Stretched forth his left hand; in his right he took
> The great long jagged sickle; eagerly
> He harvested his father's genitals
> And threw them off behind.

From the blood spattering the earth spring the Furies, the Melian nymphs, and the Giants, the brothers of the future Olympians. And from the genitals, scattered on the sea and carried as foam on the surface of the waves, Aphrodite, goddess of love, is born.

In a variant supplied in the Orphic tradition, the son repeats his father's act, and Zeus plies Kronos with fermented honey, binds him and then castrates him, as he had castrated his father. But this fragment of the tradition was not widely known, and later narrators had great difficulty (with which modern readers might well sympathize) in keeping the generations of filicides and parricides distinct. *La Bible des poètes*, illuminated as if it were a manuscript and published by Antoine Vérard in Paris in 1493 and 1507, opens with a most arresting frontispiece. It compresses the story into one vividly dramatic image: Kronos in the centre is devouring a child, while bleeding from the wound from his severed genitals; Aphrodite, Ouranos' daughter, simultaneously rises on her shell beside him. Kronos here appears holding the scythe of the planet Saturn, his Roman counterpart, with whom he was wholly identified in the Middle Ages, and on the helve of the scythe a dragon is looped, devouring its own tail—another image of cyclical time, another expression of the desire for eternal return.

For the issue at stake among ogres and cannibals of myth and fairy tale is, above all, the onward march of time. Children bear away the future with them—either thieves of their parents' store, or its guardians. Hence, the second, interwoven area of anxiety in the baby-eaters' stories: to whom do babies belong? Mothers or fathers? How can they belong to both? In what form can this doubleness of origin be expressed? How does the natural, biological origin convert into social relation? Who has control of the identity of children? What relation exists between identity and origin? How does the father affirm his continuity?

In the illustration of *La Bible des poètes* we see Kronos as an unnatural mother, a man operated on to acquire a woman's bodily functions, a kind of sex change: a man who gives birth twice over, through his mouth after he has eaten his children and through the semen frothing on the sea from his severed phallus. The medieval text's collapse of diachrony into synchrony opens a door on to one meaning of the death that the ogre and his food supply might signify: male jealousy of women's bodies as birthgivers. Such stories recognize the aggression felt towards this female capacity, because control of fertility is crucial, as we know, to the establishment of family and kinship boundaries. Michel Tournier, the French novelist, mined this misogynist side of male passions when he revisited the myth in his sinister and compelling novel *Le Roi des aulnes* (1970). He gives his protagonist the surname Tiffauges, after the castle of Gilles de Rais, and moves the action to Nazi Germany; throughout, he concentrates on the exquisite tenderness of his hero's 'maternal' love for the boys whom he holds captive in a camp. Tiffauges, a latterday ogre, identifies strongly with St. Christopher, who epitomizes for him paternal protection because he bore the Christ Child on his shoulders. Tiffauges undertakes, with voluptuous self-abasement, all the traditional tasks performed by women on behalf of his boy charges; for him, their exclusively male world brings about an ideal, blissful plenitude.

In the Middle Ages and Renaissance, the name Kronos, beginning with the Greek letter kappa (κ), became assimilated to the Greek word for time, *chronos*, spelled by contrast with an initial letter chi (χ), which had itself engendered many terms for time in the Romance languages and English. Hence, in traditional zodiac imagery, on calendars and in numerous astronomy and astrology treatises, the complex figure of Kronos/Saturn, presiding genius of Melancholy, holds a scythe and an hourglass as he rides in his chariot round the wheel of the heavens. Sometimes he is shown devouring his children, who are allegorized as the Hours. He comes to represent the unrelenting passage of Father Time, who devours all, as depicted in appropriately saturnine engravings by sixteenth-century artists like Hans Sebald Beham and Maerten van Heemskerck.

But the problem with this influential conflation is that it colludes—unconsciously—with the father's intentions and refuses to admit the defeat of the hoary old patriarch. The medieval and Renaissance allegory reassigns the laurel to the elders, to Father Time, because in terms of chronology, the metaphor of the Hours being inexorably swallowed up as Time rolls on works in a familiar way. Yet this misses the human point: the metaphor is inadequate to the task of capturing all that is happening in the original mytheme of Kronos devouring his children. The myth of Kronos and Zeus tells of time's eternal victory from the point of view of the vanquishing children who take over. Kronos is attempting to halt time; the children, representing the future generation, announce his redundancy, immortal or no. Through them, time will roll on *for him*.

Kronos devours his children in order to put an end to their independence and to their maternally derived difference. In direct contrast, in another constellation of tales, child murder is the most heinous revenge anyone can wreak on an enemy, exacerbated only by the refinement of cooking the victims and then offering them to the unsuspecting fathers to eat. In this group of stories, the mad melancholy of Saturn can sometimes take possession of the predators after they have consumed their own. Characters like Tereus in the story of Philomel and Procne, or Tamora, Queen of the Goths in *Titus Andronicus*, or the nameless father in the Grimms' tale 'The Juniper Tree' are invited to feast all unwittingly on a macabre banquet made of their own children's flesh, baked in a pie or boiled in a pudding. This startlingly common plot presents such parental cannibalism as an act of consummate revenge on their deepest interests, a principle that at one level apparently reverses the thrust of desire in the story of Kronos.

The Most Lamentable Roman Tragedy of Titus Andronicus was performed in 1592, a period when cannibal dramas were especially enjoyed by theatre audiences; part of Shakespeare's gory spectacle is patterned after Ovid's tale of Philomel, the future nightingale, victim of her

The planet Saturn, in Renaissance interpretations of the Zodiac's power over human destiny and passions, presided over the affliction of melancholy, inducing suicide and madness. Maerten van Heemskerck, sixteenth century.

Thracian brother-in-law Tereus, who conceives an irrepressible lust for her, abducts her, rapes her, and then, when she rails at him, cuts out her tongue.

In Shakespeare's play, Titus' only daughter, Lavinia, suffers the same cruelties as Philomel, but with the added horror that her assailants, Demetrius and Chiron, cut off her hands to prevent her depicting her story in tapestry, as Philomel does in the *Metamorphoses*. They know the story, and so does almost everyone else in the play, for it is referred to constantly. In revenge for the violation of Lavinia and other outrages in this most gory of plays, Titus butchers her aggressors and dishes them up to their mother, as Philomel and Procne cooked Itys for his father's dinner. The maid without hands, who is disfigured after she has been violated, is a recurring, even stock topos in medieval romance and thence fairy tales, as is the ogre's cannibal feast.

An Elizabethan ballad, which appeared soon after the play, summarizes

Titus' revenge in his own voice:

> I cut their Throats, my Daughter held the pan
> Betwixt her Stumps wherein the Blood it ran;
> And then I ground their Bones to Powder small,
> And made a Paste for Pies straight therewithal.
>
> Then with their Flesh I made two mighty Pies,
> And at the Banquet serv'd in stately wise;
> Before the Empress I set this loathsome Meat,
> So of her Son's own Flesh she well did eat.

The play itself proceeds by grim exchanges of body parts, a penitential talion exacted on the living flesh of its vast cast of characters: at the opening of the drama, Titus has lost twenty-two sons in the wars; three only remain alive. In retribution, he demands the death of Queen Tamora's son, thus unleashing her fury against him. Later, after two of Titus' surviving sons have been (wrongfully) arrested for murder, Aaron the Moor brings Titus the message that if one of the Andronici is willing to sacrifice his hand, the emperor Saturninus will grant the young men a reprieve. The paternal Titus immediately obliges, in order to save his boys, and dispatches the lopped limb. But the hand is no sooner dispatched than it is returned, scorned, along with the heads of his executed sons. There then follows 'the most bizarre exit in Shakespeare', as Jacques Berthoud has commented: Titus carrying off one of the severed heads, his brother the other, while giving Lavinia his own hand to bear offstage; handless herself, she takes it between her teeth like a dog.

This sequence of grotesque exchanges corresponds to the predominant arboreal metaphor of family descendance. Titus and Tamora, and their sons and his daughter, are limbs on the family tree, and they are cut off, one by one, tit for tat, from the trunks of the two warring lineages in the tragedy. The emperor who presides over these bloody events is called Saturninus; he remains without issue when Tamora's baby turns out to be Aaron the Moor's. It is odd, and perhaps worth noting, that Shakespeare gave the emperor this name, with its close echo of Saturn-Kronos, in a play that features child-murder and anthropophagy; the god is alluded to in the course of the drama by Aaron the Moor, who invokes Saturn as 'dominator' over his desires (Act II, sc.iii). Shakespeare thus disperses the planetary deity's characteristics among several of his characters. The childless Saturninus and the fondly paternal yet saturnine Aaron represent inversions of the Greek filicidal myth, and thereby encapsulate the profound divergence of the meaning of *Titus Andronicus* from the myth of Kronos. In the play, all are seeking to maintain their children alive—to further their interests, to be replaced in due course by heirs who will carry on the family name, renown, fortune. Here having issue is the issue; making time serve family interests drives the characters' desires. This interest turns upside down the Greek gods' attempts to extinguish the threat of usurpation by the younger generation.

Titus succeeds in his revenge when Tamora, that 'lascivious Goth' (Act II, sc. ii), 'that ravenous tiger' (Act V, sc.iii) eats her children:

> Why, there they are, both baked in this pie,
> Whereof their mother daintily hath fed,
> Eating the flesh that she herself hath bred.

A shift in the myth occurs in later fairy tales that weave different plots around the theme of incestuous cannibalism: the intrinsic thrust towards the happy ending produces lucky escapes for the child victims in 'The Sleeping Beauty,' 'Snow White,' 'Hansel and Gretel' and many others, and in most cases, the parents rejoice that their offspring are safe in spite of all. Charles Perrault's 'La Belle au bois dormant' ('The Sleeping Beauty in the Wood') features a spectacular ogress: the wicked mother-in-law, who is so jealous of her son's lovely wife and children that she orders her Maître d'Hotel to serve them one by one 'à la Sauce–Robert'. He is worried that the Sleeping Beauty might be tough, because, after all, 'The Young Queen was twenty, now, if you did not count the hundred years she had been asleep.' (This kind of cannibal joke survives unmarked by age.) An English chapbook translation of around 1750 gives the recipe. 'This is a French sauce', a gloss informs the children, 'made up with onions, shredded and boiled tender in butter; to which is added vinegar, mustard, salt, pepper and a little wine.' The butler, like the huntsman in 'Snow White', cannot bear to kill the lovely children or their mother and hides them one after the other. Eventually, the wicked ogress is thrown to stew in her own pot: 'The King could not but feel a little sad; she was his mother. But he soon consoled himself with his lovely wife and children.'

The telling and retelling of incestuous cannibal stories can be placed in a cultural-historical perspective which suggests that both social circumstances and biological imperatives contradict any claim to universality made for the Oedipal theory. *Titus Andronicus*, in Shakespeare's play as well as its associated ballad, and 'The Juniper Tree', the Grimm Brothers' fairy tale, first published in their anthology in 1812, show decidedly different ideas about the relation of children and parents. Yet Freud's own gifted storytelling has naturalized the Greek genealogical myth about murderous rivalry between fathers and offspring. Dishing up children in a pie for their own father or mother to eat unsuspectingly constitutes the sweetest and most savage revenge for Titus Andronicus, as it does for the prince's wicked mother in 'The Sleeping Beauty' or for Snow White's rival in the fairy tale, both of whom are foiled in the attempt. These stories assume dynastic survival from generation to generation as the most profound desideratum, likewise the natural love of offspring: the barbarous Tamora, Queen of the Goths, loves her own children beyond all other principles of conduct, just as a tigress does; her spectacular acts of savagery are fired by Titus' murder of her son, just as Titus' pitiless rage and madness are incited by the deaths of his children and the mutilation and rape of Lavinia; the arch-villain Aaron the Moor, when he becomes a father, grows soft and lyrical about what he will do on his infant heir's behalf. Futurity is guaranteed by the advent of children: their survival is necessary to continuing presence, power, identity.

The Grimm Brothers published their collection *Children's and Household Tales* in Germany at the time when modern concepts of horror were being formed, as they were in Goya's Spain and in Edgar Allan Poe's America. Their anthology includes the much repeated and much loved fairy tale of incestuous cannibalism, 'The Juniper Tree'. In this story, a macabre recasting of the Kronos foundation myth for the modern nursery, in which mortals take the place of immortals, the ogre's attempt to destroy a member of the future generation is frustrated, the wicked disorderly elements of family are cast out and harmony is restored around the good father.

The nameless father is portrayed as innocent, ignorant of his act of cannibal incest—or has he been shielded by the story from complicity in the dark events, as other fathers are in other tales in the Grimms' versions? However it may be, in 'The Juniper Tree', incorporation into the father—when the little boy is unwittingly eaten for dinner—does not spell absolute death for him any more than it does for the Olympians whom Kronos devours. Paternity, in this fairy tale as well as in the Greek myth of divine origin, can bring forth the whole child again.

'The Juniper Tree' narrates a father's mistaken act of cannibalism, followed by the salvation and healing of the family as it regroups around the figure of the good father and expels the wicked, controlling, murderous false mother. This conclusion mirrors the end of Perrault's 'The Sleeping Beauty' and the Grimm Brothers' 'Hansel and Gretel', in which the women, in charge of the cauldron and the oven, are responsible for all meals and what they contain. Written down in the stark affectless tone of true fairy-tale macabre, 'The Juniper Tree' fingers again many of the sore lesions in the ancient myth of Kronos. Although the wicked-ogre figure here is a woman, the father exhibits various ogreish standby traits: he is easily deceived, he eats human flesh, and he establishes his power through a sequence of consuming acts and metaphorical rebirths. Though the stories seem not to cohere, the nineteenth-century variation consolidates paternal power at a depth that eluded Kronos.

A child is born to a woman whose blood falls on the snow as she is peeling an apple—and he is as red as blood and as white as snow. During her pregnancy, she has gorged to excess on the blue berries of the juniper tree, and they have poisoned her; so, although she is able to rejoice at the birth of her son, she dies, asking to be buried under the juniper tree. The father, of course, marries again. The wicked stepmother has a daughter, and she hates the stepchild who is as red as blood and as white as snow. She maltreats him; and one day, when he asks for an apple, she drops the lid of the trunk where the apples are stored and cuts off his head; it rolls in among the red fruit. She then takes the head and adjusts it back on the child's body with a white kerchief at the neck to hide the wound and props him up on the chest with an apple in his hand. Her daughter, Marlinchen, comes in and notices that her stepbrother is looking pale; when he does not answer her wish for the apple, Marlinchen gives him a box on the ears, as her mother has suggested, and knocks his head off. She is terrified, but the mother, a veteran cannibal hell-hag, exclaims, 'What have you done! Be quiet and let no one know it; it cannot be helped now, we will make him into black puddings.' So she chops up her stepchild; Marlinchen, weeping, salts the pieces with her tears. When the father comes home for his dinner, he sups with relish on his son, not knowing of course what he is eating. He finds the stew delicious, asks for another serving, and another. Later, Marlinchen gathers up the bones he has tossed under the table, wraps them in a silk scarf, and buries them under the juniper tree; she lies down under it and feels strangely quietened, almost happy. Then a beautiful bird rises out of a mysterious fire that appears in the tree like a mist, and sings,

> My mother she killed me.
>   My father he ate me.
> My sister, Marlinchen,
>   She gathered up my bones. . .
> *Tweet, tweet!* What a lovely bird I am!'

The magic bird flies around, singing and drawing the marvelling pleasure of its listeners, who give him in turn costly gifts at his request—a gold chain, a pair of red shoes and, finally, a millstone, so heavy that twenty millers are needed to lift it up for the bird. But he dips his head into the hole and flies up easily, to sing outside the juniper tree house. The wicked stepmother hears the terrible song and feels as if she is being burned alive. The father hears it, too, and the bird drops the gold chain round his neck; then he gives Marlinchen the shoes. When the stepmother runs out of the house, he drops the millstone on her head. Fire explodes around them. When the flames have died down, the little boy who was devoured is standing there: 'He took his father and Marlinchen by the hand, and all three were right glad. Then they went into the house, sat down at the table, and ate.'

Orality in the oral tale: red and raw. The child red as blood, born after his mother is peeling an apple, the mother who then dies from the juniper berries, the boy's head that rolls down among the rosy apples in the trunk, the cooked meat on the table, the bones under it—the sequence of fatal foods climaxes with the millstone for a murder weapon. The instrument for grinding good bread ends the life of a woman who put bad food before her family; only after she is dead can the family regroup around the restored, disinfected table in a scene of domestic—and patriarchal—stability. Ingestion and gestation are so braided together in the tale, as they are in the words and their common root, that it is hard to disentangle where breeding ends and eating begins, or vice versa. The family is reborn, re-engendered, restored through the oral language of the fairy tale as a group physically born of the father, saved by the airy fiery phantom bird that was the murdered son/brother, and reassembled to feast on the right nourishment—a domestic restaurant. Biology is negated: the dead mother, after she has given birth, has no body, though she continues to affect the course of the action through the bird who rises from their common grave under the juniper tree. But she is no longer enfleshed; only the nurturant father remains to control the ongoing cycle of eating and living. In a recent opera of this fairy tale, composed by Roderick Watkins, the drama pointedly ends with the boy taking the place of his father at the head of the table.

Both the Greek myth of the infantiphagous father and this German Romantic fairy tale encode a lesson in resignation to the passage of time, the overtaking of age by youth, and the necessarily stepped character of the genealogical ladder through life. The Grimms' 'The Juniper Tree' is one of numerous similar stories that exist in different versions in different countries, but it is noteworthy that this *plattdeutsch*, or Pomeranian dialect version, was passed on to the brothers by the German Romantic artist Phillip Otto Runge, who in his own paintings insists on the almost preternatural vitality of children.

In Runge's portrait of his own parents and children, for instance, which was painted in 1806, six years before the publication of *Household Tales*, the old couple in their dark clothes, shaded and withered, are withdrawing into the shadows, but their two grandchildren, blooming with beauty and splendour, glowing with colour and energy and *élan vital*, are fingering lilies of the field. The little girl eyes her grandparents, seemingly almost sceptical of their continuing existence. In many other paintings and drawings, children symbolize day and spring and burgeoning and life, while their elders fade away. Runge may have responded to 'The Juniper Tree' and to fairy tales in general because he was living at a historical moment when the child emerges as a subject—and a hero. These child-centred narratives proclaim the resilience of the young and their eventual emergence as supreme.

Writing during the Grimms' youth, when the *Household Tales* were being collected, Thomas Paine inveighed against the callousness of provision for children within the English system, and made a brilliant leap from mythological cannibal fathers to primogeniture: 'Aristocracy has never more than *one* child. The rest are begotten to be devoured. They are thrown to the cannibal for prey, and the natural parent prepares the unnatural repast.' He then endorsed with passion the abolition of primogeniture by the French revolutionaries, which had to be done: 'As everything which is out of nature in man, affects, more or less, the interests of society, so does this. . . To restore, therefore, parents to their children, and children to their parents—relations to each other, and man to society . . .', this was the urgent task. The resuscitation of the boy with the help of his stepsister in 'The Juniper Tree' correlates with Paine and Runge's advocacy of children's interests at the turn of the eighteenth century.

In such a story, as in the myth of Kronos, the rules that define genus and species and that forbid the eating of one's own kind, govern the relationships between progenitors and the generation that comes after them. Beneath the grotesque phantasmagoria of cannibal bogeymen there pulses the biological urge to perpetuate the line; the folly and horror of child murder and abuse recur alongside other violations and terrors. At its heart flourishes anxiety about generational order, the stewardship of the future by the living on behalf of the vulnerable who should inherit. The forms the fear takes are intertwined with the idea of due order; they cast a shadow of the disorderly and the monstrous. And the idea of regularity gives rise to

The light falls on the artist's children, the coming generation, as his ageing parents recede into the shadows. Phillip Otto Runge, Portrait of the Artist's Family, *1806.*

extravagant conjugations of irregularity in myths and stories; monstrous and grotesque behaviour helps to define lawful lineage. Terrible tales of aberration and abomination constantly invoke, by inversion and trespass, an ideal of normal practice and expected categories. As Geoffrey Galt Harpham points out in his study of the grotesque, 'Genre, genus and genitals are linked in our language as in our subconscious.'

The grotesque, with its parodic harshness, its sick humour, its shivery manipulation of fear and pleasure in the monstrous, may seem an odd corner for the selfish gene to lurk, but it has emerged as a pronounced, if not dominant, method of facing down the menace that threatens survival and posterity. With the comparative easing of material dangers, this motive has shifted, towards a desire to afford psychological rather than physical protection. But as a stratagem, its efficacy is questionable. Perhaps part of the pleasure inspired by performances and images of the bogeyman arises from this indeterminacy, as children reveal when they peep through their fingers at something scary, not knowing whether to look or to look away, not knowing whether to shriek or to laugh, to be truly frightened or to mock. Not knowing where the game begins—or ends.

❖   ❖   ❖

It would be far too simple to state that a new empathy with children as victims fashions the appearances of the ogre in stories. Needless to say, his threat lingers, and its links to control and punishment have allowed him to flourish in cultures that are not child-centred in the spirit of Runge.

The myth of Kronos, as it is told by Hesiod, teaches by negative example: his assault on his progeny offends against human law. The story offers an upside-down mirror in which to view paternal love and duty in its proper, even natural, form. Unexamined acceptance of the Oedipus complex has, however, made it harder to see the affirmation of child-parent unity that cannibal stories paradoxically hold out.

The ogre as a generic father, whose sons murderously oppose and defeat him, matches some of the cases told in myth and fairy tale; but it is significantly emphasized in the nineteenth century, when legal, social and political interpretations of the material yield to universalizing domestic and psychological views. Freud's Oedipal plot has itself become a dominant tale of our time.

This master plot of the Victorian symbolic imagination assumes the hunger of the son to depose and supplant his father. In this, it remains faithful to the strand in Greek myth that sings the praises of Zeus and hymns his conquest of all comers—monsters, giants, fathers, rival gods. But this narrative came to dominate later, European retellings for cultural reasons, and in many representations the victory of Zeus over the Titans in the great battle of the giants took precedence over the Titans' assault on the younger generation, as in their murder of Zagreus: Giulio Romano, for example, in his dazzling, innovative Sala dei Giganti in the Palazzo Te, Mantua, frescoes the fall of the Titans over the dramatic vault in oblique homage to the grandeur of his patron, the young duke.

The myths of Kronos castrating Ouranos and of Zeus defeating Kronos were frequently muddled, as in the frontispiece to *La Bible des poètes*. It is interesting that no less a figure than Freud also conflated them. Like father, like son, Freud must have thought, when he wrote in *The Interpretation of Dreams*, that Zeus castrated his father Kronos. In fact, Hesiod does not tell us the fate of Kronos after he is usurped by Zeus; he fades into obscurity, joining the equally shadowy Titans in their exile from supreme power. Freud's passage targets paternal authority in his own time, using the Greek gods as examples: 'Kronos devoured his children, just as the wild boar devours the sow's litter; while Zeus emasculated his father and made himself ruler in his place.' Freud comments, 'The obscure information which is brought to us by mythology and legend from the primæval ages of human society gives an unpleasing picture of the father's despotic power and of the ruthlessness with which he made use of it.'

The emphasis of Freud's Oedipal theory falls, however, on the son's aggression towards the father, as his rival, and on the 'primal horde's' murder of their progenitors. As Laura Mulvey has pointed out, the original crimes of Kronos and of Laius (Oedipus' father) are obscured in Freud's interpretation: the father who purposefully mutilates his son and exposes him to die on a mountain does not figure very vividly in subsequent discussions of the story, compared to the prominence given to the son's crime: that of Oedipus who, in an early instance of road rage, kills his father unknowingly.

Freud, to whom the mistake was pointed out, later used the error when he examined the truth-telling value of such slips and tricks of memory in *The Psychopathology of Everyday Life*. Revealingly, he linked his mixing up of Kronos and Ouranos to a remark his older half-brother had once made to him: 'One thing you must not forget is that as far as the conduct of your life is concerned, you really belong not to the second, but to the third generation in relation to your father.' Freud explained that his own mistake, when he repressed the myth's sequence, betrayed his refusal to admit that he was young enough to be his half-brother's son. Again, the myth of the murderous father repeats a lesson about genealogical time. Freud's insistence on the son's murderous intentions towards the father effaces paternal animus—the foundation myth of Abraham and Isaac, of God the Father and Christ, of Oedipus exposed by Laius—in the interest of emphasizing the father's vulnerability.

Freud was son and father in a populous household of siblings and offspring and servants at a historical moment when the authority of the paterfamilias stood high and remained largely unchallenged; it is perhaps not surprising that Freud's personal lenses obscure the narrative about the threat—and the attraction—of women's bodies and women's power that the brutal myth of the ogre also enfolds. However, as Paul Ricoeur has eloquently pleaded:

In The God Beneath the Sea *by Leon Garfield and Edward Blishen, the dream of the male giving birth: the son emerges from the father's jaws. Charles Keeping,* Cronus, *1970.*

Is there not a possible religion of life, a religion of love? . . . in the famous myth of the primal murder, Freud encounters an episode that remains unexplained, although it is ultimately the pivot of the drama: the episode among the brothers whereby they agreed not to repeat themselves the murder of the father. This covenant is highly significant, for it puts an end to the repetition of the act of parricide; by prohibiting fratricide the convenant engenders a history . . . Why not link the destiny of faith with this conciliation, rather than the perpetual repetition of the parricide?

Leon Garfield and Edward Blishen give the story of Kronos a blazing retelling in *The God Beneath the Sea* (1970), a classic for young readers of Greek myths. Cronus [Kronos], maddened by the Furies, eats one of his children and so feels invincible:

The mad king grinned in triumph. Sooner or later, he would destroy his tormentors even as he had eaten his child. Nothing would shake his throne . . . Then Rhea bore another child. Was there a traitor in his bed? No matter. Cronus was armoured at all points. Again he ate the child.

He would reign for ever . . .

In a tingling closing paragraph to the Kronos episode, the child is endowed with superhuman foreknowledge of his triumph: Rhea has tricked Kronos into swallowing the stone, and

He reached out and stroked her cheek. Then he wiped his mouth and left the room.

When he was gone, Rhea sank to her knees beside the bed. She stared into the careless folds. Then she started. Two golden eyes were gazing out at her, and an infant's lips were curved in a prophetic smile.

Garfield and Blishen are writing within the unspoken Oedipal and Darwinian plots of intergenerational strife which translate the aggression of the old towards the young into stories of the greed and ambition of both old and young. Yet as George Devereux has wisely protested:

Through the course of history, infinitely more children were killed . . . by their parents than parents killed by their children. Likewise child sacrifices are more common than parent sacrifices. Books on history, ethnology, criminology, comparative religions . . . and even the daily press . . . all tell the same story. These are hard facts, which simply cannot be reconciled with the arbitrary thesis that the cannibalistic impulses of children are more intense than and also dynamically and genetically prior to the cannibalistic impulses of adults, and that children groundlessly fantasize their parents as potential cannibals . . . though *ultimately* everything goes back to childhood, it need not necessarily go back to a *genetic* or *biological* substratum, but may result from a childhood experience . . . i.e. from the *impact* of the adults' cannibalistic impulses upon the infants' psyche.

The ogre and his imitators present what is possibly one of those rare universal fantasies, for children are still making up cannibal stories and passing them on. The anthropologist and art historian Claude Gaignebet, working recently in France, collected several hilarious and hair-raising examples from nine-year-old boys in the Pas de Calais. These are not fairy tales but anecdotes which claim to be true—they are even presented sometimes as autobiographical. One group rings variations on the theme of paternal cannibalism and castration in a contemporary setting:

> Un coup c'était Cafougnette, y ren'tre dans une boucherie, puis y avait un grenier, alors lui y ren'tre dans l'grenier puis y voit un trou, y dit merde, qu'est-ce que c'est. Alors y prend sa bitte puis il l'enfonce dans l'trou. Alors v'là une femme et puis elle dit: alors y a plus d'saucisse, alors y [le boucher] dit: non, elle dit: si, si y'en a une. Alors 'peut-être, c'est la dernière', alors y prend, il l'coupe Zwitt. Alors y donne à la femme. La femme la mange et l'lendemain, elle revient et elle dit:—elle etait bien bonne vot'saucisse, vous n'avez pas une autre et Cafougnette après y dit par l'trou, 'Quand er r'poussra.'

> (Suddenly there was Bodger, he goes into a butcher's, then there was an attic, so he goes into the attic and he sees a hole, he says shit, what is that? So he takes his willy and he pushes it into the hole. Then suddenly there's a woman and she says: so there's no more sausages, then he [the butcher] says, no. And she says, yes, yes there is one. Then, 'Perhaps it's the last one', then he takes it and he cuts it off, Snip! Then he gives it to the woman. The woman eats it and the next day, she comes back and she says— 'it was really good your sausage, haven't you got another' and Bodger says through the hole, 'When it grows again.')

In another spin on the story, it is the *father's* willy that is cut off. This too ends with the line, 'When it grows again.'

Gaignebet does not find savage irony in the punchlines about poor protagonists who are such dumblings they do not know that penises do not grow back. He heard the boys telling the stories without cynicism, and he praises their spirit of comic optimism, the rude health of children's humour. It is the first variant, in which the child's penis is eaten instead of a sausage, that seizes on the message of the myth of Kronos: that the young suffer the aggression of their elders but comfort themselves that they will inevitably gain ground on the old, that they will, like the brothers and sisters of Zeus or the protagonist of 'The Juniper Tree', return safe and whole. Gaignebet did, however, hear another tale of sausages, which concluded, rather more bleakly: 'Well it's Dad who's eaten it'.

The second variant contains the Oedipal threat of retaliation. It echoes that epiphanic moment of wordplay in the work of Melanie Klein when one of her small patients pretended to eat one of his toys. She interpreted the episode in the light of her theory of parent-child conflict: 'We came to recognize the father's penis and a growing feeling of aggression against it in many forms, the desire to eat and destroy it being specially prominent. For example, on one occasion, my [four-year-old] patient Dick lifted a little toy man to his mouth, gnashed his teeth and said, "Tea Daddy", by which he meant "Eat Daddy." He then asked for a drink of water.' (This child is the 'little Dick' whose case Jacques Lacan explores in his seminar on naming the father, or the Big Dick of the symbolic order or language.)

Father and son face each other in infinite regression in this way of telling the conflict; the struggle will go on. Gaignebet also points out that these are boys' stories—starring them first as victims, then as heroes.

But this male perspective on the figure of the ogre, and the easy, even glib identification with masculine aggression and paternal power, obscures the ogre's importance in the fantasies of women, who have told and heard—and enjoyed—these stories, and still do. The spirited phallic content tends to draw attention to castration anxiety, of a post-Freudian character, away from the sheer hunger that rumbles in the stories. Ogre stories are about food and power, about food in the right place and who puts it there, and vice versa. This concern has grown, as monsters have proliferated and their appetites been ever more luridly dramatized, so that feeding and monstrosity have begun to coincide in meaning: from the Cookie Monster of *Sesame Street* to the dinosaurs of *Jurassic Park*.

Phillip Otto Runge did not tell the Grimms who it was who had told him 'The Juniper Tree', but we know that most of their tales were passed on by women of all classes. It is important to put the ogre back in the mouth, on

In her performance piece of 1976, An Edible Family in a Mobile Home, *the artist Bobby Baker invited the audience to tea: father, sister and baby brother were offered as cake.*

the tongue, between the jaws of female speakers—and the children to whom they were speaking. When we do this, the stories begin to yield insights into their aggressive energies and their greed, too.

When girls or young women enter the plots, the threat of the monstrous bridegroom is primarily sexual, and the metaphors of devouring stand for his engulfing desire, as in Mme de Beaumont's 'La Belle et la bête', or Mme de Murat's 'Bearskin', a fairy tale about an ogre called Rhinocéros. The potent erotic field reverberating around the word 'consuming' and its associated metaphors has been explored with baroque plenitude in Peter Greenaway's film, *The Cook, the Thief, His Wife & Her Lover* (1989), and has become the particular terrain of the vampire fiction of Anne Rice and other return visits to the Dracula legend.

The one who consumes can also run a terrible risk: eating at someone's table places you in their power, as Persephone failed to remember when she bit into the pomegranate in Hades and for that reason alone was condemned to remain in the underworld. The myth resonates throughout Peter Greenaway's *oeuvre*, and makes a modern inferno of the restaurant in *The Cook. . .*, with the anti-hero as a Lord of Death and his wife as his unwilling consort, his Persephone. However, the tensions around feeding and being fed, as distinct from eating and being eaten, have been registered most acutely in representations by women, who are after all so often cast as the mistresses of ovens and kitchens and spoons and cauldrons and larders and stews in mythic material. A poem like Christina Rossetti's 'Goblin Market', with its succulent litany of tempting and lethal fruits, foreshadows the pronounced orality in writing by late twentieth-century writers like Angela Carter, Michèle Roberts, and Lucy Ellmann. The visual and performance work of women artists in the twentieth century also returns obsessively to feeding as a metaphor for power. Under the diabolical sign of the consumer consumed, they have travelled the range of anorexic-bulimic polarities and explored the role of the nurse-provider-and-cook, who is also a mouth needing to be fed herself. The Surrealist artist, Meret Oppenheim, in several mordantly ironical mixed media objects, likewise explored the connections of the female body and food, of sex and devouring, of love and nourishment: the celebrated *Déjeuner en fourrure (Fur Luncheon*, 1937), for example, which evokes in deadpan punning the act of cunnilingus. She also explored the theme when she placed on a dish a pair of white, high-heeled bridal shoes, trussed and upturned, with butcher's frills around the heels like lamb chops (*Ma Gouvernante—My Nurse—Mein Kindermädchen*, 1936), and when she baked a bread roll in the shape of a woman showing her vulva and laid it on a chessboard as place mat, with knife and fork alongside ('*Bon Appétit, Marcel*', 1966). Her contemporary, the artist Louise Bourgeois (b. 1911), twisted eucharistic motifs into the perverse joys of parricidal myth in her 1974 mixed media sculpture installation, *The Destruction of the Father*, for which she cast animal limbs in latex to create a *mise-en-scène* of a ritual meal. Later, the artist described the imagined scene behind the work: 'The children grabbed him and put him on the table. And he became the food. They took him apart, dismembered him. Ate him up. And so he was liquidated . . . It is a very murderous piece, an impulse that comes . . . when one turns against those one loves the most.'

Soon afterwards, in 1976, in London, the performance artist Bobby Baker independently created a work entirely out of cake. She applied baked sponge layers to lifesize figures, modelled from chicken wire, and then, as if she were playing with figures in a doll's house, she set them out in the postwar prefab where she was then living, in rooms lined with newspapers and magazines: beauty pin-ups in a bedroom where a girl was lying on the bed reading, comics in the boy's room. She then invited an audience to tea, to have a piece of cake with their cuppa. The mother was made in the form of a dressmaker's dummy with a cupboard in her chest and a teapot for her head, the artist using it (her?) to pour the tea for her visitors. The installation came to an end only when visitors had eaten up the figures of the father in his armchair reading a paper, and the three children, including the baby.

An Edible Family in a Mobile Home was a profane communion, a family tea party in which the most polite, indeed genteel, national ritual of friendship became an ogre's banquet. When all that was left of the figures was a stain on the floor and a mass of twisted chicken wire, Bobby Baker realized, as she had not done before, that she had made a group portrait of her own family. The piece brilliantly enacted theories of family conflict and the place of food within them, as simultaneously the symbol of care and love and the instrument of control and authority: 'I'll be Mother' means taking charge of the teapot.

The Bahamian-born artist Janine Antoni (b.1964) has also used food to dramatize specifically female conflicts in their relation to metaphors of devouring. For the piece called *Gnaw* (1992), she did indeed gnaw a huge slab of lard and an equally huge block of chocolate, leaving toothmarks all over the massive waxy, smelly, Qa'baa-like cubes; from the fatty matter she scraped together by this extreme means, she then cast glossy lipsticks and chocolate boxes and displayed them in the kind of gleaming gilt and glass cabinets used in the most expensive stores. The insecure desire to be

Janine Antoni slips away from under her mother's night-dress at the end of
Ready or Not Here I Come! *Artist's video, 1994.*

beautiful and loved, which consumer advertising and star and model cults
play on and excite, and its connection to food disorders (illustrated so
starkly in the case of Princess Diana) resonate in Antoni's sickly and sickening installation.

More recently, in 1994, Antoni re-enacted a childhood bogey game, in a
film that offers a vivid and fresh meaning of the ogre figure from a daughter's point of view. She filmed *Ready or Not Here I Come!* in her parents'
house, where she had grown up. The camera is situated behind the eyes of
the 'He', and he is hunting for Janine who is hiding, as no doubt the artist
did as a child. Her own father is playing He in this game of Hide and Seek,
and it is his voice we hear calling out the title 'Ready or Not Here I Come!'
In the same way as David Lynch positioned the camera in the marauding
and murderous Dennis Hopper's mind in his film *Blue Velvet* (1986), the
camera here moves with her father's movements. Tracking with his eyes,
playing Janine Antoni's pursuer in the game, we too, as spectators, roam
all over the house, looking into corners, into cupboards, into bathrooms,
under tables, beds, chairs. The first two times she is found easily enough—
and slips away, barely seen, with a laugh, wearing a loose white dress that
connotes night-time and childhood. But the third time, he—we—cannot
catch a glimpse of her anywhere. Each room of the house becomes familiar
as we search it, return to it and search it again. Finally, Janine Antoni is
found: concealed under her mother's loose dress—or nightdress—as she

sits by the bathtub. When spotted, the artist darts away—and this time she is not wearing any clothes except undershorts and the father's voice is heard exclaiming at her nakedness in a mixture of shock and wonder. The artist, repeating what was perhaps a favourite game for her as a child (her work is intensely autobiographical), goes back into her mother's tummy in make-believe in order to evade the marauding father who is coming after her, and the sight—however fleeting—of her mature, sexual, woman's body dismays him. It induces in him a moment of saturnine melancholy at the passing of time, at the separation of parent and child, at this unbridgeable difference and the taboo that makes contact between them impossible. The short video captures, deftly, wittily and touchingly, the bid to overturn the laws of generation and the limits of gender that tales of consuming cannibals often explore. It takes up the tragic theme of Saturn devouring his children and defies it, lightly, in the spirit of a game.

❖   ❖   ❖

The ogre who eats babies figures forth, in medieval and early modern narratives, the spectre of death that carried off both mothers and babies in the long centuries of high infant mortality. But he also embodies a monstrous and anomalous paternal response to the anxiety that his offspring would supplant him; his wicked folly makes plain the social and human imperative that the young must be allowed to thrive and grow. In fairy tales the commingling of bodies in the cannibal act threatens to wipe out the smaller, younger characters, in the same way that Kronos' impious devouring of his children almost succeeds in exterminating any successors who might rival his rule. Baby-eating returns in such narratives to affirm in topsy-turvy the social imperatives of procreation. The new generation must be allowed to survive: forces which attempt to engulf it, to halt age and time, appear as brutal, stupid, and ultimately powerless. In this sense, fairy tales do offer allegories of time and resignation: the future belongs to the young giant-killer, to the young prince and princess; the stories press their claims to autonomy and happiness, and warn the old—the authorities, the patriarchs—that their time will soon be up. In the Christian scheme child-murder, the most heinous of crimes, is imputed to the devil and his legions. These demons can also place adults in danger, of course. Although they express a moral wrong rather than a prodigy or anomaly of nature, such agents of absolute harm are enfleshed in monstrous bodies that borrow many of their abhorrent features and functions from the bestiary of pagan mythology, as in the terrifying case of Scylla the sea monster, who was cursed with an appetite that could never be appeased.

REFLECTION

THE NYMPHAEUM OF THE EMPEROR TIBERIUS

Around A.D. 511, a band of monks, under their leader Abbot Fortunatus, settled in the abandoned Tiberian villa at Sperlonga; they entered the pleasure dome the emperor had decreed in a grotto below the promontory of the Monte Circeo, Circe's Italian home, and took hammers to the pagan idols displayed there. They smashed the sculptures into smithereens and left the pieces where they fell, in the natural basin formed by the sea. Pope Gregory the Great reports the pious act of iconoclasm with satisfaction: terrible creatures from the sacrilegious pagan imaginary had been destroyed. One sculptural group showed Polyphemus the Cyclops slumped in a stupor from the wine Odysseus offered him; the hero and four of his men, Lilliputian in relation to the slumbering giant, are about to plunge the fire-sharpened stake into his single eye. Polyphemus' massive frame is imagined with virtuoso verisimilitude, down to the last particular: hair curls from the tops of his gigantic toes and on the upper side of the arches of his gigantic feet. Celebration of the hero's exploits is the predominant tone; the sculptors' rhetorical realization of the Cyclops' heroic scale and musculature magnifies the deed Odysseus performs. But this stupendous Polyphemus lay to one side in the emperor's arrangement: the centrepiece featured an even more fearsome adversary: the sea monster Scylla.

This hyperbolic monumental group of giants and monsters from classical myth appeared to be lost, shattered beyond repair after the monks' work. But sand was swept over the shards by the sea, and the fragments preserved. The torso of Scylla, armless, headless, gradually rose again above the bed of the basin, and was noted, in its barbarously mutilated state, in 1879. By 1953, excavations had begun and the patient work of piecing the sculptures together again. After more than forty years' work, the Polyphemus and the Scylla are now partially restored.

The lost monumental sculpture of Scylla seizing Odysseus' men with her dog's heads and double sea-serpent's tail has recently been restored. Roman copy erected between 4–26 A.D. of a possible Greek original, second century B.C., rediscovered in 1957 and reconstructed from 7000 fragments.

Tiberius' sculpture at Sperlonga conveys the piteous hybridity of the sea monster Scylla. In contrast to the Polyphemus, she is caught at a moment of whirling activity: naked to the waist, she is rising above the writhing assemblage of her monstrous nether parts, like a fantasy fairground attraction, a nightmare merry-go-round; a sea serpent's double tail curls out powerfully on either side of her to pin down two victims, while six dogs' heads sprout from her middle, with victims caught in their jaws. She has seized the tiller of Odysseus' boat as if it were hardly bigger than a wooden spoon, and is flourishing it aloft. Often depicted with a nymph's young and lovely face, framed by tousled and dripping hair in the traditional pose of an Aphrodite anadyomene, *and wearing a fringed skirt of sea fronds at her waist, the sea monster Scylla offered a rare opportunity to depict the female nude in classical art outside the cult of the goddess of love herself.*

The muscly and scaly double tail is not described as such in Homer, but it implies strongly that Scylla is cloven below, split down the centre of her abdomen, and it makes her the prototype of the double-tailed mermaid of later bestiaries and other fantasies. For it is Scylla the sea monster, and not the sirens whom Odysseus has safely eluded just before, who in classical art possesses a fish's scaly tail.

The monks were not only attacking a blasphemous example of pagan fantasy. They were also smashing the claim to authority that the emperor Tiberius was making when he situated the tremendous monumental sculptures in his summer retreat, a sybarite's grotto located on Circe's mainland abode, as described by both Hesiod and Ovid (as opposed to her island home of Aeaea, named in Homer); he assembled in the sea cave there a sculptural programme that asserted his predestined imperial status.

The group of Scylla, Polyphemus and other episodes in the fall of Troy, inspired by the Odyssey *and other epics, made visible Tiberius' imaginary lineage, as such stories of giants and wonders often do. For the emperor claimed descent from Telegonus, Circe's son by Odysseus, and thus was able to trace back his legitimacy as ruler not only to the Trojan hero Aeneas, legendary founder of Rome, but also to the Greeks.*

If the sculpture of Scylla had been recovered at another, earlier time, it would have inspired fervent ekphrases written by travellers to the classical ruins of Italy, such as Winckelmann or Goethe who invoked the wonders of the Laocoön. *In our day, this stupendous work has not achieved the worldwide fame it deserves. The plaster restoration incorporates the millions of shards abandoned* in situ *by the iconoclasts, and the results are overwhelmingly powerful. It is, possibly, a first-century Roman copy after a Hellenistic bronze predecessor of the second century* B.C.; *it is signed by*

Athanadoros, Hagesandros and Polydoros, the selfsame Rhodian masters whom Pliny names as the sculptors of that other mythical group of tragic death, the Laocoön. *Alternatively, it might be an original Roman work, merely claiming a prior model to enhance its prestige.*

That the monks attempted such a violent job of pious iconoclasm is perhaps not so very surprising. They were practising the heroic method of dealing with foes, like Odysseus himself: when they found strange and frightening phenomena, they tried to destroy them. Odysseus, a figure in a book, encounters imaginary creatures that are represented as all too real to him. The monks were, however, dealing with the double imaginary: representations of monstrous and heathen beings. These were identified with the diabolical and they felt the need to resort to heroic violence to rid themselves of them. For it is in medieval ideas of the Christian hell, among its flames and its naked and writhing devils, that ideas of pagan monsters and wonders and metamorphosis were, literally, demonized and the deepest foundations of the popular concept of bogeymen were laid.

III

THE POLYP AND THE CYCLOPS

The Lamia, Emblem strong of Sin,
  Does all her Charms employ;
To draw the unwary Trav'ller in,
  And then the Wretch destroy.
(. . . as to Man, it allures him by its Snares, for lying on its Belly, and concealing all but its Face and Breasts, tempts his Approach, till seizing on him by Surprize, it tears him to pieces, and then devours him.)

A Pretty Book of Pictures, 1770

 In Hesiod's *Theogony*, Scylla belongs among the huge progeny of monsters descending from the union of Earth and Sea, of Gaia and Pontus. In some genealogies she issues from their children, Phorcys and Ceto, and is sister to Medusa and the Gorgons, and to the three Græae with their one eye between them. Homer gives her a mother, Krataiis; he does not invoke a paternal origin for her. But Hesiod gives her different prodigious parents: Echidna, who was 'a fair-cheeked girl with glancing eyes' and a speckled viper below, couples with Typho, an amorphous manifestation of pursuit, terror, storms and mayhem: 'There grew out of him numerous heads and hands and wings, while from his thighs came huge coils of snakes. He emitted all kinds of roars and nothing could resist his might.'

From this scaly and serpentine pair, children of terror are indeed born, who have many appetites and as many mouths to satisfy them: among them a son, Cerberus the watchdog of hell, and several daughters—Hydra, hundred-headed assailant of Hercules, Chimera and Scylla.

The *Odyssey* evokes Scylla—twice over, in Book XII—in some of the most extended, vivid and intense descriptions in the poem. Scylla's name means dog—or, more precisely, bitch—and her accursed hybridity includes canine as well as marine features. Dogs' heads poke out from her hips in all directions, their jaws agape. She is not, however, a mastiff, like Cerberus, her brother. Her voice sounds, we are told, like a whelp crying out. George Chapman, in the translation published in 1616 and made famous by Keats, stretches the metaphor and adds alliteration as he describes her voice 'at all parts no more base / Than are a newly-kitten'd kitling's cries . . .'. In a footnote, Chapman shows himself very proud to be the first of Homeric translators to notice that the poet has written not that she roars, but that, contrary to expectations, she whimpers. Scylla is thus a female accursed by both gender and appearance, and childlike in her wordless utterance. Or is this yelping closer to the 'sweet moan' made by 'La Belle Dame Sans Merci'? Or could the poet have been suggesting the eerie cry of the octopus, which squeals like a siphon? Scylla does recall a giant polyp more readily than any other creature, with her many limbs and her puny sound. Multiplicity and incongruity: two characteristic marks of the monstrous.

Circe, giving the first account of Scylla, insists on her dread nature. In the midst of instructing Odysseus in his forthcoming ordeals, she tells him that Scylla is 'an evil monster', her 'howling is terror', she is a 'thing to shun', so hyperbolic in her excess and multiplicity of limbs and orifices that she is indeed hard to visualize. Thus, in Chapman's tremendous, properly sublime version:

> Twelve foul feet bear about
> Her ugly bulk. Six huge long necks look'd out
> Of her rank shoulders; every neck doth let
> A ghastly head out; every head three set,
> Thick thrust together, of abhorred teeth,
> And every tooth stuck with a sable death.

She is a devourer, a snatcher, a swallower, who inhabits a misty cave under the overhang of a cliff that is 'turned towards the dark', connected to the underworld of Erebus. From this coastal lair she watches, darts out and seizes her prey with her many monstrous mouths:

> She lurks in midst of all her den, and streaks
> From out a ghastly whirlpool all her necks;
> Where (gloting round her rock) to fish she falls;
> And up rush dolphins, dogfish; somewhiles whales,
> If got within her when her rapine feeds . . .

The enchantress warns Odysseus that, if he is to survive, he must resign himself to relinquishing six of his men to her appetite.

Later in the poem, Odysseus recalls his first-hand encounter with the monster whom Circe had first conjured from a distance. He dwells on the death of his companions, and vividly compares Scylla's raid to a line fisherman landing small fry that sprawl and gasp on the shore after being hooked. Again the emphasis falls on the heart-rending cries they make as they beg Odysseus to save them. He closes his account with the lines:

> I never did see,
> In all my sufferance ransacking the seas,
> A spectacle so full of miseries.

Their devouring closes the sequence of cannibal ordeals at the centre of the *Odyssey*.

Scylla's legend is confused, and after Hesiod and Homer, fanciful accounts were offered for her monstrosity: the storytellers set to work to insert her in the stream of romance and revenge dramas. She was once a beautiful nymph, according to one source; the sea goddess Amphitrite, jealous that her husband Poseidon had fallen in love with her, tossed poisonous herbs into the pool where she went to bathe, and they deformed her. In Ovid's *Metamorphoses*, the merman sea god, Glaucus, falls in love with Scylla, and she rejects him; when he turns to Circe for a charm and a potion to help him win her love, Circe herself falls for the smitten young man, and makes passionate declarations to him; it is his turn to remain indifferent. Circe then takes a terrible revenge on her rival, her spell a hideous distortion of Glaucus' own marine form.

Glaucus himself is fish-tailed, with a sea-green beard and blue limbs, but he rejoices in his hybridity and the ocean depths where he lives. For a woman, however, for the unnatural stony-hearted nymph Scylla, her marine metamorphosis is a cruel and terrible curse. In *The Art of Love*, Ovid takes the Homeric monster to further extremes, and Scylla finds to her horror that a litter of puppies writhes perpetually in her womb.

The *Odyssey* describes how, after he has escaped Scylla, Odysseus passes the foot of a lower cliff close by, where the whirlpool of Charybdis 'sucks down the black water'—three times a day. Odysseus did not see, he says, the moment that Scylla pounced on his men because his eyes were gazing instead at Charybdis, a thundering blowhole, a vortex that swallows 'the brackish sea' and spits it up again. Again the domestic metaphor draws on human nutrition, but this time on its preparation, not its capture.

Homer does not describe the Cyclops' features, but sculptures reveal the giant's huge, single eye. Terracotta, fifth century B.C.

Charybdis is likened to a seething cauldron, spitting its contents, like polenta or other meal if the fire sets it boiling too rapidly.

Scylla and Charybdis have long been identified with the fast and tricky currents of the Straits of Messina, and there is still a village called Scilla on the coast of Calabria facing towards Sicily. But more interestingly, the three ordeals through which Odysseus passes dismember and scatter the female erotic body by synecdoche across the water in the path of his return home to his wife. It is as if, after the bidding of the sirens' song, the jaws of Scylla, Odysseus and his men must navigate the deep-throated vulva-like passage of Charybdis, and prove themselves able to re-emerge. Ovid's vicious twist to Scylla's curse draws out an allegory of perverted maternity that beats beneath the imagery of food and consuming in the language of the poem: the men like wriggling fishes, the toothed mouths of Scylla, the hot cauldron of Charybdis.

The episodes of Circe, of the descent into Hades, of the passage past the Sirens, the Clashing Rocks, Scylla and Charybdis are all recounted by Odysseus in the long section of the epic that takes place in the banqueting hall of Alcinous' palace. It is all too easy to forget this first-person framing and to read Circe's speeches as if they are being reported directly by the poem. The poem persuades us of the truth of what Odysseus is saying not only because he tells his story so well, so movingly, so stirringly, but also because his story takes place within the second frame of Circe's instructions. His account of his encounter with the sirens and other monsters and perils exactly fulfils her predictions—as he himself has relayed them. Reading the epic makes the enchantress' words appear uncannily prophetic, but, as both anticipation and fulfilment are channelled through the hero, it could be that Homer presents us with his 'Odysseus of the many wiles' justifying his actions by recourse to the famous enchantress' oracles. Thus

Circe corroborates, through her visions and prophecies, the ineluctable necessity of the course that the hero has taken. Odysseus vaunts himself—and makes excuses—to Alcinous and his company, for example:

> 'But then even I forgot to shun the harm
> Circe forewarn'd; who will'd I should not arm,
> Nor shew myself to Scylla, lest in vain
> I ventured life. Yet could not I contain,
> But arm'd at all parts, and two lances took,
> Up to the foredeck went, and thence did look
> That rocky Scylla would have first appear'd
> And taken my life with the friends I fear'd.'

It is also worth trying to think with Odysseus when considering the material and its dreadful freight of danger and death. He has lost six men; yet the episode does not diminish his stature, for his tale concentrates on his uncontainable courage and the fatal and irrevocable cannibal greed of Scylla, rather than on his failure to protect his men from a terrible death. The passage past Scylla serves to enhance his tragic role as hero of the poem: he displays his bravery, his sensibility, his favoured status with the immortals in the encounter, and he succeeds in saving the boat and continuing his voyage; her terrors also aggrandize him.

Scylla is only one ordeal in the involved sequence of adventures that takes Odysseus from one variety of cannibalism to another, as noted before. He makes a series of ever more narrow escapes, from his capture by Polyphemus, to his brush with the bloodthirsty ogres the Laestrygonians, to his self-imposed ordeal of the sirens' shore. With the exception of the sirens, all these monsters seize and eat some of Odysseus' men; and he sails on, greatest of the survivor heroes through courage and cunning and charm, the only man to hear the sirens and live (and he does not tell us what they sang). First a single giant with one eye, on his own in a cave, eats his victims live and raw, without even stopping for a quick kill like a mountain lion. The Laestrygonians, by contrast, are a whole people, with men and women, a social organization; they share the Cyclopes' gigantism but are arranged in families. Odysseus' men first meet the daughter of King Antiphates drawing water; her people live in high-roofed dwellings, and their town centres on a marketplace. These cannibals hunt down Odysseus' men by pelting them in their ships with rocks, from the top of the cliff, and then, when their quarry is floundering in the water, 'one by one they harpooned their prey like fish and so carried them off to make their loathsome meal'. The image of the princess at the well also suggests evolved cuisine: these cannibals forage for food and cook, hunter-gatherers in the human image. (The simile of the harpoon fisher returns to characterize Scylla's raids on passing ships.) The sirens do not explicitly devour their victims, but Circe describes them beckoning from the kind of corrall of displayed *écorchés* that would profoundly influence cannibal imagery of empire, including the headquarters of Kurtz' in Joseph Conrad's 'Heart of Darkness' (1902):

> They sit amidst a mead,
> And round about it runs a hedge or wall
> Of dead men's bones, their wither'd skins and all
> Hung all along upon it . . .

The sirens kill more than they need to eat, like human beings, and leave the leftovers strewn about, trophy spoils. Scylla's ravenousness on the other hand can never be satisfied. She is the picture of insatiability: her predations only stop because she runs out of mouths to engulf more and yet more. She behaves like a watchdog turned rogue: in the same way as the mastiffs in the Grimms' 'The Boy Who Went Forth to Learn What Fear Was' and in Hans Christian Andersen's 'The Tinder Box' are momentarily appeased by offerings tossed in to fill each of their terrible mouths, Scylla's appetite is never glutted, only briefly stalled.

❖   ❖   ❖

The Cyclops Polyphemus and the monster Scylla, as a diptych of Odysseus' ordeals, are also paired on wine cups. Both foreshadow the development of the monstrous in literature and art and the differences between the male and female lines. Polyphemus has the most salient, though ignoble, career, for he becomes the prototype of the flesh-eating, doltish giant, who in spite of his gargantuan size and colossal strength, can be gulled by a stripling. Odysseus the trickster gets the better of the Cyclops: fox outwitting a lion, the ancestor of *le petit Poucet*, or nimble Jack and crafty Tom and so many other boys' heroes of fairy tale.

The Cyclops' eye, which Homer, oddly, does not describe, is emblazoned across the whole area of his eye sockets and brows in Greek sculptures of the sixth century B.C.: it has no pupil or iris, and so resembles nothing more than a giant orifice, with lids for lips. He is all mouth, all appetite. When, in Book IX of the *Odyssey*, he captures Odysseus and his men, he carries them off to his cave, another gaping hole, foreshadowing his rending and swallowing of human flesh. He does succeed in eating some of Odysseus' men before he is outwitted by the hero, and Odysseus recounts the horror of his cannibalism (in Chapman's 'horrid' version, again):

> He . . . rush'd in, and took
> Two of my fellows up from earth, and strook
> Their brains against it. Like two whelps they flew
> About his shoulders, and did all embrue
> The blushing earth. No mountain lion tore
> Two lambs so sternly, lapp'd up all their gore
> Gush'd from their torn-up bodies, limb by limb. . .
> Both flesh and marrow-stuffed bones he eat,
> And even th'uncleansed entrails made his meat.

But Odysseus tricks him with a famous, riddling pun that was already probably an old device when it was introduced into the *Odyssey*. Odysseus plies the Cyclops with a special wine, which the giant eagerly and rashly quaffs; he then tells Polyphemus that his name is 'No man' or, in other versions, 'Nobody'. Once he has stupefied his captor, Odysseus blinds the felled giant by driving into his one eye the long stake that with his men he has sharpened and burnished in the fire. This moment is represented in a monumental sculpture, from Sperlonga on the coast south of Rome, as well as in mosaics and paintings and on classical vases. The Cyclops howls for help from his fellow giants, but all he can cry out is: 'O my friends, it's Nobody's treachery, no violence, that is doing me to death.' At this, his fellow giants decide that he is ill and suffering from delusions. They suggest he pray to his father, Poseidon. Thus Odysseus is nobody's fool; and so, in a perverse topsy-turvy way, is his gull, the giant Polyphemus.

A glutton and a dullard, the Cyclops is nevertheless able to call on the god of the sea for revenge. Poseidon curses the trickster on his son's behalf, and Odysseus has to suffer as his punishment another several years' delay in reaching home. In this early fairy tale, the Cyclops has a long reach and his anger is terrible; but later, though ogres frighten the little children, they also make them laugh.

The *Odyssey* revolves anthropophagy through several possible permutations with a storyteller's relish for repetition, elaboration, and nicely judged increments of horror. Polyphemus sins chiefly by flouting the rules of hospitality. This epic priority enshrines the content and preparation of food as the issue of civilization; ogres' barbarism defines human standards. Scylla, the giant's counterpart, develops the theme in a different direction:

her cannibalism is the effect of her femaleness, turned monstrous in its multiple, genital offshoots.

Polyphemus will mutate into the ogres of fairy tale, both terrifying and monstrous: he will spread alarm with his bloodthirsty cry, 'Fee Fie Fo Fum', and giant-killers will spring up to vanquish him. And Scylla, shipwrecked on the reefs of her own monstrosity, as if she, too, is being swallowed up by a body not of her species that afflicts her and drives her, might be seen as a forerunner of the Loathly Lady from medieval Arthurian legend, who is cursed with monstrous form, or of Laideronnette (Uglessa), the heroine of Marie-Catherine d'Aulnoy's fairy tale 'Serpentin vert', or of all those heroines who are cursed by wicked fairies with outer ugliness—except that these characters are redeemed, restored, according to the conversion logic of fairy-tale narrative. It is more accurate to see Scylla inaugurating a line of female monsters who are fatal and abhorrent—and past redemption.

The Scyllan double fishtail, though not invoked in the *Odyssey*, recurs in her iconography. These scaly coils later come to figure female sexual

Scylla inhabits a hideous travesty of the mermaid form, with a double tail as part of her panoply of weapons fatal to passing men. Reconstruction, Roman, first century A.D.

display, as in the Sperlonga sculpture, the incidental and playful marginalia of medieval churches and manuscripts and in early medieval floors, such as the mosaic pavement of Otranto cathedral. They then migrate to become the identifying mark of the mermaid of fairy tale, when she and the selkies and undines of Celtic and Nordic legends are assimilated into folklore.

The single-tailed mermaid and the double-tailed species have not inspired distinct strands of stories. The little mermaid of the single fishtail strikes the onlooker as rather more virginal than the siren who exhibits herself by holding up her two tails on either side of her cleft; she has survived more vigorously in subsequent fairy tales and legends that tell of female initiation to love. The double tail suggests the onset of menarche and sexual maturity (Hans Christian Andersen's Little Mermaid, for example, bleeds when her tail is divided into legs and she becomes a human), with all the accompanying threats that Greek myths like Scylla's express so keenly. Scylla acquires this double tail in her iconography, not her literature, and it serves to bind her myth's associations more closely to issues of female sexuality, its purposes, its appetite. She has come down as a particular form of the dangerous female, in the great classical throng of monsters that includes Laestrygonian ogresses, musically seductive sirens, snaky-haired, tongue-lolling Medusa, Grendel's mother in her bloody lacustrine vaults.

The serpent lurks in the reflected image of every daughter of Eve. Even Alice's transformations hint at the monstrous: in Wonderland, she nibbles at the Caterpillar's mushroom and shape-shifts, now shrinking till her chin hits the ground, now growing 'an immense length of neck'. She 'was delighted', writes Lewis Carroll, 'to find that her neck would bend about easily in any direction, like a serpent. She had just succeeded in bending it down into a beautiful zig-zag . . .' when a pigeon attacked her.

> 'Serpent!' screamed the Pigeon.
> 'I'm *not* a serpent!' said Alice . . .

Carroll illustrated the episode with two drawings of this metamorphosed Alice; they are more awkward than usual, perhaps on account of the patent erotic character of his fantasy. Tenniel did not reinterpret them.

The history of fairy-tale selection and adaptation has given far more prominence to male beasts who are afflicted with monstrosity, and then has held up the promise of redemption through love for them: the beast himself from 'Beauty and the Beast', who is restored to his human shape, or 'Riquet à la houppe' ('Ricky with the Tuft'), in one of Perrault's stories, who teaches the giddy heroine to love him for his mind, in spite of his looks. In more recent interpretations, such as the film of *The Phantom of the Opera,* or *Mask,* and *The Elephant Man* (directed early in his career by that aficionado of the macabre, David Lynch), the 'monster' solicits sympathy in the midst of exciting distress, horror and alarm.

So Scylla's monstrous afterlife is more fragmentary and complex than that of the Cyclops. Defeated giants inspire a certain patronizing affection, as mirrors of a buried and superseded ancestry, as we shall see, and they enter the comic repertory of entertaining tales. Scylla's tacit but rampant sexual symbolism raises doubts and anxieties less glibly assuaged, and, besides, Odysseus does not put an end to her. Paradoxically, it is the monsters done to death by heroes who survive gloriously, narrated again and again as part of their murderers' destinies. Scylla remains estranged, even from fairy tales, but her insatiability continues here and there to characterize the vilest pariahs and outcasts: Spenser's Errour in *The Faerie Queene,* who eats her young, Milton's Sin in *Paradise Lost.*

Milton illuminates a fundamental reason for the terrors the human imagination contrives, for his *Paradise Lost* observes Scylla's perverted role as guardian of her territory. The poet places her, with Death, on either side of the gates of hell, the scarecrow to crown all scarecrows:

> The one seemed woman to the waist, and fair,
> But ended foul in many a scaly fold
> Voluminous and vast, a serpent armed
> With mortal sting: about her middle round
> A cry of hell hounds never ceasing barked
> With wide Cerberian mouths full loud, and rung
> A hideous peal: yet, when they list, would creep,
> If aught disturbed their noise, into her womb,
> And kennel there, yet there still barked and howled,
> Within unseen.

Milton then acknowledges his source—principally Ovid's vision of Scylla—and amplifies the impact of his vision by comparing Sin's whelps unfavourably to Scylla's:

> Far less abhorred than these
> Vexed Scylla bathing in the sea that parts
> Calabria from the hoarse Trinacrian shore

Swiftly following this classical reference, another comparison, drawn from widespread fears of cradle-snatching sorcery, brings in witch-hunters' fantasies in full noxious bloom:

> Nor uglier follow the Night-hag, when called
> in secret, riding through the air she comes
> Lured with the smell of infant blood, to dance
> With Lapland witches . . .

Spellbound in a hideous travesty of women's fertility, Scylla's type of monstrosity, in *Paradise Lost*, comes to express the greatest abomination that women were suspected of committing.

Predatory killers in Scyllan dress lurk in corners of the twentieth-century imaginary: she foreshadows the cannibal greed of Shelob, for example, one of Tolkien's scarce female characters, a vast spider who lurks underground in a foul, many-runnelled mountain lair. Scylla's multiple limbs, her rearing and snatching heads and snaky coils recur conventionally in the graphics of popular aspiring satanism–Heavy Metal album covers, bikers' tattoos, some pinball and video adventure games. H.R. Giger, the Swiss artist who designed the sets and characters for the films *Dune* and *Alien* deliberately plays with Scyllan bodies in this raptly morbid, grotesque vein. Even that voluptuous black-velvet-sheathed anti-siren, the Sea Witch, in the Disney cartoon film of *The Little Mermaid*, takes the form of a tentacular polyp. Serpentine she-monsters also appear in comics—but mostly those with an adult or at least young-adult readership. They are not, however, susceptible to reform to the same utopian degree as male beasts but tend to a static, indeed archetypal fixity, as in the case of the wicked stepmother and the wicked witch.

Yet sensitivity to obvious misogyny has helped to tilt monstrosity's gender from female to male. Anxiety about negative representations of women and girls has rolled them back from recent mainstream entertainments—Disney's Sea Witch and Cruella de Vil from *The Hundred and One Dalmatians* being alluring exceptions. The reflex of these recent blockbuster movies, which have been and will be seen by several millions of children, clearly results from the women's movement of the 1960s, whose members have grown up and as mothers and grandmothers have decisive spending power. (The wicked stepmother of 'Cinderella' or the wicked queen in 'Snow White' would be sent back for a rewrite, and Milton's

OPPOSITE *Harpy, inscribed 'last spotted in Peru'. Engraving, c. 1773.*

baroque glorying in his vision of Sin as a foul mother would not pass the Disney Corporation's rules of representation today.) But this account of feminist achievement fails to take the temperature of contemporary misogyny accurately. 'Adult Only' material does not offer such a reassuringly sensitive picture: the siren, harpy and gorgon still prowl, inwardly monstrous even if outwardly lovely, through many successful movies like *Fatal Attraction* (1987) and *The Hand that Rocks the Cradle* (1991), as well as thriving in lurid corners of the horror and porn video industry, where cannibal schoolgirls and vampires rampage. It is nevertheless a symptom of the changing face of monsters that the Disney cartoon *Hercules* (1997) does not draw attention to the indisputable femaleness of the Hydra in Greek but refers to her as 'it' and dubs her voice with bestial snarls, hisses and blasts. (In the accompanying merchandise, 'Terrifying Hydra' comes Jabberwocky-like, with 'Pop-up Evil Heads!' and 'Biting Jaws!': 'Chop off head and 3 Grow Back!' urges the selling line.) Megara, the film's siren-like heroine, is given the name of a sinister Greek Fate, portrayed as the spellbound daughter of Hades and sent to do her father's fatal work on earth. But she becomes subject to a benevolent metamorphosis, and is cured of wickedness by love: the redemptive promise of fairy tale turning decisively against the Greek myth that cast sea monsters' female bodies as the engines of perpetual death.

IV

THE DEVIL'S BANQUET

It is impossible to suppose a giant the object of love.
                                        Edmund Burke, 1757

The word 'ogre' derives from the Latin *Orcus*, for Hades, God of the Underworld, hence Hell. The feminine version, *orca*, refers to that monstrous genus to which Scylla, Charybdis, Ceto, and so many serpentine others belong, and in turn lent its name to whales, titanic engulfers who swallow legendary heroes, like Jonah or Sinbad. In the shadow of Scylla and Charybdis, and of Grendel's mother, female ogres tend to more watery, submarine realms—Nessie, the Loch Ness monster, shows that the tradition is still very much alive. The gigantic octopus-like kraken from Norse lore, being a sea dragon and masculine in gender, is an exception to this cultural tendency to associate death by water with women.

Male ogres and giants predominantly inhabit the elements of fire and earth: in Greek myth, their natural haunts are underworlds inside mountains, labyrinths, caverns, swamps, bogs, volcanoes—the predecessors of the Christian hell, which is fiery, unlike Hades. Atlas the Titan is doomed to shoulder the Earth, Polyphemus the Cyclops dwells in a dark cave. Dante, brilliantly combining the classical and Christian schemata of the infernal regions, casts the giants as Satan's own bodyguards, a rampart of towers sunk navel deep into Cocytus' pit of ice. Giants are not identical with ogres, but they share characteristics, stories and meaning. Looming like towers, the *Inferno's giganti* strike terror in the poet: he names

OPPOSITE *The punishments of the damned replicate alimentary, gastronomic, digestive processes: sinners are condemned to eat and be eaten, to roast and to stew in Hell's colonic tract.* Fra Angelico, The Last Judgement, *1425.*

Nimrod, builder of the Tower of Babel, uttering gibberish; then Ephialtes, one of the Titans who rebelled against Zeus; finally Antaeus, who once took 'for prey a hundred lions'. Dante, like a scared boy peeping through his fingers, is still hungry for more sight of these man-mountains and asks Virgil if he can meet Briareus, one of the 'Hundred-Handers', but Virgil, a parent rationing thrills, rejects his request.

Size is of the essence, of course: Dante strains to express their stature, instancing one comparative measurement after another. But the effect of his casting about for relative terms—city towers, ship-masts—is to render the giants measureless. The earth quakes when Ephialtes stirs; there are hints of their chthonic consubstantiality with mountains, chasms, volcanoes and the abyss. But Dante's giants are morally 'horrible', too, in their brute force and folly. In Norse mythology, *jötuns* are 'huge, shaggy beings of a demonic character . . . [who] dwell in a distant dark chaotic land'.

The order of the monstrous, to which ogres belong in cosmic genealogies, always belongs to a past, a horrible, frightening past that nevertheless fascinates and continues to be summoned vividly to mind in the present. 'In the giants as a whole,' comments Jakob Grimm, 'an untamed natural force has full swing, entailing their excessive bodily size, their overbearing insolence, that is to say, their abuse of corporal and mental power.' Giants and ogres have been superseded, and though both frequently enjoy immortality, they are always in the throes of defeat, and the story of the battles that overthrew them is rehearsed again and again. They stand for a barbarous history: the Titans whom Zeus defeated with his thunderbolts forged for him by his brother Hephaestus; Polyphemus who, though a loved son of Poseidon, occupies an inferior niche in the Olympian hierarchy as a kind of loutish throwback; the Celtic gods who were supplanted by Christian saints; the Nephilim, who in an obscure passage of Genesis (6:4) are the heroes of days gone by, offspring of gods coupling with 'the daughters of men'. The presence of giants in effigy during Carnival in the Low Countries, for example, or during Corpus Christi celebrations in Spain, often recalls their defeat and the glorious arrival of a new, human-scale, civilized, political and religious order. Yet these barbarous figures frequently inspire great attachment in the citizens: in the chronicle of Geoffrey of Monmouth, Albion is a mighty British giant who was defeated, with all his giant cohorts and his brothers Gog and Magog, by the founder of London, Brutus. But it is Albion who is of course remembered in the most patriotic name of all for England.

The old carry the young on their shoulders. Atlas, one of the deposed Titans, foreshadows the Catholic giant St. Christopher, literally

Christo-phoros, the Christ-bearer. Further back in time, in contradiction to perspective, beings grow larger: the New World was imagined as a haunt of giants as of other wonders—men with one eye in the middle of their chests, men who shaded themselves from the sun with a single, gigantic foot. The Yeti, Abominable Snowman, Bigfoot, Sasquatch and other giant forebears who are regularly sighted and much documented by enthusiasts are the modern descendants of these heroes of legend. They too are marked out by their colossal height and girth (hence the depth and size of the evidence—the footprints). Mark Hall, a contemporary American scholar of 'True Giants', has compiled global records of their incidence; Africa and South America are the only continents where they are not widely recalled and have not left tracks. He argues that *gigantopithecus* is another species of primate, largely wiped out by *homo sapiens* (as the Neanderthals were) but clinging on to survival here and there. His wonderful palaeontology proposes a giant who falls into the mythical pattern—cannibalistic, primitive, huge, far-dwelling: 'Giants survive as remote occupants of the least hospitable terrain on the major continents.' Roald Dahl understands well this magical geography in his tremendous children's story about flesh-eating ogres, *The BFG* (or Big Friendly Giant, 1982).

Champions and heroes who inaugurate a new time, institute a new charter, establish a new faith, need to meet and engage with giants and monsters and aliens in their youthful trials: in the Anglo-Saxon epic, Beowulf overcomes Grendel in epic combat, Grendel who raids by night, carries off the Danes and feasts on their carrion: 'The Monster . . . quickly seized a sleeping warrior . . . rent him greedily, bit into his body, drank the blood from his veins, swallowed bite after bite; and soon he had eaten up all of the dead man, even his feet and hands.' Grendel's size shifts disturbingly in the poem, and his features dilate and blur under the heaped names of evil—demon, fiend, devil and so forth—names that will be repeated by Mary Shelley when she invokes the creature Frankenstein has made. But the poet of Beowulf magnifies Grendel physically, telling us that 'he strode beneath the clouds', and when the hero has severed his head, four men 'had much trouble to bear into the princely hall the head of Grendel on the spear'. Grendel and his mother partake also of dragons' nature: their lair is a misty fen fastness, lit by foxfire, where the accursed race of Cain was banished, and Beowulf, in the poem's moment of fiercest vision, descends through boiling gore into its depths to fight 'the monstrous hag'. He uses a great sword made by giants to kill her—so that in the course of the poem he moves backwards through mythic time, encountering first the anthropomorphized fiend Grendel, then the more primitive, zoomorphic

St. Christopher, much loved patron saint of travellers, began life as a savage, dog-headed giant. Byzantine, seventeenth century.

mere-wife-mother in her primeval swamp with her crew of sea monsters and water spirits. Her blood is like dragon's fire: 'the sword was already melted, the damasked blade burnt up,—so hot had been the blood, the fiend so poisonous . . .' After Beowulf has brought this weapon back as a trophy, the Danes find engraved on the golden hilt the tale of the giants' destruction by the flood: 'that was a race alien from the eternal Lord . . .', progeny of the first murder. 'Thence all evil broods were born, ogres and elves and evil spirits—the giants also, who long time fought with God.'

Even the occasional major Christian saint begins in monstrous form, with paganism written on his body. St. Christopher, patron saint of travellers, had a dog's head before his conversion. According to early Byzantine legend, he came to his humble occupation as ferryman in repentance for a rampaging career as this cynophelous giant, but Christian scholars were at pains to reject the story: 'Some marvellous and miraculous relations concerning this saint are current in some quarters', one protested in the tenth century, 'as that he was a dog-headed man-eater until he was metamorphosed at his conversion. This is not the fact, only some supposed him such because he was a heathen wild and grim.' But icons of Christophoros Cynocephalus, looking somewhat like Anubis, the jackal-headed Egyptian ferryman of dead souls, survive long after this pious denial—in a seventeenth-century icon, for example, in the Byzantine Museum, Athens. Barking was the noise expected of giants, as the sixteenth-century explorer Antonio Pigafetta reported he heard when he sailed past Patagonia.

Cut into the chalk of the downs at Cerne Abbas, Dorset, the 180-foot-high Cerne Giant represents a vanished barbarian past. He may have been brandishing a carcass or a severed head in one hand and still wields a mighty club; his nipples, ribs, navel and phallus are delineated against the deep green turf. From a drawing of 1926 by the archaeologist Flinders Petrie, it seems that the navel was originally the glans at the tip of the phallus, making it even longer than its present twenty-six feet. The giant's origins are not precisely dated or understood, and the earliest records of his present appearance date back only to the mid-eighteenth century. But the Cerne Giant is considered prehistoric, or at least very ancient, and has been identified with several legendary figures—including the pre-Roman British god Helis or Helith, the Roman hero Hercules, Herne the Hunter, and an unspecified ogre, who ate up children like 'rashers of bacon'. The most suggestive proposal is that Harlequin evolved from Hellequin, just such a scary master of death as the Cerne Giant. Harlequin, when he first makes his appearance in medieval French plays, ushers the band of lost souls to their doom.

The giant of Cerne Abbas is only one of several such figures in the British Isles: giant chalk carvings of Gog and Magog on Plymouth Hoe and on Wandlebury hill fort near Cambridge were recorded, but are now lost. These enigmatic colossi served on the face of it as imposing reminders of a superannuated pagan rule. But at the same time, the massive presence of the Cerne Giant, complete with his uncensored phallus, has kept alive the power and the magic of an imagined old faith; so does the Long Man of Wilmington, in spite of his 'castration'. Even the vanished Gog and Magog chalk figures beckon from the outer reaches of the past to the present, however delusory their reality. Maypole dances were held near the Cerne Giant, and the local people traditionally turn out every seven years to scour the chalk channels of his outline and renew him; children can dependably be conceived, it is reported, by making love within the precincts of the giant's body.

Giants' powers over fertility animate the pagan fantasies of the Romanesque, later. On the façade of the eleventh-century church of San Petronio, Tuscania, for example, there appears a fantastic carving of a figure with three heads. The one facing us is pulling his tongue, while from his three mouths there grows a labyrinth of looped and intertwined foliage without end, transforming his snaky limbs into leafy or thorny rinceaux and coils of greenery—is he spewing up this fertile thicket, or is he swallowing it down? On the other side of the rose window, over the front portal, is another carving, of the Lamb of God, the Saviour; the two magnificent, vertical bas-reliefs proclaim divergent concepts of the future. The Lamb promises redemption and the resurrection of the body. By contrast, the serpentine, tricephalous, vegetable demon presents the possibility of metamorphosis across not only species, but genera: he represents an anti-Christian system of natural metamorphosis. From his position above the left side door of the church (as you leave), the Doomsday side of the

The Giant of Cerne Abbas, cut in chalk downs, still possesses vigorous and fertile powers. Romano-British (?) second century A.D.

damned, he reminds the faithful that in death bodies decompose and turn into—not other bodies, but plants, trees. Belief in metamorphosis was central to paganism, from the Christian point of view.

In the same way as the demons of the new faith are pictured in the image of the pagan gods, so the classical, Pythagorean idea of fluid, interchangeable bodies over time informs the eternal cycle of the Christian underworld. It is significant that engulfment by monstrous male appetite supplants a horrific version of female birthing that characterized the afterlife in Norse mythology. There, Hel is the daughter of the joker god Loki and swallows the souls of the dead into her insatiable mouth. The Christian hell has lost this connection to metaphors of female bodily process, except in so far as Satanic torments parody an endless rebirth. In one of his many polyvalent aspects, Satan, the Christian Lord of Tartarus or hell, sits enthroned in the underworld, acting as judge and executioner in the manner of the Olympian who also presided over the kingdom of the dead and the damned. Satan assumes the unholy terrors of Moloch, the Canaanite idol to whom babies were sacrificed in burnt offerings and whose rituals were explicitly condemned in Mosaic law (Lev. 18: 21; 20: 2-5; Deut. 12: 31; 18: 10). Later, the devil powers the metaphors that clothe the ogres of nursery entertainment, in both their terrifying and their comical aspects.

The signature activity that these figures share, which represents their horror, is cannibalism.

❖   ❖   ❖

The cannibalism of demons offers a vision of eternity that refashions space, time and identity in direct contradiction to the conditions of salvation and paradise, and this divergence runs through Christian metaphorical language. According to the beliefs of Pythagoras, souls could vacate the body in which they were housed and migrate to another, at any level of creation; Pythagorean metempsychosis underpins Ovid's *Metamorphoses*. But salvation promises immutable bodily integrity in the afterlife: in the Christian scheme there is no migration of souls, no transmogrification of bodies, no changing from girl to laurel tree or spring or star or animal . . . Every human being keeps his or her form, integral, recognizable, essential.

The status of the resurrected or eschatological body of eternal bliss has always inspired lively speculation: where would the trimmings of toenails go, what would be the age of the blessed, and what was the fate of those who had indeed been devoured by beasts, by sea monsters and others? But the restored union of body and soul in eternity entered the Nicene Creed in the fourth century and remains an article of the Christian faith. It places

The great dragon is cast down into the pit of his kingdom, the many-headed Mouth of Hell. Lambeth Apocalypse, c. 1260.

belief in the preservation of everyone's unique enfleshed identity at the centre of ideas of personhood.

Hence, cannibalism of the perpetual variety practised in hell becomes the preferred and potent metaphor for the obliteration of self that is the fate of sinners. The infernal body is forever devouring or being devoured: hell is a devils' banquet and Satan its master of ceremonies, and the damned are trapped in a perpetual cycle of metamorphosis without closure. The cycle by which sinners are eaten, then regurgitated or excreted, serves as the dominant metaphor in Dante's great poem *The Divine Comedy*, and his scheme directly inspired artists throughout Italy: further afield, orgies of gluttonous cruelty with Dantesque echoes erupt from the more northerly fantasies of Hieronymus Bosch. The metaphor of perpetual consumption conveys the cyclical stasis of hell, the ever-present and ineluctable eternity of pain.

Dante's vision of Satan in the grip of the terrible ice of Tartary, the lowest circle of hell, draws on these earlier definitions of the eschatological body and the survival of individuality in the afterlife. Dante's Satan is all orifice, and each one stuffed with another victim:

A three-headed image of Satan, inspired by Dante's vision in Inferno, *mangles for all eternity the traitors Judas, Cassius and Brutus. Sandro Botticelli, graphite, fifteenth century.*

con sei occhi piangea, e per tre menti
gocciava 'l pianto e sanguinosa bava.
Da ogni bocca dirompea co' denti
un peccatore, a guisa di maciulla,
sì che ne facea così dolenti.
A quel dinanzi il mordere era nulla
verso 'l graffiar, che tal volta al schiena
rimanea della pelle tutta brulla.

(With six eyes he was weeping and over three chins dripped tears and bloody foam. In each mouth he crushed a sinner with his teeth as with a heckle and thus he kept three of them in pain; to him in front the biting was nothing to the clawing, for sometimes the back was left all stripped of skin.)

The principal victims of this carnivorous mangling are named in *The Divine Comedy*: the traitors Judas, Cassius, and Brutus. But artists relished the opportunity to feed Satan's ravenous appetite in ever more terrifying envisionings of the fate of the damned (Pl. 5). Taddeo di Bartolo in San Gimignano, in his fresco painted in 1396, Giovanni da Modena, in his fresco, of around 1410, in the Basilica of San Petronio in Bologna, and Fra Angelico in San Marco, Florence in 1425 depicted in detail the monstrous gastric tract of the Dantesque underworld, its colonic channels and pouches, and its cloacal depths; they materialize with lubricious excitability the cycle of ingestion, digestion and regurgitation, in order to convey eternal suffering, the loss of blessedness, the annihilation of the damned.

So the gnashing of teeth describes not so much the activity of the damned, as they wail and weep and bemoan their fate, as the response of the devils as they seize hold of their prey and hustle them towards the blazing ovens of hell's mouth. Hell is frequently configured as a profane restaurant, in which all the guards are vampires and cannibals. The haunters of nurseries, the child-stealers, the bogeys behave indistinguishably from these emissaries of death.

The *Malleus Maleficarum (Hammer of Witches*, 1484–6), written by the Dominicans Jakob Sprenger and Heinrich Krämer, crystallized the circulating fantasy that the devil was the ultimate cradle-snatcher who demanded sacrifices of babies at his Sabbaths: Goya, in *Los Caprichos* and several small oil paintings, returns to this popular and persistent fantasy still recounted in Spain three hundred years later. In *The Witches' Sabbath* of 1797–98, the hags are holding up babies to sacrifice to the large, seated goat-headed devil; in *The Spell*, from the same period, the crones are leering as they gather, handling baskets of infants. Both omophagy and anthropophagy take place at Satan's profane banquets, for diabolical predators do not always prefer their meat raw. Sometimes, cooked meat is to their taste, and the fires of hell then turn culinary. In hell's kitchen, in an apocalyptic vision from *The Hours of Catherine of Cleves*, painted in Utrecht around 1440, devils deal with sinners on barbecues, in cauldrons and kettles, on spits and griddles, with pitchforks and brazing irons; in other images, sinners are cast down, to be eternally gnawed like bones strewn on a kitchen floor. The need to encompass both aspects of the cannibal penalty—raw and cooked—sometimes inspires artists to depict a cauldron boiling *inside* hell's mouth, as in the Last Judgment carved in bas-relief on the façade of Ferrara cathedral, as well as in countless medieval and Renaissance manuscripts.

In 1376, coinciding with the time of the Black Death in Europe, there appeared for the first time the word 'macabre'. It is as rare for a new affect to be named as a new planet, but the macabre is one such response, a particular *rasa* or flavour on the taste-buds which had probably existed but

From his three mouths, a colossal pagan spirit of nature gives rise to interlaced vegetation without beginning or end. San Petronio, Tuscania, eleventh century.

not been isolated and identified before. The mysterious phrase enters Jean Le Fevre's poem 'Le Respit de la mort' where he writes, 'Je fis de Macabré la danse' ('I made a dance of Macabré'). Dances of Death, inaugurating a new frenzy of activity on the part of the devil and his death squads, and the type of tomb called *transi* which depicts the body of the deceased decomposing as worms feast on its flesh, appeared around the same time. Whereas Satan, an obese and indolent giant puppet, presides over his banquet in the northern Italian frescoes, French and, later, German artists and poets animated the concept with ferocious kinetic energy, so that Death himself becomes the most lively—and hence the most unbearably uncanny—figure at his own dance.

The *danse macabre* on the walls of the Cimetière des Innocents in Paris famously formed the backdrop for metropolitan scenes of picnicking and soliciting and revelry, and the subject became so popular in art that nearly thirty different editions of woodcut versions were illustrated and distributed throughout Europe, the most appallingly vivacious being Holbein's great sequence, showing King Death drumming and piping pope and pauper, princess and nun to the grave. The images are interesting, too, because in the terrific pageant of death levelling everybody, regardless of age or state or degree, all kinds of occupations are incidentally recorded.

Nobody is spared: the roll-call is all inclusive. In a text like *The Hours of Simon Vostre*, printed in Paris in the early sixteenth century, the engravings of the *danse macabre* show working women in various trades—from the more predictable abbess to the unexpected *sote*, or female fool, as well as working men of all conditions. It was also customary for the spectre to wear a tatterdemalion version of the costume of his prey and to imitate with grotesque exaggeration the victim's usual activities. Death is a double; each of us has our own death in the mirror. Death is oneself on the other side, beyond reach.

Paul Binski situates the dance of Death, as well as the skeletons and *écorchés* on tombs and other memento mori, within the long-range view of subjectivity that Christianity held out, and then places them at the root of the development of the secularized individual identity: 'The image represents a future state—what the subject will become—and so contributes to the subject's sense of self. In this case the thing that is constructed . . . is the notion of the sinner . . . The macabre implicates us in a *mise-en-abyme*, a hall of mirrors. And by means of its use of defamiliarization, it offers the capacity for self-examination.' He reminds us that many of the tombs in which the deceased was shown devoured by worms were actually commissioned and carved during the subject's lifetime: thus, Archbishop Chichele, founder of All Souls, Oxford, may have contemplated the artistic progress of his own decomposing body on the tomb in Christ Church while he was still alive. These funerary monuments are 'designed not to engender memory in the narrow sense', writes Binski, 'nor prayer, but to provoke . . . the pondering of self'.

The process of individual self-discovery, which begins, as we shall see, with the first steps into language, continues in stories about devouring and death, cannibals and bloodthirsty giants. The spectres haunting fairy tales are Death's associates: 'When I am gone, / And the great bugbear, grisly Death,/Shall take this idle breath . . .' writes Thomas Randolph, almost absent-mindedly, in the mid-seventeenth century.

❖   ❖   ❖

Death apes the condition of his victims: when he comes for a knight, he appears in chain mail and impales him on a lance. Dance of Death, *c. 1530.*

Hell's torments were also frequently burlesqued, for cannibalism invites grotesque jokes, as do many of the deepest assaults on the security of self. A rollickingly ribald ballad, 'Cock Lorrel's Treat', was originally performed in Ben Jonson's *Masque of the Metamorphosed Gipsies,* in the presence of James I, on no fewer than three occasions in 1621. The verses are a delirious and extreme example of the popular English tradition of merry jesting and mirth. They set the scene by describing one Cock Lorrel, who is captain of a Ship of Fools, thronged with the members of various professions as in a traditional dance of Death. Cock Lorrel sups with the devil, but in this ballad, the devil is his guest: 'Never the fiend had such a feast/Provided him yet at the charge of a sinner.' He devours the population of London:

> the bawde and the bacon . . .
> Six pickl'd taylors sliced and cutt,
>   Sempsters, and tirewomen, fit for his palate;
> With feathermen and perfumers putt
> Some twelve in a charger to make a grand sallet.

The Eucharist consumed as gingerbread:
William Hogarth,
Enthusiasm
Delineated,
c. 1761.

In the manner of an accumulative nursery rhyme, the courses pile up, one vicious pun following another as the devil gorges on

> A rich fatt usurer stu'd in his marrowe,
> and by him a lawyers head in greene sawce . . .

At this jolly trot, the devil then dispatches

> A London cuckold hott from the spitt . . .
> The chine of a letcher too there was roasted,
> With a plumpe harlots haunch and garlicke . . .
> A large fatt pasty of a midwife hott;
> And for a cold bak't meat into the story,
> A reverend painted lady was brought . . .

After these predictable sinners, the devil concentrates on the hypocrites. Guardians of the law are not spared: a justice of the peace, a jailer, a constable, two aldermen, a holy sister ('who almost makes his devilshipp sicke'), a teacher, a courtier and clown, tradesmen and merchants, church-men and lawyers . . . player and whore . . . countess and servant, and so on through all kinds and labours, classes and conditions, 'All which devour'd'.

Finally, the devil breaks wind, and that wind is tobacco, 'which wicked weed . . . that's feast for the fiend', James I wholeheartedly detested.

The jocular tone recognizably passes into gleefully childish—even scatological—nonsense. But the ballad's jubilant spouting of mock horrors also develops an implicit satire on religious iconography, with an Erasmian contempt for the lurid imagery of Roman beliefs as well as for clerical and other official hypocrisy. The ballad lampoons the orality of Christian eschatological mysticism; but in doing so, it merely takes to savage extremes of burlesque the cannibalism that structures not only hell but also the comestible metaphor at the core of the mystery of the Eucharist.

William Hogarth, also a great mocker of human folly, took up the motif in a savage print of *c.* 1761, *Enthusiasm Delineated*, in which he satirized the rising Methodist movement. Hogarth expresses the common fear that Methodists were simply Roman Catholics under another name, and he draws the congregation in various states of religious excitement. Many of them are biting into figurines of Christ, as if he were simply a gingerbread man with a radiant halo, and some wear the bestial expressions of the damned as they munch, gnaw and chew. Above this 'realm of tormented unreason . . . with its air of a feverish Black Mass', as Jenny Uglow describes it in her biography of the artist, hangs a globe chandelier, with the gaping maw of a John Dory, its fanged jaws marked 'Eternal Damna-tion Gulf'. Thus William Hogarth, with the fury of a rationalist and an Anglican, condenses cardinal symbols of the Catholic faith into a diatribe against barbarism.

The print was extensively reworked before publication: revealingly, Hogarth's friends advised him that his mockery of the Eucharist would be taken as attacking all Christians. The Christ poppets were replaced by models of a contemporary ghost who had been haunting Cock Lane, in London—more evidence of vulgar superstition and a glimpse of Hogarth's dismissive view of miracles as such, if a famous hoax could supplant the Saviour. Hogarth's self-censorship reveals, in an artist who did not mince his words, how sensitive the issue of communion was, and how deeply abhorrent the imagery of anthropophagy associated with the 'real pres-ence' remained for a Londoner in the period when ogres, giants and other flesh-eating monsters began to thrive in stories for children.

❖   ❖   ❖

The imagery of both hell and its penalties on the one hand and the Eucharistic feast on the other continue to shape satirical and carnival rituals that are performed today, with ever greater popular success. Sometimes such festivities seek to raise hell in smoke and riot—pandemonium itself. Hallowe'en conjures the whole crew of demons from Gothic nightmare as well as the infernal regions. Such carnivals draw on excess, flourish, grimace and caricature to make their impact: they deploy giants, mannikins and masks, scarecrows and bugbears; they unfurl banners, wave placards, brandish staffs, explode fireworks, bangers, crackers, bang rattles and drums. Seasonal cakes and sweets and biscuits, often stamped with devices particular to the feast day in question, commemorate the gathering and its common petitions—in Sicily, pastry in the shape of the eyes of St. Lucy and the breasts of St. Agatha; in Berga, Catalonia, devil biscuits for the Patum.

In some cases these ceremonies have been revived, with innovations, but many have been recently devised, usually in the name of authentic tradition, to guarantee the future safety of a community. Three-dimensional simulacra in such public carnivals and performances purposely dislocate our sense of size and relation, diminishing us by comparison with the giants, aggrandizing us by contrast to the occasional puppets and the child participants. But the makers of the often elaborate, ingenious and magnificent masks, effigies and costumes consider their creations precious not because they are works of art but because they act as instruments of magic continuity.

The popularity of Hallowe'en in Britain and the United States has never been stronger, for example, and grows year by year, spreading upwards through the ages: airline clerks now dress as ghouls for the day, a ball and chain shackled to their ankle; young executives go to work with axes through their skulls and bloody eyeballs. The range of costumes for children encompasses the full cast of hell and all hell's servants, as well as random figures from later Gothic invention: Frankenstein's creature is a great favourite, as is Dracula, of course, both of them taking their place alongside the devils of the medieval inferno from the mind of Dante and other high thinkers of Christianity. In England, on Bonfire Night (November 5), a Catholic conspirator, Guy Fawkes, is thrown in effigy on to the flames, with great jubilation and explosions of fireworks, though the 'guy' has become, in most places, a generic figure of sacrifice, and the political story of the Gunpowder Plot lingers on only in the rhyme, 'Remember, remember the Fifth of November / Gunpowder, treason and plot' and is otherwise not much invoked or discussed. In the village of Sticklepath in Devon, the annual Bonfire Night pageant in 1996 staged a remarkably

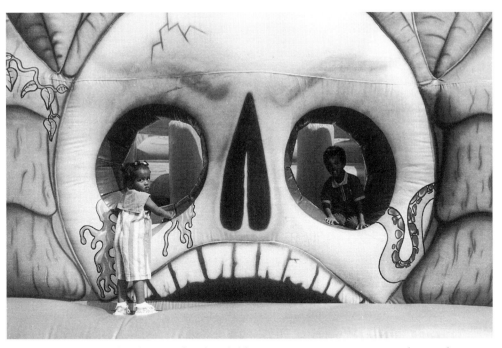

At a summer fair, bouncy fun for children in a memento mori, *complete with worms. London, 1997.*

ambitious comic carnival drama: a series of adventures with animated effigies—including a giant fourteen-foot Guy, a Rastafarian singer, a game host, and some enormous snails racing in a snail race. The pageant culminated in a combat between the devil and an angel over Guy's soul. 'Guy ultimately fell into the devil's clutches,' reported a local participant, 'and spent the money in a giant one-armed bandit (appropriately anthropomorphized). He won—and a cascade of children each carrying oversize coins slid out from the belly of the fruit machine'—the metaphor of consuming children aptly updated.

In Bolsena, Italy, on July 25, the feast of their patron Santa Cristina, the local people create bloodthirsty *tableaux vivants* throughout the town that dramatize the prolonged and ingenious torments of the child saint and virgin martyr: she is bound to a fiery wheel, bitten by venomous snakes, and her tongue is cut out—among other trials. In the final 'station' of her cross, her father, who masterminded her torments because she refused to reject Christianity, is thrown into the pit of hell by devils with pitchforks. This is the only point in the cycle when the characters are not frozen into position but move, with glee, to throw him in. During Easter week in Spain, as well as in Mexico and other parts of Latin America, effigies of Judas are

A ram lives up to his name in the feast of Los Carneros *(The Rams), while* Caravinagre *(Vinegar Face)* RIGHT *with his fool's bladder inspires a child's confident imitation. Photographs by Cristina García Rodero, Spain, 1980s.*

exploded in a blaze and cacophony of rockets. They are often made in the semblance of some well-known hate figure: taxman, local politician, official or local dignitary—only sometimes in jest. Elsewhere, new figures of imaginary enemies are sacrificed in riotous secular ceremonies that unite whole cities and even countries. Sacrifice, that principle of the religious imagination and worship, is shedding its sacred character in late twentieth-century rites and making a strong return in secular rituals of communion and display, from rock concerts to performance art and even street parties.

Children are frequently involved as subjects and players, and not only during Hallowe'en. Guaranteeing their survival is a central part of the story, and different festivities face up to dangers that can assail from any number of directions—sickness, animal predators, witchcraft, devils, cannibals, ogres, succubi, fire and flood and famine. The magical attempt to secure safety takes two predominant forms: either the participants impersonate the danger itself, as in the carnival masks and fancy dress of Hallowe'en, and thus, cannibal-like, absorb its powers and deflect its ability to inflict harm; or they expose themselves and by surviving the ordeal, prove their invulnerability.

Over the last twenty years, Cristina García Rodero, a remarkable

anthropological photographer, has travelled through her native Spain taking pictures of such celebrations and rituals, and published the images in *España Oculta* (1989) and *Festivals and Rituals of Spain* (1992). She photographed, in Redondela (Pontevedra), the *coca*, or she-bogey, which takes the form of a large dragon, or *tarasca*. On the feast of Corpus Christi, half-proud, half-scared young children are seated in its papier mâché body and pulled along in procession through the town—as if by entering the belly of the beast in masquerade, such a calamity could not befall them for real. But it is moot whether children understand ritual as semblance; in their mixed excitement and dread they are closer to the gestures' intention, for magic cannot work if it appears to be empty make-believe. Rodero has also published an image of a masked guiser from the festival in Frontera (on the Canary island of El Hierro) called *Los Carneros*

(The Rams), who butts the crowd with his ram's horns, and especially homes in on children; another of her photographs shows *Caravinagre*, or Vinegar Face, on the feast of St. Fermin in Pamplona, as this lantern-jawed Mr. Punch-type bogey was being cheerfully mimicked by a child in the street. She has caught the stark fear on a baby's face and body during a St. John's Day ritual in Mallorca, when infants are passed naked, high above the crowd, through osier bushes in order to cure them of hernias.

The word *tarasca*, used in Spain for the feast-day dragons, comes from Tarascon in southern France, where the cult of St. Martha flourishes; she delivered the area from a flesh-eating dragon and enjoys in consequence a special guardianship of children. This monster, known as the *Tarasque*, is brought out at Pentecost and on the feast of St. Martha, on July 29. Handled by a team of men, the *Tarasque* rushes the crowd in mock assaults, as can be seen from eighteenth-century woodcuts.

Sometimes the risk-taking is no masquerade but, as in bullfighting, places the participants in real danger: on feast days throughout Catalonia, confraternities form troupes of acrobats to build human *castells* or towers, living giants composed of eight or more tiers of men, girls and boys climbing one above the other, gripping thighs, backs and shoulders, until at the end the whole perilous edifice is crowned by the *anxaneta*, a small child who shins up to the pinnacle, which towers 40 feet or more above the ground. A Corpus Christi rite in the town of Castrillo de Murcia (in the province of Burgos in northern Spain), first mentioned in 1621, revolves around the usual procession of the Eucharist through the town. But on the following Sunday, two *colachos*, or devils, armed with horsehair switches, clicking loudly with their castanets and harrying onlookers with their whips, sweep through the town past prepared altars in the street. In front of each of the altars lies a mattress on which the year's newborn babies are laid out, in their Sunday best, against lacy pillows. To the rising excitement of drumming and castanets, one of the 'devils' then takes a death-defying six-foot jump over the assembled, happily oblivious infants. He thereby secures health and happiness for them in the future, it is believed.

Secular rejoicings like Hallowe'en and Guy Fawkes night might blur the distinction between the show and the crowd more effectively even than religious ceremonies. They create, within an urban architectural space, a riotous drama in which everyone is an actor; they conjure the spectral and the demonic, introduce puppets and effigies, masks and costumes to

OPPOSITE *St Martha freed the city of Tarascon from a dragon, who is brought out yearly to celebrate her feastday. The* Tarasque, *1850.*

represent perennial themes—the combat between good and evil, between outsider and insider, between authority and rebellion. They excite contact and euphoria, noise and havoc, with the overt purpose of re-establishing harmony, overcoming common terrors, and reinforcing a sense of identity and belonging among the participants and the spectators. Imagery is made, often in three dimensions, as in the traditional celebrations of Hallowe'en, to achieve this exorcism; fantasy representations are staged to summon the worst in order to establish its opposite. Participants and spectators merge into one another: bodies involved in the performance are also present as themselves, and break from one mode to the other as the day's rituals wind on. Performance is the nearest term for this type of representation; simulacrum implies likeness, even replication, and does not therefore serve, since the figures and the dramas they perform do not usually replicate lived experiences or known subjects. Their population is fantastic: giants, devils, angels, dragons. When the cast includes Moors, Christians and other historical characters, as often happens in Spain or in Italy's carnivals, they tend to be exaggerated to an otherworldly scale: 20 feet high, in spectacular outfits. Such performances adapt ancient magical uses of simulacra; the effigies are used in the same way as figures, puppets, miniature images in sorcery, both benign and malignant: vessels of identities that are to be controlled by imitation.

Public festivals stitch private people into the very fabric of the stonework and attempt, in so doing, to name pervasive age-old terrors and drive them out. The traditions of Catholic imagery confront the dark through representation, as vivid and lifelike as possible, and this magical approach is gaining ground over the Enlightenment preference for critical analysis and the Protestant Reformation's rejection of such practices, of the use of icons and relics and prophylactic rituals. Of this late twentieth-century tendency, the Patum of Berga, performed in Catalonia on the feast of Corpus Christi each year, offers one of the most startling examples taking place today.

REFLECTION

THE FEAST OF CORPUS CHRISTI, 1996:
THE PATUM OF BERGA, CATALONIA

During the days when the Patum takes place, the main square of Berga, a small mountain town in Catalonia, becomes a natural arena, even a pit: the space is asymmetrical, approached down steep inclines on three sides. The crowds are packed into it, without barriers or police cordons, so that the distinction between performer and audience breaks down. Watching from a safe distance is possible only at the farthest edge of the throng, and many of those spectators plunge in as the turmoil begins to build.

The Patum is a festival, a carnival, a ritual, a party; its name evokes the roll of the drum—pa-tum, pa-tum—that opens the performance and is connected to words for explosion, as in English 'petard'; it consists of a series of repeated tableaux, combats and dances, and it climaxes at night-fall in a prolonged salvo of rockets (Pls. 4, 6, 7, 8).

The first bout of the ritual cycle features guitas, *long-necked green drag-ons, rather like the Loch Ness monster—though the word actually means kicking mules. Their serpentine necks are crowned by gloss black, fanged masks with rolling eyes, and the rockets are fixed between their red jaws with wrought-iron clamps: from a distance in the crowd, these heads look small, but when they approach, they are large, heavy, and the crudeness of the enciphered monstrousness—the livery black and scarlet, the teeth, the stare—makes them genuinely frightening. The* guitas' *manipulators rush the crowd, dipping the beasts' heads all of a sudden on one group, sweep-ing furiously across it, showering the bystanders with sparks. Then they suddenly swerve and mob another section of the throng, moving at break-neck speed along the length of the front lines, the lighted firecrackers in their monsters' jaws spluttering and hissing all the while. The crowd wears heavy cotton hats and coverings as protection from the fiery saltpetre, but young participants want to confront the danger. Later, they display the scorched and holey trophies of their encounters like battle scars.*

Meanwhile, during these skirmishes, two pairs of gigantes—*Old and New Giants—brought out for the occasion, are standing in the square, outside the town hall. They are like colossal national dolls, richly cos-tumed, bewigged with real (horse) hair, and have bright glass eyes, so that*

1 & 2 *Francisco Goya, in* Saturn Devouring His Child, *revisited the Greek myth about the god's jealousy of his off-spring and fear that they would usurp him.* Judith BELOW *another of Goya's Black Paintings, 1821–3, formed its pendant: a father's cannibal assault on his children and a young woman's beheading of a warrior exemplify polar extremes of unnatural and savage violence.*

3 RIGHT *In Goya's painting,* The Burial of the Sardine, *c.1812–9, raucous revellers wearing masks of Death, the Maiden, Beauties, Beasts and other characters, dance a traditional* sardana *under a banner painted with one of the artist's recurring emblems of human folly, a leering fool.*

4 BELOW *The feast of Corpus Christi, celebrating the miracle of the Eucharist, still inspires carnival celebrations. In Berga, Catalonia, Spain, a guiser in the Patum festival wears a devil mask and fireworks for horns and carries a drum with another popular and grotesque symbol – the poking tongue.*

5, 6, 7 & 8 *Satan's monstrous minions, befanged and beclawed, drive the damned into hellfire* LEFT *in Hans Memling's,* The Last Judgement, *right wing, c. 1480. The Patum* ABOVE *climaxes at nightfall with the dance of the devils who raise hell in a storm of exploding rockets.*

9 & 10 Bugs and devils are linguistically and visually associated, as in the swarms of fallen angels from Hieronymus Bosch's image of the Fall LEFT, *while his vision of Hell* RIGHT *imagines devils as fantastic jumbles of parts—monkey bodies, moth wings, insect proboscies and feelers.* The Haywain, *left and right wings, early sixteenth century.*

11, 12 & 13
*Supernatural beings
can change their shape,
simulate, deceive and
disappear, as insects do.*
LEFT *Fairies, painted by
Richard Dadd, inhabit
insects' teeming,
microscopic world and
possess their powers of
metamorphosis and
disguise.* The Fairy
Feller's Master-Stroke,
1855–64.
BELOW LEFT *In a vivid
example of Batesian
mimicry, a harmless
moth imitates a lethal
hornet while* BELOW
RIGHT *a cricket's
perfect rendering of a
leaf makes it almost
invisible as it feeds.*

Mimicry: a moth-hornet (Sesia apiformis)   *Camouflage: Cryptic katydid* (Aegimia elongata)

14, 15, 16 & 17 *In biological mimicry and human signing, games of* Boo! *share a language of colour and form:* LEFT *Joshua Reynolds borrowed a motif from antiquity when he painted one sister frightening another with a mask in* The Fourth Duke of Marlborough and Family, 1777–79 *(in the Red Drawing Room, Blenheim Palace, Oxfordshire). Today, from religious festivals to rock music, the aggressive postures and coloration of different species offer human points of identification:* BELOW RIGHT *the larva of a Puss Moth (*Cerura vinula*), in its characteristic threatening pose;* BELOW LEFT *The 1997 poster of a crab in lurid battle dress promoted the Prodigy, a hugely successful English band;* FAR BELOW RIGHT *a Spanish* guita, *or fire-breathing dragon, acts to chase away evil.*

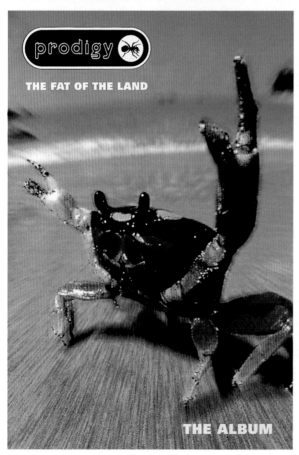

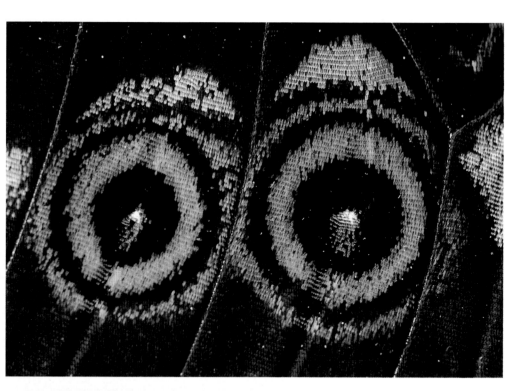

HANDLE CAREFULLY
RADIOACTIVE
CONTENTS................
NO OF CURES...........

18, 19 & 20 A comic Spanish cabezudo *or big head* LEFT *delivers an uncanny frisson with its staring eyes.* ABOVE TOP *The ocelli on the wings of a South American butterfly have evolved, down to the last detail of the highlights in the pupil, to match the gaze of a creature far larger and more fearsome than itself.* ABOVE *Danger notices use the stark hues of animal offence and self-defence.*

21, 22, 23 & 24 *Lambs in wolves'
clothing: the Viceroy butterfly* TOP
*(Basilarchia archippus) evolved to
resemble almost indistinguishably the
foul-tasting Monarch variety (Danaus
plexippus)* ABOVE RIGHT. *Role-playing
games like Dungeons & Dragons,
Spellfire and Skaven draw on a biological
language of alarm and aggression:* LEFT *a
Chaos warrior from the Warhammer
Catalogue of figures with* ABOVE *a
froghopper (Cercopis vulnerata) in
warning livery.*

*their stolid immobility gives them the unsettling, uncanny effect of wax-
works. The two couples are kings and queens, one Moorish, one Christian,
and they emanate directly from the copybook of romance and chivalry, as
parodied by Cervantes: more than twelve feet high, turbaned and crowned,
noble, beautiful, mirror images, but enemies. Such colossi are also paraded
in many other parts of Spain on this same feast—in Barcelona, Valencia
and elsewhere. They represent the victory of the Catholic kings and the
vanished power of heathen Islam in Spain, though nobody refers to this
past history any longer. The* gigantes *are held in high esteem by Bergueans,
who attribute detailed lives and characters to the four of them, and invoke
them for help with love affairs, marriages, and the birth of children.*

After the guitas' *rockets have burned out and they have retired from the
fray, chosen bearers raise up the* gigantes *and whirl them to the music—but
at a stately pace, since they are bulky and very heavy. Then follows the
combat of St. Michael and his angels with the devil and his minions, all
costumed in chivalric style, the devils in grimacing black masks with curly
horns; the fighting is ritualized, and the devils eventually lie prone in
defeat. Next it is the turn of the dwarfs to dance. Theirs are the most vivid
masks of the celebrations, and their performance the most eerie; again,
such* cabezudos, *or big-heads (Pl. 18), occur in many Spanish festivals,
today and in the past, as numerous sketches and drawings by Goya reveal.
The dwarfs also come in two couples: the Old Dwarfs are costumed like
municipal councillors of Catalonia in the eighteenth century, the New
Dwarfs are dressed up comically as housewives and traders of more recent
date; the female roles are played by cross-dressed men. These vivid, gaudy,
caricatural masks are donned proudly, by participants who guard hereditary rights to the privilege of guising in this character. They, too, like the
giants, perform a kind of reel to the brass band. But the guisers' legs—
kicking out beneath the massive gaudy heads with their fixed expressions,
some even coiffed in mob caps and wearing aprons—produce a most
grotesque effect, poised between ridiculousness and horror, like Bosch's
fantasy of the eggshell doing a jig.*

*The most solemn phase of the Patum occurs when the Eagle, a symbol
of authority and faith, bows to the mayor and the dignitaries on the town
hall balcony and then spins three times on the spot to a high, slow melody
from the band; there is only space inside the big, glossily varnished wooden
brown bird—which looks more like a pigeon—for one pair of shoulders,
and it is colossally heavy. So this feat, also performed by a member of a
hereditary family, earns the crowd's admiration and awe. The crowd falls
silent and keeps still, as the stately music from the brass band swells,*

The Old and New Giants, kings and queens from the legendary history of the Moors and Christians, whirl above the crowd.

creating what the anthropologist William Christian, Jr., calls a 'true ritual moment' and communicating a liturgical feeling for the only time during the secular celebrations of the Patum.

These episodes are enacted and re-enacted over and over again in the course of two days, until, finally, on the second day, darkness falls and it is possible to stage the ecstatic conclusion: the salt de plens, *the dance of the full devils.* Rockets—the petards—are attached to the bodies of participants dressed as devils in scarlet and black and dark green, to their rumps as tails and to their foreheads as horns. These masked dancers are not acting as in the theatre but acting as in the sense of agency: there is make-believe in the costumes and scenarios, but not in the performance, which is all too real.

The men guising as demons let loose from hell—and they are all men,

The Old and New Dwarfs, cross-dressed in carnival spirit, dance a jig.

not women—put on the towering mask/head-dresses over their faces, and their heads and bodies underneath are swathed in fresh and sappy vidalba *vines from the river valley nearby so that they will be protected from the blast of the fireworks. Each of them is accompanied by a friend carrying a taper, and at the signal from the drum, this* accompanyant *lights the fuse. The crowd presses in close, the square masses into a solid human wave as the rockets catch and sulphur rises in the air, flaming grapeshot bursts out and great sprays of yellow gold and scarlet fountain from the devils' horns and rumps. Flames, smoke and bangs fill the small town square in a terrifyingly effective scene of hell-raising, of pandemonium. Aspects of the Patum echo the medieval Carnival of Devils, to which the ballad of Cock Lorrel alluded, in which everything is topsy-turvy and diabolical wind signalled the anal birth of new souls. (The word 'Patum' could also be related*

Making sure there is nothing to be afraid of, fingers poke at the eye sockets of a devil mask.

to the word for fart, as in French 'péter'.)

At the height of the excitement, the crowd breaks up into rings around each human firework, who whirls in the centre, spattering the fire away from him in an arc as he spins—failing this, he would probably be burned. Each ring of dancers also wheels round the plaza, always turning counterclockwise, in the contrary movement of the satanic powers, the witch's widdershins. The cacophony that explodes sounds like artillery fire in a siege or massacre; the square seethes like a giant brazier on which fat drips and turns into hissing plumes of flame; gradually the rockets sputter and die (peter out), and the disoriented, deafened devils are led away by the jubilant participants in the ritual.

The whole cycle is repeated again the following night; but before that, the next afternoon, comes the turn of the children to perform the Patum.

The children's Patum is a novelty—children began participating in the 1950s—and its introduction illustrates very well the innovatory and contemporary meanings with which old images and traditions and rituals, like the dance of Death, are invested. The public ritual, defining generational responsibility as the burden of the performance, offers a remarkably potent example of the contemporary use of horror in confronting imagined dangers and inspiring strength and confidence. Girls and boys, some of them as young as six years old, re-enact the sequence. They wear small, similar masks for the dragons, the combat of Michael and the devil, the Giants, the Dwarfs, the Eagle.

At the climax, they are costumed in red and green devil suits and swathed from head to toe in damp weed like their elders; this swaddling is entrusted to experienced older men who have done it for decades. In some cases they bandage the children's ears and then tie on the rockets to explode from their horns and their tails. Completely encased in their green masks, the now blind 'devils' are conducted by their parents—fathers, mostly— up the steep alley from the dressing area to the square, and coaxed to take part bravely. Some show signs of unwillingness, but this is not encouraged. It is a high honour to play a devil, and only the young of Berga's best and most influential families are included. Fathers and grandfathers dominate the preparations and the explanations; in the dressing area, preparing them for the dances and performances, as well

Before the dance, a child playing a devil is swathed in damp greenery for protection against the fireworks.

as in the crowd, carrying many members of the next generation shoulder-high in order for them to see better, they instruct them in the meaning and importance of the ritual for a Berguean. Meanwhile, the 'trash', the young who do not have access to the privilege, hang close to the edges of the arena, showing off the holes in their hats and sweaters to display that they have what it takes to dance in the salt, *if only they were allowed to. The excitement in the atmosphere builds before the* salt de plens; *the tension for parents, children, bystanders grows palpably.*

The anthropologist Dorothy Noyes took part, unusually for a grown woman, in the salt de plens, *and she describes the experience:*

> *The music begins and you begin to jump for your life, the crowd pressing, the sparks falling on your hands and inside your mask. You hear explosions inside your head; the texture of the* plaça *changes beneath your feet; a second of open space and air is too quickly resubmerged in smoke and crowd for you to catch your bearings. Helpless, you follow your* accompanyant *until it's over and he lifts your mask and the lights come up. You gasp for air*

and gape at the plaça; *emerge to a place you had forgotten . . .
Birth must have been like this: the long descent in the darkness;
the helplessness; the struggle to push up, out, through; the
release when the* fuets *explode—and the ones on your tail hit
you like the doctor's slap to a baby. As you do the* salt *through
the years and 'learn the place with your feet' more adult
sensations supervene. Now it is the 'oulde dance' towards an
anticipated climax; a familiar pleasure made new in eerie
re-enactment. In a single moment, the* plens *condense the beginning and the end of generation.*

Concentrating on this Dionysiac incorporation—perhaps similar to
other forms of orgiastic communal jubilation, as at raves for example—
Noyes overlooks the festival's larger, moral function: to invest the forms
and strokes and blows of evil so intimately that they can no longer harm
you. And this is not some primordial ancient or medieval rite, steeped in
Christian antiquity or the Moorish wars, though clearly the imagery of the
giants retains links to Spanish history. It was only in 1820 that the Patum
emerged under that name. The Eagle appeared at the end of the eighteenth
century; the festival was then closely connected to the Church and to the
processional display of the host for Corpus Christi (as still takes place in
Barcelona, for example). But many of its other, most important and distinctive features are only around a hundred years old. The New Giants
were added to the Old ones in 1891, while the plens, or full devils as such,
were first mentioned in documents in 1877. The children's replica was
introduced as late as 1956. Even more surprisingly, since the fire dance
bears every mark of antediluvian paganism, the euphoric salt de plens
reached fever pitch only in the 1960s. Its popularity is growing: a comparison of photographs showing the crowd over the years reveals that the
square is yearly becoming more and more of a terrifying compression
chamber. The celebrations pass on a modern sense of Catalonian identity,
and destiny.

The Patum's historians and local people insist on the atavistic, unchanging authenticity of the tradition, claiming it as a time-honoured ritual. It
should however be understood against the background of the bloody
struggles in recent Spanish and Catalonian history, which it re-enacts, confronts, and subdues in the deep disguise of its effigies and masks. The
Patum does not look modern, but it is; and it is symptomatically modern,
in its cruel forging of community and its risk-taking quest for annihilating
ecstasy. It follows from the follies that transfixed Goya, at an earlier time

During the Corpus Christi festivities in Burgos, El Colacho *(the Devil) takes a leap over the year's newborn babies. Photographed by Cristina García Rodero, 1975.*

of terrible violence and turmoil in Spain; it is a twist on the grotesque he explored and epitomized, a medium to induce horror, to create a state of contemporary 'scariness', where terror and pleasure meet.

Noyes sums up the Berguean ritual's significance: 'The dancing effigies of the Patum counterpose "respectable" bodies—socially located, controlled, and clearly bounded—with figures of the "popular"—ambiguous, improvisatory, and open to contact. The festival's techniques of community—drinking, noise, fire, contact, vertigo, and others—work to dissolve this polarity and incorporate the community into one body. This wholeness is the festival's acknowledged goal, and release from everyday factionalism.' The interplay of the feast with clerical and political authority before and during the Franco years conferred on it a dissenting, *revolutionary character: it expressed popular desires and antagonisms. Here Noyes is following the highly influential, utopian interpretation of the carnivalesque in Mikhail Bakhtin's work on Rabelais; Bakhtin, from his perspective as a Soviet scholar working at a time of profound cultural oppression, argued for the liberating energies of mass expressions of vulgar exuberance and mockery of authority.*

The Patum was first banned; then later co-opted for Fascist-patriotic purposes—the children being hardened in an ideal of invincibility—but since the dictator's death the Patum has again metamorphosed, into the living theatre of Catalonian identity: 'the plaza after the Patum', writes its leading local historian, 'looks like a battlefield after combat, where the spirit of a people unwilling to die has achieved one more victory.'

Noyes adheres to the Bakhtinian line in her positive reading; but she modifies her interpretation with regard to the last decades, when, as she admits, the disorderliness of the feasting has been recast as an ideal of community and selfhood. She argues that in place of the ancient enmities (Moor and Christian) 'a living civil religion, an enactment of Berga's unity and identity' has emerged. Drawing in her conclusion on Victor Turner's perception of ritual functions, she writes, 'The individual's vertigo is an "as-if" of possession and self-loss; the con-sensus of 14,000 people is an "as-if" of community. When the earth stops moving, everything is in its proper place.'

However, as critics of Bakhtin's utopianism have argued, it is difficult to agree that Carnival, charivari and other topsy-turvy popular merry-making effectively undo the power of authoritarianism and mock tyranny. The grotesque body of Carnival, as Bakhtin evoked it, displaying bodily functions and appetite, glorying in excess and transgression of polite mores, does not figure in the Patum; in its conjuring of power, control and invulnerability, the festival expresses a characteristic late twentieth-century resistance to mortality and weakness. The afflicted, gaping, spewing, consuming and joyously ungoverned grotesque body Bakhtin so eloquently evoked has yielded pride of place in this contemporary version of the carnivalesque to a body that overcomes the ordeal it sets itself. The organization of the Patum affirms existing ethnic, class and gender hierarchies in the town and in the wider Catalonian setting. The anarchic or subversive potential of masking seems in a state of collapse; there is no social or political satire, but rather an aggressive jubilance about Catalonian identity and statehood. The children are mustered for a very late twentieth-century ordeal by noise and fire and terror, and their heroic-stoical survival, unscathed and unflinching, serves to define them within their community. An outsider like myself felt only the oddness of the thrill-seeking and a fear of being burned or of finding oneself watching while someone else—a child?—caught fire. A stranger cannot join in the wild communion of the prolonged ritual, and its hazards and harshness maintain an unsettling alienation. But an anthropologist like Dorothy Noyes, who embraced the community and was embraced by it, unreservedly entered into the locals' euphoria, in memory as well as at the time.

The Patum of Berga is a local event, a peculiarly Catalonian expression of identity born of the changing circumstances of Spain. But it also throws light on points at issue in this discussion of ogres and bogeymen and related phantasmagoria. A general movement makes itself felt through this single Catalonian feast: the failure of carnival riot to draw the sting of common terrors, the implication of a standoff between notions of individuality and community. Berga is not the only town in Spain or the only place in the world where people face terrors and evils by investing in them, by assuming their identity. The children of Berga, dressed as devils and exploding with the fires of hell, are play-acting the disorder that all individuals embody in potentia, *and children above all, in the late twentieth century. In participatory performances from the Patum to rock concerts, in spectator entertainments, thrillers like the film* Seven *or adventure blockbusters like* The Lost World: Jurassic Park, *even through reading, as in the new line in juvenile horror literature, adults and children submit themselves to extreme experiences—to endurance tests—that act upon their bodies with often ferocious impact to produce fear. Coming out of such ordeals alive delivers a 'hit', the high of surviving, it defines the living, impervious, sovereign self, and becomes a cause for ecstatic release.*

The reasonable aims of the Patum—to confirm harmony and social order through public catharsis and spectacle—cannot efface the festival's delirious conjuring of the fears it claims to defeat; such intensely involving, joyous exorcism tends to erase personal identities with their freight of different sorrows and terrors; it effectively abolishes the subject. A feast like the Patum of Berga enrols its agents into orderly community. It invokes chaos in order to subdue it. It initiates the young into declarations of belonging. It constitutes, it could be said, a kind of official hazing. In this respect, it does continue, as performance, one historic function of nursery tales which is about overcoming death and other evils.

V

'HOC EST CORPUS'

Behold my hands and my feet, that it is I myself: handle me, and
see; for a spirit hath not flesh and bones, as ye see me have.

Luke 24 : 39

The feast of Corpus Christi has not declined today, as have
other great medieval feasts, such as Pentecost, but still provides the occasion for remarkable processions, imagery and
performances that have become acts of communion beyond
the ecclesiastic authorities' reach. It continues to celebrate the miracle of
transubstantiation which lies at the centre of the Catholic belief system.
This central doctrine has enhanced, far beyond the writ of the Catholic
faithful, a contemporary sacramental relationship among bodies, images
and their meanings. It informs the theme of ogres and bogeymen more
vividly than might at first appear, because its religious meaning attempts to
purify cannibalism, to turn the pollution of anthropophagy into a means of
salvation. The feast of Corpus Christi celebrates the central sacrificial meal
of Christianity, the holy mystery of the true presence of the body and blood
of Christ in the consecrated bread and wine of the Mass.

According to Robert Graves in the *Greek Myths* (1955) and to M.L.
West, in his study of Orphism, the sacrificial meal during which worship-
pers partake of the god structures the story of Zagreus' death. Both writers
interpret the baby's encounter with the flesh-eating Titans as an account of
the Orphic ritual feast for initiates into that mystery religion, which was
practised in Crete. The connection with the later Christian Mass and the
sacrament of communion with divine flesh then stands out clearly, though
Graves emphasizes that the Orphic commemorative banquet, recalling the
god's death, was not a simulacrum or performance but an actual human
sacrifice of a youth elected to be Zagreus-Dionysus and rule for a day. In

In a walled and flowery mead, God the Father sits enthroned, with the Lamb beneath him; the waters of salvation rain hosts into the basin below them, but unbelievers are prevented access by a blindfolded High Priest. Juan Belasco, The Fountain of Life, *sixteenth century.*

direct contradiction to this interpretation, however, the French classical scholar, Marcel Detienne, stresses that the Orphics were early vegetarians and censured the killing of animals for food. They were also radical opponents of the mainstream religion of the Olympians, and resisted its worship. Consequently, Detienne sees the baby's slaughter, in the myth and in its ritual recapitulation, as a vehement and appalled imitation of traditional blood sacrifices to the divine pantheon on Olympus.

Whether Zagreus' death foreshadows Christ's as a ritual sacrifice, or whether the Orphics were horrified by the gruesomeness of such ceremonies, the issues of divinity, magic and authority traverse the story through the performance of a meal: the Titans, ingesting Zagreus, are attempting to absorb him into themselves, to incorporate his virtues at the

The homely metaphor of a flour mill conveys vividly the doctrine of the real presence in the Eucharist: here the wafers tumbling from the hopper take the form of the child Jesus. The Mystical Mill, *Swabian, c. 1440.*

same time as extinguish his threat to their power. The cannibal assaults in stories express a desire for possession of another's essence, as does, in a hallowed manner, the sacrament of communion. But the divergence of interpretation also reveals how profoundly disturbing the idea of eating a person, human or divine, actual or symbolic remains. These tender and ambiguous zones of fantasy and desire are the main breeding grounds of the sacred.

The feast day of Corpus Christi was formally instituted by Pope Clement V in 1311, to proclaim the truth of transubstantiation, that is, the miracle that the bread and wine are truly changed by the priest's reiteration of Christ's words at the Last Supper: 'This is my body, this is my blood— do this in commemoration of me.' Corpus Domini, as it is also known, is kept two weeks after Ascension Day, which falls forty days after Easter; it is therefore locked into the unfolding cycle of Christ's resurrection and its salvific meaning. Both Easter and Corpus Christi declare that death shall have no dominion, that the divine image—the pattern of the human creature—lives for ever, and that, in the case of Jesus, it lives on as flesh; this mystery looks forward to the day when all will rise in their flesh, too.

A miracle had taken place, in 1263 or 1264 when a priest from Prague, who was suffering from doubts about the Eucharist, was saying Mass in the church of Santa Cristina in Bolsena, Italy; as he came to Christ's words, the moment of consecration, and pronounced, 'Hoc est corpus meum', the bread began to bleed, staining the corporal, or linen cloth that is used to cover the chalice, on the altar beneath his hands, and then dripping on to the marble floor. The miracle of Bolsena inaugurated the great feast of Corpus Christi, one of the major holidays of the Catholic year, when, with solemn and public ceremony, prelates reaffirm to the faithful the central mystery of the faith. The bloodstained cloth, now vulnerably threadbare and wan, was enshrined in an exquisite silver and enamel reliquary made by Italian artisans and removed to the diocesan seat at Orvieto, to its own side chapel. Bolsena retained the altar at which the miracle took place and the russet marks of the blood on the floor, and Raphael later painted one of the walls of the papal suite in the Vatican with a sumptuous and reverent interpretation of the Mass at which God gave this visible proof of his presence in the host.

Catholics who were brought up after World War II remember the many hours spent anxiously pondering the mystery of the consecrated host: we should not bite into it, we were instructed by the nuns, but let it melt on the tongue and swallow it whole. I was frightened to experiment and nibble at it—in case it might turn bloody in my mouth. Any crumbs were caught in the paten that the serving boy held under our chins and open mouths, and gathered together later; then the priest mixed them up in the wine and drank them down, because Jesus was present in every fragment, infinitely divisible and ubiquitous.

Thomas Aquinas wrote a sequence for the Mass, the 'Pange, lingua, gloriosi', which affirms Christian Eucharistic doctrine in pellucid, dancing pairs of images:

> Verbum caro panem verum
>> Verbo carnem efficit,
> Fitque sanguis Christi merum
>> Et, si sensus deficit,
> Ad firmandum cor sincerum
>> Sola fides sufficit.

(The Word made flesh converts true bread into flesh by his word, and wine becomes Christ's blood. If the senses fail, faith alone is sufficient to confirm the pure heart.')

The last two verses of this sequence were sung regularly at Benediction, the evening service adorning the exposed host that I went to twice a week when I was at my convent school.

Like the miraculous Mass of St. Gregory, during which Christ appeared in person, naked, wounded, bleeding in the tabernacle, the miracle of Bolsena confirmed the dogma of the Eucharist—the eating of Christ's body by the faithful during the sacrament of communion. This central tenet of the Catholic faith inspired some fantastical extensions of the Eucharistic metaphor: books of hours and portable altars show Christ in a wine-press, his blood running out as wine into a chalice; sometimes he is being ground in a grain mill, while the hopper at the bottom delivers the wafers to his votaries. *The Fountain of Life*, possibly by Juan Belasco, a sixteenth-century Spanish painter, shows this flow of manna-like hosts into the eponymous fountain. On its left, in the Doomsday place of the damned, figures of unbelievers are being deprived of the host's resuscitatory powers by a blindfolded figure of the Synagogue personified. The painting acts as a pertinent reminder that faith needed its Others to be affirmed and that, where there was a mystery defying rational belief, there were those who defined it, by inversion (witchcraft) or by rejection (Muslims, Jews).

Although Eucharistic topoi have faded from devotion since the Reformation, they resurface in secular thought, often with far more force than generally accorded to miracles or fantasies in early modern societies. An incident occurred in 1750 in Paris which illuminates the workings of the metaphor in a historical and political context. Serious rioting erupted that year after children began disappearing; the most violent occurred when feelings mounted so high that one of the officers suspected of involvement was pursued by a mob and lynched. Beyond the immediate circumstances of the injustice, a persistent, traditional fear, endemic in folklore about ogres, may have incited the rioters. For it was widely rumoured in the workers' *quartiers* before and during the violence that either the king himself—Louis XV—or one of the princesses was failing. Leprosy was mentioned. This royal disease required magic physick: bathing in the fresh blood of vigorous young bodies was necessary, it was believed, for recovery from this sickness. Hence the snatching and stealing of children from the streets of Paris: their limbs were to be hacked off so they could be bled into tubs.

In an anti-French satirical print, a king lies sick: blood is 'the best cordial'. The Four of Spades, English playing card, *c. 1710.*

The idea of the bloodsucking despot figured vividly elsewhere during the same period, in British satires against the French above all. As early as the first decades of the eighteenth century, a set of playing cards included, on the Four of Spades, an image of an ailing monarch and two bedizened aristocrats approaching the royal bedside, urging, 'Give Him Blood to Drink'. From the woman's mouth issues a bubble, inscribed, 'The best cordial.' Similar stories of a 'blood carriage' that was rumoured to roam, collecting victims of future butchery, also circulated in Holland.

Such terrors not only arose from the 'low' superstitions of popular scaremongering. Drinking the blood of the young had been advocated as a reliable elixir by no less a scholar than Marsilio Ficino in the fifteenth century, who wrote in his treatise *Della Religione Christiana* of the belief that witches procure babies to suck their blood in order to refresh themselves. He endorsed the practice's therapeutic power: 'Then why might not our elderly, finding themselves all but without hope of survival, suck the blood of a lad? Of a lad, I say, of stalwart forces—healthy, cheerful, well-tempered, having excellent blood . . . Let them suck, then, like a leech . . . This should be done precisely when they are very hungry and thirsty, and at the waxing of the moon.' Ficino explicitly addressed his advice on extending life to *persone letterate*. The divergence between the inclinations of learned Christian culture then and the intense anxiety aroused today by bodily fusion and exchanges could not find a more starkly illuminating text. Medical learning continued to explore the theme; chemists mixed human blood, oil and flesh for invigorating powders and poultices in the seventeenth century, while anatomists experimented with cadavers (of criminals, since no others were legally available) to make 'the quintessence of human blood', giving instructions for preserving it in a glass jar '[like] any jar of jelly or marmalade, canned at the appropriate season each year . . .', comments Piero Camporesi.

Bologna was the site of the first public dissection of a human body, as early as 1302, and citizens' alarm about such operations, and about the consequent disinterring, transportation and use of corpses, resulted in a law of 1442 permitting only two dissections a year, to be performed on bodies taken from outside a fifty-mile radius of the city. The art of making detailed models of the human body began in Italy, and then spread: the Imperial Museum of Physics and Natural History in Florence, more commonly known as La Specola, opened in 1774. Similar cabinets followed, in Vienna (1785, the Josephinum) and in France, where the ancient medical school of Montpellier had acquired its own collection by 1793. Napoleon visited it and instantly ordered a duplicate set for Paris (it never arrived).

Using wax sculptures for students' anatomical research was inspired by public horror at the dissection of cadavers; Pope Benedict XIV initiated the wax cabinet in Bologna in order to forestall experimentation with real bodies. Yet the pioneer and virtuoso Ercole Lelli (1702–66) modelled lifesize figures of a man and a woman on real skeletons, using no fewer than fifty cadavers for accomplished freestanding *écorchés* demonstrating musculature and the nervous system. Wax anatomical modelling failed altogether to put an end to the need for corpses: the porter of La Specola was piteously petitioning, as late as the mid-eighteenth century, that he be granted 'an oilcloth hat, an overcoat and a pair of boots, to be used in going to get the cadavers at the hospital and in bringing them back, so that he may be able to protect himself from the wet and cold since he is not able to stop anywhere'; the report added that 'the tasks endured . . . have been unspeakable, for, besides the continued handling of the dead bodies, he has found himself on many occasions without sufficient time to get something to eat in order to attend to his unceasing work'. Even the grave-digger in Hamlet had less acquaintance with the dead.

Against this background of advances in medical knowledge, the deep fear of pollution excited in the eighteenth century converges with the body-snatching terrors and other scientific abuses that underlie the cultural rise of the vampire and the Frankenstein creature, who in the Gothic tale is

William Hogarth communicates the unease provoked by pioneering surgery and its methods of inquiry with a gruesome warning to the wicked: criminals finish up on the dissecting table. The Reward of Cruelty, *1751.*

stitched together from boneyard remains. When William Hogarth engraved, in 1751, the grim series entitled *The Four Stages of Cruelty*, he mapped the moral sequence that begins with boys tormenting animals and leads to rape and murder. In the final macabre image, *The Reward of Cruelty*, the perpetrator has finished up a ghastly shrieking corpse on a

The rhetoric of revolution on all sides invoked monsters: unnatural appetites loomed large as the defining activity of the enemy. James Gillray, Un petit souper à la Parisienne, *1792.*

surgical dissection table, his innards rummaged by doctors and spilling in profusion on to the floor and into pails, his bones in the anatomist's cauldron, while above on the operating theatre walls are suspended the skeletons of criminals who have preceded him under the scalpel.

The rumour of a bloodsucking monarch circulating in Paris in the 1750s thus coincided with the spread of this form of medical experiment, in fact and in the fantasy of contemporaries. The fear it inspired was rooted in the same terrain as the cannibal apparently made manifest in the figure of the native, the Caliban or wild man: chapbook stories, ballads and fairy tales, all of which were beginning to be published successfully at this time, refracted it as clearly as more adult and mainstream representations, like Hogarth's prints. Louis XV and his family assumed the features of the traditional ogre, but in earnest. The rioters' fantasy conveys, under the appearance of ignorant tale-telling, the social predicament in which they were caught, as the concept of the ogre slipped between fact and superstition, between description and metaphor, with the inherent instability of the ogre and cannibal mytheme.

New, swingeing laws against loitering had been instituted by the king, and bounty offered to the police in pursuit of their new duties. Consequently, police zeal led to a number of arrests of children who were in some cases merely running an errand on their own. When the anxious families eventually traced the missing offspring, they had to pay heavy fines in order to obtain their release from custody. Levies for the colonization of Louisiana were also taking place, and these inspired further terror in the populace when children or young people vanished. Thus the bloodsucker of street rumours materialized for real in the figure of the king. These Paris riots foreshadow 1789, when metaphors of monsters informed the language of the debate about Liberty—they were summoned in the rhetoric of the Jacobins and other revolutionaries, in the rationale of the Terror, in the denunciations of the mob by Edmund Burke. The 'Marseillaise' itself does not shirk the 'cruelty' Hogarth excoriated when it makes its appeal through the blood metaphors of rejuvenation:

Aux armes, citoyens! Formez vos bataillons!
Marchons, marchons!
Qu'un sang impur abreuve nos sillons!

(Citizens! To arms! Make up your battle lines!/ Forward march, forward march!/ Let's quench our furrows with polluted blood!)

In a Catholic setting, stories and images about flesh-eating and the circulation of bodies through other means, such as surgery, expressed deep anxieties, which suffuse the structure of hell and damnation, as well as beliefs about witchcraft. The correspondences were repulsed, as a perversion of the truths of Christian doctrine. Thus in Spain, as Goya's art reveals, the devil's works were invested in the signs and wonders of the faith, hellishly inverted. (The structures of such beliefs still govern the drama of a feast like the Patum, however recently it has developed its present popular features.) In Protestant England, by contrast, the same mysteries of the Eucharist and the resurrection of bodies also shaped the vocabulary of terror but were dismissed as foreign practices and popery. The ogre was seen to be Other in both situations, but neither means of repudiation managed successfully to keep him quiet.

From nourishing to devouring, metaphors of feeding course through the stories we tell ourselves about identity, survival, redemption, and their opposites. The songs and tales that feature ogres and cannibal devils and other monstrous eaters raise questions about the very nature of desire and our ways of expressing it: do our appetites make *us* monstrous?

VI

'HOW...WE CAN BEGIN TO FEED'

'Nurse! Do let's pretend that I'm a hungry hyæna, and you're a bone!'

Lewis Carroll, *Through the Looking Glass*

How could a bird that eats another bird be pure?

Aeschylus, *The Suppliants*

 The ever-present hunger in ogre stories, those recurring pots of porridge and pudding, sausages and pies, haunches and joints, cakes and gingerbread, currants and berries, communicate a world of literally frustrated physical appetite. Tom Thumb jumps into the king's 'firmity pudding' when the cook is taking it to the table and later slips into the giant's pocket in order to feast by filching food from his unwitting host's supply; Hansel and Gretel are ensnared when they begin to break off pieces of the witch's cottage and feast on them; Snow White bites into the (near) fatal apple. When shortages and illness deeply imperilled infants' lives, and material scarcity shaped dreams and drives, the world of stories was one in which glowing, ripe plenty beckoned elsewhere. As an anonymous critic wrote in 1820, in an early essay about children's literature: 'The child builds puddings in the air, instead of castles . . . palaces of apple-dumplings . . . pavements of pancakes . . . A pastry-cook's shop . . . becomes . . . what America was to Sir Walter Raleigh—a fairy land, an Atalantis [*sic*], Utopia, the *summum bonum*, the goal of life's race.'

Sheer physical hunger can explain the food fantasies in the stories: food, more food, more varieties of food, hotter, sweeter, juicier, flowing in an ever more easily available supply: fairy tales and nursery songs dream of this plenitude. (Angela Carter, in one of her deft and offhand sallies,

At a puppet play of Chinese shadows, the audience cast animal shapes, while on screen a cook with a pig's head meets a pig with a ... French, c. 1890.

famously remarked that a fairy tale is a story in which one king goes to visit another king to borrow a cup of sugar.) Hunger dominates the passions expressed in such materials; the same hunger that takes possession of ogres and witches.

This hunger in fairy tales reveals its keen edge even more clearly against the historical background. Actual orphans and fairy-tale foundlings coexisted in eighteenth-century culture, and food was stodgy and often scanty. Consider, for example, the bill of fare at the Foundling Hospital, London, founded by Thomas Coram in 1739, and the insistence on the topic of food in printed nursery tales seems not unreasonable. The Tables of Diet of the children in that pioneering institution make very dismal perusal indeed: in 1747, the General Committee minutes show that during one week 'in the Pork Season' the menu offered 'Gruell' for breakfast, 'Potatoes' for lunch, and 'Milk & Bread' for supper on Monday, 'Milk Porridge—Boiled Mutton' [and] 'Bread' on Tuesday; 'Broth—Rice Milk', 'Bread & Cheese' on Wednesday, 'Gruell—Boiled Pork' at last, and 'Bread' on Thursday,

'Milk Porridge—Dumplins—Milk & Bread' on Friday, 'Gruell—Hasty Puddings [and] Bread & Cheese' on Saturday, and then, the climax of the week: 'Broth—Roast Pork [and] Bread' on Sunday.

Yet this was a remarkably rich and varied diet for the times, far better than the fare of many children in working families.

In their preoccupation with hunger, early modern stories about ogres and their like were addressing a fundamental question about life: If living requires eating and eating requires the death of another living thing, how is it that I can be exempt? How will I avoid eating wrongly? And becoming what I eat? Or, even more sharply: how can I avoid being eaten?

The question has gained urgency in more recent fantasy materials which revolve around the issue of human monstrosity and our cannibalistic modernity. The French philosopher Jacques Derrida comments:

> The question is no longer one of knowing if it is 'good' to eat the other or if the other is 'good' to eat, nor of knowing which other. One eats him regardless and lets oneself be eaten by him. The so-called non-anthropophagic cultures practise symbolic anthropophagy and even construct their most elevated socius, indeed the sublimity of their morality, their politics, and their right, on this anthropophagy . . . The moral question is thus not, nor has it ever been: should one eat or not eat, eat this and not that, the living or the nonliving, man or animal, but since *one must* eat in any case and since it is and tastes good to eat, and since there's no other definition of the good (*du bien*), *how* for goodness' sake should one *eat well* (*bien manger*)? And what does this imply? What is eating? . . . The Good can also be eaten. And it must be eaten well.

Consumption was always a topic of popular stories, and it has remained a much-revisited theme: tales and rituals tell of the defeat of the bad eaters, and proclaim the identification of good eaters and their survival. Because of the intrinsic interdependence of life and food at a material level as well as in the mystical meaning of the Christian sacrament, the bad eaters—ogres and their avatars from the fantasy realms of alterity, monsters, dragons, giants, and other swallowers and devourers—turn up with regular and vivid inventiveness on religious feast days and in other cultural expressions. Unlike most of the world religions, Christianity does not observe dietary proscriptions: Christians are omnivorous. This has two broad effects: first, the imagery of eating pervades the very language of the culture, its beliefs and its rites; second, it provokes anxiety about impurity—an anxiety that used to be partly contained, for Catholics, by minor rules of abstinence, such as no meat on Fridays and fasting before communion, but is no longer. The taboo on cannibalism—on eating your own kind—offers the apparently unbreakable standard of propriety and hence ethics. Yet it is always being broken through performance and metaphor, thus plunging the system of discrimination between the good and bad eaters into continual disarray.

❖　　❖　　❖

Eating and being eaten inspires one of the most common games adults play with babies. Animal noises—gobbling, if not barking like giants—are what adults make when they play-act monsters with their young. It is instinctive, as instinctive as kissing or crying, to growl and grit your teeth and curl your fingers as if they were clawed and bring your face near the baby's and bare gritted teeth, going 'Grrrrrr, you're good enough to eat', or 'Yum yum, you're a sweet little morsel and I'm going to pop you in my mouth and eat you all up . . .' In French, the expression *faire barbo* refers to just this ancient game of clenching your teeth and grunting and making as if to claw the little body in fun.

We can catch the mother's voice, that acoustic mirror of early childhood, in some children's playground games in which girls as well as boys take part: these feature ogres and ogresses with names like Mother Cripsy-crops and Old Mother Hippety-hop (who limp, like the devil). The game begins when the mother leaves her children behind—warning them not to admit any strangers. The witch arrives—the It or He of the games—captures the children one by one and makes off with them, sometimes enticing them with special delicacies. She then play-acts turning them into pies and giving each of them a name: apple pie, cherry pie, peach pie. The living, bodily mother then returns, to scold roundly but reanimate her brood; she directly counteracts the ogre's devouring and annihilating acts and defeats the child-guzzler by baking and serving the right kind of meats. (My own favourite bedtime treat was when my mother agreed to 'bake' me: I'd beg her, far more often than she herself wanted to, to pat me and knead me and roll me and then pop me in the oven to cook for the night. The traditional nursery rhyme, 'Baby and I were baked in a pie/The gravy was wonderful hot' catches some of the primal bliss of this bedtime ritual.)

Needless to say, it is equally instinctive not to play ogres or even bakers at first encounter with someone else's child; the risk of mistaken meanings is clear. A Creole lullaby incorporates the baby-eating game:

Fais dodo, bébé, pour mama
Fais dodo, bébé, pour mama
Si bébé ne fait pas dodo
Gros chat est là que manger li
Gros chat est là que manger li.

The mother pretends to be the big cat; then there comes the *grand loup-loup*, and so on through a menagerie until the mother herself eats up her babe . . . A South African song also catches the risky thrills of the fantasy, as the mother makes believe an even more violent assault and then reassures her infant again:

Siembamba, Mama's little child
Wring his neck, throw him in a ditch.
Trample on his head
Then he is dead
That I shall not do.
I like to keep my little child
So why should I cut his head off?

The same impulse can arise in adult love-making, but orality there is not usually accompanied by monster faces or jaw-snapping and munching sounds. In sex, the eating fantasy does not often twist and turn through comic exaggerations and parodic beastliness. As Adam Phillips has commented, 'If . . . kissing could be described as aim-inhibited eating, we should also consider the more nonsensical option that eating can also be, as Freud will imply, aim-inhibited kissing.'

The interplay of these two ways of connection sometimes tilts, in the changing representations of poetry, play, images and songs, towards eating, sometimes towards kissing; in today's climate, the public emphasis falls on food. Food may stand in for sex, the oral gratifications perhaps interchangeable at a psychic level, but in terms of shared, overt expression, the promised satisfactions of food eclipse mutual exchanges of kisses and caresses. And these satisfactions include power over the hungry, control of the consumer.

Max und Moritz, a children's classic, widely translated—even into Latin—and still in circulation, dances with mischievous audacity on a tightrope drawn between sheer menace and joyous fun. Children do not appear to be altogether repelled by these adult threats. Or perhaps I should say they are schooled, by the conventions that developed within children's materials in our culture during the last century, into finding them joky and meeting with robust equanimity fantastic variations on the motif of eating and being eaten. Wilhelm Busch, born in Lower Saxony in 1832, was writing in the grotesque comic tradition of the Grimm Brothers. His scapegrace heroes stage a series of pranks against adults, but receive their comeuppance. In their sixth act of mischief, they climb down the baker's chimney and land in his trough of dough:

> He seized upon this precious pair
> Kneaded them thoroughly, and there
> You see him put them both to bake
> Inside the oven, like a cake.

However, the young hellions are not destroyed by this; like cartoon heroes of later *Tom and Jerry* popular films, they rise again to work more

Eins, zwei, drei! — eh' man's gedacht,
Sind zwei Brote d'raus gemacht.

In dem Ofen glüht es noch —
Ruff!!! — damit ins Ofenloch!

Good enough to eat: Max and Moritz, merry young scapegraces, try to steal some biscuits—and fall into the baker's dough. Wilhelm Busch, 1874.

mayhem: though baked to a crisp, the two rascals break out of the pastry crust and run away. In the last episode of the story, they slit open the miller's sacks of grain, whereupon, like a bogeyman with his bag, he pounces on them and ties them up in the sacks and feeds them into the hopper, where, crick-crack, they are ground into little pieces, and that is the last of Max and Moritz.

Even Lewis Carroll, whose imagination seems less down-to-earth, is at his most effervescently inventive when his fantasies are trained on eating and drinking. For a man who was so austere in his own tastes, jam and other treats held Lewis Carroll's interest and dominate the imagery of his jokes from his juvenilia onwards. Indeed he sounded a nostalgic note for such childhood pleasures as early as 1854, when he was already recalling lost times of 'pinafores, treacle and innocence'. In *Alice in Wonderland*, Alice loses a sense of who she is as her body keeps changing, growing now tiny, now huge. Carroll shows his awareness of the exciting possibilities when he writes: ' "I know *something* interesting is sure to happen," she [Alice] said to herself, "whenever I eat or drink anything; so I'll just see what this little bottle does" ' (not a sentiment that would be allowed in children's writing today). This closeness to children's primal appetites Carroll retained all his life: risky experiments with mysterious bottles appear alongside the familiar stodge of puddings and pies, tarts, cakes and treacle wells, while a parody of High Table pomp characterizes adult fare—oysters and lobsters and mock turtle soup. In one early story, the villain—an early Boojum—gets reduced to 'mashed potatoe' (sic). But the Boojum does not always suffer. Carroll submits the recurring problem—who eats and who gets eaten—to his most brilliant parodic wit in 'The Walrus and the Carpenter':

> 'Now if you're ready, Oysters dear,
>   We can begin to feed.'

> 'But not on us!' the Oysters cried,
>   Turning a little blue.

But the Oysters are 'eaten every one', as the Walrus and the Carpenter weep crocodile tears.

In 1889, after meeting Princess Alice, Queen Victoria's granddaughter, Lewis Carroll wrote to Isa Bowman, one of his 'child friends', 'If I made friends with a dozen Princesses, I would love you better than all of them together, even [if] I had them all rolled up into a sort of child roly-poly.' So

The rats fear it will not be a good pudding, after all. Beatrix Potter, The Tale of Samuel Whiskers, *1908.*

the tea-time treats he dangled in his *Alice* books return to convey just how sweet and spicy is the stuff little girls are made of. If eating can be 'aim-inhibited kissing', then Carroll's fascination with tea parties and jam tarts and his recurrent fantasies about jaws that bite, about babies who turn into pigs and get their faces peppered, about old men devouring little oysters, become moves in his unconscious—and in his plot.

Within twenty years of Carroll's instancing of a child roly-poly, Beatrix Potter wrote *The Tale of Samuel Whiskers, or the Roly-Poly Pudding*, in which Tom Kitten, the naughty boy hero, rapscallion son of fussy Mrs Tabitha Twitchit—and clear point of identification in the story—is rolled up in pastry by the rats in the attic:

> Tom Kitten bit and spat, and mewed and wriggled; and the rolling-pin went roly-poly, roly; roly, poly, roly. The rats each held an end.
>
> 'His tail is sticking out! You did not fetch enough dough, Anna Maria.'
>
> 'I fetched as much as I could carry,' replied Anna Maria.

'I do not think'—said Samuel Whiskers, pausing to take a look at Tom Kitten—'I do *not* think it will be a good pudding. It smells sooty.'

Tom Kitten is spared, unlike Max and Moritz, unlike the Oysters dear. The children in the tale share his relief at his escape; but they are left with his lifelong terror of rats.

❖   ❖   ❖

In the 1960s, the anthropologist Gregory Bateson developed a theory of play, according to which testing the limits of safety and entertaining the terror of murder and torment help to confirm the child's sense of security with the parent or caregiver. It was one of Adam Phillips' girl child patients who told him, 'When we play monsters, and mummy catches me, she never kills me, she only tickles me.' Butterfly swinging—when a child is held by the arm and leg and flown round and round in the air as the adult turns— stirs the same thrills of surrender; the adult is giving full expression to the power of life and death that he or she holds during infancy and childhood and is expressly refraining from using it to extreme ends. But many remember as adults the fear they experienced as children: the lessons in vulnerability were well taught.

The Irish novelist Kate O'Brien, for example, recalled in her memoir *Presentation Parlour* (1963) her grandfather's 'sickening gaiety' as he dandled her to the song 'Cuc-a-nandy':

> I knew—and it always happened—that I would be snatched from the quiet perch I occupied, and slung up and down between the ceiling and his watchchain while he sang:
>> Dance her up and up, and
>> Dance her up on high . . .
> I hated that. I was sure that one day in excess of vitality he would dash me against the ceiling.

Her grandfather appeared rarely, and so the child Kate was suspicious of him. This kind of terror-play can comfort and thrill at the same time only when there is deep, familiar trust between the players—one of the latent messages of lullabies, nursery rhymes and fairy tales is not to trust the stranger, especially the big stranger of the male kind, but to remain at home, at rest in the familiar small world close to hand.

Games of thrills and spills, stirring phantoms of bogeymen, snatchers and watchers, then become part of the process of learning the norms of social languages, and of differentiating oneself within them. But while the rhymes, songs and play serve the child's needs—it is rare for adults to perform in this way alone (though sometimes they do with pets)—they also define the caregiver's place. The ogre or bogeyman is a character in a family drama, written and directed by someone who is often the mother or the nurse. In Cinderella and many other fairy tales, the wicked stepmother may represent the narrator's rival for authority in the household, whom she consequently attacks and defames by means of the story in order to win the allegiance of her hearers, the children. A similar structure may govern the singing and playing and acting out of bogeyman fantasies: we may be hearing the fear, anger and other emotions of women, for whom infants' vulnerability acts as a pretext. The ogre is the witch or wicked stepmother's counterpart: the unacceptable bad father. Greek myths about Kronos' attempts against his offspring, fairy tales about giants lusting for human flesh—preferably young and tender—define crimes against the duties and dues of paternity, as we have seen. The scaremonger who seems to be inviting bogeymen into the nursery even as she banishes them is also setting out ideas about authority distorted, care perverted. The ogre's appetite expresses nothing more than the wrong kind of desire, love in excess.

But why does the food source become the children themselves? Why do popular ceremonies place babies and youngsters in the fattening coop of the witch, in the belly of the dragon, or on the ogre's table, or threaten them with a roasting, as in the Patum? Are the imagined ogres cannibals, strictly speaking? Are they consuming their own kind? Or are they different in species, and merely anthropophagous, in this respect, like werewolves or crocodiles? Are ogres to humans as animals are to humans? Or are they as humans are to animals? Or as adults to children? Or, more particularly, are baby-eating giants to their nourishment as adult humans are to the succulent young meat of lamb or calf that they relish at their table?

The question is not easy to settle: giants are different from humans and yet very like them; ogres are people, too, but also inhuman in their desires. The identifications revolve from character to character. For ogres not only are large adult humans but have a remarkable affinity with children. Infants are very different from giants but are at the same time represented as rather like them. The monsters of popular dread, with their unbridled appetite, insatiable tyranny, unappeasable desire for gratification, are just like . . . babies, big babies, as big as babies are when they explode into a life and change it. Ogres are voracious, stupid, clumsy, bumbling, vulnerable to the cleverness of human wits; they have big heads; they are, in spite of their size, rather easily overcome; they eat human flesh. Mythic stories frequently proceed with the punning literal-mindedness of dreams while all the time inverting experience in a form of negation. So, is it not possible that the ogre contains a concealed portrait of an infant? The English cartoonist Heath developed a Gargantua-style baby for a highly successful series in the 1980s; Martin Amis, the novelist, lampooned with bravura hyperbole the consuming appetites of another newborn, the horrendous (and horribly funny) Marmaduke, in his 1989 novel *London Fields*.

At the most literal level, babies are not carnivorous, and the cannibal metaphor has only recently been extended to cover their excited suckling, and to psychologize it as expressing a whole range of darker passions. The physical hunger children experience only lends itself to allegory in this way during times when the memory of want has faded. Voracious at the breast, the child does drink his mother's substance in a form of omophagous consumption of like by like; the stories about ogres and giants—and cannibal witches—cast them as throwbacks, superannuated types of perverted and barbarous behaviour, stuck in the infancy of unappeasable demands and violent greed. Again, the stories may be teaching by negative example: they might be saying to the child receivers, Soon you will have to stop behaving like a greedy ogre, and learn how to restrain your appetites and not to eat (or consume) your own kind.

This message is only latent in most fairy tales about 'firmity' or blood puddings or other delicacies. But today the word 'want', which used to mean 'need' at a material level, more commonly denotes emotional desires. Post-1950s conditions in the consuming West have changed the relation of many infants to scarcity and need: death does not bear them away as it did—thankfully, though poverty and all its attendant ills (which include junk food) still bedevil many families in most prosperous and stable societies, including Britain and the United States.

Simultaneously, psychoanalytic theory, most particularly in the work of Melanie Klein, has staged a primal chamber of horrors with the infant as unstoppably, murderously voracious. One consequence is that the ogre who used to stalk children has now been internalized as the image of inner compulsions, especially greed and the ferocious survival instinct. The bogey *Doppelgänger* defines self: it is the child who can be understood to be the potentially insatiable devourer, the possible monster of greed and gratification and excess. And this ogre within corresponds to the ungovernable id, which is pictured as somehow fitted inside, as if the prompter concealed below threatened to take control of the performer on the psychological stage of the ego. All the soppy talk about the inner child has not laid to rest deep fantasies about the inner ogre.

A perfect example of such contemporary psychological exegesis occurs in a passage about one of Leonardo da Vinci's several drawings of all-engulfing floods. These are small, so densely worked that the paper has changed texture in places, and their imagery of catastrophe, even at a reduced scale, inspires the depths of awe and terror associated with the sublime. Eric Charles White, commenting on *The Deluge*, makes the connection with the all-engulfing, apocalyptic character of hell, as the vehicle for the threat of annihilation that death represents. Writing in 1987, he takes this Dantesque metaphor of final extinction, drawn around 1514, as an image of Leonardo's innermost tendencies 'subduing his surroundings so as to remove the possibility of further traumatic encounters. He thus produced as oral sadistic fantasy of consuming the totality of existence not simply in order to obtain an increased yield in pleasure but to ward off the terrifying possibility of personal dissolution . . . That is, the artist's famous curiosity about the nature of reality is really a sublimation of the child's cannibalistic rage.'

This idea of the child as cannibal simply constitutes another instance of fallacious and defensive projection, working according to the same mechanism as in the fantasy about Oedipus and Zeus, of the child as parricide. It is adults who eat children, if anyone is doing any eating of this sort—as unfortunately happened during shipwrecks and sieges. The French nursery song, 'Il était un petit navire' ('Once there was a little boat') insouciantly records such a disaster at sea: 'Le sort tomba sur le plus jeune./C'est lui qui sera mangé/Olé olé (The lot fell upon the youngest/It's him who shall be eaten/ Olé Olé'.)

Where the Wild Things Are, Maurice Sendak's exhilarating children's book of 1963, opens with its young hero wearing his wolf suit and making 'mischief of one kind and another'. When his mother—who remains invisible throughout—scolds him for his naughtiness, calling him 'Wild Thing!', Max responds in wolfish kind, threatening to eat her. The oscillation between food as boon and food as bane continues, for his mother then punishes him, by sending him to his room without his supper. There, as everyone knows who has read this inspired classic, a forest grows and Max sails across the sea to the land 'where the wild things are'.

Sendak's wild things are monsters who instantly threaten to devour Max. They have fangs and claws and horns and goggle eyes, huge lolling heads and scales and tails, and they bristle and snap and roar at him from the shore as his little barque approaches and then, over five glorious double-page spreads of Sendak's graphics, they cringe and cavort and gambol and

The most lovable beasts of nursery lore today, raising a 'wild rumpus' in Maurice Sendak's classic picture book, Where the Wild Things Are, 1963.

lollop, goofy, comical, baggy giant dumb creatures. For Max has tamed them; an Orphic dragon slayer, he simply used words to charm them and his 'magic trick of staring into all their yellow eyes without blinking once . . .'

Staring into their eyes, he might see himself reflected, as he is indeed reflected in their larger being, which they acknowledge, calling him 'the most wild thing of all' and making him their king. At the end of the 'wild rumpus', Max deals out the punishment his mother dealt him: no supper.

The next illustration shows a woebegone Max, still in his wolf suit and spiky crown in his royal pavilion, surrounded by the giant wild things all slumped in sleep with their claws dangling limp and their overbites slack

over their massive jaws; his mind is on food, and he decides to leave. The wild things repeat to him his earlier threat to his mother: 'We'll eat you up—' and they add, following the logic of all-consuming passion, 'we love you so'.

The story ends with an image that inspires in listener and reader alike, no matter how many times the story is told, a sigh of supreme satisfaction: Max finds his supper waiting for him [page turn] 'and it was still hot'.

Sendak's pared-down narrative pulses beside or under his excessive, hyperbolic, crowded and gargantuan cartoon creations to create a dream-world of gratification, power and, ultimately, consolation and safety. The still-hot supper stands on a table under a full moon shining in through the open window: a hunting moon, a werewolves' moon. It consists of a bowl with a spoon in it, a glass, a small pile of sliced bread; this restrained, wholesome meal encapsulates the secure place of home, in contrast to the lunar kingdom of the carnivorous beasts, within and without. The books pushes that traditional confrontation in giant-killing tales between the small hero and the huge monster towards sympathetic identification of the unruly passions and power inside children according to the Freudian schema of the psyche: the id below, bubbling and troubling, corresponds to the youth of the species. The wild things themselves—cuddlingly lumbering though they be—congrue with this plan; they figure as so many antediluvian throwback giants along the evolutionary lineage. Sendak's brilliant and poignant work may reflect an inherent empathy children have with feral creatures—it would be hard to argue that their attraction to soft toys and teddy bears has been formed entirely by consumer interests. But his classic is also a classic of its time: it reflects adult perception of children today; it forgoes the usual combat tale between hero and ogre in favour of a reciprocal recognition of resemblance, of doubling, of twinship. The ogre—the wild things—no longer appals, like the cannibal giant in the classical myth, or in *Beowulf*, or in Jack the giant-killer tales, but has become much more clearly the little boy's *alter ego*. And that slant on the ogre theme arises from a decisive change in attitudes to children that began in the mid-eighteenth century and was crystallized in ours.

David McKee, in his mordantly comic, brilliant and laconic picture book *Not Now, Bernard* (1980), focuses even more clearly than Sendak on children's monstrousness in adult perception. Bernard sees a monster and tries to get his parents' attention, but the refrain continues, 'Not now, Bernard.' When he tells them 'there's a monster in the garden and it's going to eat me', they still turn a deaf ear. Bernard, drawn by McKee as a pudgy, squat, round-eyed naïf, two or three years old, in T-shirt and sneakers, goes out and greets the purple-faced, shaggy, shark-toothed and snarling monster in the garden.

Turn the page and the story simply reads, 'The monster ate Bernard up, every bit.'

This is a devastating surprise—richly comic and also terrible, a grotesque effect. The purple monster then takes Bernard's place in the house—biting his father's leg, eating his dinner, breaking his toy, sleeping in his bed, always to the same refrain from the mother and father. On the last double-page spread, the monster protests, 'But I'm a monster' and still Bernard's mother says, as she puts out the light, 'Not now, Bernard.'

The twenty-four-page book is hideously funny and also sad; the patent message makes fun of parents who are so automatic in their oblivion—and

Child or monster? It's all the same to mother. David Mckee, Not Now, Bernard, *1980.*

rejection—that they do not notice when their child has been eaten. But the latent message whispers that they cannot tell the difference between a tiny tot and an angry beast, because the two are all the same to them: that is how they see Bernard. The imagery of identity flows through the act of eating: Bernard does not turn into the monster, he is incorporated by it. McKee makes readers laugh when he purposely upsets all expectation, refuses a happy ending or a moralizing warning, and Bernard simply gets eaten; but his story also runs counter to psychological ideas of taming the monster within, of achieving integration with the id. Sendak's *Wild Things* follows a more conventional Freudian line in this respect when Max discovers the wildness inside him, but returns tamed and docile; in McKee's *Not Now, Bernard*, it makes no difference to be Bernard or the monster. Only a kind of rueful resignation to the condition of monstrosity is offered there to the child reader. It is rather the parent, reading the book at bedtime, who might take away a lesson in better behaviour!

In a teeming variety of ways—through food, toys, endearments, cartoons, stories above all—children have been associated with little beasts, adorable and repellent at once. Pet names range from 'dumpling', to 'piglet' to 'lambkin' to 'ducks'. Children are not simply identified with the young of other species, as in the once only American but now widespread 'kid'; the metaphors are decidedly more gastronomic. 'Sausage', for example, is becoming increasingly popular. In Italian, the most common expression of endearment is *ciccio* or *ciccia*—meaning roly-poly, plump—often accompanied by a strong flesh-testing pinch. In the United States, child beauty pageants are held to win titles like 'Sweet Niblet'.

Food packaging and advertisements aimed at child customers have continued to reinforce the kinship between monster and human in the case of the child, stressing the affinity between them, gliding between creatureliness and monstrosity without much pause for distinctions. Packagers direct their appeal to children—and to adults—through a variety of fantasy animals. Umbrellas for strollers now come equipped with animal ears that stick up; pick-and-mix candy selections include snakes, piggies, crocodiles, and various other reputedly monstrous eaters, as well as the inevitable dinosaurs. Cereal packets and biscuit wrappers illustrate how monsters and other creatures flourish on the contents, assuming children will take the message as directed at them. Sugar mice and sugar dentures and 'Cheeky Bottoms' (pink buttocks) are all making the same joke about the childish omnivore; jelly tots, and especially jelly babies, of course, which come in every colour, pose the delicious problem of where to start—by nibbling the feet, or biting off the head? Eliza Haughton, aged six, when asked what she preferred, said she started at the feet. Why? 'Because,' she replied, 'then they can't run away.'

Defiance of the lord of death can also unite, in mocking mode, songs, toys and treats: it is not only in Mexico on the Day of the Dead that skeletons and skulls furnish sweetmeats' shape; during the Napoleonic wars with France, there was candy called Boney's Ribs for sale in England. Sugar skeletons can still be bought there from the loose selection that includes witches' hands (knobbly, with claws), vampire teeth as well as bloody, veined horror movie eyeballs, with Vampire, Demon, Ghoul, Dracula, Living Dead, and so on stamped on them.

Distinctions between different meats are hardly nicely maintained by these comic and inventive transmutations of food for children. It would not be very difficult to think you were ogreish in your appetite when cuddly animals surrounded you as your closest associates and at the same time their real counterparts were set on a plate in front of you at meal-times.

Animal anthropomorphic fantasy aimed at a child audience deepens the confusion: Lewis Carroll in *Alice's Adventures in Wonderland* stages a ferocious culinary assault on a baby in the 'Pig and Pepper' episode, when the Duchess fails to ward off the battery of pots and pans hurled by the cook. The baby then turns into a piglet in Alice's arms: 'And she began thinking over other children she knew, who might do very well as pigs . . .' (Harry Graham may be echoing the scene in one of his *Ruthless Rhymes for Heartless Homes*:

> Nurse, who peppered baby's face
>   (She mistook it for a muffin),
> Held her tongue and kept her place . . .
> Mother, seeing baby blinded,
> Said, 'Oh, nurse, how absent-minded!')

The Alice stories empathize with children's appetites for tea-time food, and throughout, they approach meat with caution. The generally more anxious sequel, *Through the Looking Glass*, gives direct expression to the trouble inspired by animals' fellow creatureliness when Alice is commanded by the Red Queen to carve the joint:

' "You look a little shy: let me introduce you to that leg of mutton," said the Red Queen. "Alice—Mutton: Mutton—Alice." ' But when Alice takes up the knife and fork, the Red Queen reproves her with a Carrollean pun on adult manners: ' "It isn't etiquette to cut anyone you've been introduced to." '

The plum pudding then arrives at the table, to Alice's protests that she must not be introduced this time, ' "or we shall get no dinner at all." ' But the Red Queen goes ahead with her usual contrariness, and when the hungry and imperious Alice does serve up some pudding, the Pudding talks back: ' "What impertinence! . . . I wonder how you'd like it, if I were to cut a slice of *you*, you creature." '

At the end, as the Looking-Glass world shatters into the most alarming mayhem, the White Queen echoes Alice's earlier remark about eating:

' "Take care of yourself!" screamed the White Queen . . . "Something's going to happen!" '

The 'something' that fills her with such screaming fear is a meal at which all the food is animate and alive—the uncanny state of the *Doppelgänger*, of the kinetic deaths in the *danse macabre*. Carroll takes the nonsense logic of topsy-turvy even further:

'. . . instead of the Queen, there was the leg of mutton sitting in the chair. "Here I am!" cried a voice from the soup tureen . . .'

This voice turns out to belong to the White Queen, who 'disappeared

The leg of mutton takes a bow in Through the Looking Glass: *Carroll liked playing with food to make havoc with sense. John Tenniel, 1871.*

into the soup'. The eaten have become the eaters.

Alice realizes the danger: 'There was not a moment to be lost. Already several of the guests were lying down in the dishes, and the soup-ladle was walking up the table towards Alice . . .'

Before she becomes another dish, Alice wakes.

It is worth noting that Lewis Carroll campaigned against vivisection, as did Christina Rossetti, with whom he became friends, and whose imagination also conjured the temptations of food. In her fantastic poem 'Goblin Market', the oozing berries and juicy fruits with which her little girl is seduced in another wonderland have a similar uncanny vitality, as if possessed of animate spirits.

As the writer Joyce Carol Oates has asked, 'Mankind's place in the food chain—is *this* the unspeakable knowledge, the ultimate taboo, that generates the art of the grotesque?—or all art, culture, civilization?'

Imaginary children, like Alice, embody this general human conflict about survival. The relation between the child and flesh becomes isomorphic with the relation between the ogre and his meat in stories: both are eating their own kind by association, if not physical identity. A show of *Ombres Chinoises*, as illustrated in 1890, plays wittily with this theme: on the screen a shadow cook with a pig's head on a platter comes face to face with a shadow pig with the cook's head on his dish. The human lets his trophy fall, aghast at his inverted mirror image. Meanwhile, the spectators' shadows take the shape of animals they resemble: a donkey, a monkey, a turkey. There is a pleasure, too, in acknowledging this cannibalistic human self: butchers and fishmongers in England today still display jolly effigies of human-sized fish or pigs dressed not for slaughter but to kill—poised with carving knife to eat.

The question has become more acute, as factory farming and industrial food production are increasingly challenged on ethical grounds. It is not unusual for parents to have to disguise food, as reluctant young eaters grow even pickier when faced by cooked animals whose species they are encouraged to be attached to—especially baby sheep and cows, let alone sucking pigs.

Certain nursery rhymes catch at this anxiety about the origins of food: *Gammer Gurton's Garland* (1783) included verses that robustly addressed the dilemma in the figure of a very fine ram going to market. The merry story ends in gore:

> The butcher that killed this ram, sir, was up to his knees in blood,
> The boy that held the pail, sir, was carried away by the flood;
> The flood, the flood, the flood;
> The boy that held the pail, sir, was carried away by the flood.

Even the whimsical and delicate Walter Crane included a blithely callous ditty in his collection *The Baby's Opera*:

> 'Oh, what have you got for dinner, Mrs. Bond?'
> 'There's beef in the larder, and ducks in the pond;
> Dilly dilly, dilly, dilly, come to be killed
> For you must be stuffed, and my customers filled!'

Children's association with animals has deepened since Crane copied out the music for this nursery rhyme and illustrated it with Mrs. Bond enticing the ducklings with onions and sage to their fate. The successful film *Babe* (1995), featuring real animals that talked, focused on this anxiety: would Babe, the charming and innocent little piggy, get eaten, and was the wicked fat cat right when she cruelly opened his eyes to human beings' reasons for their care of animals: that they were nothing but meat to them?

Roald Dahl, whose mixture of the macabre and the jolly continues to bring his books millions of readers worldwide, worked with uncommon accuracy on children's food fantasies, their pleasures, their terrors, their fundamental ambiguities and confusions, in *Charlie and the Chocolate Factory* (1964) (the ultimate dream, turned nightmare for some), *The BFG* and other stories. In the earlier, highly unusual *James and the Giant Peach* (1961) the boy hero takes refuge inside a magic fruit that suddenly appears in his wicked aunts' garden. There he finds himself with lots of other hungry fugitives; they escape, by rolling away, and incidentally squashing the two aunts as they go. The huge, soft, furry, dark peach becomes James' home, getaway car and murder instrument, but it also turns into the only source of sustenance—for him and his new friends—and they gradually eat it as they wander through many adventures. After the fruit and its cargo have arrived safely in New York, the children of New York want a taste, too, and by the end of the story, 'the whole gigantic fruit had been completely eaten up, and only the big brown stone in the middle, licked clean and shiny by ten thousand little tongues, was left standing on the truck'.

Dahl avoids the problem of James' own appetite in an interesting way, for James' new friends, the inhabitants of the peach, all turn out to be insects—and implicitly inedible; they can therefore feast happily on the flesh of their magic fruit vehicle, without doing one another harm. The film version (1996), a gentler treatment than Dahl usually inspires, drives home a related point only barely suggested in the book, that James himself was always treated like a worm, called 'you little bug' as well as 'you little grub' by the appalling Aunt Sponge and Aunt Spiker. So when he finds himself among his new family of bugs—Spider, Ladybird, Grasshopper, Centipede, Earthworm, Glow-worm—he is merely accepting the insult but turning it topsy-turvy, making it positive.

Those ten thousand little tongues and sets of teeth have been the successful subject of children's materials since Tom Thumb fell into the giant's pudding and Hansel and Gretel nibbled at the gingerbread house, and the adults behind the stories change the same material's impact. The illustrator Quentin Blake's sweet-tempered pen transformed Roald Dahl's brooding obsessions, in *The BFG* and other books, into a mood of blithe light-toed comedy, whereas Rosemary Jackson's lurid and distorted illustrations for *Dirty Beasts* underlined the author's preoccupation with children's voraciousness and adult bullying and malice, as Jeremy Treglown points out in his critical biography of Dahl.

Raymond Briggs offered in *Fungus the Bogeyman* the most brilliant and most determined affront to the growing identification of children with monsters; his flagrantly foul creation plays exuberantly with the theme that the beast is father to the man—or rather that inside every child is a bogeyman. Fungus epitomizes the grotesque body of carnival writ large: he inhabits the slimy, reeking, puddle-strewn world beneath the visible shell of home, in the bath pipes, in the sewage system, and he—and his bogey family—stink, spew, crap and fart. His preferred sport is to terrify respectable DCs (Dry Cleaners, alias adults) out of their wits: a mum in her bathtub and a vicar in a cemetery become the victims of his sudden apparition. Fungus eats unspeakable things, of course, but he is also endowed with 'four stomachs', still attached to 'the Umbilical Cord' that Bogeys retain all their lives—they are big babies, not even yet out of the womb. 'By this means,' writes Briggs, 'they can draw food and drink directly into their four stomachs . . .' Their purpose is not to nourish themselves, however, but 'to discharge noxious stomach gases into DC bedrooms'. (Fungus also sticks his finger up his nose: Briggs, who footnotes a 1646 dictionary definition, as we saw, also knows the meaning of that other kind of bogey.)

Briggs' invitation to revel in disgustingness, to surrender to the pleasure of the monstrous and abject body that evacuates and smells, is issued with tonic high spirits; his book refuses to erect a barrier between adult seemliness and childish beastliness because the author sides so patently with the bogeys. This Rabelaisian unbuttonedness matches the artist-writer's political sympathies: he wants to rescue the degraded and the down-trodden, and has created other zestful books for children in this spirit, about nuclear war and the solitude of a man who cleans toilets for instance. (He also lampooned Mrs Thatcher's Falklands war policy in a vicious, Swiftian comic strip.) *Fungus the Bogeyman* springs to the defence of bogeymen by blowing up the accusations against children into a hyperbolic comedy of filth and greed.

It is not surprising, given the ambiguities about children's orality in so much of the material aimed at them, that this source of gratification has become an area of tension. Food and health panics erupt with accelerating frequency in Europe and the United States; as identity becomes even more intensely corporeal, what the body takes in, absorbs, and consumes defines destiny beyond the individual's control. Anorexia, bulimia and probably a whole attendant host of ever more finely analysed food disorders are increasing among young people, men now as well as women. Fashion consciousness about silhouette, about thighs and tummies, underlies 'the slimming disease', but the turn against fat also springs from deeper causes.

Patrolling contamination and pollution by external substances or agents has become one of the most active political enterprises today, undertaken by numerous pressure groups; it is also one of the tenderest areas of present psychological insecurity. In the aftermath of Chernobyl and in the age of the HIV virus and BSE ('Mad Cow Disease'), there are reasonable grounds for the sense of danger. But this acute anxiety about poisons passed down the food chain also affects the symbol of the child in a particular way: children no longer communicate a lost world of past bliss, as they did for the Romantics ('trailing clouds of glory do we come'), they present an image of a lost future of carefree self-pleasuring. We are living though a historical phase of unprecedented attention to childhood, but the cult of the child often reflects adult dreams rather than children's interests. Indeed, children incur blame for failing to correspond to the fantasy ideal.

Children have murdered children in the past; but there is no historical precedent for the public expressions of rage and disgust excited by the two boys who killed James Bulger in 1994. When Mary Bell was tried, in 1968, for the murder of two small boys, the mood was aghast, but more perplexed and sorrowful than avenging. By contrast, her memoirs, *Cries Unheard* (1998), written by Gitta Sereny nearly thirty years later, stirred violent rage against Mary Bell and drove her into hiding. The Jonesboro playground killings in 1998 were a terrible tragedy, but in such cases, too, the horror of children's crimes appears to have been compounded, not mitigated, by their youth at the time they committed them. Children imitate their elders: they cannot generate moral standards independently of the adults who surround them. Some will be Red Guards and denounce their grandmothers if their schoolteachers expect it of them; some will see visions of the Virgin Mary. They are not the keepers of our good conscience, and their aberrations reflect, and, in some shocking instances, magnify our own, as William Golding, in his terrifying allegory *The Lord of the Flies*, understood so pitilessly as long ago as 1954. Meanwhile, many adults who have killed adults with premeditated callousness and conscious motives do not excite such righteous indignation—indeed, having served their sentences, they emerge into new lives, often undisturbed. Childhood is a special, coveted realm of enchantment, and children (and adults) who profane it can no longer be forgiven.

Family portraits show that children used to be outfitted like their parents. Now, in the well-nourished West, adipose, amorphous, squidgy adult bodies grow larger and more shapeless in cushiony shell suits and bright Babygro colours, with squishy air-filled trainers on their feet and travel mugs in hand so that they can suck every now and then and the dread day of weaning can be postponed forever. The visual lexicon of American identity in particular has changed emphasis; bigness still defines

OPPOSITE *From* A Parents' Survival Guide *by Laurie Graham, the cartoonist Heath's giant baby with appetite to match, 1986.*

it, but a bigness grown pillowy and flaccid and fluffy and fat, like babies, or pneumatic and engorged, like the hard-bodied flesh of athletes—the aesthetic of the animated cartoon writ large over aspects of the culture far beyond the world of entertainment where it began. The new aesthetic seems to me part of a generalized cult of childishness, a widespread, let's-pretend infantilism. This then fosters the image of the monster babies: they have something which we lack, which we desire. Baby envy has eclipsed penis envy. It is the enviable young who are perceived as all-consuming: adults are looking for their inner child, while children themselves all too often are thought to harbour an inner ogre.

Father Flog goes to punish the squalling children.

He does not go into the houses where the good children are.

Father Flog corrects the obstinate little boys and girls.

If the lazy children will not learn their lessons, he punishes them.

Madam Flog hides herself in the saucepan to catch the greedy ones.

Mamma calls father Flog to correct a little story-teller.

Father Flog goes to fetch the wicked children.

He takes home with him those who are disobedient.

Father Flog puts into prison, the children who do not attend to what their parents say to them.

Father Flog gives a whipping to the idle boys.

Madam Flog gives a dunce's cap, to a lazy little girl.

Father Flog, takes the untruthful children and cuts their tongues.

He puts into a cage the little girls who run about too much.

Madam Flog makes a journey to catch the boys who play truant from school.

Madam Flog gives sweets to the children who obey their parents.

Madam Flog sets free a little boy who is penitent.

Imagerie d'Epinal. — Pellerin, imp.-édit.

"Printed expressly for the Humoristic Publishing C°., Kansas City, Mo."

VII

'TERRORS PROPERLY APPLIED'

Now, as fond fathers,
Having bound up the threat'ning twigs of birch,
Only to stick it in their children's sight
For terror, not to use, in time the rod
[Becomes] more mock'd than fear'd
The baby beats the nurse, and quite athwart
Goes all decorum.

Measure for Measure, I, 3: 23–31

Bigotry has cast bogeys and ogres with certain features; the feared intruder comes in the shape of a stranger, any stranger who does not belong to the known and immediate community and family, who does not come from 'home'. When a parent, grandparent or other caregiver threatens a fractious child, and places centre stage the horrible possibility of being taken away, devoured, or otherwise destroyed, the characters invoked are frequently drawn as enemy Others in their own time and place. Gypsies, Jews, Turks, blacks have all been used to scare the young into obedience, to play the part of disciplinarian *alter egos* on behalf of adults and to provide the harsh treatment that appears necessary but for which it is uncomfortable to take responsibility. In the process of nursery projection, these bogeys have been imputed many diabolical practices—including stealing away children. The conventional character and appearance given to devils or bogeymen in medieval Judaeo-Christian culture unfortunately drove in the pilings on

OPPOSITE *Father Flog and Madam Flog come to the aid of parents with bad children in a French nineteenth-century comic strip, translated for the US market, c.1930.*

which modern forms of racism and xenophobia, including today's nationalist excesses, have been built. Certain absolutely traditional and symbolic features—the blackness of hell, for example, which signifies the absence of the light of God among other metaphors—have been applied literally, with grievous social and political effects (Pl. 5). Thus the common parental scapegoat, who threatens to do what the mother or father would rarely own up to wanting to do, grew in size and power until it cast its shadow far beyond the cradle or the home.

In Italy, one particularly bad-tempered lullaby goes like this:

> Fai la nanna, che tu crepi,
> che ti vengano a piglia' i preti!
> Ninna, oh! ninna, oh!
> Questa bimba a chi la do?
> . . . La darò all'Omo nero
> che la tenga un giorno intero.

> (Go to sleep, may you die in your sleep,/That the priest come to take you keep!/Ninna . . . oh Ninna . . . oh!/To whom shall I give this little girl?/ . . . To the bogeyman I'll give her./ For a whole day he will keep her . . .)

Predictable inversions of the danger occur, from another perspective. A lullaby from the plantations of Gran Canaria begins gently enough but then issues the recurrent threat:

> Duerme duerme, negrito
> que tua mama esta en el campo, negrito
> Duerme duerme, negrito
> que tu mama esta en el campo, negrito
> Te va a traer lindas flores para ti,
> te va a traer codornices para ti,
> te va a traer ricas frutas para ti.

> (Sleep, sleep, my dear little black boy,/For your mummy's in the fields, little black boy/She has gone to pick pretty flowers for you,/She has gone to find quails for you,/She has gone to pick rich fruits for you.)

It then continues, half-jokingly, half meaningfully,

Y si el negro no se duerme
viene el diablo blanco u zas!
te come la patita al chiquitin . . .
tumba tun, tumba tun . . .

(And if the black boy won't go to sleep/The white devil will
come and—snap!—/eat the little foot of the little one. . . tumba
tun, tumba tun . . .)

So the bogeyman here figures not as the usual black devil of European
folklore—*l'omo nero* of Italian fantasy—but, as one might predict, as a
white devil.

It is very hard to date popular materials like these lullabies, and the
identification of bogeymen with foreigners, especially any of a different
religion or race, becomes intense during the period of the Crusades, as
revealed by medieval portrayals of figures like King Herod. Christian anti-
Semitism routinely ascribed Jewish clothes, customs, and even the Hebrew
language and Hebrew script, to the devil; the persecutors of Christ, who
were identified with all Jews at whatever point in time, were depicted in
medieval and Renaissance art with monstrously distorted physiognomies.
Secular contexts in the early modern period do not see much diminution of
the tendency, unfortunately. Isabella de Moerloose, the seventeenth-
century Dutch autobiographer, noted that in her country the dreaded
bogeyman was invoked as a bat (*vleermuis*), a werewolf, a toe-cutter
(*tenesnijder*), and as a *nikker* (black man) and *Jood* (Jew). The prejudices
pervade popular culture: bogeymen were often physically identified with
Jews. Maria Edgeworth, in her novel *Harrington* (1817) specifically under-
took an act of reparation for her unconscious anti-Semitism. An earlier
novel, *The Absentee* (1812), had elicited a complaint from an American
Jewish reader. So, in *Harrington*, she used fiction to tackle her own prejudices and her society's, to produce a radical re-vision of *The Merchant of
Venice*. She set the scene in childhood: when her protagonist will not settle
at bedtime, his nursemaid, Fowler, threatens him, 'If you don't come
quietly this minute, Master Harrington, I'll call Simon the Jew here . . . and
he shall come up and carry you away in his great bag.'

The blood libel of cradle-snatching, which cost many Jews their lives in
medieval and Renaissance Europe, here twists into and taints nursery lore
with racial terror and hatred. In *Harrington*, the boy is terrorized by the
'secrets' his nurse tells him, then bullied by his father into violent reprisals
against the source of his fears. But he grows up to confront both this

female and this male mode of demarcating and dealing with Us and Them, and, following the ritual sacrificial structure of the fantasy, to make atonement.

But every Maria Edgeworth who challenges the signs and symbols of her upbringing is shadowed by many who do not question the contours drawn by the languages of intolerance and ignorance. And Jews were not the only group perceived as dangerous.

Since the time of the Crusades, Saracens offered the readiest portmanteau image for any feared or hated outsider. Turks were literally demonized: in *Macbeth*, the witches toss 'nose of Turk' into the cauldron. The famous pub sign—The Saracen, Moor, or Turk's Head—

Tilting targets of courtly jousts included Moors' and Turks' heads as Aunt Sallies. Swedish, 1776–1800.

was perceptively glossed by John Selden in the seventeenth century: 'Do not undervalue an Enemy by whom you have been worsted. When our Countrymen came home from fighting against the Saracens & were beaten by them, they pictur'd them with huge bigg terrible faces (as you still see the Signe of the Saracens head is) when in truth they were like other men, but this they did to save their owne creditts.' Tilting targets, set up in the lists for knightly exercises at the court of Denmark, also in the seventeenth century, included Turks' heads as well as Moors'—ancient military enemies who had come to symbolize generic Others. Turban, scimitar and flowery pantaloons continue to act as ubiquitous labels in any number of children's illustrations in the nineteenth century, from the foe of 'Puss-in-Boots' to Bluebeard himself. Thomas Percy, when giving instructions for the illustration of the ballad 'Guy of Warwick', specified that the Giant Amarant should be 'in a Coat of mail, with a Turban on his head'. The tilts at the court of Christian V of Denmark included the effigy of a Turk who struck back if the jousting knight did not pierce him through the eye. Turks survived, alongside Fat Ladies and other Aunt Sallies, as the target of fairground shies into modern times.

Prejudice affects reality even when it is based in fallacy not misinterpret-

*Knights' armour adopted ferocious features to terrify
assailants, as in this helmet presented to Henry VIII.*

ation; it has the dangerous power to make things happen. For this reason,
the language of rumour, fairy tale and fantasy needs to be treated with
sceptical calm. It never identifies culprits with any accuracy: needless to
say, unusually tall men and wizened old women are unlikely candidates for
child-stealers. One of the reasons, however, that the faces of serial child
murderers today—Frederick West or Ian Brady or Jeffrey Dahmer—
dismay the public so profoundly is that we are all disposed to imagine that
murderers of children cannot look like ourselves, or our neighbours, but
must be marked out as monsters by visible and determining signs. It would
be telling to conduct a survey asking listeners to draw Identikit portraits of
suspects in a crime—from their imaginations.

Sporadic attempts were made, even before the eighteenth century and
the rise in interest in children and their well-being, to put an end to rank
intimidation and scaremongering, and to mitigate the terrors of the bogeyman. 'It is a common custome in many places,' wrote a Swiss pastor, Loys
Lavater, in 1572, 'that at a certain time of the yeare, one with a nette or
visarde on his face maketh children afrayde, to the ende that ever after they
shulde laboure and be obedient to their Parents, afterward they tel them
that those which they saw, were Bugs, Witches and Hagges.' Beating
children was preferable, he thought, to stories telling them 'they shall be
devoured of Bugges, Hags of the night, and such lyke monsters'. Gulliver

reported after his voyage to Lilliput, 'And if it be found that these Nurses ever presume to entertain the Girls with frightful or foolish Stories, or the common Follies practised by Chamber-Maids among us; they are publickly whipped thrice about the City, imprisoned for a Year, and banished for Life to the most desolate Part of the Country.' Jonathan Swift's ironies aim at many, shifting targets, but he frequently used Lilliput's differences to portray the follies around him. Fear was the widespread, recommended method of stilling fractious children. Even a genial chapbook, printed in London around 1760, containing a mischievous, merry version of Tom Thumb's adventures, advocated a bit of terror to keep them quiet. A nurse threatens the baby that she will give him to the wolves if he does not stop crying, and the wolf at the door, depicted in the woodcut, licks his chops, according to the iconography of traditional editions of Aesop's *Fables*. But when the beast comes to claim the promised feast, he finds the baby

M. and Mme. Croquemitaine, the French nursery bogeyman and his wife, become a child's paper cut-out toy, complete with tongues that pull and hands that grab. French, c.1900.

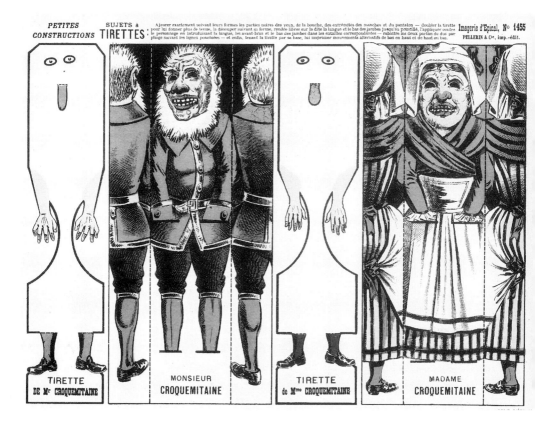

already hushed and the nurse cooing and clucking to it, murmuring endearments. The writer comments, giving an insight into the emptiness of these threats: 'He that waits for a nurse's doing to a cross child what she threatens, will certainly be disappointed.' But he still concludes, *'terrors, properly applied*, are as necessary to quiet froward spirits, as praises and rewards are to encourage the tractable' (emphasis added).

❖   ❖   ❖

One of the most profound and puzzling features of the bogeyman is his seductive power: he can charm at the same time as he repels. For it is not only parents or nurses who resort to impersonating him; children are also ready to identify, to adopt his ways and, far from being successfully intimidated, are often quick to learn and to mimic the adult game. Thus the demonization of figures is never stable and the devil's attractions can never wholly be undone, even by the skill of a Christopher Marlowe. Clearly some children enjoy taking part in the Patum, for instance. The traditional comic drama of Punch and Judy, still a staple of summer fairs and parks, is staged specifically for the amusement of very young children in the UK, who stay and watch and scream between fits of giggles at the mayhem. Mr. Punch, a descendant of Pulcinella from the *commedia dell'arte*, hook-nosed, hump-backed, red-faced, brandishing a club, chants his part in an uncanny fluting voice created by the use of a 'swazzle' stuck against the puppeteer's palate. He embodies the strangeness of the bogeyman, though unlike many others, Mr. Punch is well and truly planted in a recognizable here-and-now where there are frying pans and sausages and burglars and policemen.

In the course of the play, Punch gleefully lays about him in a series of violent assaults. His victims include his own baby—whose torments raise the shrillest squealing from the audience. Mr. Punch is left to baby-sit by Judy (also the butt of his big stick), and when he fails to put the baby to sleep, he batters it. Punch and Judy is considered good family fun, though in recent performances, in deference to contemporary sensitivities, the baby is merely (!) shaken about by the exasperated Mr. Punch, not killed. His abuse is the play's only running gag, now and then punctuated by the puppeteer's up-to-date jokes inspired by the week's news and television. Children find it very funny.

After the death of his 'babby', the ugly, obstinate, brutal gnome overcomes all obstacles—the policeman, a crocodile, a thief—which culminate in Mr. Death himself, whom Punch tempts to place his head in his own noose. The structure of the drama follows the traditional shape of ritual

In defiance of death, the motif of erotes *or* putti *playing with the armour of Mars, god of war, appears in reliefs on the tombs of children. The 'Sarcophagus of Germanicus', Roman, second century A.D.*

combat, and Punch's sequential victories can be read as affirming the inextinguishable vigour of Everyman against all comers, including Death. The artist Susan Hiller has explored this theme in an ambiguous and powerful installation called *An Entertainment*. Harrison Birtwhistle and his librettist Stephen Pruslin in their sinister Opera *Punch & Judy* (1968) set Punch's furious bludgeoning to one of the most playful of dandling songs, 'Dancy baby diddy, / What shall Daddy do widdy? / Sit on his lap, give it some pap, / Dancy baby diddy.' Reading against the sense, contradicting the sweetness of the words, the composer has turned the song into a torturer's anthem.

Children's resilience springs from their laughter: Punch and Judy is often performed with a commentator on the side, who eggs on the audience to find Mr. Punch's antics ridiculous, and guides the children's mockery. If they did not laugh at Mr. Punch's antics, they would be very frightened. But they do not always need steering by an adult; in the right circumstances children can spontaneously make fun of intimidation, and turn its threats hollow. Or they may use it to establish their own power—over other children. But to both ends, they love—apparently almost by instinct—to play the bogeyman and scare themselves into fits. The pretence appears to match the observed pleasure in fright that children take:

it defies fear at the very same moment as conjuring it. It exemplifies a defensive response that is frequently adopted in real experience: internalizing the aggressor in order to stave off the terror he brings.

Some of the oldest child's play in the world, as represented on Greek pots and Roman sarcophagi, throws light on cannibal and murder games and their magical powers of defence and protection. The images show putti gambolling, but their fun includes frightening the wits out of their playmates—by playing monsters, as adults do in fun, by pretending to be an ogre. The theme is scattered through Renaissance imagery under classical influence, as in a spirited sepia drawing of the school of Mantegna, which shows one child thrusting his hand through the mouth of a satyr mask as he play-acts seizing his friends. A terracotta bas-relief by François Du Quesnoy, later taken up and reproduced by Gerrit Dou in his self-portrait, makes an analogy between the play-acting of art itself and children's games. Sir Joshua Reynolds in turn borrowed the idea for his magnificent family portrait of 1777–79 of the Fourth Duke of Marlborough with his wife and children, which still hangs in Blenheim Palace (Pl. 14). The story goes that when Lady Ann, one of the daughters, first saw Sir Joshua, she shied away from him, crying out, 'I won't be painted!' The artist was so taken with her expression of fear that he was determined to represent it in his portrait, and introduced the device of a grotesque satyr mask brandished in her face by one of her sisters. The dogs, too, are shown starting back, hackles raised, taken in by the make-believe.

One child runs away, another falls down scared, at the make-believe of their masked playmates. School of Mantegna, Putti Playing, *sepia, fifteenth century.*

In 1883, the American folklorist William Wells Newell reported, 'Half a century since, in eastern Massachusetts, it was a pastime of boys and girls for one of the number to impersonate an *Ogree* [*sic*] . . . who caught his playmates, put them in a coop, and fattened them for domestic consumption. From time to time the Ogree felt his captives to ascertain if they were fat enough to be cooked . . .'

Lewis Carroll, in his stiff, but eloquent illustrations to *Alice's Adventures Under Ground* shows her arm poking out of the window of the doll's house, snatching at the White Rabbit, who has fallen over in dismay: 'she suddenly spread out her hand, and made a snatch in the air'. (Tenniel's variation on Carroll's sketch magnifies Alice's giant hand and the rabbit's

A small person erupts all of a sudden in a satyr's mask, expecting—and getting—a frightened response. Engraving, Amsterdam, 1803.

helpless fear under her spread fingers, but leaves out the aperture of the doll's house window and so loses the connection with traditional jack-in-the-box play.)

The ghost-story writer and scholar M.R. James, picking up on the 'winter's tale' that the young Mamillius begins in Shakespeare's play, recounted a similar game. Mamillius begins, 'There was once a man dwelt by a churchyard . . .', but he leaves the story untold. M.R. James filled it in: the man has stolen a bag of gold from a grave, but the corpse rises and comes after him, drawing closer and closer until 'the figure whipped round, stood for an instant at the side of the bed, raised its arms, with a hoarse scream of "YOU'VE GOT IT!"' James concluded: '—At this point H.R.H. Prince Mamillius flung himself upon the youngest of the court ladies present, who responded with an equally piercing cry.'

The folklorist Jacqueline Simpson identifies this as a known tale type and comments that M.R. James may well have played the game himself, as a boy or even as a schoolteacher. Carroll may also have seen some of his 'child friends' playing at grabbing and catching one another in this way, and joined in. The game deflates monstrosity by showing it up as a sham, as a guise that can be assumed through masks, accoutrements, performance; but it simultaneously places monstrosity in its potent, magic aspect within gleeful reach of the least potent and most vulnerable. It is sobering that the theme also occurs in a place that Carroll may have known, on the so-called *Sarcophagus of Germanicus* in the Ashmolean Museum, Oxford. The classical relief shows the scene after Venus has seduced Mars: mischievous Cupids are carrying off his weapons of war, dwarfed by his armour, helmet, cuirass, and sword. Botticelli developed this motif in his painting *Mars and Venus*, in which the god of war lies in a 'lover's ordinary swoon', while Venus sits, quietly watchful, opposite him; attendant putti are making mischief with his weapons, tilting with his lance and trying on his helmet. This wishful image of aggression's undoing at the hands of love, women and infants takes on sharper significance in relation to the bogeyman of the nursery, for the theme usually appears on the sarcophagi of children, as is thought to be the case in Oxford. The spectre of Death, summoned in so many nursery tales and nightmares, has snatched this dead child. Yet the game depicted on the tomb itself insists in the face of reality that the victory is hollow.

This tactic—assuming the assailant's imagined characteristics in order to forestall his assault—is often adopted to confront fear and turn its discomfort into thrills, as in the case of the Patum. Masking, guying, and other devices in adult rituals (and entertainment) also animate the most basic child's play, as in the game of Boo! A board book for babies, for example, called *That's Funny!* runs through the range of scary-but-nice games that make babies squeal and gurgle: tickling, startling (a jack-in-the-box), chasing and catching, throwing in the air, Peek-a-boo, and finally, a close variation on Peek-a-boo, jumping out and crying, 'Boo!' 'I'm funny,' says the child in the book. 'Can you be funny, too?' The putti playing with Mars' weapons are saying Boo! to the god of war, no less; on the tombs the powerful god stands in for Death itself, whose power they are also trifling with—however deep the irony.

❖   ❖   ❖

When the game of Boo! is played today, as it is increasingly, in a variety of forms, the accoutrements and weapons of fear are no longer purloined from the god of war, or even from the cannibal fathers of fairy tale or the giants or despots. The features, character and gestures of power and terror are now often borrowed from territory close to the old chthonic cave dwellings of the primeval and medieval dragons as well as from the analogous realm of insects. Insects are universally considered the most ancient surviving species, the most numerous, the most adapted and adaptable: for this they are feared—and provoke awe. Hieronymus Bosch introduced moths, beetles and ladybirds into the landscape of hell; his devils are often miniaturized, like insects, and wear veined wings, frail antennae and crests (Pls. 9, 10). Though Bosch also populates his fantastic worlds with uncannily large shellfish and birds, insects suggested concealed worlds below, secret underworld haunts of beings normally invisible to humans, fairy realms hidden inside mountains, goblin territory. Insect metamorphoses offered a special menacing connection with the aberrational processes of hell, where, as we have seen, forms lose their integrity.

Shakespeare hints at fairies' insect-like size and character. In *Romeo and Juliet*, Queen Mab, 'the fairies' midwife' inhabits a miniaturized elfland, staffed by insects and fitted out with their body parts:

> Her waggon-spokes made of long spinners' legs;
> The cover, of the wings of grasshoppers;
> Her traces, of the smallest spider's web . . .
> Her whip, of cricket's bone; the lash, of film;
> Her waggoner, a small grey-coated gnat . . . (I, 4:54–64)

The names of fairies in *A Midsummer Night's Dream* also convey their entomological character and small scale: Mustardseed and Moth. Henry Fuseli, who profoundly influenced later artists, was inspired by Shakespeare's tiny, eerie concept of fairyland; Romantic and Victorian painters, like Richard Dadd in his sinister, distorted vision *The Fairy Feller's Master-Stroke* (1856–64, Pl. 11) and John Anster Fitzgerald, crystallized the convention, visualizing fairyland as a near-invisible teeming world of tiny creatures, as if seen at the end of a microscope. The distance from bug (devil) to bug (insect, virus) has gradually been closing.

Such monstrously entomological and miniaturized hybrids have also been flourishing in the multi-level cosmos of fantasy games: Dungeons and Dragons, Chaos, Empire, Skaven are popular Warhammer products, and they teem with various orders of enemies and aliens (Pl. 23). 'Orcs and goblins,' declares the catalogue of Citadel miniatures (the figures used in the games), 'are arguably the most war-like race in the Warhammer World. In fact, if they didn't spend so much time warring with each other, they

Every ingenious variety of fur and fin, knob and knuckle, horn, tooth, tail, hoof, claw, wing, trumpet, spine, nose, cere, beak, lobe, plume, pod, flap and sucker clothes the preposterously anomalous, hybrid confections of devils who assault Saint Anthony so viciously they lift him in the air. Martin Schongauer, fifteenth century.

would have crushed most of the Human, Dwarf, and Elven Empires long ago.' As they generate their evil legions, the games' designers shuffle parts in restless combinations to create cockatrices and scorpions, spiders and harpies, while 'Squigs' are 'giant heads with teeth', like hell's mouth on the rampage.

The film *Alien* (1979) pictured the invaders as reptilian bugs hatched from a monstrous maggoty queen ant; this visual lexicon has proved durable, though the gender has shifted towards male broods of monsters. *Men in Black* (1997) treated the threat of an alien global takeover with a sense of the absurd when it personified it as a colossal cockroach, known as the Bug. Insects reverse the historical perspective on dragons and the Titans; they have come to seem the future, and their form consequently can give new, satisfying expression to the horror and desire that reaches for weapons of self-defence, for costumes and stratagems of power.

In several cases popular artefacts and writings adopt and cherish the metamorphoses of the insect world for the same purpose as the creatures themselves: to scare off predators. As adults would sometimes use the spooky night-raiders to assert their own authority, so young audiences now thrill to entertainments that raise spectres of aliens and ghouls, and identify strongly with the fantasy of power they represent. In scaring themselves at such films, or with such imagery, they are still playing a game of Boo!, making believe presence and strength, like scarecrows. The more fragmented, drifting, incoherent the technological world of the late twentieth century feels, the more terrifying images are produced by today's imaginings, and they revealingly mix and shuffle elements from varying species, extrapolate from a stag beetle's antlers and a fly's feelers, a crab's claw and a pig's snout to create fantastic new hybrids, the modern chimerae of celluloid nightmares.

Never have insects provided so much imagery: the quest for strangeness, for the monstrous, for the not-human points today towards the non-mammalian, the invertebrate; the cold-blooded. Insects' exoskeletal structure gives a mechanical character to a beetle's scuttling; like the figure of Death in the *danse macabre*, it wears its bones on the outside, as if it were not enfleshed at all. Scales, tails, fangs, crests, fins, horns have streamed into monstrous modernity from those draconian and reptilian avatars of the devil: Satan himself, 'that old serpent . . . which deceiveth the whole world' (Rev. 12:9), Leviathan, Behemoth have all contributed their dragon-like characteristics. Beetles' gleaming carapace, insects' heavy mandibles and bristling antennae, the barbed feelers of ants and flies have similarly migrated from the richly stocked arsenal of medieval diabolical portraiture. The cockroach, for all its solidity and even weight, speaks of a shadowy underworld: Kafka's *Metamorphosis* would hardly have achieved its effect had Gregor Samsa become a bear or even a bat. The non-mammalian metallic chill of insects' chitin has been adapted for many shivery techno-horror hybrids, like the robot itself, as in films like *Robocop* (1987), *The Terminator* (1984) and *Tetsuo: The Iron Man* (1991).

It is difficult to know how instinctive recoil is or whether cultural attitudes determine the horror in which so many people hold insects. One of the earliest films to be made showed worms crawling in cheese: it was censored. Fear of disease, spread by the invisible attacks of bacteria, has been given graphic validity by optical advances that vividly picture the interior of the body: metaphors of warring parties frequently colour accounts of viruses' devastations. Certainly reformers' attempts to introduce succulent worms as protein into Western diets have not succeeded, though many peoples in Africa and Australasia nourish themselves on grubs and crickets with expert knowledge of their nutritive value. In the European tradition, insects are not even redeemed by characteristics seen as entirely winsome in mammals: how many people have brushed away furry contact with a spider or a caterpillar when they will happily stroke a gerbil? The first sign that the scientist-protagonist is turning into a fly in David Cronenberg's film *The Fly* (1986) are the stiff hairs growing out of his back. But these confected and metamorphic bodies are founded on certain axioms; the fantastic body of horror and fear is pinned together over a ghostly dressmaker's dummy of another actual body—the human— that it contradicts and obliterates. And this principle repeats in itself a principle of animal behaviour that is most marked in the insect world: mimicry as self-protection (Pls. 12, 13, 16).

Mimicry is a fundamental principle of self-protection, and it sometimes pretends to harmlessness, or even inertia, as in familiar forms of camouflage: soles lying invisible against the sandy sea bottom and, most famously, chameleons changing colour to match their surroundings. In other cases—stick insects, cicadas and grasshoppers, moths—the creatures have evolved a form that disguises them in such detail that they cannot be deciphered in their natural habitat (Pl. 13). The katydid's imitation of the mulch in which it forages includes ragged edges to its leaf-like wings so that they look as if they have already been half-eaten; the Chinese character moth even looks like a bird dropping.

A familiar example of such camouflage mimicry occurs in hawk moths, as explored in *The Silence of the Lambs,* with its leitmotif of the death's head insect that lies concealed against a mottled background. Significantly,

*The eerie mimic gaze of the Hawk-eyed Moth (*Smerinthus ocellata*), evolved before humans to stare out predators.*

the plot contrasts two lethal killers: Hannibal Lecter, who eats his victims raw, and 'Buffalo Bill', the transvestite, who flays them in order to sew their skins into suits that will metamorphose him. Thus the book and the film contain both the Christian view of the afterlife—death as a devourer (the hell's mouth trope)—and the Hellenistic, pagan belief in metamorphosis, the eternal return of self in another outer form, as bear or wolf, laurel or spring.

But insects are also disguised in the image of their predators, and in this they throw light on some aspects of the human desire to assume a different shape, or at least to costume and guise and play and project difference, violence and survival. Their mimicry consists of shifting into others' shapes, as Zagreus does to escape the Titans, as Circe's victims do under her spells. The huge eyes, or ocelli, on the wings of lepidoptera, the hawk moths and the peacock butterflies, imitate the reptilian stare of creatures much larger and more ferocious than they are themselves, in order to deter marauders; the puss moth larva, fearsomely gaudy in emerald and scarlet with black ocelli, looks like a samurai in full armour and bristles at possible attackers. Even though harmless insects exhibiting this sightless stare bring to mind panthers or owls, their false eyes are reptilian, these markings having

Whiteness as menace, or as portent: a barn owl hunts at night, liveried in the ghostly pallor that startles its victims so that they freeze.

evolved before mammals appeared. This same round, well-like, unblinkingly steady eye has entered the make-up chest of special effects for scary films, as well as having migrated to the wings of fighter planes. When a moth or other creature displays one, it is displaying, most probably, a picture of a dinosaur's eye created by natural selection (Pl. 19).

One kind of animal mimicry is called Batesian, after the explorer H.W. Bates who first documented it; it describes one species imitating another, more harmful one. The technical name for such creatures' borrowed clothes is 'aposematic colour'; the word 'aposematic' reveals its relation to the apostate, who defects from a belief system, or to the apotropaic gesture that deflects harm and danger. Biologists have confined themselves to noting this remarkable capacity in insects, reptiles and amphibians: there is a South American plant hopper that can fool assailants by turning itself into the image of a young Cayman crocodile—so Peter Parks tells us in his survey of the phenomenon. The hover fly *Volucella bombylans* can imitate different species of bumblebees, so that 'it is possible to see several individual *Volucella bombylans*, each looking completely different from the next'. The most famous pair of mimics are the monarch and the viceroy butterflies (Pls. 22, 23); the latter has evolved to resemble the former, which tastes very nasty indeed: not a wolf in lamb's clothing, but vice versa.

The yellow and black bands of the wasp have been imitated by numerous more harmless insects. The wasp family is extremely well defended by its terrible sting, and has proved one of the most popular evolutionary patterns: hornet moths look much more like hornets than like moths (Pl. 12), but the wasp beetle looks beetle-like despite its bright yellow and black stripes. The range and extent of such camouflage is extraordinary: it is a memorable experience to look at a tray of hover flies in an entomological cabinet and observe the exact mimicry of the wasp in the elongation of the abdomen, the narrowing of the waist, the stripes. Even more remarkably, the innocuous flowerfly has so perfected its imitation of a hornet that it now displays shading on the lower edge of its wings in order to give the impression that, like a wasp, it has another pair concealed beneath its fly-like single set. 'If a model is lethal,' comments the entomologist John Rawlins, 'there will be almost infinite selection to look like it.'

The existence of 'true Batesian mimicry' has been disputed, however, as the mimics are not themselves completely without sting, bite, stink, juice or other method of inflicting hurt in order to defend themselves; this could also be said of humans. So biologists have developed another term, Müllerian mimicry, also named after the scientist who first documented it, to describe a further adaptive stratagem for survival that occurs among poisonous or foul-tasting species of insect. In these cases, the insects' cunning crypsis—or alteration of external signifiers—imitates another

ABOVE *At Punch and Judy puppet shows, children shriek to warn Mister Punch that Death is just behind him. Devon, 1997.*
RIGHT *One child sits on another's shoulders to play a masked ghost in George Dance's 'Whence and what are thou?', c. 1780*

species that is repugnant, and even poisonous. This could illuminate the stratagems of play and camouflage in some children's and adults' games of mock horror and fear.

The entomological palette spells danger, too, in colours that startle: sometimes a moth or butterfly will 'flash', opening its wings all of a sudden and giving a glimpse of some blazing sign on its underwing, often red, sometimes orange and yellow. Again, this may mislead a hungry hunter into believing that the insect is another, much nastier sort, and should be avoided. Beetles are also striped or spotted in colours that 'flash' unmistakably in the eyes of a passer-by: oranges, yellows, saffrons and scarlets dominate—their closeness to the flaming and sulphurous palette of hell is not fortuitous (Pls. 5, 24). These bright tones cannot easily be missed. Designers of traffic signs and chemical hazard notices have gravitated to a similar range: in the United States and the UK signs of low clearance are striped black and yellow, for clear visibility, as are taxicabs in many different cities (New York's old chequer cabs!). There are, it seems, inherent values of legibility and temperature that distinguish some colours; beyond that, cultural history modifies their meanings. The biologist Peter Parks makes the point that there exist 'basic warning colours . . . that humans also have adopted . . . for warnings on vehicles, waste tips and office signs'. But he does not extend the analogy to ritual combat against evil, to a survival response in the face of danger (Pl. 20).

The gleaming scarlet and black masks of the Patum's devils, the use of fire itself in their flaming horns and tails, belong to a similar gaudy vocabulary of alarm as the defensive panoply of beetles, ladybirds and butterflies. Contemporary rock bands' liking for virulent colour schemes on their record covers and posters also borrows from nature's own palette and range of signals: a certain tropical crab that displays a ferocious gamut of hot colours when it raises its claws in battle was recently chosen for a poster of the Prodigy, the most popular techno dance band of the late 1990s (Pl. 16). This reflex is hardly new; totem animals appear in the heraldry of medieval knights, the insignia of regiments, the mascots of cars and the trademarks of companies. But whereas MGM, in the Twenties, chose a roaring lion for its emblem, the bug, that old cousin of the devil, dominates popular means of expression arising in the present magical and millennial imagination.

The most frightening colour of all, interestingly, is absence of colour: the whiteness of negation, found in night-flyers such as barn owls and certain moths. White flashes in the corner of the eye: like orange and scarlet and black, it is unmissable. The owl that hunts and screeches, gleaming ghostly in the shadows, its spectral appearance and sound announcing its presence rather than concealing it through imitation of the surroundings, has a paralysing effect on its prey. And this phantom colour returns in the range of scarecrow apparitions, imbuing the revenant, the undead, the Gothick hero and heroine, the ghost, the psychic mask and the ectoplasmic apparition with the shadow of death, like the gypsum-daubed faces of the Titans around Zagreus' cradle.

Such colour- and shape-shifting provides a most suggestive conceptual model for human crypsis in art, drama and other representations. There is a fundamental distinction, however: the mimicking metamorphoses of insects and reptiles have developed through natural selection over millennia, unconsciously. Human beings, by contrast, are choosing, as individuals and as groups, to guise and play at being other than they are, and at being far more dangerous. What has changed is the metaphorical and visual vocabulary used to evoke imagined enemies. The diabolical or beastly used to draw on mammals, especially the predators among them, for its arsenal. Wolves persist, in the great modern lexicon of lycanthropy; bats survive, undiminished, in the continuingly proliferating annals of vampirism, and cats have furnished some notable modern *frissons*, for instance in the film *Cat People* (1942), a chilly tale of animal metamorphosis. But recently, effective scaring has plundered promiscuously the multiplicity of insect species and morphologies. The bogeys are becoming more complexly hybrid, more terrible, in step with the magnified sense of human capacity for harm and a corresponding need to mount a spectacular defence.

Inspired by the eloquent work of Roger Caillois, in his book *Méduse et Cie.* (1960), Jacques Lacan became interested in the phenomenon of Batesian mimicry. But he comments, ironically, that its clever optical illusions do not seem to make much difference to survival: as many disguised victims are found in the stomachs of their natural predators as others who cannot or have not transformed themselves. This rueful view is perhaps a guess rather than a statement of fact, since we cannot know what the statistics would be if none was capable of such performative make-believe. Lacan relates the phenomenon to his theory of the gaze, suggesting that the ocelli on a moth's wings represent acutely the distinction he makes between the eye that sees and the gaze that is sensed but does not see, 'the underside of consciousness'. By making visible the predator, the intruder, the stranger whom we fear lurks beyond vision, like the *coco* in Goya's print, by dragging the object of terror into shape in the common light of day, by imitating its imagined assaults and power, it can be controlled, or so it is hoped. This returns us to scaring and to the function of play-acting and masking: to summon up the terrors that are only sensed, to give them such form as they seem to possess in that eerily enfolding field of inner consciousness, to bring them out into the field of vision, and then to imitate them so that we will be as big and strong as they are, and they will be diminished.

However, when Lacan draws this distinction between seeing and being the subject of the gaze, he rejects Sartre's consoling argument that the gaze of another, which excites shame and trouble when it is noticed, melts away when the eyes of the beholder and the beheld meet. He cites Goya's use of masks and disguises: under the gaze of a masked or hooded man, however much we might exchange glances, the fear continues: the children shrinking in fright at the appearance of '*el coco*' inhabit their own subjectivity (are behind their own eyes, at one with what their look is telling them). But the *coco* himself looks at them from the wide, borderless field of the world's gaze, which shatters the subject and scatters him or her across a blurred and terrifying wilderness where control of knowledge through sight expires. The bogeyman, still shrouded, still invisible under his hood, continues to stalk on the edges of the gaze, unseen.

Thus consciousness possesses the unsettling capacity to summon objects that lie beyond its control, in the intractable and ungovernable realm of actual events, communicated in distorted forms and through unintelligible signs. The game of Boo! in all its permutations, great and small, can work—but only up to a point. What is imitated is only imagined, since by its very nature the object of fear eludes the grasp of understanding; in the fearful mind's infinite recession of images, an unknown enemy inspires mimicry not of his features, since they are not known, but of another's who is not him but who seems equally frightening and powerful and can stand in for him. The imitator, arrayed in this panoply of terror, then inspires further imitation as an object of alarm and force in himself; and so the phantasmagoric sequence generates more reflections and exacerbates 'the plague of fantasies', as the psychoanalyst Slavoj Žižek has called it.

❖   ❖   ❖

Nowhere does this cruel trick that the imagination plays with anxiety show more vividly than in lullabies. Ostensibly songs to soothe and lull, they reflect the rich range of feelings that the young and vulnerable inspire. Soothing through repetitive song and sound is used to conjure away fear of

OPPOSITE *Satan as a bug: the 'Lord of the Flies'. German, sixteenth century.*

the dark; the singers of these ancient, often anonymous songs desire above all to protect the infant from all dangers, known and unknown. But surprisingly, the songs do not always seem to bless the baby or even placate possible furies; they sometimes issue curses and threats themselves. In their unexpected variety—and perversity—lullabies are fulfilling many tasks, at once magical, pedagogical and psychological.

PART TWO

LULLING

Sing lullaby, as women do,
  Wherewith they bring their babes to rest,
And lullaby can I sing too
  As womanly as can the best . . .

Then lullaby my youth, mine eyes,
  My will, my ware, and all that was.
I can no more delays devise,
  But welcome pain, let pleasure pass.
    With lullaby now take your leave,
    With lullaby your dreams deceive . . .

George Gascoigne,
'Gascoigne's Lullaby', 1573

REFLECTION

CARAVAGGIO: THE REST ON THE FLIGHT INTO EGYPT

 Mary and the child are sitting on the ground, both drowsing, the baby at her breast but no longer suckling, her head bowed over him. She is not dressed in Marian azure, and the Christ child does not appear naked, as he does against all practical logic in so many Madonna and Child paintings in order to foreshadow the pietà. *As was his radical custom, Caravaggio has translated the divine cast of characters into recognizable contemporaries, an Italian mother and her baby, both of them falling away from consciousness into the sleep that follows feeding. But beside them, in the centre of the painting, an unearthly visitor from the inner eye of the artist has alighted: an angel in floating* déshabillé *playing on the viol, with Joseph facing him, apparently acting as music-stand and page turner. Within the single moment of this static and silent image, the consolation of the music gradually enfolds listeners both inside and outside the frame, lulling the Holy Family and the viewer.*

Though hardly medieval in character, Caravaggio's painting The Rest on the Flight into Egypt *(Pl. 26) grows from the early mystical practice of grounding the infancy of Christ in daily life. It conveys in visual terms lullabies' musical sympathy with consolation and ironic prophecy, communicating the reprieve that the Holy Family are enjoying as they flee Herod's Massacre of the Innocents. Painted around 1595–96, it is a comparatively early work by Caravaggio, and may have been commissioned by a cardinal in Rome—Pietro Aldobrandini—who had a connoisseur's collection of musical instruments.*

Joseph often sees angels in the New Testament: he receives one visitation, when in a dream 'the angel of the Lord' tells him to marry Mary even though she is having a child (Matt. 1: 20–21). Then, again in a dream, the angel warns him that Herod is planning to kill every first-born son, and orders him to take Mary and the baby and flee into Egypt (Matt. 2:13). At the Annunciation, Mary is not asleep and she answers Gabriel, but artists often imagine that she drops her eyes at his approach as if his radiance was too dazzling; she may have been wise not to look him full in the face, unlike Semele, who was blasted when she looked at Zeus in his panoply of

OPPOSITE *The angel plays on a viol . . .*

Joseph holds up the sheet music . . .

celestial light and thunder. In Caravaggio's Rest on the Flight, *only Joseph is wakeful, and looks across at the musical angel.*

Angels travelled with the Holy Family, disorienting Herod's soldiers by sowing miraculous wheat fields that sprang up to obstruct their pursuit, and bending down the boughs of fruit trees to nourish the fugitives with cherries, dates or apricots, and guiding them through the desert to watering places. Hosts of angels sing and play at the child's birth, and frequently flock around his crib with viols, trumpets, flutes and even portable organs. But Caravaggio's single angelic youth with his fiddle is an innovation. He is an intimate guest, introducing his music at a moment when the New Testament and the Apocrypha do not mention any such performance.

The score that Joseph is holding up for the angel to read contains three pieces. Two of them have been identified, as motets for four voices by Noël Bauldwyn, a choirmaster in Flanders in the early sixteenth century. The angel is playing the soprano part, and though it is written in a major key, it sounds mournful, solemn, stately, slow and 'liturgical'; the rhythm is very steady and would lull, or rather, certainly not arouse a listener. The

Mary and the child drowse . . .

capacity of music to soothe, calm and console could not be more strongly implied by the scene: the wayfarers, exhausted, stopping to rest, without shelter, with almost no supplies, no travelling clothes, are visited by a truly angelic being, who has alighted in bare feet that seem hardly to touch the ground on which Mary and the baby are slumped.

The motet was aptly chosen, for it sets a variation on verses from the Song of Songs invoking the Beloved; these amorous lyrics have been applied allegorically to praise the Virgin Mary since the thirteenth century at least. The passage opens, 'Quam pulchra es':

> *How fair and how pleasant art thou, O love, for delights!*
> *This thy stature is like to a palm tree, and thy breast to*
>   *clusters of grapes.*
> *I said, I will go up to the palm tree, I will take hold of the*
> *boughs thereof: now also thy breasts shall be as clusters of the*
>   *vine . . .*
> *Come my Beloved, let us go forth into the field . . .*
>   *. . . let us see if the vine flourish, whether the tender grape*
> *appear, and the pomegranates bud forth: there will I give thee*
>   *my loves.*
>   *(Song of Solomon 7: 6–2)*

*Caravaggio has connected the rhapsody to his theme, wrapping the Virgin
Mary in associations with the fruitfulness of the Beloved in the canticle.
Her cradling of the child to her breast, his look of sleepy repleteness, shifts
the eroticism of the imagery of a woman's breasts; tenderly, she lays her
face gently to the baby's head, as if smelling his warmth and comfort, as
mothers do. Other flowering elements characterize her side of the picture.
Light falls warmly, glowingly from behind her, where a stretch of water
freshens and irrigates the earth.*

*By contrast, the space in which Joseph is sitting is parched and withered
and lies in shadow. He appears close to the donkey, lowly, humble,
quotidian, linked to a beast of burden, symbolic of humility and toil. The
donkey is rolling its luminous eye, an almost bizarre note near the very
centre of the composition. Perhaps, like Balaam's ass, it can not only see
the angel but also foresee the sufferings that lie in store for the sleeping
infant. Or the creature, also a symbol of folly (our* alter ego *in the world),
might be rolling its eye because it knows that this moment of time in which
the Holy Family are now safe will come to an end: the animal visibly
wears, on its shoulders, the stripes of Christ's cross.*

*The right wingtip of Caravaggio's angelic viol player touches the picture
plane itself, in a deft, even exhibitionist display of illusionistic skill, as if the
artist had seen that the act of bowing with the right arm would indeed
make the right wing lift and arc. His figure divides the painting down the
middle, superimposed on the tree that gives the composition an unusual
central axis. The tree could be typological, a reference to the Fall, as in* The
Allegory of the Old and New Testaments *by Hans Holbein the Elder, who
also bisects his painting with the tree of knowledge, and shows it withered
on one side, where Adam and Eve are fatally tempted, and blossoming on
the other.*

Similarly, in Caravaggio's Rest on the Flight into Egypt, *sere foliage
clings to the oak tree on the left side of the painting, as the dry leaves do on
this kind of oak until the spring breaks. A cabbage, the kind stored for
winter provision, also lies in the foreground. Thus Joseph's side of the
painting is freighted with a sense of seasonal and historical change. He is
keeping vigil; the activity of the angel is taking place in an immediate
present tense, but this present turns into the past as the angel reads the
notes and the sequence falls through time: history unfolds in spite of the
painting's inherent stasis. Joseph has brought the Holy Family to safety
from the rage of Herod, but they are moving towards the pusillanimity of
Pilate, the balancing pole of wickedness in the mystery plays.*

On the right side of the painting, by contrast, the sky is lightening, and sleep has caught up mother and baby in its uneventful atemporality. The mediating figure between these contrasted halves is the angel, who is also, as so often in Caravaggio, sexually indeterminate: androgynous, epicene, a boy-girl, a short-haired youth with a round rosy bottom like a nymph's. He is wearing the wings of the bird sacred to the goddess of love, but they have been purposely studied from their most humble, even degraded form: a town pigeon's duskiness, not the ring-dove's pearls and pinks. The angel hyphenates maleness and femaleness; on the left, in Joseph's half, the space of time as narrative spools backwards as the music plays; on the right, in Mary's half, the narrative has been lulled to a standstill, and appears to be holding its breath before its own futurity. Caravaggio achieves this by communicating so richly and so tranquilly music's effect of translating present passions (fear, grief) into hope and calm. This is the work of lullabies.

The doubleness of angelic gender also embodies the double tongue necessary to the function of such music: the melody should catch the feelings of the hearers, speak for the audience, in the same way as the singer of a lullaby projects into the mind of the restless child and attempts to allay the fears she apprehends are there. The music itself is not androgynous, but doubled, as the voices of the lullaby can be plural in other ways, too—shared between siblings, friends, minders, nurses. Mary and the child—their escape from the Massacre of the Innocents at Herod's command, and their future griefs—are being sung by the angel in the tranquillity created by the music. They have averted danger—for the time being.

Ordinary lullabies, sung not by angels but by nurses, mothers or grandparents, attempt to work the same magic for ordinary human babies.

VIII

'SING NOW MOTHER...

WHAT ME SHALL BEFALL'

Cebes laughed. Suppose that we are afraid, Socrates, he said . . .
Probably even in us there is a little boy who has these childish
terrors. Try to persuade him not to be afraid of death as though
it were a bogy.

What you should do, said Socrates, is to say a magic spell over
him every day until you have charmed his fears away.

But, Socrates, said Simonias, where can we find a magician
who understands these spells now that you . . . are leaving us?

Greece is a large country, Cebes, he replied.

Plato, *Phaedo*

 Lullabies, an ancient form of poetry, are sung all over the
world to settle infants to sleep, to banish the fear of the dark in
older babies and children, and to ease the drop into oblivion
against which babies often seem to struggle so hard. The
sound of the steady rhythm and simple repetitive melodies, accompanied
by patting, walking, swaying, cuddling, or rocking of the cradle, can help
soothe the fractious child. But while this primary function defines lullabies,
the songs also calm the mother or caregiver, and make the daily struggle
bearable. They appear to express the child's angle of view and meet babies'
dominant needs, but they also carry female voices and concerns across
time on their words and in their tunes. Far from being instinctive creatures
of basic animal drives, infants often show themselves highly reluctant to
sleep or to eat, provoking frustration and even rage in their parent or
baby-sitter; these feelings are often reflected in the lyrics (in the seventeenth
century, the expression 'a lullaby cheat' was used of a baby who would not
respond to this kind of caress). Like fairy tales, fables, ballads and other
vernacular forms of storytelling and poetry, these songs have been made by

Not only herald angels proclaimed the birth of the Saviour: around his crib angelic choirs and minstrels, often playing instruments of the artist's times, were gathered to hymn his coming and lap him in song. Piero della Francesca, The Nativity, c. 1472.

the nameless mass of illiterate and forgotten people 'whose labour made our world,' as Angela Carter remarked.

Anthologies and ethnographical records include hundreds of examples of nursery music from all over the world, alongside cradle and dandling songs, finger games, counting-out and other nursery rhymes that also help to amuse and occupy children and anchor speech patterns. Yet these forms of sung verse have been studied surprisingly little compared to, say, the ballad. The word *nenia* in Latin was used to mean silly trifles and nonsense as well as nurse's songs, and lullabies continue to be generally overlooked as sentimental fribbles, fit only for mere women and babies. But with a moment's care, these worldwide, frequently anonymous songs can be opened up to disclose some of the secrets, light and dark, that the most disregarded means of communication, lives, and pursuits often contain. They are among the very first utterances directed to babies as persons; this alone makes them worth analysis.

❖   ❖   ❖

Sleep figures in lullabies as a journey into a place about which nothing is known, which may hold terrors; the surrender to the mysterious state of consciousless life not only conjures death, the biggest of all the bogeys, but also inspires thoughts on the unknowability of destiny, of life itself. The child must cross from the world of watching into the glimmering of a doze and thence into the mystery zones of sleep and dreams; lullabies reveal how the watcher by the cradle then peers into that child's future, which is as opaque as the mind of another far away in slumber. So although they aim above all to expel the phantoms of the unknown and the night, lullabies also cast a spell against the metaphorical resonance of sleep, its twinship with death.

But lullabies are not only sleep songs. They include predictions, singing imaginary lives for the infant in the form of blessings; they attempt to ward off dangers, as the fairies do in *A Midsummer Night's Dream* over Titania's rest, and to forestall harm to the child; they explicitly attempt to keep the bogeyman or bogeywoman from the home, to anticipate—and prevent—the raid of the Titans around Zagreus' cradle. But more peculiarly, the lullaby also invokes figures of death and punishment, brings the stalkers and the cradle-snatchers before the infant's eyes. Both kinds of charm over the child's cot are often repeated over and over, sometimes almost tonelessly, a form of incantation. A lullaby is weak domestic magic, alert to its own inadequacy.

The verb 'lull' is possibly related to a Greek word for the sound of lapping water, and to *lallatio* and *lallare*, in late Latin. The word for lullaby in Latin, *nenia*, shifts to an *n* sound, the earliest that infants make, and this connection recurs in many languages' names for the song as well as in their refrains: *ninna-nanna* means lullaby in Italian, with an aural connection to the word for old woman in Latin, giving Granny, *Nonna*, as well as 'Nan' and 'Nanna' in English. Saint Anne, the mother of the Virgin Mary and hence the grandmother of Jesus, does not appear in the Bible, and her name may have developed from these etymological associations, among other connections. The importance of 'nan-songs' was acknowledged as early as the fifteenth century, when the Neapolitan humanist Giovanni Pontano dedicated a book of lullabies to his son with the words: 'Neniae Luciolum verbaque ficta iuvant' (Lullabies and fantastic stories delight little Lucius).

Yet the imagery and patterning of such chants and charms have not been much analysed; nor has the history of transmission and of changes in taste and outlook been reviewed. The fortunes of the form reflect the fashion in fairy tales and nursery lore, in that the early printed tradition includes much riskier examples (harsh and sometimes even bawdy lyrics) than the versions and selections which now circulate. An early selection, *Tommy Thumb's Pretty Song Book* of 1744, compiled by one N. Lovechild, contains this bedtime rhyme:

Piss a Bed
Piss a Bed
Barley Butt —
Your Bum is so heavy
You can't get up.

Rhymes like these were left out of the anthologies which found modern nursery literature, in favour of far more innocuous and gentle *berceuses*, the kind set to music by Brahms and Chopin in the nineteenth century. The earliest extant collection of nursery rhymes stressed their musical character in its title, *Songs for the Nursery, or Mother Goose's Melodies*. The book reportedly appeared in Boston, in 1719, but it is a 'ghost volume' and a copy has never been found; its famous successor, published around 1765 by the pioneering children's publisher John Newbery, carried a similar title, *Mother Goose's Melody, or Sonnets for the Cradle*. This original was packed with tongue-in-cheek glosses that have been attributed to Oliver Goldsmith. The volume reappeared, much expanded, and its adult ironies cut, in Boston around 1825, as *Mother Goose's Quarto, or Melodies Complete*. It includes many if not most of the famous English nursery rhymes, but 'Rock-a-bye, Baby' and 'Bye, Baby Bunting' are the only lullabies, strictly speaking.

Literary interest in the form mirrors the interest in national folk culture and fairy tale that grew from the late eighteenth century onwards. Clemens Brentano and Achim von Arnim, for example, chose to conclude *Des Knaben Wunderhorn* with a lullaby, the only one in the book and the only poem they print that is not in German but in Latin, thus breaking with the whole enterprise of the collection. Nevertheless, the lullaby's position, closing their great work of literary recovery and national memory, underlines the lullaby form's accepted connection with authenticity, with a quality of ahistorical transcultural truth-telling, along the lines of the figure of Mother Goose in Romantic perception. Composers interested in popular melodies and folksong, like Béla Bartók, Alban Berg (in *Wozzeck*) and Stravinsky, set versions of traditional songs, including lullabies, while writers committed to a vernacular diction and rhythms, as well as to identification with 'Anon.', also composed new ones or borrowed the form: William Blake, Christina Rossetti, Robert Louis Stevenson, and, in the twentieth century, Federico García Lorca, and W.H. Auden. The ethnic imprinting of children becomes important to commentators: Lorca stressed the lullaby as formative of Spanish melancholia with its particular savour of '*aguda tristeza*' ('acute sadness'). Although the measure of a lullaby echoes the regular intake and exhalation of breath and, by extension, the rocking of a cradle, the habitual mood of the melody is melancholy. The minor third dominates lullabies, internationally; even songs as simply loving as the Russian lullabies set by Stravinsky, for example, seem almost to keen, so plaintive are the tunes.

It is the Romantic cradle song, with its rocking rhythm, its sentimental icon of mother and baby intimacy, and its sweet untroubled domesticity that on the whole dominates perception of the lullaby. Authored variants of the lullaby are frequently by male writers—by Shakespeare or Thomas Dekker or Isaac Watts—and they tend to coax and soothe the child more smilingly than examples surviving in the anonymous, oral tradition. It is when such songs do not own up to their origins, when 'Anon.' remains indeed nameless and might for that reason be female, perhaps unlettered, certainly forgotten, that these apparently naïve and uncomplicated songs of reassurance touch on complex anxieties. Lullabies often situate the child—and those who care for it—in a perspective of life's risks; their thoughts surprisingly wander into zones of suspicion, aggression, violence and fear.

Lorca has written the only substantial essay on the topic of lullabies, 'Las Nanas infantiles', in which he fancies he has heard, in the voice of 'a beautiful Andalusian . . . a joyful young woman, without the slightest hint of melancholy, the ancient imperious voices that ran through her blood'. 'These melodies,' he continues, 'in which sadness is strongly accentuated, accompanied by texts of highly melancholy expression, seem to colour the first dreams of [Spain's] children.' In one of his own ballads, he exchanges verses with a group of children, who possess, the poet declares, the secrets of poetry itself. They urge him to steep himself in 'the antique song'. In the poem, which is itself modelled after the antique in its whimsy and prosody, Lorca exclaims:

> Yo: ¡Voy en busca de magos
>   y de princesas!
> Los Niños: ¿Quien te enseñó el camino
>   de los poetas?
> Yo: La fuente y el arroyo
> de la canción añeja.

> (I: I go in quest of wizards and of princesses!/The Children: Who taught you the way of the poets?/I: The fountain and the stream of the antique song.)

For Lorca, an 'antique song', such as a lullaby, orients the poet in relation to his language's history, as well as to the personal past.

But an extended chronological account of the lullaby's development would be likely to put an audience, including readers, to sleep. What interests me, in relation to the theme of terror, are the songs' multiple psychological and social functions for children and for adults.

❖   ❖   ❖

Lullabies imply two narratives at least: the relationship of the singer to the child and, within the words—and to some extent in the melody as well—another story. Many such nursery songs, like the most famous English example of all, 'Hush-a-bye, Baby', tell a tale that is characteristically set in the future, but the dominant tense of the form is conditional. If something were to happen, then there would follow . . . *Gammer Gurton's Garland* gave this variant:

> Rock-a-bye baby on the tree top,
> When the wind blows the cradle will rock;
> When the bough breaks the cradle will fall,
> Down will come cradle and baby and all.

The end foreshadowed may on the other hand be benign, as in the caressing song attributed to Thomas Dekker, which the Beatles echoed with nostalgic irony on *Abbey Road* in 1969:

> Golden slumbers kiss your eyes,
> Smiles await you when you rise:
> Sleep pretty wantons, do not cry,
> And I will sing a lullaby.

George Gershwin echoes this strain in the famous opening song of *Porgy and Bess* (1934–35), in which Clara dreams of the sweets of life with honey-rich, slumbrous but wistful lyricism: 'Summertime and the livin' is easy . . .' DuBose Heyward's lyrics, slightly altered in composition by Gershwin, catch the melancholy lilt of the Negro Spiritual 'All my trials' and its resigned entreaty— 'Hush lil' baby, don' yo' cry / Fadder an' mudder born to die . . .' For a shadow falls across even this pictured summertime bliss:

> One of these mornin's you're goin' to rise up singin'.
> Then you'll spread yo' wings an' you'll take to the sky.
> But till that mornin', there's a-nuttin' can harm you . . .
> So hush little baby, don't you cry.

Space and time coincide in the lullaby: the place where the song is sung, that secure place of the breast, the lap, the crib, intersects with the dreams and often the forebodings of the future, drawn by the singer from the blank of the infant's life. The narrative voice can be doubled, for the lullaby sings to the child, opening up vistas on possibility, but can also sing for the child, as if in the child's voice. In several Middle English poems, the child Jesus is imagined singing to the Virgin Mary of the sorrows and the joys that await her and the trials that he will himself face. In one example, from a commonplace book dated 1372, Jesus presents himself as a divine king as well as a human infant and announces his steadfastness: 'I shall be tempted by Satan . . . / The same way Adam was, / But I shall withstand him better.' In medieval devotions, especially those of the Franciscan temper, prayer was aimed at stimulating personal identification with the mysteries of Jesus' life. But, in order to imagine his experiences, the texts necessarily draw on the poets' or singers' own lives, and the lullaby's characteristic human fearfulness seeps into these religious cradle songs, frequently transcribed alongside laments and threnodies for Passion Week.

In that Middle English lullaby, the verses not only imagine Mary and the child in dialogue, but cast their exchanges within another literary trope, the dream of the poet who comes across a vision of them in dialogue:

> The maiden wolde with-outen song
> Hire child o slepe bringge;
> The child thouthte sche dede him wrong,
> & bad his moder sengge.
>
> 'Sing nov, moder,' seide that child,
> 'Wat me sal be-falle
> Here after wan i cum to eld —
> so don modres alle.'

But she is baffled, for, like all mothers, she does not know:

> 'Suete sone,' seyde sche,
> 'Wer-offe suld i singge?
> Wist i neuere yet more of thee
> But gabrieles gretingge.'

The child then responds, precociously predicting his future and her sorrows, to the refrain, 'Lullay, lullay, la lullay,/ Mi dere moder, lullay.'

Thus lullaby and elegy are linked in a duet between them. Again, in this recurrent formula, prophetic ironies work a kind of sorrowful magic: the lullaby as future personal narrative opens into a universal commentary on the frailty of human life. The undertow of grief pulls hard, towards the future: these songs mourn future memories, not past events. The effect can be very bitter: in the Russian film classic *War and Peace* (1967), the nurse sings a lullaby to Prince André's son over scenes of carnage at the battle of Borodino.

Hans Christian Andersen captures this morbid characteristic in 'A Mother's Dream', a poem that Robert Schumann set as a chilling *Lied*. The song evokes the cosy picture of the title, then shatters it with the morbid intervention of that sinister harbinger of fairy tales, the raven:

> Her dreams of hope drift to the future —
> as mothers often will dream in their hearts.
> The raven with his brood meanwhile
> shrieks a tune outside the window:
> your angel, your angel will be our prey . . .

In this shivery, proleptic character, lullabies resemble charms and magical wishes: spelling out what might happen in order to bind it is witchcraft. And this performative speech, this act of spell-binding, can either determine the future (make it come true) by chanting it into being or prevent it through articulating it. Worries about children, as most parents know, proliferate along these magical axes of prevention and cure.

The songs also offer an origin of subjectivity, for the exchanges between singer and child frame the self in relation to the evoked outside world. The mother acts as an 'acoustic mirror', in the telling phrase of the cinema and psychoanalytic theorist Kaja Silverman. She proposes superseding Jacques Lacan's mirror phase, in which infants learn their individual separateness from their mother by seeing their difference in a mirror. Instead she argues for substituting the experience of hearing another voice, which responds, echoes and initiates new sounds in the duet played when language begins to form in children's mouths and brains and they start acquiring speech, expressiveness and thought.

The answering voice that shapes perception of self and the world fuses with the fictionalized voice of narrative, as it takes shape according to the conventions of disembodied voice-over narration in novels and movies. Silverman quotes in particular the work of the French film historian and musicologist Michel Chion: 'The first to display images is the Mother, whose voice before the [eventual] learning of written signs, makes things become detached in a living and symbolic temporality. In the fiction of the fabulator and teller of stories as in the traditional voice-over of the commentary, something always remains of this traditional function.'

Yet this maternal voice-over, so often first heard in lullabies, does not always reassure or give comfort. Early lyrics are saturated in apprehension or even dread: fear writes or speaks the boundaries, and the phantom of death, always just around the corner, defines the life. As Lorca later questioned, 'How is it that the most bloody songs, the least suited for the [child's] delicate sensibility, have been kept to name the dreams of a child?' An impending chill colours the song, and the words include a threat as well as a warning, the familiar 'Down will come baby, cradle and all' so insouciantly—and liltingly—repeated down the generations.

The image of the cradle in the tree, central to both 'Rock-a-bye, Baby' and 'Hush-a-bye, Baby', has puzzled many minds. Some fanciful and ingenious solutions have been proposed, notably that the lullaby is American in origin and was indeed even written by one of the first European settlers. This young *Mayflower* Pilgrim Father, the story goes, was inspired by the native practice of hanging a papoose in a birch-bark cradle from a branch in safety from predators. However, it seems possible that another, far more common use of arboreal imagery meets the case: the family tree, which usually represents time as growing upwards, with the youngest members among the topmost branches. 'When the bough breaks' could refer to the death of parents and its effect on children—another shadow from the future crossing a baby's path.

Odd as it may seem, lullabies obsessively spell out such dangers, attempting to encompass every possibility. The cradle blessings over Baldur the Beautiful in Norse myth list the metals and woods and materials that might harm him, but fail to include mistletoe—and so it is with a mistletoe arrow that he is killed. Lullabies dip infants prophylactically in the imaginary future of ordeals and perils; nightmares are uttered in order to chase them from the impending dreamworld—a manoeuvre akin to a blessing in the form of a curse: as in 'Break a leg'. 'In bocca al lupo' (Into the jaws of the wolf)—the traditional Italian good luck wish—actually harks back to one of the most common bogeys of the lullaby and nursery tale. But in so doing, such verses name those bogeys and, as in fairy tales like 'Rumpelstiltskin', naming can undo evil forces and banish them.

Prophecies of danger can never be comprehensive: there will always be something, someone omitted, some fate or death round the corner who has not been counted. Even when a goddess like Thetis wanted to ensure that her son would be invulnerable, she failed: when she plunged the infant Achilles into the water of the Styx, she held him upside down by his foot, and so left his heel a point of weakness—which Paris' arrow would home to, unerringly.

❖   ❖   ❖

Lullabies are related to work songs, spinning songs, shanties, chain-gang songs, waulking songs from the Scottish isles sung to accompany the fulling of the tweed, and even to liturgical repetition in such prayers as the litany of the saints and the rosary. In all these different forms, experience is interwoven into rhythm and language to give a structure to daily life and make its tedium more tolerable. Walter Benjamin, in his essay 'The Storyteller', pointed out that drudgery and tedious, repetitive chores on long winter evenings provided storytellers with their natural, nesting places. More specifically, lullabies, as Leslie Daiken has commented, 'are diffused with all the ups and downs of a mother's housebound brooding'. A very early, undated example, found interpolated in the fourteenth-century Welsh heroic epic *The Gododdin*, strikes an unusually dithyrambic note for a cradle song, but also registers the inevitability of a noblewoman's confinement. The mother of Dinogad begins to sing in the enclosed, domestic household where she plies her needle:

> Dinogad's smock, pied, pied,
> It was from martens' skin that I made it . . .

But soon she is remembering the origin of this particular baby bunting's suit and is mind-voyaging far beyond it, with the child's father and his exploits:

> I would sing, eight slaves sang.
> When thy father went a-hunting,
> A spear on his shoulder, a club in his hand . . .
> He would kill a fish in his coracle
> As a lion kills its prey.
> He would bring back a roe-buck, a wild boar, a stag,
> A speckled grouse from the mountain,
> A fish from Rhaeadr Derwenndydd.
> Of all those that thy father reached with his lance,
> Wild boar and lynx and fox,
> None escaped which was not winged.

This woman of substance does not lack for anything but mobility. At the other end of the social scale, and at least six hundred years later, an anonymous Italian mother in the Abruzzi in the 1960s was recorded, in a haunting, unaccompanied, almost tuneless voice, looking out from the confined and vulnerable sanctuary of home (the words incidentally give a startling, grim picture of a bogeyman as another hooded, monk-like predator):

> Babbo tornate
> che l'è arrivato un frate
> un frate cappuccino
> che ha portato via la pappa e 'l pentolino . . .
> Babbo venite
> che ci da un po' di pane
> che non si muoia dalla fame . . .

> (Come home Daddy, for a Capuchin friar has taken the baby's pap from the pan . . . Come Daddy, bring us some bread, otherwise we'll starve to death . . .)

A song advises that the Bogeyman will catch you, unless you pretend that you are a crocodile or put salt on his tail. London, 1930.

Like the storyteller in Walter Benjamin's account, the lullaby singer is soothing herself—very occasionally himself—from daily routine burdens as much as communicating to another. Repeating words and melodies which have offered that consolation before she sang them, she can feel herself joined to others who, like her, were frustrated, exhausted, bored, hollow. Gilles Deleuze and Félix Guattari in their essay '1837: Of the Refrain' lay out the function of music in defining territory and group: 'Now we are at home. But home does not pre-exist: it was necessary to draw a circle around that uncertain and fragile center, to organize a limited space . . . marking out a wall of sound, or at least a wall with some sonic bricks in it.' They go on to argue that chants, snatches of song, Muzak, humming to oneself as one works, putting the radio on, serve to mark the boundaries, as stones do. They mention lullabies, for these songs are often the first way the edges of a world are fumbled out for a newborn by a mother or nurse, and their essay is called 'Of the Refrain' because familiarity through repetition inscribes the territory until it is known by heart.

The two philosophers' connection of familiar refrains to the idea and identity of home deepens one crucial aspect of lullabies. In a very quirky piece of etymological guesswork, an eighteenth-century lexicographer tried to gloss the word 'lullaby' in order to forge a similar link, making the suffix *by* mean house and home: 'The common compliment at parting, good *by* is good *house, may your house prosper*; and Sel*by*, the Archbishop of York's palace is a great *house* . . .' so that lulla*by* means literally 'to sleep at home, or in one's bed'.

Several cradle songs give a regional accent to the sound of the nursery. 'L'Canchon dormoire', the lively lullaby known as 'Le P'tit Quinquin' (the same one that features a punitive St. Nicholas) was written in 1853 by the Romantic poet and musician Alexandre Desrousseaux in local dialect; it is still so widely sung around Lille that it has become a kind of regional anthem for northern France. The future holds the possibility of riches and pleasures and rewards:

> Come on, close your eyes, sleep my little one,
> I'll say a prayer to Baby Jesus,
> So he comes here while you sleep . . .
> So he brings you a lovely bun
> With golden syrup running down your chin,
> You'll be licking yourself for a good three hours . . .

Here again, the temporal and spatial axes intersect in the arms, on the lap of the mother figure, and it is the unknown future ahead and the unknown terrain beyond that swell with menace, while the here-and-now represents safety, ideally to be prolonged and extended. But envisaging zones beyond the home consistently stirs anxieties: when the bough breaks, it is clear that the ground will not be soft enough to break the cradle's fall; it is only till that morning when the child leaves, spreads its wings, and takes to the sky, that 'a-nuttin' can harm you'.

The dreams of the anonymous singers are simple: they imagine an end to want and toil, an increase in comforts—a chicken in the pot and a warm place by the fire. These were the desires that Angela Carter located at the modest heart of fairy-tale wishes, as in the affectionate Italian song:

> Go to sleep my little chicken-thighs!
> Your mother has made a skirt for you.
> She sewed it up all around.
> Go to sleep my little chicken-thighs!
> Go to sleep! If you sleep
> May your bed be made of violets,
> The mattress of soft down,
> The pillow of peacock feathers,
> And the sheets from cloth of Holland.
> Close your eyes, and go to sleep!

There are many such tender, poignant lullabies, crooning and cooing cradle songs, and contemporary selections on the shelves in public libraries featuring these are much borrowed by mothers who only vaguely remember the songs from their childhood or no longer know them at all. The gentleness of the scene is emphasized, naturally enough: 'These are sleeping songs for you and the baby, having a cuddle or gently rocking to and fro or side to side.' There follows 'Bye, Baby Bunting', 'Golden Slumbers', and other mild nursery ditties and sleep charms:

> Sleep, baby, sleep,
> Your father tends the sheep,
> Your mother shakes the dreamland tree
> And softly fall sweet dreams for thee,
> Sleep, baby, sleep.

When I was first sent to my English convent boarding school at the age of nine, we—the youngest children there—would beg Mother Barbara to sing to us at night. Sometimes she agreed. It was always a fantastic treat, but also a source of great pain, because as she stood in the corridor between the line of curtained cubicles and sang to us, unseen, unfelt, without a kiss or a cuddle, she reminded us that indeed, we were not at home with the familiar figures:

> So lulla lulla lulla lullaby bye,
> If you want the moon to play with
> Or the stars to run away with,
> They'll come if you don't cry.

> So lulla lulla lulla lullaby bye,
> In your mammy's arms be creeping,
> And soon you'll be a-sleeping
> So lulla lulla lulla lullaby bye.

But singing against the dark paradoxically invokes it, the gentleness of the music often running counter to the message of the song. Consider the savage turn taken in the second verse of the traditional American cradle song 'All the Pretty Little Horses':

> Hush-a-bye don't you cry, go to sleep you little baby
> When you wake you shall have all the pretty little horses
> Blacks and bays, dapples and grays, coach and six-a little horses.

> Hush-a-bye don't you cry, go to sleep you little baby,
> Way down yonder in the meadow lays a poor little lambie
> The bees and the butterflies peckin' out his eyes
> The poor little thing cries 'Mammy'.

American commentators traditionally interpret this as sung by a black mother remembering her own baby, left behind in the fields while she looks after the white folks' offspring. But even if the background to the elliptical story behind the lyrics is not filled in, the song includes a bizarre image of death: the song conjures, with a sweet piping tune, a lamb so tender that like a fallen fruit it attracts insects—and is this a dead child, who is being compared to a lamb, or a live child suffering cruelly, since he is still able to call for his mother?

OPPOSITE *'Bye Baby Bunting' from* Mother Goose's Melodies, *Boston 1833.*

In its unexpected morbidity, 'All the Pretty Little Horses' is nevertheless a most characteristic lullaby. For in its earliest known public history, this humble, domestic verse form projected suspicions and forebodings into the larger world, and its chants against evil were associated with the longed-for overthrow of tyrants and the casting out of foreign bodies.

'HEROD THE KING, IN HIS RAGING'

In a verse play, the contemporary English poet Tony Harrison imagines the mother of Commodus, most bloodthirsty of Roman emperors, thinking of her son's infancy when she nursed him at her breast. In bleakly ironical rhyming couplets, the poem then foreshadows other mothers of other tyrants far off in the future, the twentieth century of massacres and pogroms:

> cradling Adolf's or Benito's tons
> of other mothers' meat that once was sons,
> and with Yekaterina, whose cradled darling
> sucked milk, and then sucked blood as Joseph Stalin.

Harrison has this mother referring to her words as 'this abattoir's black lullaby', thereby placing her despair in the classical tradition of female mourning, of which he is acutely aware. My own mother in Italy was taught a *ninna-nanna*, or Italian lullaby, which opens with a scene of twelve women stitching bonnets for

> I marmocchi non giunti ancora,
> ma che ben presto, forse all'aurora,
> avrebber messo il capino biondo
> in faccia al sole, in faccia al mondo.
> Ninna-nanna, ninna-nanna . . .

(For little babies who haven't yet been born, but who very soon, maybe at dawn will have put their little blonde heads to face the sun, to face the world . . .)

Giuseppe Arcimboldo assembled the features of King Herod from the bodies of the Holy Innocents: a pittura infamante, *or defamatory painting, such as was made in the Renaissance to brand criminals with their crime. Sixteenth century.*

But by the end of a song which sounds as if it might have been written after the First World War, the women have white hair:

> dodici vecchie testine bianche
> vegliano sempre ma non son stanche . . .
> dodici mamme, dodici cuori
> dodici affetti, mille dolori
> dodici pianti, così va il giorno . . .
> dodici attese, nessun ritorno.

> (Twelve little old white heads always keep watch but they aren't tired . . . twelve mothers, twelve hearts, twelve attachments, a thousand griefs, twelve laments, and so it goes . . . twelve vigils, not one returns.)

Women's voices—in the *mater dolorosa's* laments, the sirens keeping vigil at gravestones, professional keeners hired for funerals, commentators from the chorus on the unfolding of the tragedy in Greek drama—have been allotted the task of keeping the record, of observing and relating the pains of events great and small, from the sidelines. The modest, even paltry, and sometimes sentimental verse form of the lullaby paradoxically reflects this work: though it blesses and caresses with melody, it also foretells, observes, comments on disasters that must be averted.

One of the earliest English texts in which a lullaby appears bears out this unexpected character of the song. The Middle English mystery play cycle, known as the *Ludus Coventriae* or Coventry Play (now renamed the Hegge or N-Town Cycle) was probably written down in the early to mid-fifteenth century, but is earlier in composition and in performance. It was staged for the feast of Corpus Christi and it introduces mothers singing to their infants just as the Massacre of the Innocents is about to take place.

The gospel of Saint Matthew first tells the story of the massacre and of the Holy Family's Flight into Egypt to escape it (Matt. 2: 13–22), as depicted in Caravaggio's *Rest on the Flight into Egypt*. But in later, medieval elaborations, Herod, King of Judaea, is a universal tyrant, who has absorbed characteristics of flesh-eating ogres, of mythical Cyclops and fairy-tale giants of the 'Fee fie fo fum' variety. From the mystery play stage, he proclaims himself a slayer of giants, a pitiless foe, a ruthless tyrant, and a wicked wizard. He is, as well, an overweening, even ridiculous, braggart, whose claims are demonstrably untrue, since the powers he arrogates to himself belong to both God and the devil:

[I am] the mightiest conqueror that ever walked on ground;
For I am even he that made both heaven and hell
And of my mighty power holdeth up this world round.
Magog and Madroke, both them did I confound,
And with this bright bronde [sword] their bones I brake asunder,
That all the wide world on those rappis [blows] did wonder.

I am the cause of this great light and thunder,
It is through my fury they such noise do make.
My fearful countenance that clouds so doth encumber
That oftentimes for dread thereof the very earth doth quake.

Herod continues in this vein for six blustering stanzas.

The three kings then arrive and seek audience with him; when he hears their news—about the birth of a new king—he rages:

I stamp I stare! I look all about!
Might I them take, I should them burn at a glede [fire]!
I rant! I rave! and now run I would!

The stage directions describe how Herod should then descend into the street and 'in the pagond' and run and rage there, that is, the actor should leave the dais and, in the manner of the Living Theatre of the 1960s, mingle with the crowd and probably even assault them directly. (It was this braggadocio that inspired Hamlet to warn the players against excessive histrionics, when he railed: 'O, it offends me to the soul to hear a robustious periwig-pated fellow tear a passion to tatters, to very rags, to split the ears of the groundlings . . . I would have such a fellow whipped for o'erdoing Termagant. It out-Herods Herod. Pray you, avoid it' (III, ii: 8-14). Villains of the mystery plays were the only characters to enjoy such robustious mobility on and off stage: Pilate, Cain, Noah's wife, and Death, (Mors) sometimes played as a female scarecrow (the word's gender in Latin), who grabs at mortals as her partners in the *danse macabre*.

Royal, judicial, and local power was consciously targeted for derision beneath the surface histrionics; this was the public level of the assault. But the scene also demarcates women's sphere of responsibility and its raw edges, it draws attention to women's particular concerns with brutality, to male jealousy of children who might supplant them, to kings' regard for political expediency and ambition; it assumes specially acute female and infant vulnerability to these threats. As Hugh Haughton has commented, bitter burlesque portraits are often 'bound up with the idea of travestied authority and spurious dignity', not only public and political but also private and domestic.

Herod gives the order for the massacre to his Armiger, his hit-man; but Joseph, meanwhile, is warned in a dream by the angel, and leaves with Mary, whereupon the stage direction is given: 'Here the Women come in with their children, singing.' The 'Coventry Carol', one of the most ancient known lullabies, follows, with its chorus:

> Lullay lullay thow littell tine child
> By, by, lully lullay, thow littell tyne child.
>   By by, lully lullay!

In the verse, the mothers are heard trying to keep the children quiet in their arms, to save them by lulling them to sleep so that they can hide them from the marauding killers:

> O sisters too,
> How may we do
>   For to preserve this day
> This pore yongling
> For whom we do singe
>   By, by, lully lullay . . .
> Herod the king, in his raging,
> Chargéd he hath this day
> His men of might, in his own sight,
> All young children to slay . . .

The mothers' attempts fail—and the stark direction to the Armiger's band of armed men reads, 'They kill the boys'.

Depictions of this scene often suggest a strong influence of liturgical theatre, with the figure of King Herod, on a balcony or a box upstage, gesturing his order for the slaughter, as the soldiers rush the huddled group of mothers and children; or looking on impassively as soldiers, mothers and babies whirl in the frenzy of the massacre in the foreground, in the shallow space of a chancel, as it were. Occasionally, he is even painted over life-size, sealing his intimate relationship to ogres and flesh-eating giants, as in the Matteo di Giovanni di Bartolo fresco in Capodimonte, and in another painting, by the same artist, in the church of S. Maria dei Servi in Siena.

Two short church dramas, surviving in twelfth-century manuscripts, represent this episode. In the version from Orléans, France, the mothers of the Innocents with their children carried on a little lamb; when the angel appeared to give warning of the impending atrocity, the children protected the lamb, who was therefore able to escape and run off—the stage directions give every impression that a real lamb took part in the drama. The mothers then interceded with Herod's assassins in a six-bar phrase of pleading music, but to no avail.

As the tableau froze over the devastation, the emblematic figure of Rachel, invoked by Matthew in the gospel account of the massacre, entered, weeping for her children and singing an elegy: 'Heu, alas you tender babes . . . Heu! piteous mothers . . .' She was joined by a group of Comforters, and the voices combined; she rallied, and cried out, 'Heu! Heu! Heu! how can I be joyful; forever those mangled limbs seeing; when my whole being is rended by emotion?' The scene closed with her exit, supported by the Comforters, while an angel encouraged the Innocents to rise up and enter the choir (the child actors must have been strewn further down the church) and then appeared to Joseph again and told him that Herod was dead and that the Holy family could return to Israel.

The Coventry Carol's 'lully lullay' chorus of mothers represents a decisive change in medieval drama from an allegorical threnody—Rachel weeping for the slaughter—to a domestic lullaby; from a biblical, quasi-symbolic, generic figure of motherhood, remote in time and place, to an ordinary crowd of contemporaries in a situation they fear they might encounter. The comic horror of Herod's raging—*furore accenso*—is met and, in theatrical terms, annulled, by the entry of the singing women; burlesque yields to lyric directness, the complex mixed feelings of thrills and shivers are soothed into simplicity by both melody and emotional eloquence. Simultaneously, the historical past—what are perceived to be the great and momentous events surrounding the beginning of the new age of Christ—collides with an ordinary, unnamed throng suffering from a human fear. Tony Harrison makes the link apparent in his variation on a school nativity play, *The Big H,* in which the biblical massacre is moved to a Leeds primary school where a 'Chorus of Mams', led by Rachel, intones the names of the dead boys.

The Massacre of the Innocents formed part of the cycle of Christ's infancy, as painted or sometimes sculpted in medieval churches. Giotto painted the scene in the Arena Chapel in Padua (1305) and another in Assisi, taking place on a wider stage, with Herod supported by three henchmen; in both, he set the action in a contemporary north Italian city street, with the tyrant presiding from a municipal balcony. Fra Angelico

*Herod towers like a giant of fairy tale, in the oriental turban that often marks
ogres and Bluebeards, presiding over the Massacre of the Innocents he ordered.
Matteo di Giovanni di Bartolo, Siena, late fifteenth century.*

painted a panel around 1425, which supplies the scriptural texts on scrolls
above and below as if voicing the liturgical reading; making the association
with public utterance and performance, Giovanni Pisano carved the
massacre on the pulpit in the Duomo in Pisa. For the Baptistery in Padua,
Giusto dei Menabuoni actually brought the scene indoors, creating an
illusion of a chamber within the existing architectural setting, by painting
lancet windows on the back wall and placing Herod and his advisers to the
side as if looking on from the sacristy; this fresco and another in Siena
represent the frenzied massacre as if it were taking place there and then,
with no feigning of historical retrospection.

In these works of art, painting's suspended timelessness is denied and
instead time unfolds, punctured, shredded and pierced by protest, struggle,
fury and then lamentation over the pitiful victims almost from left to right

in a narrative sequence, as the soldiers enter, stage left as it were, and the mothers and children fall to the ground stage right.

Such pictures attempted, often with painful success, to convey the tragedy through an evocation of noise: the bodies of the protesting and flailing mothers form a frenzied syncopation across the image. The compositions pack the soldiers, mothers and children into the foreground as if on the narrow rostrum of a mystery play; the artists show a terrible ingenuity in the variety of childish corpses at different stages in the massacre. Some women cradle the morsels, limbs, severed heads of their infants. As in Christ's Passion and some saints' martyrdoms, judicial punishments and executions of the time shadow these pictures: they are phantasmagoric in intensity, but not detached from lived experience.

The traditional iconography also reveals the *coup de théâtre* that the lullaby sung during the mystery play must have achieved. For these are paintings in which the women are screaming: rarely in Western art have there been so many mouths open, cursing and then keening. In Guido Reni's ferocious painting of 1611–13 (Pl. 25), the slaughter is captured *in medias res*: one mother has fallen to the ground, mourning the marmoreal corpses of two infants in the foreground, while behind her five others, packed into the high-pressure vertical composition, attempt to flee the two rampaging executioners. One of the ruffians has a mother by her kerchief and is yanking her head back to hold her as she yells; another mother is trying to flee with her bundled baby; she too has her mouth open, while an older woman is also howling from her gaping mouth. In Poussin's violent interpretation of the tragedy (1632–35), now in the Musée Condé, Chantilly, forms part of a series of four paintings dramatizing tyrants' excesses. The artist has also closed in tightly on the ferment: he shows one mother screaming at the centre of the image, as her head is forced back by a soldier who hauls her by her hair; he is trampling her child and at the same time lifting his sword, about to strike.

These images hardly represent lulling, nor do they hint at the tragic irony which the English mystery play makes clear: that the mothers are trying to hush the infants so that they will not be discovered. But the artists have found in their rendering of the mothers' shrieks and tears a visual equivalent for the horror. The imagined respite of the flight into Egypt, which follows this massacre, stands at the opposite pole of all this anguish and cruelty and horror. Herod's slaughter of the Innocents exemplifies the wickedness of paganism's might but also announces its collapse. He flouts humanity's proper care for children, and the women's voices rise to keen for them, the first Christian martyrs. The drama screams against carnage, and so implies what might be, the blessed life and love epitomized by soft singing. The founding massacres and catastrophes of contemporary identities—the Shoah, the Great Hunger—correspond to this biblical atrocity: those innocents stand for all victims of injustice and hatred and holocaust. The massacre differs, however, from today's historical narratives because it forms part of a salvation story—the promise of the cycle of Christ's infancy and death is that it will lead to something else. Hope is the result of the images' act of mourning, not despair.

With regard to women's lives, the Massacre of the Innocents and its representations assume segregated worlds: they do not feature fathers weeping for their babes, attacking the soldiers, or even negotiating a peace. The scene maps female territory in distinction to men's: their screaming— their singing—defines the function of maternal care, with its accompanying griefs, as it outlines the boundaries of women's powers and their accompanying vulnerability to encroachment and assault. The implied lullaby here dramatizes home territory as analysed by Deleuze and Guattari— not a fixed abode or a geographical address, but 'a reorganization of functions and a regrouping of forces'.

The women throw their voices to refuse death. When they lull their babies in the mystery play, they are announcing the possibility of security and bliss; for this is the sort of music that resonates in heaven: angels are above all musical and proclaim the birth of the Saviour to the shepherds with song, a chorus that inspires the tradition of serenading seraphim, so common in painted cycles of Christ's early life as to have become invisible, the accepted imagery of countless Christmas cards. The two types of music—the keening, the lulling—were intertwined liturgically and resonated together through the imagery in a manner lost to the viewer today. For, when Joseph is warned by an angel about the Massacre of the Innocents, he takes the Holy Family to Egypt, and in traditional iconography angels frequently minister to them on the way, their ministry featuring serenades—or, perhaps, lullabies, as we saw in Caravaggio's serene painting. What was coupled functionally as well as symbolically in the Coventry mystery play has been lost to modern consciousness with the disappearance of the Apocrypha from common knowledge. But this was not the case in the Renaissance: Tintoretto's cycle in the Scuola di San Rocco, Venice, retains the diptych character of the two scriptural stories: his swirling *Massacre of the Innocents*, which inspired a rhapsodic *tour de force* from John Ruskin, is followed by the calm pastorale of the Holy Family's flight, against a sky where light is breaking, though, unlike Caravaggio, Tintoretto does not introduce an angel to sing to them on the way.

The infancy narratives of Christ routinely set up a stark, dramatic antithesis: lullaby and terror, escape to a haven of timeless oceanic infantile bliss versus history, accident, process, rupture, death.

❖   ❖   ❖

The enemy, those figures of terror, like Herod, in the micro-narratives that lullabies tell, is predictably defined as Other, according to the social and historical circumstances and prejudices of the context. As in the folklore of ogres, it is Welshmen or Thracians or other giants beyond the borders who are the barbarians. Herod himself, in the mystery play, invokes Mahounde as one of his presiding genii; Mahounde was the diabolical name for the prophet Muhammad, used as a Christian anathema on the heathen, and so here the English drama is blithely disregarding both Jewish and Roman religious affiliations of the historical Herod, King of Judaea, so as to place the ogre figure firmly in the camp of the enemy—the pagan opponents of the crusader period during which the drama developed.

Some lullaby lyrics start at shadows in the corners, and then flesh them out with the features of familiar devils. The traditional Aesopian fable about a wolf at the door, retold by La Fontaine, and by William Godwin in his pseudonymous anthology of fables, develops the familiar cautionary sequence of danger threatened, then allayed: as we have seen, a marauding beast hears the exasperated nurse threaten the baby that if it does not go to sleep she will abandon it to be eaten by wolves. The wolf's mouth waters with delight at the promised feast: but he is discovered and immediately shot by the villagers, or by the baby's own father. The antiquarian Joseph Ritson made an ingenious, but far-fetched phonetic connection between 'Hush-a-bye, Baby' and this cautionary tale: 'Hé bas! là le loup!' was his phonetic rendering of the opening line.

The disturbing content of such songs is surprising enough; what is even more so is that lullabies often threaten the infant directly, the infuriated singer of a cradle song summoning the monster or bogeyman to work on her behalf. It is often the baby, not the barbarian at the gates, who is the target of the threat. This kind of lullaby conjures the terrors of the night, not always to silence them, but to flourish them.

As Adam Phillips writes, 'The first world we find outside is, in part, a repository for the terror inside us, an elsewhere for those desires and objects that bring us unpleasure. And that world we make outside is the world we need to get away from . . .' He concludes with a characteristic flourish of a paradox: 'To be at home in the world we need to keep it inhospitable.'

Strangers and enemies are defined at home, in the singer's abode, in babyhood, with all the prolonged repercussions that this entails. In Lermontov's disturbingly relevant poem, 'A Cossack Lullaby', the poet ventriloquizes the patriot mother of the fatherland:

> I can see the Terek falling
> Over rocks and land
> And an angry Chechen crawling,
> Crawling knife in hand . . .
>
> You will grow and go into battle
> With the Cossack force;
> I will decorate the saddle
> For your handsome horse . . .
> Only wait till you are bigger,
> *Bayúshki bayú.*

Sometimes, however, the 'angry Chechen' is not held at a distance, but courted and invited into the nursery. Herod has his counterparts in the nameless boo-baggers and bugbears and bogeymen used to intimidate children into at least lying quiet if they will not go to sleep. Herod's descendants, the Sandman's counterparts and the devil's minions have included Cromwell and Bismarck and Boney (Napoleon):

> Baby, baby, naughty baby,
> Hush you squalling thing, I say.
> Peace this moment, peace, or maybe
> Bonaparte will pass this way.
>
> Baby, baby, he's a giant,
> Tall and black as Rouen steeple,
> And he breakfasts, dines, rely on't,
> Every day on naughty people . . .
>
> And he'll beat you, beat you, beat you,
> And he'll beat you all to pap,
> And he'll eat you, eat you, eat you,
> Every morsel, snap, snap, snap.

Iona and Peter Opie, in their edition of nursery rhymes, point out that versions of this ditty have cited Menshikov, the commander of Russian forces in the Crimean War, and 'Black Old Noll'—Oliver Cromwell.

The phenomenon is widespread. The Spanish bogeyman, *el coco*, made an appearance in the lullaby that inspired Goya's frightening spectre, as we saw; in Brittany, the spooky words of 'Le grand Lustucru' are still sung, performed and published in anthologies of lullabies for sale to prospective parents. They invoke the coming of a clanking monster:

> Entendez-vous dans la plaine
> Ce bruit venant jusqu'à nous?
> On dirait un bruit de chaines,
> Se trainant sur les cailloux.
> C'est le grand Lustucru qui passe,
> Qui repasse, et s'en ira,
> Emportant dans sa besace
> Tous les petits gars qui ne dorment pas.

> (Do you hear in the plain this noise that's reaching us here? It sounds like the noise of chains, dragging on the pebbles. It's the great Lustucru who is passing, passing by and will go away, carrying off in his knapsack all the little children who aren't asleep.)

More northerly European lullabies make even less pretence at cajolery. A collection edited by the writer Hans Magnus Enzensberger in the mid-1960s in Germany includes an alarming section of grim cradle songs. In one, the recurrent plot of the fairy-tale wicked stepmother returns, communicated in four brief lines:

> Sweet little babykin, what are you whispering in the straw?
> Your mother is dead, your father is happy,
> If he marries a new young wife
> Then the children will get a beating.

But such verses should be viewed with more sympathy than a first glance inspires. More often than not, the songs are filled with the difficulties of mothering, and far from diffusing a sentimental ideology of blissful union, they catch the tension and the exhaustion of dependency—maternal ambivalence. They may also act to defuse it, by allowing it harmless—and even perhaps funny—expression.

In such a song, the singer's violent and violating narrative is at variance with the music and the lullaby's prime function, for if the baby could understand the words, she or he would be likely to wake up with a start of terror, far from lulled. But if the child is still an infant, the words are likely not to be understood: as the mother or grandmother or nurse or sibling sings rockingly, caressingly, she is able to give vent to her anger, and often her exhaustion at the task—without the child taking in the words: 'Hee-o, wee-o, wha' can I do wi' ye?/ Black's the life that I lead with ye,' sings the Scottish mother in 'O Can Ye Sew Cushions?', a traditional cradle song,

A versatile bogey, Lustucru (whose name means 'Would you have believed it?') menaces his victims with abduction and annihilation in lullabies, broadsheets and stories. French, c. 1900.

first collected at the beginning of the last century, and now sung far beyond its Scottish birthplace. 'Mony o I hae little to gie ye/ Black's the life that I lead wi' ye.'

The woe the mother expresses shadows forth tales of abandonment, too, not simply penury: sometimes the two themes combine, when it is hinted that the father left because the child stretched the family's resources beyond capacity. Yet other circumstances leave a trace: Lorca was gleeful when he found a type of Spanish lullaby, with variants across the peninsula, in which the mother begs and complains for another reason—her lover is waiting in the garden for her to come out to him.

So the lullaby's contradictory stories have two separate receivers in mind, for whom the tiny texts and melodies will have a different purpose. Sometimes the voice is clearly that of a frustrated baby-sitter:

> *Heidschi bumbeidschi* sleep long,
> Your mother has gone out . . .
> She has gone out and will never come back
> Leaving the little one all alone at home.
> *Heidschi bumbeidschi, bum bum*
> *Heidschi bumbeidschi, bum bum*
> *Heidschi bumbeidschi*, sleep sweetly,
> The angels send their greetings,
> They send their greetings and want to ask you
> If you'd like to go for a ride in Heaven,
> *Heidschi bumbeidschi, bum bum, bum bum*

The refrain, sung to a sweet, lilting tune, then takes shape as a bogey itself as the baby-sitter imagines, with evident satisfaction, an end to her labours:

> The *Heidschi bumbeidschi* came
> And took my little boy with him
> He has taken him and has never brought him back,
> So I wish my boy a very good night.
> *Heidschi bumbeidschi, bum bum, bum bum.*

This seems a cruel sort of playfulness. Yet it does not appear to have done its young receivers much harm (my informants were startled when they stopped to consider the meaning of words that had hitherto been an unexamined childhood memory).

Lewis Carroll, with his quick ear for adult behaviour towards children, parodies this type of nursery song in the 'Pig and Pepper' episode in *Alice in Wonderland*. The Duchess nurses her baby with 'a sort of lullaby . . . giving it a violent shake at the end of every line':

> 'Speak roughly to your little boy,
>   And beat him when he sneezes:
> He only does it to annoy,
>   Because he knows it teases.'

W. H. Auden, in the spirit of the Duchess, reported from Iceland that he had collected another 'sort of [no-nonsense] lullaby':

> Sleep, you black-eyed pig
> Fall into a deep [foul] pit full of ghosts . . .

The singer here curses the infant directly, without resorting to a phantasmic surrogate. The poet commented, 'It's a great pleasure to think that all the best nursery poetry shocks the Neo-Hygienic-child-lover.' However, the insults may represent a superstitious measure, to divert dangerous attention away from the child's preciousness: according to widespread belief, vaunting one's pride in one's children may stir the gods' jealousy and alert the fates, as Niobe learned when she boasted of hers and attracted the murderous mayhem of Hera. Parents often disparage their offspring, long after the lullaby stage, out of some unaccountable worry that praise will somehow do them damage.

These violent lullabies count on the infant's incomprehension. In the Aesop fable, the nurse did not mean what she threatened; the baby understood only her tone of voice, its cadence and rhythm. In the story it is the wolf who understands the words and is misled by them, to his destruction; the uncomprehending infant stays safe.

Nevertheless, a passionate plea on behalf of the squalling infant comes as a relief after all this frustration, anger and violence. One Dubliner passed on to me a song her mother sang her—in which she takes on the bogeyman fair and square and threatens him with abduction: 'Ah Bo Bu/ I'll beat you/ If you touch my baby/ Ah bo back/ I'll put you in a sack/ If you touch my little paddywhack.' 'It was always very comforting,' Maeve

OPPOSITE *The slaughtered firstborn of Bethlemen are venerated as the first Christian martyrs. Holy Innocent, Spanish, seventeenth century.*

Casey remarked. 'I was always aware of the underlying violence the mother is prepared to mete out in answer to a threat.'

Even when the songs target the child, the singer may be acting to protect them both. Many animals use such a feint to confuse invaders. The film *Jurassic Park* dramatizes the velociraptors' particular cunning. When under attack, they will glance in another direction, as if there was something else there threatening them. The predator, following their eyes, will lose concentration for an instant, allowing the velociraptor time to escape or even to attack. In *Jurassic Park*, it is the white hunter who is tricked in this way—fatally. He dies with the words 'Clever girl' on his lips. Similarly, if an intruder appears, some species of monkey will cry out, but not directly at the object of alarm. Again, the female feigns the presence of another danger and raises the alarm in that direction in order to muddle the real enemy. This decoy technique deflects the primary attack by positing an imaginary one. Could this stratagem throw light on the human phantasm of the bogeyman? Of course, several of the enemies invoked are all too real: famine, illness, sudden death truly threatened the lives of infants—and still do. But the restless return of the bogey in the songs may also represent a parental diversionary tactic. By conjuring the phantom assailant, that wolf at the door, that bagman with his sinister booty, that stalker in the shadows, it is possible that the mother or minder is giving out analogous signals that she and the child need genuine protection against danger. Nor can such an enemy, should one appear, count on the advantage of surprise; instead he learns that his target is vigilant.

Infant vulnerability is not accepted with stoicism, let alone indifference, in raw, violent lullabies; part of their function is not to let anyone slacken in preventing danger from taking its toll.

X

'AND THOU, OH NIGHTENGALE'

> Music is pervaded by childhood blocks, by blocks of femininity.
> Children's, women's, ethnic and territorial refrains, refrains of
> love and destruction: the birth of rhythm . . . The motif of the
> refrain may be anxiety, fear, joy, love, work, walking, territory
> . . . but the refrain itself is the content of music.
>
> Gilles Deleuze and Félix Guattari,
> '1730: Becoming–Intense, Becoming–Animal'

Women's voices, especially singing at night, have long been associated with the nightingale. Penelope in the *Odyssey* compares herself to the bird: 'I lie down on my bed, and care comes with a thousand stings to prick my heavy heart and turn dejection into torture . . . You know how . . . the brown nightingale . . . makes her sweet music when the spring is young, and with how many turns and trills she pours out her full-throated song in sorrow.'

In Homer, the nightingale has killed her own son by mistake, hence her nightly lamentation. But the savage story usually turns less on a mother's fatal inadvertency than on the issue of her voice, which has been deliberately silenced. The legacy of Philomela's 'sad tale' from Ovid's *Metamorphoses*, one of the most savage and terrifying of the Greek myths, underpins the bird's persistent femaleness in poetry. There are also Greek sources, such as the *Metamorphoses* of Antoninus Liberalis (second to third century AD) whoever the author, however, the nightingale plot always permutates themes of incest, rape, murder, mutilation, infanticide and cannibalism, as we have seen in Shakespeare's *Titus Andronicus*, for which it was a source.

With regard to ideas about women and their singing against horror, it is Ovid's attention to Philomela's voicelessness that is of most importance

Procne with Philomela brandishes the head of Itys in front of Tereus, his father; before Tereus takes his revenge in turn, they are all three changed into birds. Johannes Steinman, Ovid, Metamorphoses, *1582.*

here. For Tereus, after he has raped his sister-in-law Philomela, cuts out her tongue so that she can no longer scald him with it. Ovid follows the horrific assault in gory rapture, recently powerfully rendered by Ted Hughes:

> . . . he caught her tongue with bronze pincers,
> Dragged it out to its full length and
> Sliced it off at the root.
>
> The stump recoiled, silenced,
> Into the back of her throat.
> But the tongue squirmed in the dust, babbling on —
> Shaping words that were now soundless.
> It writhed like a snake's tail freshly cut off,
> Striving to reach her feet in its death-struggle.

The gods show their pity on dumb Philomela by a characteristic ironic retribution, turning her into the nightingale, for all eternity pouring forth her soul abroad, 'infesting poetry', Francis Celoria comments with impatience in his fascinating glosses on Antoninus Liberalis. Meanwhile Procne, her sister and accomplice in revenge, becomes a swallow, and Tereus, the rapist, a hoopoe. In other versions, members of the doomed family variously become a swallow, a woodpecker, and a halcyon or kingfisher.

The classical myth of violated and muted Philomela gruesomely dramatizes the relation of utterance and freedom, silence and deprivation, song and desire. Its range of themes is shadowed forth in many lullabies, too, though more gently and far less luridly. In the *Odyssey*, Penelope hears the bird as she is trying to sleep: if the blackbird or robin or lark's song flows and spills as fluently, these songsters belong to dawn and to daylight, not to the nightingale's darkling hour, the threshold between waking and sleeping. Comparatively early lullabies, from the literary rather than oral tradition, acknowledge through metaphor the form's kinship with bird-song, and the nightingale is often invoked as the singer's *alter ego*. Bedtime naturally announces the hour of the nightingale, which the fairies, for example, invoke in *A Midsummer Night's Dream* when they sing to Titania:

> Philomele, with melody,
> Sing in our sweet lullaby,
> Lulla, lulla, lullaby, lulla, lulla, lullaby.

Before Keats contrasted his aching soul with the nightingale's 'happy lot' and 'full-throated ease', before he identified the bird's ecstasy with heedless joyousness, Philomel was far more commonly associated with doleful threnody. Thus a mother's song, taken down in 1802 by a clergyman, laments her state: 'Thy father is cross' and gone 'to see an Old neighbour' (it was ever thus), while she watches alone and 'does nothing but weep'. The song opens, 'Indeed I do love thee, my dear little child . . .', but the mother soon turns sorrowful, finding sympathy with the emblems of nocturnal melancholy:

> The moon on thy window is shining so bright,
> And Philomel tells her sad tale to the night.

A poet faced with a family tragedy might incline naturally to such symbolism. Thus, the Revd. Mr. Frampton 'extemporized' a song for his niece, the infant Lady Maria Howard, after the death of her mother in childbirth:

> Hush ye winds! My Baby dear
> No ruder noise than this must hear . . .
>   And thou, oh Nightengale
> Whose Warblings sad, but sweet
> The evening Pilgrim greet . . .
>   Join, Philomel, O join
> Thy plaintive melody to mine . . .
>   Join Maria's Lullabies.

Keats' ode strikes a strong contrast between his heaviness ('My heart aches') and the bird's light-winged joyousness ('While thou art pouring forth thy soul abroad/ In such an ecstasy'). But he does modulate the mood of the ode in accord with his mythical sources, and closes the poem on a more mournful note: the birdsong becomes a 'high requiem' and fades from his hearing as a 'plaintive anthem'.

John Clare, needled by Keats' antiquarian and mythologizing observation of nature in his ode, observed the nightingale in the wild: 'mouth wide open to release her heart/ Of its out-sobbing songs'. In *The Progress of Ryhme (sic)*, he transcribed its melody as spontaneous poetic language:

Chew chew chee chew chee
chew chew chew chew chee
— up cheer up cheer up
tweet tweet tweet jug jug jug

Wew wew wew—chur chur chur
woo it woo it tweet tweet
tweet jug jug jug

tee rew tee rew tee rew—gur
gur—chew rit chew rit—chur-chur chur
chur will-will will-will tweet-em
tweet em jug jug jug jug

grig grig grig chew chew

Clare made the crucial connection between wordlessness, as in birdsong, and the expressiveness of nonsense vocables, which have no meaning but at the same time exceed verbal eloquence in their communication of free-wheeling joy in utterance itself. T.S. Eliot, quoting Clare twice over in *The Waste Land*, familiarized readers with Clare's precise anti-lyrics: 'And still she cried, and still the world pursues/ "Jug Jug" to dirty ears.' But Eliot switched the emphasis from Clare's wondrous, blithe, delicious acoustics to Philomel's rape and mutilation.

The variations in historical response to the nightingale pose charged questions about the inherent emotive qualities of music, that stout defence against fear. Is the bird's song intrinsically 'plaintive', or do human ears hear its mood through other, extraneous conductors? And is a dirge consoling in itself, however melancholic the melody and the pace? Do requiems and laments steady us, like lullabies? And could it be that this power of music is linked to the nature of language? Are they both systems that order disorder, that have a calming, soothing and hopeful effect on the listener, enabling him or her to let go of fears and sorrows? This would explain how the same musical sequences—the nightingale's—can strike the human ear as 'out-sobbing songs' or as 'joyous' outpourings. Unlike bird-song, however, human song is a willed representation, attempting to match feeling and sound. Yet human song echoes birdsong in that its effect does not depend on the emotional content of the music, and, oddly, it lifts the spirits, however doleful it sounds. This is the power of artifice, that it can induce feelings different from those it represents. Singing is a charm against the dark: in their whole range of expression, verbal and musical, however peculiar, sad, harsh and bitter, lullabies work.

❖   ❖   ❖

The doubled and contradictory nature of lullabies which express aggression and even terror towards infants is grounded in another of the song's functions: the lullaby is intriguingly important to language acquisition. While the singers vent their feelings, the squalling and wide-awake infants are probably learning—but not from the manifest content. Again, a comparison with birds is instructive: 'Baby birds distinguish the song of their species by responding to individual sounds making up the song. That process seems to parallel the one seen in human infants, who recognize individual vowels and consonants before they learn words, phrases, and sentences.' It is important to note that there is a very short period during their first year of life when birds can acquire their species' song; if they are deprived of the chance, through segregation or isolation, in many species they will remain mute. The exceptions are the fly-catchers, for whom song is 'genetically encoded' and who can consequently still vocalize even when raised in silence. All other songbirds—robins, thrushes, blackbirds, nightingales—will slur and gibber if they are not raised within earshot of members of their own species in the brief time of the 'learning window' that opens. Mimics, like mockingbirds, put the crucial character of this early exposure into sharp focus, for they 'borrow bits and pieces of the songs of many other species, and weave them into an exuberant and highly varied outpouring. But mockingbirds living in urban or agricultural environments, where there are few models to imitate, sing relatively barren and uninteresting songs.'

For humans, language formation also depends on acquiring sequences of sounds, like tunes, before grasping single syllables or words, the lyrics of language. Phonetic and prosodic patterns are laid down before semantic understanding, which explains why it is so much easier to reproduce the cadences of a second language when it is heard and acquired at an early age. It is the case, however obvious it might seem to point it out, that, setting aside difficult sounds like *r* or *th,* even a consonant like *d* differs in French from English, and can rarely be reproduced accurately late in life. Infants absorb cadence and tonality before they can understand meaningful phrases, and it is now thought that contact with such prosodic variations 'may facilitate speech processing and language comprehension'. A language's characteristic vowels and consonants recur in the patter of nonsense songs, imparting the intrinsic music of that speech to the infant, and refrains, ritornellos, choruses and catchlines return to typical sound clusters: *ninna-nanna* in Italian and Greek, *heidschi bumbeidschi* in German, *baya bayu* in Russian, *shoheen-shal-eo* in Irish, *dodo dodo* in French, *cha-chang cha-chang* in Korean, and so forth.

Myths and natural history do not always congrue, despite Ovid's programme of explaining the phenomena of creation in the *Metamorphoses.* Philomela's story sails past the problem that in nature the singing nightingales are male, wooing females in the spring and proclaiming their territory, their home, where their mate will be or is nesting with her young. Even Clare, making his notes direct from explorations of the countryside, heard the nightingale's song as female; in Stravinsky's opera *Le Rossignol* (1914), based on a Hans Christian Andersen fairy tale, the part of the real nightingale, as opposed to the mechanical toy, is sung by a soprano, following the pitch of the birdsong rather than the gender of the word. Only Coleridge, who rebelliously acclaimed 'the merry Nightingale', writing, 'in Nature there is nothing melancholy', referred to the bird throughout this 'Conversational Poem' as male.

Research shows that birdsong correlates with high levels of testosterone, and in experiments 'those [females] that received testosterone implants sang more.' There are, however, exceptions: robins—females as well as males—sing, and sing all through the year. Among familiar species in the Old World, a few other mother birds sing full-throatedly—marsh tits, during the fledging period. North American redwings, which live in polygynous groups, give voice in two different modes, one song elicited by the presence of other females, and another in response to the male. In the tropics of the Amazonian forest, many females sing duets with the males, sometimes in counterpoint, sometimes in reciprocal phrasing, antiphonally.

But on the whole, females give signals: they shriek, scold, twitter, and call rather than warble. I have seen and heard a hen blackbird in my small

London garden try to defend her young from a raiding magpie by setting up a frenzy of noise as she mobbed it, fluttering and whirling on the ground in an attempt to distract it from the nest in the tree above—unavailingly. The magpie snatched the tiny hairless hatchlings and was not even hungry enough to eat them, for I found one mangled carcass on the lawn later that day. I have also been dive-bombed by a screeching mother tern, her beak stretched so wide her face seemed all sharp tongue and pink barb, on a walk in Scotland when I came too near the nest. These are cries, ejaculations, birdscreams, not birdsong.

These glimpses throw light on the human nestling and on cultural attitudes to motherhood and childhood. First, the mistaken poetic assumption that the nightingale, embodiment of twilit singing, was a mother mourning the loss of a child and her own tragic predicament reveals the human apprehension about offspring predominating in the lullaby. But the traditional simile also proves fruitful in two more ways: birds sing frequently to warn off intruders, and they signal their presence to one another through their song, which their neighbours then recognize as uniquely theirs. Though it can be glib—and tendentious—to deduce human characteristics from animal behaviour, birdsong does give an angle of view on uses of language as well as language acquisition in infants.

The charting of self, same, other, and different which the lullaby's oppositions dramatize (Herod and the Innocents, the wolf at the door and the baby in the cot, the mother's lap and the bogeyman's bag) can be understood in relation to the functions of birdsong, to singing to defend territory, to defining identity against enemies, trespassers, usurpers and parasites. Birds are not the only species to take these measures: vervet monkeys chutter and utter the sound *rraup* and chirp in order to give precise warnings about which predators—snakes, eagles, big cats—are approaching. Female birds' vocalizations thus contribute to this recognition of identity and habitat, and help orient their young in a certain group, marking the boundaries around the home, figuratively and metaphorically. The young of both sexes are exposed to these conversations and learn from them, even though their own oral expression will differ later.

New research by psycho-linguists on the relation between sounds and language draws increasing attention to the importance of parents' speech, especially the mother's, and to the role that patter and nonsense play in the development of imagination as well as the acquisition of language. They also emphasize the predominance of women's voices at this early stage: all kinds of linguists' and paediatricians' measurements in different social groups and countries observe consistently that fathers—and grandfathers or other males—do not vocalize in contact with children with as many variations of frequency, pitch, exaggerations of tone and cadence, additions of 'tags', stresses, and repetitions, all devices that help imprint language and impart speech. In many respects, the phrase 'mother tongue' can be taken at face value with maximum force.

Although lullabies are above all charms to soothe care, they also had—and still have—a crucial practical function. Walter Benjamin was scornful of the notion that babies' rattles originated as tools to develop hearing and reminded his readers that they were first placed in infants' hands to scare away evil spirits. Despite art and magic seeming more artful and more magical when separated from use values, lullabies do form a vivid part of what psychologists call 'the maternal melody', by which they mean not simply singing but the whole palette of clucking, whispering, patter and prattle, coos and babble, and even kissing. 'Mothers reassure partly through sounds—to make the link, the mother offers her feelings through touch, gestures, facial expressions and particularly through sounds. These sounds compose a melody without many or any words which shows a remarkable similarity in tune across cultures. The mother's voice is known to the infant; her melody is tuned to the infant's needs and responses.'

In jargon, this early communication is also sometimes termed 'Motherese' or 'BT', acronymic for 'Baby Talk'. (By analogy, 'PT', or 'Pet Talk', has also been clinically observed: communication in the larger, extended family of dogs, cats, birds and other animals.) There is a huge and ever growing scholarly literature on the subject. Briefly, Motherese encompasses more than caressing, rhythmic play and talk; lulling is a primary source of this kind of 'smiling' web of sound, woven with babble and nonsense in patterns characteristic of the local language. It is not always mothers who communicate in this way to infants, of course; a range of grandparents, neighbours, minders and siblings do too. Isaac Watts, who included 'A Cradle Hymn' in his *Divine Songs*, specifies in a footnote to the line, ''Tis thy [Mother] sits beside thee', that 'Here you may use the Words Brother, Sister, Neighbour, Friend, &c.'

The range of voices heard in these songs thus extends well beyond the mother's. Robert Louis Stevenson dedicated the collection *A Child's Garden of Verses* (1896), to Alison Cunningham, 'Cummy', who nursed him during his many illnesses as a child; she recited to him ballads and metrical psalms—and told him scare stories—learned during her upbringing in Scotland as the daughter of a fisherman. In one sense, these early exchanges, through song, poetry, whisperings and cuddling are a kind of secret, shared in childhood, and their intimacies, sometimes perverse and sometimes fanciful, are hidden from history.

The fundamental need to acquire sound systems, cadence, in order to develop children's speech may also explain the odd recurrence, among human beings, of holding babies on the left arm. A recent medical study of 'left side cradling' discovered that 80 per cent of newly delivered mothers and new fathers hold the baby on the left. Girls from the age of six choose this side instinctively (boys show no marked preference until they become fathers). This holds for the higher primates, too—gorillas, chimpanzees and orang-outangs, 80 per cent of whom also carry their young on the left. That the position leaves the right hand free to do other things might offer a quick explanation, except that the research found that 70 per cent of left-handers also perch their offspring on their left hip.

As the Virgin Mary has been represented more than any other mother in the history of culture, it is worth pausing over the traditional images of Madonna and Child: any wander through a medieval and Renaissance collection will reveal that Mary very rarely carries Jesus on her right arm. Examples are far too numerous to survey, and they are by no means confined to high European art. Left-cradling Madonnas appear far and wide, high and low: in Mexican votive images, in seventeenth-century Ethiopian paintings, as well as in numerous cult icons and statues of popular devotion—Our Lady of Antwerp in her stiffly jewelled and embroidered festive vestments, or Notre Dame de Bon Port, patroness of sailors in Antibes.

The tradition does not appear to be knowingly connected with any doctrinal purpose, though the conventions and secular symbolism of right-handedness may influence the iconography in some instances. The Byzantine theme of the Virgin Hodegetria—the Virgin who points the way—depicts Mary indicating the child Saviour with her right hand; he returns her gesture with blessing with his right hand, too. It is also possible that an almost unconscious sense that the mother should take her place on the child's right hand, as she does as the supreme mediatrix in scenes of the Last Judgment, influenced the iconography. Still, it is striking that when the Madonna does hold Jesus on her right, she is either nursing him or dandling him or holding him for another to touch, as in scenes of the mystic marriage of St. Catherine.

For some time, this prevalence of left-side cradling was attributed to the place of the heart, pulsing, lullaby-like, to pacify the infant. But observations have shown that the preferred sound of both foetus and infant is the mother's voice, not her heartbeat. The newly offered hypothesis looks at the phenomenon from the ever-burgeoning interest in consciousness, and takes as its premise the bilateral division of function in the brain where language, expression, and communication are concerned. The evidence gathered from patients who have suffered strokes or brain damage through accidents reveals that the interpretation of sound and visual signals is separated from semantic understanding: 'the left hemisphere controls word content, grammar, and syntax; the right controls intonation and affective intent (prosody).' A baby's brain, as it grows, learns to read facial expressions and to understand pitch and tonality with the right side of the brain which is connected to the left ear and eye; by contrast, verbalization is linked to the left hemisphere and the right ear and eye. Consequently, this fresh line of inquiry proposes that a baby cradled on the left, with the left ear and eye free, will be absorbing facial and vocal expressiveness, independent of verbal meaning, embedding the aural and visual foundation of communication.

A strikingly harsh example from an Icelandic song may clinch the argument about the phonetic importance of lullabies and nursery rhymes and nonsense songs: in 'The Child in the Sheepfold', a baby sings to its mother, with the added macabre twist that the baby has been exposed to die. The song opens with the mother complaining that she has nothing to wear to go to a *vikivaki*, a dancing and storytelling festival. While she is in the sheepfold, milking a ewe and lamenting her lot to another dairymaid, they hear a voice rising from under the wall, consoling her with a lilting song:

> Mother mine don't weep, weep,
> As you milk the sheep, sheep;
> I can lend my rags [swaddling bands] to you,
> So you'll go a-dancing too,
> You'll go a-dancing too.

The chorus goes:

> Móðir mín í kví, kví,
> kvíddú ekki, þvi, þvi,
> eg skal ljá þér duluna mína,
> að dansa í,
> og dansa í.

An Old Norse and Icelandic scholar, Carolyne Larrington, wondered why the song was so popular, and even sung as a lullaby, but she points out the recurrence of the two unusual consonant groups, *kv* and *þv*, tricky to pronounce, and, consequently, necessary to introduce at an early age.

Even 'Hush-a-Bye, Baby', still so popular at bedtime, does contain several characteristic English phonemes: the aspirate *h* of 'Hush'; the voiceless *wh* in 'When the bough breaks . . .'. According to the linguist Edward Sapir, the *wh* is learned by English speakers in relation to other sounds through its difference from them, and especially through the nuances that distinguish it from close neighbours, such as the sound made when blowing out a candle. Arguing for the formal and symbolic structure of communication as distinct from the utilitarian models, Sapir was inspired to make eloquent claims for such native skills: 'the articulation of the *wh*-sound in such a word as "when" has no direct functional value; it is merely a link in the construction of a symbol . . . In brief, the candle-blowing *wh* means business; the speech sound *wh* is stored-up play which can eventually fall in line in a game that merely refers to business. Still more briefly, the former is practice; the latter, art.'

The force of this argument for language learning as 'stored-up play' can be felt, I think, by taking a step sideways and looking at human aptitude for learning a second language, which is so much greater in childhood than maturity. When the French Symbolist poet Stéphane Mallarmé was working as a teacher of English in Paris, he became fascinated with English nonsense rhymes, ditties and catches; he translated them into French for his pupils, expounding the rules of the language through such verses as:

> For this little cock-sparrow would make a nice stew
> And his giblets would make a nice little pie, too.
>
> 'Oh! no,' says cock-sparrow, 'I won't make a stew,'
> And he fluttered his wings, and away he flew.

A schools inspector chanced to come in just as Mallarmé was teaching the following rhyme to the children at the Lycée Fontanes in 1880, and translating it word for word:

> Liar liar lick spit
> Your tongue shall be slit
> And all the dogs in the town
> Shall have a little bit.

The report was withering: 'M. Mallarmé, as he is to remain a teacher of English . . . should learn English . . . he should not dictate . . . foolish rubbish like "Liar liar lick spit".' He then gave, in full, Mallarmé's polished version of the rhyme, and concluded, blustering, 'One is tempted to ask oneself if one is not in the presence of a sick man.'

However, it is likely that Mallarmé's pupils learned English rapidly and with relish. They may even have been young enough to learn to master *th*.

Nuances of pronunciation, mastered only by native speakers in infancy, can be used to tell friend from foe, sometimes in times of conflict. Though it seems harsh or even perverse and ugly to point to such connections, lullabies form the ground in which shibboleths are sown.

'Shibboleth' was the word with which Jephthah and the Gileadites challenged their enemies the Ephraimites:

> Then Gilead cut Ephraim off from the fords of the Jordan, and whenever an Ephraimite fugitive said, 'Let me cross', the men of Gilead asked him, 'Are you an Ephraimite?' If he answered 'No', they said, 'Then say Shibboleth'. He would say, 'Sibboleth', since he could not pronounce the word correctly. Thereupon they seized and slaughtered him by the fords of the Jordan. There perished in this way forty-two thousand men of Ephraim. (Judges 12: 4–6)

This righteously gory Old Testament episode institutes pronunciation at the core of tribal identity, and gives rise to the current prevailing meaning of 'shibboleth' (an empty formula to which a member of a sect or cult or group must pay obeisance). In Holland, during the German occupation in 1941–45, it was said that the Dutch Resistance could identify German infiltrators by their failure to sound the right Dutch consonants in the word Scheveningen. Native tongues announce belonging, proclaim descent: and the converse can also be true, in that what is heard as a characteristic acoustic pattern can become the mark of ethnicity; it is no accident that such a nonsense refrain so resembles infantile patter.

'Lillibullero', sung to an upbeat variation on the tune of 'Hush-a-bye baby', throws light on this function of nursery songs and rhymes. The jaunty nonsense refrain—'Lilli burlero bullen a-la'—was said to have been a watchword of Irish insurrectionists in their massacre of Protestants in 1641. However, in 1686 the musical catch changed sides, when King James II appointed a fellow Catholic as Lord Lieutenant of Ireland. At a time of bitter religious antagonism, his choice roused the future Orangists' rage, and 'Lillibullero' was taken up by the Protestants in mockery, to become the taunting chorus of a brutally ironic anti-Papist ballad:

Dare was an old prophesy found in a bog,
　Lilli burlero bullen a-la
'Ireland shall be rul'd by an ass, and a dog,'
　Lilli burlero bullen a-la.
And now dis prophesy is come to pass,
　Lilli burlero bullen a-la.

This gibe against Irish vocables, dialect—and jollity—was sung by the English army 'perpetually' in the campaign; 'and perhaps never had so slight a thing so great an effect,' commented the historian Burnet in wonderment. However, by the early eighteenth century, the time 'my uncle Toby' is depicted whistling 'Lillabulero' in *Tristram Shandy* at any point where this genial and lovable man finds himself at a loss for words or otherwise ill at ease, the song had simply become the badge of the brave British patriot. Effectively declawed and defanged, 'Lillibullero' had passed into the happy-go-lucky meaninglessness of the mundane. The song's history nevertheless reveals how identity can inhere in a merely phonetic humble sequence of nonsense syllables. A tune, a lyric, a way of pronouncing and cadencing a phrase, a simple catch can take their place beside other more imposing symbols of belonging, such as a sacred site, a national monument, or a holy talisman like the Stone of Scone; such monuments, on account of being highly prized, are especially vulnerable to vandalism and mockery.

Passing on distinctive sounds, singing on behalf of another, ascribing speech and babble to the infant and for the infant, transmitting cadence and language, telling the child of imaginary fates it has avoided, or, some-times, of fortune lying ahead, bear a relation to the arbitrary arrangements of that kind of first-person fiction which women writers pioneered and whose development they have profoundly influenced, in which the teller is there living the scenes recounted and, *ipso facto,* cannot be there to write them simultaneously: he or she is, as it were, spoken for, as the earliest formulators of omniscient thoughts near a child form that child's fears and longings on its behalf. Deleuze and Guattari argue that such melodic landscapes of tunes and songs constitute art, that they are too individual, too fragmentary for ritual and, like art, they extend representations to include fabrication. After setting up the markers around the abode, 'one opens the circle a crack', they write, 'opens it all the way, lets someone in, calls someone, or else goes out oneself, launches forth . . . As though the circle tended on its own to open on to a future . . . This time in order to join with the forces of the future, cosmic forces. One launches forth, hazards an improvisation. But to improvise is to join with the World, or meld with it. One ventures from home on the thread of a tune.'

Thus earliest shaping of infantile character literally sketches out the possibilities ahead, writes the part: 'Smiles await you when you rise', or, 'twelve vigils . . . and not one returns'.

Richard Kennedy, who worked as a boy in the offices of the Hogarth Press, recalled in his memoirs how he was given a lift in the Woolfs' car and how 'Mrs Woolf kept up a flow of absolutely absurd conversation with the child in a high-pitched voice, using a crazy language made up of unrecognizable sounds.' This was what Virginia Woolf called her 'pixerina-witcherina' language which she had invented with her sister's daughter Angelica.

Language in its early patternings sets the course of a life; the importance of expressiveness cannot be overstated: without linguistic agility we are poorer, clumsier, less fit—in the true sense of less adapted and adaptable— just as, without song, fledglings are fatally maimed. Nonsense, babble, patter, ditties, verses, dandling and cradle songs, all the threads of tune and talk that adults spin around growing children in the home, in the street, and in other spaces where they interact, play a crucial part in this development. They dovetail into the nursery rhyme repertory, along with skipping, clapping, counting-out rhymes, tongue twisters, riddles and other early inventive wordplay that children themselves go on to enjoy and invent, what Paul Muldoon has called 'Lillibullabies'. This infantile language imitates an imagined form—the incoherent babble in the infantile brain, while it projects what might be the state of that consciousness in other ways, too. The adult plays the fool to draw the child into adult ways.

Fright and lulling have been only two responses sought after by entertainers, storytellers, artists, by mothers, grandparents and other caregivers: bogeymen can also be figures of fun. Children have not knuckled under to the threat of their fell presence; they have prompted a reinvention of the ogre, have turned his voracious appetite and dread into a series of games and stories that, surprising as it may seem, make them laugh.

PART THREE

MAKING MOCK

There are three things that are real: God, human folly and laughter. Since the first two pass our comprehension, we must do what we can with the third.

Valmiki, *The Ramayana*, *c.* 200 B.C.

REFLECTION

LOUIS DESPREZ: THE CHIMERA

On the pediments of classical temples, Medusa grins, splitting her gorgon mask into a wide and ferocious leer, baring her tusks, lolling her tongue. Athena wore the Gorgoneion— Medusa's head—on her breastplate, a trophy of the protection from harm that she offered, as well as a talisman that shielded her. The Etruscans set up fierce lions with protruding tongues and rows of bared teeth at the entrance of tombs to guard the corpses from desecrators and to prevent their spirits wandering and disturbing the living, too. Kali, goddess of destruction and the hearth, also puts out her bloodstained tongue as she dances in her necklace of skulls. Medusa and Kali may have exerted reciprocal influence over each other as monstrous figures of household protection. The sexual exhibitionist who appears on Christian churches, frequently in Celtic areas (Ireland, Cornwall, the Outer Hebrides) but also in England, may have a related role to play. The sheela-na-gig, with her vulva defiantly exposed—the nether mouth—dances and displays herself, often grimacing open-mouthed, showing her teeth and tongue; she is usually placed high up on a tower or on gates, wells and bridges. The Egyptian dwarf god Bes, worshipped in Hellenistic Egypt as the god of bedrooms, held special propitiatory powers against the capriciousness of the fertility goddess Hatwa and the envy of other women; he similarly makes a face, poking out his tongue like a naughty child as he spits against the evil eye and stands in a straddling pose, his genitals exposed, his penis dangling as if in imitation of his tongue. 'Such beasts,' comments Jean-Pierre Vernant, 'often perform the role of guardians, even scarecrows, barring the way to forbidden places.'

These images are not simply grinding their teeth or snapping their jaws or spitting fire. They are, well, laughing, in a mirthless way, baring their teeth at the same time as making a funny face, in the simian grimace that signifies a double greeting: hello, but beware. Their communication is complicated: they are, after all, pulling their tongues as well, just as children do in rude (and comic) defiance, or perhaps just as adults would, if they were not taught to control the impulse. The expression is more instinctive than a culturally bounded gesture, such as giving a finger or

Chimera, of the monstrous kin of Scylla and Cerberus, came to signify the principle of illusion itself, the very embodiment of the fantastic. Louis Desprez, La Chimère, *c. 1777.*

thumbing one's nose: it reveals the animal within, the beast under the mask of the human. It is perhaps worth noting that grunnire *(Latin for 'to grunt'), belongs in the same sound cluster as Greek* gryl, *also 'to grunt', and to many English words that catch the child's Grrr!—such as 'grin' and 'grimace' and 'growl'.*

The gesture verges, riskily, on the absurd, and it reappears in that profane mood on the edges of official representations: on medieval chimney pots, seventeenth-century automated effigies for Carnival, and in a nineteenth-century cut-out paper puppet of M. et Mme. Croquemitaine, bogeys of the French nursery. In this last instance, the tongue protrudes when the child pulls on a tab. The more unholy images are in their snarling, in their instinctive ugliness and grotesque menace, the more endowed they become with the apotropaic powers of turning away danger: as scarecrows, gargoyles, sentries.

The brood of serpents, dragons and other monsters imagined thronging the pantheons of polytheistic religions has this function of warding off imagined and as yet unimagined evils, which Christian devils have necessarily shed. In the fantastic prehistory of the divine genealogies, when all the powers and creatures born to Earth and Ocean combine into fantastic and ferocious features, Echidna and Typho give birth to monsters. Scylla, as we have seen, is sometimes numbered among their progeny, which includes another daughter, Chimera, a fiery hybrid with three heads:

> *. . . who breathed awful fire,*
> *Three-headed, frightening, huge, swift-footed, strong,*
> *One head a bright-eyed lion's, one a goat's,*
> *The third a snake's, a mighty dragon-head.*

Of all the hybrids and monsters fabricated by the Greeks and their cultural descendants, it is this amorphous Chimera, described in Hesiod and in Homer, who encapsulates the complex mixture of horror and comedy in the mind's illusions, the nightmare fabulations of reason. The word 'monster' resonates with the word for 'to show' monstrare, influenced by monere 'to warn', thus implying a portent, a warning. All monsters are to some extent chimerae, impossible in nature, explicitly described yet also unimaginable, and the very display of such outlandish inventions inspires strong emotions of dread—against which laughter can be the best defence.

A magnificent antique bronze of the monster, found in Arezzo, in Tuscany, gives every impression of being conceived life-size; it shows her three heads disposed along her body, not sprouting from her shoulders, like Cerberus'. A goat's head rears from her dorsal ridge, and her tail spouts fire, like an amphisbaenic gargoyle doodled in the margin of a medieval manuscript; in the usual place of a head, she roars through lion's jaws, and her whole form, brilliantly tooled and chased by the ancient bronze sculptor's skill, tenses with further, impending violence.

Chimera's fate, like that of many she-monsters, was to meet death at the hands of a hero, her fearsomeness aggrandizing his feat. Her killer was Bellerophon, astride the magic flying horse Pegasus. Pegasus had risen fully formed from the blood spilled on the ground when Perseus struck off the head of Medusa—the progeny of another murder by a young hero and another founding massacre of due, human order. Chimera dies when the lead from Bellerophon's spearpoint melts in the flames that her dragon's head has breathed out and the pellets choke her. Her lair was located on a hillside in Lycia, in modern Turkey, where flames spurt spontaneously from gases trapped in the rock; the crews of boats passing offshore can still see the flickering light on the volcanic slopes, where low-lying fumaroles erupt spontaneously with blue flames, like the rings on a gas burner lighting. Scattered at random through the scrub and rocks, the fires flare here and there, vagrant, like will-o'-the-wisps. The zone is still identified with the fire-breathing creature of myth whom sailors out at sea imagined prowling her barren, scorched terrain. The classical bronze Chimera, for all its skill and tension, cannot fully convey the nature of this beast, for the sculpture solidifies and stills her, failing to catch her foxfire ubiquity, her evanescence, the changeable and elusive nature which makes her a spectre that can never really be seen. It is interesting, as Ginevra Bompiani points out, that Bellerophon's later career takes a melancholy turn very different from the glories of other dragon-slayers: he succumbs to a profound depression after his attempt at Olympus fails when Pegasus throws him, at Zeus' urging, and Bellerophon crashes to the ground in Lycia and is blinded. Illusion is a treacherous and elusive opponent, and a hero can never be certain to have quelled it utterly.

Unlike other monsters who have remained embedded in their native stories, as protagonists and individual creatures—Echidna herself, Scylla, Cerberus, Atlas—'Chimera' acquired a definite article, by analogy with her monstrous kin the Sphinx, the Medusa, the Hydra, the Cyclops, and thence lent her name to a wide, generic concept. Like the grotesque, the chimera combines antithetical parts (those three beasts' heads) to produce a phantasmagoric assemblage, a heterogeneous being. The word has come to mean, since the Renaissance, illusion itself, an impossible and delusory figment of the imagination: in the 1740 edition of Bailey's Dictionary, 'a strange Fancy, a Castle in the air, an idle conceit', or, as Bompiani puts it, 'the creature of language, the metaphor of metaphor'. Jorge Luis Borges, in his incomparable bestiary, aptly quotes Rabelais' witty question: 'Can a chimera, swinging in a void, swallow second intentions?'

From the populous bestiary of the classical and medieval imagination, it is the Chimera above all fantasy creatures who, for her protean elusiveness, should take the stage as a prime figure of ambiguous fantasy since the Counter-Enlightenment. If the Medusa inspired one of the last century's most symptomatic and enduring theories, the castration complex, the Chimera stands at the root of another fundamental contemporary mental state, the fascination with the fantastic, the longing for escape and relief in

Scarecrows, guardian angels, or fools fooling? Gorgon LEFT *Greece, fifth century* B.C.; *sheela-na-gig* CENTRE *Kilpeck, England, twelfth or thirteenth century; chimney-pot* RIGHT *Oxford, fourteenth century.*

the vivid, created presence of the imaginary, however grotesque.

Louis Desprez, a French eighteenth-century proto-Surrealist printmaker and illustrator of Rabelais, engraved one of the most remarkable examples of the late grotesque imagination. His flayed dragon, drawn around 1777, conveys savage monstrosity in a mood of ghastly hilarity. Desprez departed from the Homeric description of the monster's anatomy and created instead a walking cannibal skeleton with bat wings and three heads on three necks protruding from her shoulders. Her whole carcass is rendered even more ghoulish by its sectional, see-through quality, for Desprez did not stint on imagining the victim's torments: we see him lie, his head flung back upside down, inside the body of the beast, stuffed halfway down the oesophagus under her ribs into her innards, as she grimly devours him with exaggerated hell-hound determination. The long, beaked carrion bird head in the middle is snapping at his jaw, while the other two heads, identical horned and elephant-eared gargoyles, Tweedledum and Tweedledee, are munching on his hands, rolling their eyes and flaring their nostrils with horrible Jabberwocky relish. Desprez has marked the monster's sex with a row of udders hanging so that the teat of the central one actually brushes the edge of the moon that lies huge and full on the low horizon; fire issues from a phallus-like tail.

A small Bosch-like winged hybrid and a snake attend the scene; skulls and bones litter the beast's lair. This excessive horror, proliferating with signs of monstrosity—the multiplicity of limbs and heads, mix-and-match elements of species, ferocious cruelty and greed—straddles with funambulist poise the line between the portentous and terrifying, and the lugubrious and comic.

A late state of the print bears a caption, which reassures the reader: once again, the dread Chimera has been conquered. It catches the elusiveness of the Chimera's form, for it is intrinsic to this monster that she cannot be pinned down: 'This Monster was always on the march,' it says, 'she had wings and Fins; She was seen now on the ground, now on the Waters. Her girth was larger than an Elephant's; it had taken a great number of armed Soldiers . . . with Dogs trained in battle' to rid travellers of this menace. Desprez's Chimera *is an Enlightenment artist's image of illusion, who inflicts on her victims a metamorphosis of negation and extermination, but inspires in the onlooker silent, incongruous laughter.*

XI

'IN THE GENRE OF THE MONSTROUS'

Ce que nous voyons de laid, difforme, des-honneste, indessant, malseant, & peu convenable, excite an nous le ris, pourveu que nous n'an soyons meus à compassion . . . Il et parelhemant des-honete, de moutrer le cu: & quand il n'y ha aucun dommage qui nous cotraigne à misericorde, nous ne pouvons ampecher le Ris.

(What we behold that is ugly, shapeless, rude, indecent, unseemly & hardly suitable, excites laughter in us, provided that we are not moved to compassion by it . . . It is likewise rude to show one's bottom: & when there is no harm in it that constrains us to mercy, we cannot help laughing.)

Laurent Joubert, 1579

Children will ask, sometimes, if something is Funny Peculiar or Funny Ha-ha, and oddly there is no better way of putting the distinction. Some mutations of the monster figure, especially in contemporary culture, induce both states simultaneously, and indeed, Funny Ha-ha and Funny Peculiar are combining into a late twentieth-century taste for the grotesque. This late grotesque is a style, a mood, a sensibility, and in the sense used before, a *rasa*, or flavour that finds expression in art; it has a history, within the history of art and of taste, and its aesthetic appearance has changed and continues to change. As Mark Dorrian has commented, 'The monstrous figure has an erratic pulse—monstrosity erupts at specific historical points.' In the last years of this century it has achieved a new prominence, and is exercising deep attraction over numerous artists, writers and performers today.

Fascination with the monstrous and the grotesque has become the dominant tone in representations of fear and its objects, its savoury juice detectable in a wide range of material: in the gallows humour of Quentin Tarantino's films, in the bestselling new niche market for juvenile horror fiction (R.L. Stine's thin little shockers, in a series called 'Goosebumps', feature ghouls, vampires, and ventriloquist's dummies that come to life, and have titles like *You Can't Scare Me!*). The Japanese *couturière* Rei Kawabuko added macabre, Quasimodo humps and lumps and lopsided pads to her designs for the spring 1997 collections for the high-fashion popular label Comme des Garçons. This chapter will follow a strand in this richly tangled tradition of comic defiance and look at its function in confronting the terrors that come in the dark.

The grotesque style beats to a double pulse: *terribilità* on the one hand, *capriccio* on the other. The poet Horace was clear about the comic effect of this style, though he did not consider it intentional. At the start of *On the Art of Poetry* he wrote: 'Supposing a painter chose to put a human head on a horse's neck, or to spread feathers of various colours over the limbs of several different creatures, or to make what in the upper part is a beautiful woman tail off into a hideous fish, could you help laughing when he showed you his efforts?' But Horace meant that one laughed in mockery, surely, not mirth. The mockery perhaps defends against the painful potential; though this early grotesque does not claim to represent the reality of phantasms at a deep level, it continued lightfootedly, capriciously, safely contained in the abstract realm of representations.

The laughter it inspired in Horace does not express trouble at realignments of the self, or even at the shuffling of the natural order. Yet the style's capacity to provoke unease has excited reproof throughout its history. For the grotesque's fancifulness also strikes observers as horrible; it indulges in inconsequential whimsy but its very detachment from logic and biology can take a disturbing turn. The Roman architectural historian Vitruvius scoffed at its incongruities, and he was echoed, in the Renaissance, by the equally influential Florentine biographer and artist Giorgio Vasari. These critics were sensitive to something diabolical about the arbitrary playfulness of the artists. They distrusted the pleasures of fancy, which mocked sense and called into question the very morality of art. From the Renaissance, artists were symbolized as apes, after the animal's cleverness at imitation, and they even devised *singeries*, ornaments and images and furniture that mischievously accepted and played with this identity. But the devil is also the ape of God, mimicking divine creativity with his perverse works, and he laughs—as monkeys also do. The devil mocks nature, mocks sense: James Joyce was knowingly working in this tradition when he invented, punned, compounded words. Dorrian develops this point:

'The language of the devil is a punning language pieced together from word-fragments . . . It seeks not to conserve categories, but rather constantly deforms them, dismantling, truncating, combining, inverting. The grotesque word (or image) which is the point from which this satanic language of incessant inventions flows, in fact holds, as the Creative Word, the very essence of the divine.' That other name for the grotesque—*diablerie*—catches the anxiety and the ambition that surround its fancies and fabrications.

The word *grottesco* arose, as is well known, from a misapprehension: that when Nero's Domus Aurea was excavated, at the end of the fifteenth century, the decorated chambers found buried under ground level had indeed been subterranean grottoes. Yet this underworld origin of the style seemed wholly appropriate and would match Freud's much later architecture of the unconscious, in the basement of the mind. The drolleries and fantastical ornaments of Mannerist artists in Italy and France gave the grotesque its earliest character and artistic meaning; hybrid creatures, masks, strapwork, floral wreathing and *rinceaux* covered the walls of princes' palaces. More Roman fancies were later unearthed round Naples and Rome, and they influenced the ornaments by Raphael and his *bottega* at the Vatican (1518–19); these parade characteristic giddy inventions: herms with wader bird legs, mastiffs mooning alongside herms and sphinxes and cherubs. But the grotesque was expanding as well as deepening, far beyond these playful decorations. When the style spread northwards in the fifteenth century, artists like Hieronymus Bosch and Bruegel the Elder gave it more eerie and disturbing metaphysical content.

Dürer recommended, prophetically, 'Whoever wants to do dreamwork must mix all things together', and in his printmaking he delineated the diabolical predators and angelic champions of the Christian apocalyptic tradition, by mixing and matching the monstrous paraphernalia of pagan gods and wonders. But Dürer and other Christians were working in an intellectual landscape in which the devil and his angels were considered not as products of the imagination but as existing beings whose embodiment, as conveyed in visual and verbal imagery, was considered more than a symbolic approximation. Botticelli's drawings for Dante's *Divina Commedia*, Dürer's own ferocious *Apocalypse*, and his fellow engraver Jean Duvet's even more hair-raising and tumultuous interpretation of the cataclysm prophesied in the Book of Revelations, represent the reality of the supernatural: Satan is not simply metaphorically conveyed by a monstrous triple-headed dragon, he is indeed 'that serpent which deceiveth the whole world'.

An exuberant mingling of elements epitomizes Renaissance grotesques, like this costume for a masque. Engraving, Denis Boutemie, 1638.

By contrast, Michelangelo, in a conversation reported by Francisco de Olanda around 1540, foreshadowed the turn to secret fantasy about non-existent beings that the grotesque later took. He picked up a phrase that Horace had let drop in passing and dramatically expanded its meaning. Horace had written, in the course of his dismissal of the grotesque style, 'Painters and poets have *always had the prerogative of daring anything (quodlibet audendi potestas).* We know it, and both demand it and grant the same licence. But not so far as to unite the mild with the savage or that snakes should be coupled with birds, lambs with tigers' (emphasis added). Replying to a question about monsters and hybrids in art, Michelangelo quoted Horace's aesthetic axiom about artistic daring and formulated a forceful defence of the imaginary as a means of expressing inner truths without offending against rules of decorum. He advocated the grotesque as the resource of artistic metaphorical expression, and defended the imaginative untruths of 'the genre of the monstrous' in the name of reason itself:

> But if it so happens . . . a work . . . under pain of otherwise becoming shameful or false, requires fantasy . . . [and that] certain limbs or elements of a figure are altered by borrowing from other species, for example transforming into a dolphin the hinder end of a griffon or a stag . . . these alterations will be excellent and the substitution, however unreal it may seem, deserves to be declared a fine invention in the genre of the monstrous. When a painter introduces into this kind of work of art chimerae and other imaginary beings in order to divert and entertain the senses and also to captivate the eyes of mortals who

> long to see unclassified and impossible things, he shows himself
> more respectful of reason than if he produced the usual figures
> of men or of animals.

This passage breathes a tranquil sense of the separateness of the monstrous from the human; Michelangelo's taxonomy brings fantasy with happy confidence under the individual artist's control. But his wilful development of Horace's critique into a humanist affirmation of the artist's creative mind does foreshadow the future contours of the grotesque in our times.

After the Renaissance, the fantastic moves from an external world which existed in the supernatural order of creation, independent of an individual's imagination, and comes instead to find a new, paradoxically modern and wholly unstable habitation in the single mind of a person, for good or ill; it becomes one with the subject or writer or artist's vision. The grotesque, which nests within the larger field of fantasy, likewise travels from an imagined world of more-than-natural phenomena into an inner landscape that represents the human mind and its phantasmagorias. In the mid-eighteenth century, another related shift begins to take place: monsters constituted of marvels in nature yield pride of place to wonders of the imaginary realm—the witchcraft creatures assaulting the sleeper in Goya's famous etching, *The Sleep of Reason Produces Monsters*. And fables, fairy tales, fantasy narratives and images begin concomitantly to grow in popularity in order to meet this modern appetite for wonders—and horrors.

When the late grotesque finally emerges in all its corrosive comic temper in the late eighteenth century, it no longer dances with frivolous, mischievous delight in its own cleverness and charm, as in Raphael's grotesqueries in Rome; it does not inspire Horace's burst of confident and derisive laughter, or more earnestly exude Michelangelo's identification with the rational genius who dares all; it begins to move to more northerly, macabre rhythms of *terribilità*, rather than *capriccio*, and twists into the personal psyche and its unassuageable terrors.

Goya is the artist who inaugurates the late grotesque—which could perhaps be called 'millennial grotesque'—from the post-Revolutionary, Terror-struck *Caprichos* of 1793–99 to the nightmare visions he painted in the Quinta del Sordo a decade and a half later. The artist's innovatory quest to reproduce his own troubled dream of reason culminates in a painting like *Saturn Devouring His Child* and founds an aspect of modern sensibility, in its ghastly hyperbole, despair, and rage. But Goya does not resolve the tension between observation of the world and inner imaginings: the strength of his art rises from this troubled conflict.

One of his notebook pen-and-wash drawings contrasts these two ways of beholding, the outer and the inner eye, and the two corresponding modes of the grotesque. It shows a boy looking through a peep-hole at the visions inside a camera obscura—so rapt at the sight that he does not sense a younger child behind him, who is gleefully looking up his exposed bottom, with a huge grin on her face. 'Tuti li mundi' ('All the world') wrote Goya on the drawing, the name given to the peepshow or magic lantern. His melancholic words refer ironically to this spectacle—the common human fundament that makes all equal—as well as to universal human prurience, no doubt. The curious girl confronts experience directly, an Enlightenment empiricist, as it were, looking at a natural phenomenon—a boy's bottom—while the victim of her mirth is a proto-Romantic, enjoying the fantastic world of spectacle, through the medium of an optical, fairground device. Thus, in what appears itself to be a documentary sketch, Goya records with mordant humour two modes of looking, two kinds of spectacle, and two varieties of excitement delivered by entertainment.

We cannot know whether the peep-show reveals to the boy wondrous sights of the real world, or ghosts and apparitions and other supernatural inventions; both types of marvel were popular fare in this kind of amusement. But as it is thought that Goya's own phantasmagorias were influenced by itinerant showmen in Spain at the time, the drawing may encapsulate his artistic span, from an observed record of the world, with all its forbidden, monstrous and singular elements, to invented representations that do not necessarily have a referent in the natural world, that make manifest what exists only as spectre or phantasm.

The grotesque and the monstrous are closely associated, but a workable and helpful distinction can be made: one belongs to the order of representation, the other to the order of nature. The first would describe, possibly, the hidden image inside Goya's peep-show, the other the sight of the boy's bare bottom. Two ways of experiencing the world, yet both are used to amuse, perhaps to shock, and both can give pleasure, or are at least supposed to be able to. The difference between them informs the history of entertainment and, within that, the changing character of pleasure and of laughter, which is one of its signs.

The transition in taste was taking place in Goya's lifetime, and it brings about the new *frisson* of the modern grotesque. Modern sensibilities have undergone a profound change in this respect: laughter at madmen and -women, or at cripples in real life now offends profoundly against social custom. While a child at Hallowe'en today, pretending to a crook-back and a limp in a witch mask, shares in the pleasures of the grotesque, a child

Two ways of seeing, two kinds of peeping: Goya's sketch of a magic lantern or camera obscura, c. 1803–24.

who could not restrain his (or her) laughter at the sight of a hunchbacked old woman with a hooked nose and warts would probably be referred for treatment. Needless to say, Bedlam or its equivalent is no longer considered a fun outing for the family. But around 1667–70 Carlo Dolci, supremely melodramatic and soupy purveyor of baroque saints' ecstasies, taught his daughter to draw by copying Jacques Callot's album *I Gobbi (The Hunchbacks)*, a bitterly comic sequence of caricatured Mr. Punches from a *commedia dell'arte* troupe whom the artist had seen performing in France. Yet this way of marvelling—and accepting—the diverting diversity of the world was giving way. John Newbery, publishing a lively alphabet in 1765, was already fighting a rearguard action against the rise of fantasy when he illustrated a 'Raree-show' under the letter 'R'. This peep-show is similar to the one in Goya's drawing, but the writer gives a clear preference for actuality over representation, for 'the real thing' as opposed to its imitation:

> Here's Ralph with his Raree-show,
>   Calling so loud
> But I'd rather give two-pence
>   To look at the crowd.

It was nevertheless Newbery's line in fairy-tale publishing that brought him success, not his efforts at fantasy-free education for youngsters in the style of Jean-Jacques Rousseau's *Emile*.

Spectators of the high Renaissance delighted in the terrible beauty that occurs in nature, and their representations or reanimations of abnormalities fill the cabinets of anatomical museums. Francis Bacon had described the contents of the earliest cabinets of curiosities at the end of the sixteenth century: 'whatsoever singularity, chance and the shuffle of things hath produced . . .'. Nature, as observed, collected, preserved and classified used to put on enough of a show to provoke wonder and awe, and continued to appeal; scientific inquiry into the prodigious, even freakish diversity of phenomena filled the medical study centres of the Enlightenment. The Hunterian Museum of the Royal College of Surgeons in London, founded in 1773, still displays, for example, the Irish Giant, who exhibited himself in travelling shows as 'The tallest man in the world, eight foot and two inches high'; beside him in the same vitrine stands the skeleton of 'the Sicilian Fairy', Caroline Crachami, who was shown by an unscrupulous doctor who had promised her parents he could help her; her miniature thimble and her tiny slippers are arranged near her bones: she stood only 19.8 inches high when she died in 1824, at the age of nine, or so it was claimed. In a laboratory jar, miscarried quintuplet foetuses, their flesh blanched by the chemicals in which they are preserved, are apparently ascending, their closed lids and open mouths making them appear to be singing, a quintet of ghostly choristers. This is 'the real in the extreme', to quote a phrase of Thomas Mann: nature's prodigies of difference on display.

The cult film classic *King Kong* (1933) illustrates the difference between the taste for the monstrous in the not so distant past and its presence in contemporary entertainment. King Kong is 'the eighth wonder of the world', an exceptional natural phenomenon like the Ifish Giant or the

Sicilian Fairy, hunted and discovered by a team of explorer-adventurers who want to show him, like a circus freak. But when he is captured and brought to New York and put on stage at Radio City Music Hall, the sympathy of the film changes and veers to identify with his plight. He has been portrayed up to this point as a brute, a giant, cannibal ape and pagan god, who demands human sacrifice and eats his victims raw, like the Cyclops. But a new feeling for him begins to flow until his final tragic destruction on the pinnacle of the Empire State Building. Within the film's story he is a spectacular monster, but the effect of his automated figure, his rampage, his rolling eyes, his flaring nostrils as he examines Fay Wray in his huge palm produces the *frisson* of disgust and pleasure combined, the response that can be caught under the rubric of the grotesque. Horror and laughter are appropriate responses; fascination and disgust coexist.

The contemporary taste for this state of mixed feelings no longer requires that the objects of the representation be monstrous in the first place: the atmosphere of a work can be utterly grotesque, exciting ghastly merriment, even when the forms it deploys are not disfigured, unnatural, outlandish or even curious; the thrust of the grotesque today, in comics, in the *X-Files* television series, in fashion, even, pushes the ordinary into the realm of the peculiar and alarming, so that the light of common day itself clouds and curdles.

When Goya inscribed his print of the dreamer at the table, 'El sueño de la razón produce monstruos', did he mean that monsters arise when reason relaxes its vigilance? Or did he mean, rather, that reason itself dreams up monsters? The Spanish *sueño* means dreams as well as sleep, and Goya had originally planned to banish monsters and creatures of the dark with his series *Los Caprichos*—they were to express 'the solid testimony of truth'. This most famous etching of all Goya's graphic work was intended as the frontispiece and can thus be read *prima facie* as a plea for reason to wake up and banish the monsters. (This interpretation recurs in later, children's materials intending to reassure.)

An early drawing for the print was also enigmatically inscribed 'Universal Idiom', and this communicates how universally vulnerable humans are, in an unconscious state, to such figments. These are nightmares, but the sufferer—with whom Goya identified himself as 'El autor soñando' (the author dreaming)—has fallen asleep by day: he is fully dressed and slumped at a table, perhaps even a desk—suggesting that, in the midst of ordinary 'rational' tasks, consciousness can be assailed by terrors and be

In a sketch for the most famous image of Los Caprichos, *Goya shows himself haunted by human spectres, rather than the owls and bats and symbols of witchcraft in the final print.* The Dream of Reason Produces Monsters, 1793–99.

made the means of their expression. In another preliminary drawing for the print, the top left-hand corner swarms with human faces, some with oddly familiar smiles and confiding looks, very much like apparitions in a dream of persons, known and unknown, but turned insinuatingly intimate by the quality of dreaming itself. Others are more diabolical, one screaming, another grimacing, like the demons under the dancing *bobalicón's* arms. There are owls in the drawing, but the birds do not dominate the monsters troubling the dreamer as in the final print, where the phantasmagoria of witchcraft has crowded out the uncanny human phantoms, and one of the owls actually grasps the artist's chalk holder in one claw and appears to be prodding him awake with it.

The owl's urging also prompts a different, more deeply troubling reading of the print's title. The genitive—the 'sleep/dream *of* reason'—makes the sentence ambiguous, for it can read that reason's own dreams are filled with demons; that reasonable men (and women), like the artist himself, are prey to irrational forces. Are the owls and bats—creatures of the Sabbath orgies—conjured by the sleeper's mind, even while they swarm to attack him? Or are they rushing in from outside, emanations of a supernatural that does exist, the moment reason lets down its guard? Is such a dreamer able to see that what others fail to acknowledge is all too much there, doing its worst? In the print version, a cat—an animal that prowls by night and is gifted with seeing in the dark—lies alert at the sleeper's side, its pale, inner-lit eyes open wide.

'I'll have you know,' wrote the painter in a letter, 'I'm not afraid of witches, spirits, phantoms, boastful giants, rogues, knaves, etc., nor do I fear any kind of beings except human ones.' His work savages ignorance, superstition and stupidity: he derides his fellow human beings. But his scepticism about the phantasmagoric, expressed overtly and consciously, is conveyed rather more waveringly by the imagery he deploys than by his protests and his political courage and enlightened stand. These restless questions enrich Goya's work, keying up the feverishness of his imaginings. Similar problems with meaning, and consequently with appropriate responses, permeate the grotesque, which gives above all an experience of conflicting feelings: horror and derision, amusement and fright all at once.

Goya's scabrous vision of human folly often draws on popular merrymaking and its rituals; though it is difficult to register the spirit in which he made his images, he was observing laughter and fun, Carnival and celebration. He represents again and again the *gigantes* and *kilikis* (giants), the *cabezudos* (big heads), *botargos* and *botargas*—devils and she-devils—*tarascas, cocos* and *cocas*. His painting, *The Burial of the Sardine (c.*1808–14, Pl. 3) captures an enigmatic Ash Wednesday ritual, which is still performed in certain parts of Spain: a grand reception for Momus, the god of mockery, opens the proceedings, and the day ends with the solemn interment of a fish, to mark the *carne vale*, the farewell to flesh at the start of Lent. The composition packs in a cavorting crowd; above the revellers, a banner shows a grinning fool, another great booby, or *bobalicón*. And in his notebooks Goya sketches the street parades and merrymaking, including the statues, giants and masks that were and still are brought out on certain feast days, like Corpus Christi, as in the case of the Patum. Goya lingers on the compelling and unsettling ambiguity of such inanimate figures; he chooses to represent Carnival banners and to paint games involving dummies and puppets. Popular effigies clearly held alarm and fascination for him; he vividly communicates their dread animation and uncanny jollity, in numerous fluid pen-and-ink drawings. But his emphases and exaggerations only ironize the sense of vitality he communicates so surely: a male scarecrow figure capers, a golliwog-like masked merry-maker with a huge head and bristling hair stares out goggle-eyed, a bedizened duenna cavorts. All of them seem trapped in their raucousness—fools of fun.

For Baudelaire, writing about caricaturists, Goya was a 'far more modern [spirit] than Cervantes . . . [with his] love of the ungraspable . . . [his] feeling for violent contrasts, for the blank horrors of nature'. Goya understood fantasy's overmastering power from within more intensely than most. The last years of his life saw the making of not only the *Black Paintings*, but also that other searing set of prints, the *Disparates* (1819–24), meaning 'follies', so called after the captions that Goya wrote on the proof sheets of thirteen images. Again, Goya's scathing method excites contradictory emotions in the viewer, for in the midst of satirizing the absurdities of human behaviour, he summons objects of terror, like the *bobalicón*.

In the *Folly of Fear*, for example, a huge ghost-like shrouded spectre, not unlike the *coco* from *Los Caprichos*, rises up before tiny men, whom it dwarfs. The artist mocks the soldiers' panic, for the small figure concealed inside the phantom, like the manipulators of Carnival *gigantes*, can just be glimpsed, clutching the grey, shroud-like wrappings. In *Feminine Folly*, a ring of four women toss a figure up and down in a blanket; another group in *Merry Folly* also appears to be giving someone 'the Bumps'. For Goya, stone-deaf at the end of his life, such larking and roistering would have been wrapped in silence, effectively cutting him out: such scenes then turned into pure spectacle and, through the equally muffled medium of art, he draws us into his experience of alienation and nightmare, of savagery and greed.

Modern eyes that envision the grotesque and then make it palpable for others are turned inward. Vision in this case does not gaze at horrifying or awesome objects outside itself but conjures spectres within. It is interesting that terms for new, inner fantasies are nineteenth- or even twentieth-century introductions into English (and French), such as the imaginary or *imaginaire* (the adjective used as a noun), phantasm or *phantasme*, and phantasmagoria *(phantasmagorie)* itself. The dreams of reason, as dreamed by modern imaginations since the eighteenth century, as evoked by Goya in his art, conduct us into painful subjectivities, where disturbing fantasies provoke powerfully mixed feelings. Terry Castle, in her entertaining and cogent book *The Female Thermometer*, argues that the eighteenth century invented the uncanny: 'the historic Enlightenment internalization of the spectral—the gradual reinterpretation of ghosts and apparitions as hallucinations, or projections of the mind—introduced a new uncanniness into human consciousness itself.' The familiar and unfamiliar shift, collide, and merge. Scepticism becomes one of the best defences against such fantasies, but it proves difficult, as Goya shows, to hold fast to its paradoxical conviction.

The late, or millennial grotesque contemplates monsters of its own creation that exist outside the borders of the actual and take visible forms in every state of the unconscious or hyperconscious mind—dream, reverie, fantasy, phantasm, hypnagogic hallucination, trance, vision, rapture, nightmare, plain night thoughts when sleeping—and its vehicles have increasingly become popular entertainment, from print to celluloid to pixels. If such materials put forward a claim today to make manifest objective phenomena, as in religious belief, it is a very weak one, but the reflex of laughter at demons and monsters still arises, and its efficacy seems more and more trusted. Monsters no longer swarm in religious imagery, but in science fiction and in children's books. They are not identified—and this must be progress of a kind—with prodigious births, sports of nature, exotic marvels. They have taken up their dwelling place inside the minds of people instead, and this poses certain new problems as to their control. The thrill they inspire blends shuddering, wonder, laughter, even sniggering. This function is related to placatory and apotropaic uses of horror and terror, as we have seen, but that does not exhaust its range of uses. Jean-Pierre Cèbe comments in *La Caricature et la parodie dans le monde antique*: 'Besides, it should be noted that from any point of view it is the laughter that is provoked by the grotesque and not the grotesque in itself that was considered apotropaic.'

The squealing laughter that erupts during horror movies, or even at moments of violence in adventure films and thrillers, expresses an attempt not to be touched, not to be moved, to overcome the more usual response of fear. The cultural change that has taken over since the 1980s can be felt in the difference between Hitchcockian suspense, in the cult classic *Psycho* (1960), for example, and pitiful horror in David Lynch's early film *The Elephant Man* (1980), between the tension of spare, superb thrillers such as Billy Wilder's *Double Indemnity* (1944), or Henri-Georges Clouzot's *Les Diaboliques* (1954), and the baroque glut of Peter Greenaway's *The Cook, the Thief, His Wife & Her Lover*, a film that brilliantly caught the flaunting greed and brutality of the Thatcher–Reagan years. Although the conventions of *film noir* still profoundly colour some movies, the taste of contemporary fear has become less double espresso; its flavour has more of the flaunty cocktail about it, mixed, coloured liquors swirling, as dread and pity mingle. The Elephant Man's physical deformities inspire complex emotions compared to the psychical perversities of Hitchcock's killers.

The types of monster conjured in *The Thing* (1951) or *The Fly* (1986) once belonged in a speciality genre aimed at a minority taste, but they now exercise a new, sympathetic charm in commercially released children's films like Steven Spielberg's *E.T.* (1982) and *Gremlins* (1984). The phantasmagoric imagination of the writer H.P. Lovecraft, mining the bizarre

A colossal spectre looms and threatens an encampment of soldiers: Goya may be mocking their terror by suggesting the ghost is nothing but a prank. Or is this another bitter allegory of war? Folly of Fear, *1819–24.*

recesses of ghastliness and pleasure, has exercised a profound influence on the trooping aliens and hobgoblins of contemporary entertainment. Visual technology has almost caught up with his linguistic ability to invent: 'Radiates, vegetables, monstrosities, star spawn—whatever they had been, they were men!' Ever more ingenious special effects and computer-generated imaging intensify the impact of the grotesque, which has migrated from marginal categories of science fiction and splatter movies into the multiplex venues of the high street. Fantastic alien predators inhabit horror movies like *The Day of the Triffids* (1962) but have been entirely domesticated now in popular entertainment, like *A Nightmare on Elm Street* (1984), *The X-Files* and related cult movies such as the unhinged suburban nightmares of David Lynch: *Blue Velvet* (1986), the television series *Twin Peaks* (1992) and *Lost Highway* (1997). Jeunet & Caro's spookily imaginative *The City of Lost Children* (1995), a powerful, dark fairy tale, explores the ancient terror of child-snatching against a monochrome cityscape of industrial ruins, dripping hulks and looming oil rigs, roamed by the one-eyed robotic henchmen of Krank, a lugubrious mad scientist. Krank, who recalls such spectres of the early cinema as the vampire Nosferatu (1921), kidnaps children, shuts them in sarcophagi and wires them up to his sick mind (he lives up to his name) in order to provide him with innocent dreams. His endeavour is not entirely successful, since the children have nightmares as well (of course).

These developments in movie entertainment are shadowed by publishing: the success of juvenile horror stories has been followed by new lines in tales of 'psychic adventure', also thronged with hybrids, chimerae, monsters of ever more ingenious and horrific devising. They seek to place the monstrous at a very great distance from ourselves: as a third kind, with whom we might have close encounters but who remain different. In this way, the frighteners and the bogeymen are expelled into space. They threaten, they invade, they snatch bodies and take possessions of minds, but these late fairy tales often promise deliverance and victory. It is for this reason, perhaps, that they have settled so well in children's books and on video shelves.

But the phenomenon is not confined to graphics and spectacles that portray the bogey as less than human. The late grotesque is a mood, not only a style, and the despairing raillery at human folly that Goya epitomizes reverberates in thrillers like *The Usual Suspects* (1995), and *Seven* (1995). They do not stage any out-of-body experiences or fabricated monsters but render the world strange and monstrous through innuendo and excess; they also connect with the diabolical terrors of the past, for they presuppose forces of evil actively at work, though furtive and concealed. The devil's laughter echoes in the characters' behaviour (the arch-plotter in *The Usual Suspects* fools everyone and even, in the last shot, limps away like Old Nick himself). But it is also incited in the audience: Quentin Tarantino crystallizes this contemporary grotesque humour of mockery in the scene in *Pulp Fiction* (1994) when Vincent Vega (John Travolta) kills the passenger in the back seat by mistake, bespatters the car with blood and gore and bits of brains, and then can only think about how on earth he and his co-hit-man (Samuel L. Jackson) are going to clean up the mess. The disparity between the callous, domestic trivia of their anxieties and the magnitude of the horror is appallingly funny—it induces the new laughter of what I have called the late grotesque. It is another symptom of the new sympathy

OPPOSITE   *Aliens, both benign and malign, live amongst us.* Men in Black, *1997.*

which this type of amusement inspires that the aliens in *Men in Black* are for the most part benign, in some cases larky and funny and winning. A terrifying Scylla of an alien mother gives birth, her tentacles whiplashing the hero, in an emergency delivery in the car on the way to hospital; once delivered, however, the alien baby is photographed as tenderly as if it were a falling star, not a squid, as it blinks into new life and waves its snaky limbs. Laughter greets these entertainments: a new kind of laughter, full of rancid sympathy. The monstrous are not strangers, after all, but the appalling potential of human evil. 'The plague of fantasies' does indeed reflect the unbearable features of the real.

A crucial distinction between Renaissance grotesque and this newly spawned late, irrational, Counter-Enlightenment derivative can be made in terms of the response. Horace may have mentioned scornful laughter as one possibility, but the contemporary popularity of the mood excites a new *rasa* which identifies far more closely with today's chimerae. Far from remaining an atavistic, rustic, antique, even fusty area of imaginative life, the grotesque style has undergone a change and expanded its reach. The treatment of monsters in fairy tales, first for an adult readership in the late seventeenth century, and progressively for a young audience thereafter, has contributed decisively to this shift in taste. The anti-heroes of popular stories, like the ugly suitor in Charles Perrault's fairy tale of 1697, 'Riquet à la houppe' (Ricky with the Tuft), or the hissing *Serpentin vert* or Great Green Worm in Marie-Catherine d'Aulnoy's tale of that name, offer a vision of the monstrous redeemed by the grotesque. Fantasy beasts may ape human beings in order to mock them, but representations stage their presence in order to think with them, through them, about what it means to be human, as we shall see in the next chapter, which looks at the transformations of men into beasts under Circe's spell.

XII

CIRCE'S SWINE: 'WIZARD AND BRUTE'

There was a lady loved a swine,
'Honey!' said she;
'Pig-hog, wilt thou be mine?'
'Hunc!' said he.

'I'll build thee a silver sty,
Honey,' said she;
'And in it thou shalt lie!'
'Hunc!' said he.

'Pinned with a silver pin,
Honey!' said she;
'That thou mayest go out and in.'
'Hunc!' said he.

'Will thou have me now,
Honey?' said she;
'Speak, or my heart will break,'
'Hunc!' said he.

Walter Crane, *The Baby's Opera*, 1877

Changes of shape underpin the imaginative structure of Ovid's universe; they constitute the fundamental principle of nature, a rationale for its mysteries. Metamorphosis explains the song of the nightingale, the deformities of Scylla, the constellation of the Little Bear, the brittle florets of coral, the hyacinth's curly petals. Shapeshifting restores order by rationalizing the phenomena, by telling stories of origins and trajectories.

One of the companions of Odysseus, changed into a swine, squats by Circe's loom; in this comic representation, the enchantress offers a grotesque Odysseus her drugged wine. Black-figure vase painting, Bœotian, c. fifth century B.C.

The Christian commitment to an embodied self by contrast envisages identity inhabiting a particular form whose unique integrity will be perfected in heaven. Yet the seductive invitation of metamorphosis—of turning into something other—has continued to suffuse fantasies of identity, on the one hand holding out a way of escape from humanity, on the other annihilating the self. The hope of shape-shifting underpins many fairy tales, of the 'Beauty and the Beast', 'Ugly Duckling' or *Water Babies* type. Metamorphosis is possibly the most inventive and rewarding manœuvre that can be made in the face of fear: to change into a beast, to turn the monster into a person can effectively reverse the process of demonization and correspondingly place the terror in a different perspective. This alteration of angle is one of the blessings that comedy can also bestow.

Circe, the Homeric goddess who turns Odysseus' men into swine, is a mistress of such changes of shape, and in her case she has been commonly inculpated for the degradation—the loss of self—they signify. And yet, in Books X and XII of the *Odyssey* and in later tradition she is also a wise woman, who knows all kinds of secrets of survival, as well as an enchantress, an expert in love and pleasure who presides over a bower of bliss, as Calypso did before her, detaining Odysseus for seven years. Circe's charms are more ambiguous than her counterpart Calypso's; her figure poses a crucial dilemma. Responses to her myth reflect ideas about humanity and inhumanity, duty and pleasure, heroism and effeminacy, chastity and sensuality. But above all Circe is comic in the true sense: she can be read as embodying a denial of the importance of being earnest. She occupies the area where humour overlaps with amusement, not jokes. She does not seem so on the face of her story, because the moralizing tendency in her aesthetic history has glamorized her vice and dalliance, turning her into a terrifying witch, a serious *femme fatale*. But she represents the comic in a deeper, less uproarious sense than jesting. First, her story enjoys its own sophistication, as it conveys irony about serious, high matters, and claims lightness as a good; second, her realm embodies the grotesque, another form of mordant humour, when she mocks human littleness and vanity with her transmutations of men into beasts. Milton was not sympathetic to Circe, but he caught this central trait of her literary function when he invented a son for her and gave him the name Comus, personification of revelry and enchantment. In Milton's masque, Comus has inherited his mother's magic and, from his father, Bacchus, wicked ways with wine, women and song. From St. Augustine to James Joyce, male imaginations have worried at the fascination the figure of Circe exerts.

Flanked by two of his transformed men, Odysseus rushes on Circe with his sword; to her surprise, she cannot change him into a beast as well. Etruscan sarcophagus, mid-fourth century B.C.

In *Endymion* Keats exclaimed, with over-zealous recoil:

> And all around her shapes, wizard and brute,
> Laughing, and wailing, groveling, serpenting,
> Showing tooth, tusk, and venom-bag, and sting!
> O such deformities!

Imagining transformations has provided a lively enduring framework on which hang definitions of what it means to be human and, hence, what it means to lose human status—a comic position, when it is not tragic. Inventing faces for terrors or redrawing their features in a changed shape represents a way of coping with them, of making them familiar, of turning them into sources of pleasure and even merriment. The invention of anomalies, aliens and whole teratological systems develops a theme and supplies characteristic visual and verbal imagery that first enters the tradition with the classical genealogies of the gods and their monstrous brethren, and, more psychologically, with the figure of Circe. Homer's witch has the power to abolish the human order and re-establish the monstrous one and she consequently offers a richly polyvalent figure for the exploration of this area of human definition. When the question of virtue seems more complicated than controlling the brutishness in human nature, figures who have cast brutes in a different light offer a way out of the moral impasse around sexuality and greed, and they help to redefine the passions with ironical self-knowledge, and in a lighter mood. Still, the laughter that the grotesque and the monstrous inspire can leave a tart aftertaste.

❖   ❖   ❖

Circe's knowledge is 'baneful', so Homer tells us; she is *polypharmakon*, skilled at many decoctions and philtres, a fitting match for Odysseus, who is *polymetis*, of the many devices and *polytropos*, of many shifts and turns. Her powers of enchantment are transformative, above all: she can change men's shapes. In the *Odyssey* she turns the companions of the hero into swine, but mountain wolves and lions also roam her grounds, and in later mythographers' and poets' interpretations, her zoomorphic range extends even beyond mammals: Machiavelli lined up a menagerie, including a giraffe, and the Italian cobbler *savant* Giambattista Gelli even included, in his *Circe* of 1548, a hare, a snake, an ostrich and an oyster, who all defend life in her merry zoo. This was a highly successful work, quickly translated into French and English and Spanish, that disseminated a sanguine vision of the animal state.

One of the earliest monumental works to depict the first Circean episode of Book X of the *Odyssey* is an Etruscan sarcophagus from the late fourth century BC; one sculpted end shows the hero at the moment when he rushes on Circe with drawn sword as Hermes instructed him to do. The god has given Odysseus the magic plant moly with a milky flower and a black root, possessed of such mysterious protective powers that Circe is unable to harm him or change his shape. When she sees that he—alone of all men— is able to resist the wave of her wand, she exclaims that he must be the promised Odysseus. She then proposes that they make love, as Hermes had predicted she would. On the tomb, the couple—for they will become a couple—are flanked by two of her more predictable victims: they are standing upright, but one has been metamorphosed into a tusky wild boar, the other into a horned ram; both ciphers of lustfulness and violence have retained their men's bodies. On the other end, Odysseus is shown sacrificing the ram, on Circe's instructions, in order to descend into the underworld and commune there with the shades, unharmed. 'No doubt,' writes Richard Brilliant, 'that the representation of Odysseus, Kirke and the monstrously deformed companions on Etruscan cinerary urns reflects the Etruscans' understanding of the perils of the journey to Hades . . .'

The hybrid character of her victims in such images departs from Homer, however, who tells us, a little later, that Circe specifically drove Odysseus' companions into pens and sties as if they were 'swine'. So the man-beasts the artists represent stand in for their internal consciousness of themselves as men, which has not changed, for all their loss of memory and con- science. Homer details the metamorphoses: he tells us that the twenty-two companions were transformed in head, shape, voice, and skin (he specifi- cally mentions bristles sprouting from their flesh): 'But their minds were as human as they had been before the change.' He describes how the meta- morphosed men now fawn, having been made servile in their bondage to the sorceress. This is the tragic doubled condition that the images of war- rior figures with animal heads convey: her victims are not sub-human, but are experiencing being trapped as humans in not-human form, unable to express themselves, only, sometimes, to weep. An arresting vase painting of the late fifth century BC in the Ashmolean Museum, Oxford, painted in the grotesque comic style popular in Bœotia, shows one companion, half-boar half-man, squatting by Circe's loom, vulpine, feral, yet tamed and thereby demeaned.

P.M.C. Forbes-Irving, in an excellent study of metamorphosis in Greek myth, has commented that beings who command ambiguous, transforma- tional powers, like Proteus, Minos, and Circe, do not take their place as full members of the divine pantheon, but remain intermediate figures, unreliable, immoral, wilful, but ultimately powerless before other, higher gods, as Circe is herself subject to Hermes' magic. 'Circe and Proteus' transformations lack the religious or moral motivation that is a basic feature of the later pantheon,' he writes. Their activities are somehow 'inimical to gods and heroes'.

In Homer, Circe is neither an Olympian nor a mortal, but a figure in between, shaman-like in her liminal straddling of different worlds. She is daughter to Helios, the sun, and her island, Aeaea, is the abode of Eos, the dawn; she comes from a family distinguished for witchcraft, Medea being her niece. The derivation of her name is not clear, but one cluster of associations is worth noting: *kirkos* means falcon, or carrion bird, and is related to the Latin *corax*, raven, and thence to Sycorax, the blue-eyed hag and sorceress; Shakespeare, who knew his *Metamorphoses*, catches an echo of the Circean realm in *The Tempest*, where he dramatizes another island that returns to due—patriarchal—order through the magic of Prospero, who has supplanted the island's former ruler, Sycorax, mother of that fishy hybrid Caliban. His protagonist recalls how powerful a witch she was, who could control the moon and tides; later, in the course of one of his magician's speeches, Shakespeare's good wizard takes on the phrases and the cadences of Medea, from Ovid's *Metamorphoses* and Seneca's play. The figure of Circe, the dread goddess associated with sounds and airs, flits behind the shadow of Sycorax, mistress of the isle that is full of noises and sweet airs, peopled with fantastic creatures, dogs and sprites summoned by Prospero's borrowed sorcery. It also reverberates, distantly but surely, in another insular dystopia, H.G. Wells' *The Island of Dr Moreau* (1896) whose protagonist lives surrounded by Beast-Folk generated, in this case, by surgical grafting. Classical metamorphosis thus prefigures contemporary nightmares about possible perverse uses of scientific knowledge, from transplantation of organs to genetic engineering to mutation of cells by other means.

Apollonius of Rhodes, in *The Voyage of Argo*, written in the third century BC, describes Circe on her island surrounded by 'a number of creatures whose ill-assorted limbs declared them to be neither man nor beast'. He draws on a pastoral metaphor for Circe's relation to her menagerie: she presides, he says, 'like a shepherd over a great flock of sheep'. The fawning which in Homer conveys the emasculation of her victims' bewitched condition returns here as contemptible domesticity, tameness, loss of individuality, sheepishness. Apollonius' text sharpens a fear and reproach underlying the encounter with the enchantress in Homer: that the unmanned state of the creatures she has transformed returns them to a literally primitive state, coming before civilization or, rather, set apart from its higher forms. As Christine de Pizan writes in her learned way, in 1400, the story teaches how Circe, 'a lady full of wantonness and idleness', places in jeopardy the manly ideals of Hector, the hero of her didactic text *L'Epitre d'Othea*. Thomas More translated a cautionary letter written by the humanist Pico della Mirandola to his nephew, in which he allegorizes the tale in Christian terms, aligning flesh and spirit with unreason and reason: 'In like wise the flesh, if it make us drunk with the wine of voluptuous pleasure, or make the soul leave the noble use of his reason and incline unto sensuality and affections of the body: then the flesh changeth us from the figure of reasonable men into the likeness of unreasonable beasts, and that diversely: after the convenience and similitude between our sensual affections and the brutish properties of sundry beasts.'

For Christian humanists, the stress fell less on the animal form *per se* than on deformity: in his poem about Circe, 'L'Asino' ('The Ass'), Macchiavelli described her brutes as *disfatti*—'undone'—they are missing ears and tails, jumbled like a game of consequences. The Dutch engraver who illustrated a seventeenth-century emblem book by Joost van den Vondel inverted the noble classical prototype of the upright animal-headed hybrid, and gave one or two of Circe's victims—a pig, a bear—ungainly animal posteriors beneath men's faces and crawling, creeping or rampant motion. In Circe's zoo, systems break down and labels are mixed up and mismatched. Hybrids and monsters result from this mingling of species; she brings generic disorder to natural phenomena, assembling around her a freak show, a variant on the cabinets of curiosities and medical museums of biological monstrosities that were popular among the learned in the seventeenth and eighteenth centuries.

An assemblage of parts not proper to the form—natural bricolage, combinatory synecdoche—epitomizes the condition of the monster in the Aristotelian tradition that was disseminated through Aquinas' teaching. If the transformed men had been wholly lion or hog or boar they would not have transgressed the propriety of natural things; their singularity makes them not individual but spare and strange, irregular and therefore accursed.

Circe's witchcraft also implies mastery of the natural properties of things, which gives her command of their perversion, too: in Homer, she puts something unnamed in the refreshing meal of cheese, barley, honey and Pramnian wine that she gives the companions of Odysseus. As supping together in myth, epic and fairy tale is usually far more dangerous than sleeping together, this refreshment fatally alters their minds; they lose

In Renaissance imagery, Circe's island menagerie grew in variety and strangeness of species; this engraving shows some victims hybrid from the waist up or from the neck down, regardless. Dutch, 1622.

memory of their homeland, and become vulnerable to another of her magic instruments, a wand, which she waves over them, to turn them into beasts. The wand is the *maga's* recurrent, identifying attribute, as Prospero's staff is imbued with his 'art' in *The Tempest*.

Both these methods of enchantment—the drugs, the stroke of her wand—are interwoven with Circe's most potent gift of all: her voice, and its command of experience through language. Circe for Chapman had 'a voice divine'. A modern translator, like E.V. Rieu, calls her a 'dread goddess with a human voice'. Robert Fagles, in his 1996 translation of the poem, renders the lines: 'Circe/ the nymph with lovely braids, an awesome power too/ who can speak with human voice.' *Audeessa*, human-voiced, is her defining epithet, and it is unique to Circe in the Homeric lexicon. Sometimes translators emphasize that Circe expresses herself in language rather than noise or music. But this unusual word interestingly echoes the

Bestial metamorphosis still underlies contemporary fears, as with the science fiction nightmare of the Beast-Folk, victims of surgical experiments in H.G. Wells' fable, The Island of Dr. Moreau, *filmed in 1977.*

word for 'swallow', *aude*, which returns in the *Odyssey* to describe the noise of the string when Odysseus takes up his great bow in challenge to the suitors. The poem compares the action to a bard's stringing of his lyre, then follows this, to intensify the effect, with the singing of the swallow:

> And now, as easily as a musician who knows his lyre strings the cord on a new peg after looping the twisted sheep-gut at both ends, he strung the great bow without effort or haste and with his right hand proved the string, which gave a lovely sound in answer like a swallow's note *(auden)*. . .

The image of a swallow may lie hidden within the epithet that character-izes the sound the men first hear when they approach Circe's domain: a bird no longer much associated with song but with home, nesting in the eaves and returning loyally each summer. The swallow's migratory habits render the bird an ironically apt image to be encrypted within Circe, the woman who tempts the most famous wayfarer of them all to an alterna-tive, eternal dwelling.

The human-voiced, swallow-noted enchantress does not appear before us as an *image* of a beautiful woman. We do not *see* her, as we see, when Eurylochus describes it to Odysseus, her house of polished stone with its beckoning smoke, standing on open ground after the dense screen of oak scrub and forest where her drugged victims, the mountain lions and wolves, are gambolling, fawning not fierce, unmanned by her magic. But Circe does not make a visible entrance into this mind picture: she is conjured up, before us and before Eurylochus and the men, as a *sound*—she is first heard, from inside the house, as she weaves some airy, delicate cloth at her loom, 'singing sweetly'. Polites, dearest of Odysseus' men, exclaims, so that (in Chapman's version) 'the pavement rings/With imitation of the tunes she sings'. We are told later she has 'lovely braids', but the poem insists far more on the quality of her voice.

Circe not only commands through language but is commanded by it: she respects its binding force, its sovereignty over the speaker's desire; though 'baneful', she does not betray her promises, perhaps cannot, since the syntax of magic lies beyond her control. Hermes tells Odysseus that after counteracting her magic with moly, he must impose an oath on her; when she has sworn not to harm him, she will not be able to: words here are indispensable support to magic herbs and permanently binding. Machiavelli later moralized on the potency of Circe's verbal arts, likening her tongue to a snake's:

> I denti più che d'avorio eran begli;
> e una lingua vibrar si vedeva,
> come una serpe, infra le labbra e quegli:
> d'onde uscì un parlare, il qual poteva
> fermare i venti e far andar le piante,
> si soave concento e dolce aveva.

> (Her teeth were more lovely than ivory; and you could see her tongue that quivered like a snake between them and her lips: whence there issued utterance that could halt the winds and set feet dancing, so gentle and so sweet it sounded.)

Artists have made ingenious attempts to represent Circe's linguistic arts, her spellbinding in visual terms. The innovative and allegorical Ferrarese painter Dosso Dossi, for example, in an unapologetically sensual image of around 1518–25 (Pl.28), now in the National Gallery, Washington, DC, strips Circe, twists her at the waist into an extreme contrapposto in order to display her nakedness, with only her fair tresses for drapery, and shows her writing on a chart, her lips parted as she instructs her transformed victims. She is captured in the act of singing—or speaking—with that legendary human voice, and a book lies open at her feet in the manner of a sibyl. In a sumptuous baroque painting attributed to Gerard van Honthurst, in Ludlow Castle in England, lumbering monsters are guzzling her poisoned meal, one of the mutants actually munching on a paper inscribed with the spell, in rather the same way as St. John ate the small book in the Apocalypse before starting to prophesy again—word incarnate as voice-flesh—or, perhaps, in the way the inhabitants of Laputa thought they could learn languages. However, Circe's beasts will lose not gain the power of speech.

It is necessary to read the text closely to see that Circe the legendary witch does not behave malignantly; after she has been disarmed by the hero's moly, she takes the part of a storyteller, a wise teacher, a sibyl, giving detailed, clear instructions to Odysseus about his destiny, telling him how he must descend into the underworld and invoke Tiresias, enumerating the steps he must take to summon the old seer's shade, and stressing the prohibitions he must observe. Prohibitions are the stuff of fairy-tale magic, the knowledge of which Circe is mistress, and which she willingly imparts. As she is Helios' offspring and thus privy to the secrets of light, so she is an insider in the realms of darkness and can disclose the laws by which darkness operates. Her wisdom encompasses these mysteries as well as those of metamorphosis: after turning Odysseus' men and so many others into beasts, she is shown doing nothing more than illuminating the shadows and revealing secrets, for the survival—for the good—of Odysseus.

Circe, dread goddess of the lovely voice, is acquainted with the Sirens and their irresistible song: she warns Odysseus about them and gives him the way of becoming the first and only man to hear them and to live when she tells him to deafen his men with wax and bind himself to the mast. The Sirens, contrary to popular readings of Homer, do not explicitly exercise sexual charms and overcome men through desire. George Chapman overdetermined the meaning influentially when he rendered their song as 'shrill, and in sensual appetite so strong', and made Circe warn Odysseus, 'How strong in instigation to their love/Their rapting tunes are.' Wildly imaginative renderings in this vein proved popular. But Homer's account of the Sirens' charms rather reflects Circe's own prescience and profound magic. They, too, are not envisaged but overheard, and they are attributed 'foreknowledge of all that is to come'. Like singers of lullabies, they soothe and charm and sing of what might be. Circe clearly enjoys this gift, too: she also foresees Odysseus' passage through Scylla and Charybdis and instructs him how to negotiate these—and further—ordeals.

Knowledge of female monstrosity and of ways to overcome or at least avoid its force belongs in the domain of Circe's expertise. In later myth, her black magic, her goety, often includes carnal knowledge. Witchlike, she holds sway over the risky and polluting effluvia of the body, able to curse as well as to bless, to make monsters, to restore youth. Minos turns to Circe, for example, when he has been cursed by a jealous Pasiphae to the effect that he will ejaculate nothing but scorpions and other insects. Circe gives him a brew to reverse the spell. When Ovid makes Circe responsible for Scylla's monstrous transmogrification, he is simply stitching the associations more tightly together: Circe commands monsters because in some sense she is herself monstrous, as witches are.

Yet in Homer, the enchantress' oracular benevolence towards the hero is not limited simply to helping him defeat her own kind. She foreshadows Penelope in more ways than one: her home-making for Odysseus includes the airy webs she weaves at her loom. It is also striking that the metamorphosis her victims undergo explicitly reinvigorates them; once they are restored and free from the hog bristles that disfigured them, they not only become men again, but 'looked younger and much handsomer and taller than before'. Her enchanted castle conceals a fountain of youth, it seems, and it has inspired many successive bowers of bliss where wanderers are made captive to the equivalent of her beautiful bed: the castle of Love in Apuleius' 'Cupid and Psyche'; the island of Alcina; the Grotta della Sibilla near Norcia; the magic castle in 'Le Serpentin vert' by Marie-Catherine d'Aulnoy; even the central brothel scene of James Joyce's *Ulysses*.

For as everyone knows, although Odysseus and his men weep out of longing for their native land, they still delay a year in 'Circe's sacred halls, feasting on abundant flesh and sweet wine'. After they have been restored to human shape, the exiles still have not recovered their full *nostos*, the drive to return to the homeland. Something of her original, mind-altering drug lingers.

The Homeric adjectives—the recurrent stress on 'baneful', 'evil'—characterizing Circe's works, the weeping and laments of the men in her vicinity push hard in the narrative to convince the hearer/reader of the horrors of Circe's sorcery. But this strong conventional opposition between Circe, representative of temptation, unruliness and decadence, and Odysseus or another manly opponent, committed to the return home and all that that means, this insistent and perennial interpretation of the Homeric story does not cohere with the Homeric episode, and it inspired a witty challenge. For the events that unfold in Circe's company and her duct towards Odysseus and his men belie the terror that the traditional exclamatory, morally outraged reaction ostensibly maintains. While evoking the men in tearful and homesick disarray, Homer's story also continues to sing the sweets of Circe's sensual paradise. Any receiver of the Homeric story could hardly fail to notice the contradiction, and a story entered the legends clustering around the figures of Odysseus and Circe, to upset the conventional, patent meaning of the bestial metamorphoses her enchantments brought about.

❖   ❖   ❖

Circe's powers of animal metamorphosis became the point of departure for philosophical discussion of the difference between the human and animal states; the seventeenth-century French prelate and tutor to the Dauphin's heir, the abbé Fénelon, called her victims 'la secte brutale' (the brutish party). Issues of principle and definitions of virtue focused on the loss—or gain—that the companions of Odysseus underwent in their change of shape.

Plutarch, in an essay from his *Moralia* that was once a well-known favourite, introduced a rebel: a certain Gryllus, one of Circe's victims, who refuses to be restored to human shape and to return to Greece with Odysseus. He defends his companions who, like himself, choose to stay with Circe. A pig speaking fluent Greek, Gryllus engages Odysseus in a fleet-footed debate about virtue and speaks up wittily but passionately against the assumed superiority of the human condition.

Montaigne, who was deeply influenced by Plutarch, took the dialogue as an attack on human barbarity and a defence of animals; in Italy, Lorenzo Valla developed this line of argument. As Plutarch also wrote on animals' skills and intelligence, invoking the swallow's nest and the nightingale's song as evidence, and furthermore advocated vegetarianism, his dialogue about the rebel pig was taken as a ringing manifesto in the debate on animal rights. Ever since a 1930s study of 'theriophily', or the love of animals, by the classicist George Boas, the 'Gryllus' has been chiefly interpreted in that light. Michel Foucault's comment that Gryllus' fate expresses 'how the soul of desiring man had become a prisoner of the beast' oddly misses the comic and subversive force of the figure. This pessimistic emphasis also overlooks an accompanying tradition that listens more accurately to the ironic flippancies of Plutarch's dialogue; for the 'Gryllus', as the essay itself came to be known, is a joke against us, against people, rather than a plea for just dealings with animals; it is an inspired early satire in the great fabric of the literature of folly. Recognizing the brute in the human can be one of the most effective ways of dealing with fear, more subtle than confronting figures of terror in heroic combat or in aggressive mimicry, but more ambiguous, since acknowledging our kinship with monstrosity does not bring simple consolation. Gryllus illustrates the long historical relationship between comic resistance and the category of the brute. Thinking through beasts punctures pride; beasts are good to think with (to quote the famous axiom of Claude Lévi-Strauss in *La Pensée sauvage*), especially when it comes to laughing at the very disturbance that beasts and monsters, distorted reflections of the human, hold up before us.

Plutarch's witty, paradoxical exchanges among Gryllus and Odysseus and Circe introduce Gryllus' defiance for the first time in written literature under the resonant title 'On the Use of Reason by "Irrational" Animals'. At the start, Circe tells Odysseus that a return to human shape will bring 'ruin' on his men. Odysseus rejoins, ' "You're definitely trying to turn me into an animal now, by getting me to believe that it is disastrous to change from an animal into a human being." ' Circe presses her point with catty comments about the home Odysseus is returning to, including a reminder that Penelope will be getting on, after all this time, whereas she, Circe, enjoys eternal youth. Throughout the argument, Odysseus remains the mouthpiece—though a rather gagged one—for the superiority of human beings. But Circe summons her champion from the crowd of pigs and asses and lions and wolves surrounding her to speak up for animal virtue, reason and natural integrity. This interlocutor is not the only one of Circe's entourage who has refused to be restored to human shape, as the dialogue will reveal. But he is cast as the spokesman for all those who choose Circe's pleasure gardens rather than restoration to human form.

Gryllus' name itself is a joke, presented as a kind of rude, almost children's nickname, for, when Odysseus asks Circe, ' "Who was he when he was human?" ' she replies (lighthearted hussy): ' "What relevance does that have? Call him Gryllus, if you like." '

Gryllus was a proper name, but Plutarch is mining a pun: it sounds like the Greek *gryl* which gives the stem for the verb 'to grunt'. It thus picks up the imagery of the Homeric 'swine' in Circe's 'sties', as well as returning us to that sound cluster of beastly Grrr! words. *Grylos* (later *grullos*) is not, however, the word that Homer himself uses, but *sus*. Nor does Plutarch's Gryllus show many piggish qualities: he rather engages Odysseus in urbane cut-and-thrust, and soon overwhelms him, Plutarch clearly warming to his theme and deploying his convictions with relish. Odysseus offers to take Gryllus and his fellow-victims with him when he leaves the island—including even the non-Greeks among them, he adds magnanimously. But

Gryllus rejoins sharply, ' "Stop right there, Odysseus. Even you are not impressing any of us!" ' Although Circe dubs him with this jocular, disparaging name, Gryllus himself takes the high ground to defend his choice. Plutarch's spokesman proclaims that the condition of a beast surpasses humankind in 'morality, intelligence, courage and all the other virtues'. Beasts have a soul (*psyche*), and furthermore, 'the animal mind is better equipped by nature for the production of virtue, and is more perfect,' he declares. 'I mean, without being instructed or schooled—without being sown or ploughed, as it were—it naturally produces and grows whatever kind of virtue is appropriate . . .'

Furthermore, animal appetites are restrained, by contrast to human, especially in the sexual sphere, since beasts mate only to propagate their species (good evolutionary biologists!); nor do they choose partners outside their species or from their own sex. Animals are more faithful, and they are temperate in eating and drinking, since they only meet their needs. Their continence extends to material things: they are not covetous of gold, or status, or power. In all these points, Plutarch is taking issue with Aristotelian arguments that animals cannot exercise justice because they lack reason and cannot therefore choose to act justly, any just act on their part being unconscious. Aristotle linked this incapacity to animals' speechlessness; naturally, Plutarch is too sly to draw attention to the difficulty that Gryllus can still talk and furthermore out-talk Odysseus, the tale-teller, the riddler. In this respect at least, his exemplary apostate belongs to that eloquent species with whom casters of spells and mistresses of voice like Circe are identified.

Models of exemplary behaviour in the animal kingdom were frequently cited in European literature, and they made their way into the lively, storytelling bestiaries of the Middle Ages and Renaissance. Gelli's Circe later affirms natural harmony: 'This is just the case with the propensions of mere animals, under the influence of their proper nature, which can't be called force, as it acts always for the best for them, and what effectually most tends to their preservation and perfection.' In this arch extrapolation from Plutarch, Gelli even demonstrates the superiority of the oyster, whose shell offers an impregnable natural defence as well as a mobile home.

But Plutarch was being deliberately contrary and outrageous to the predominant thinking—and delightfully so. The fundamental notion that beasts were ruled by instincts and irrational passions prevailed and was adduced to exclude even a mother's ferocious defence of her cubs from the virtuous sphere of righteous anger. In one of Plato's *Dialogues*, the sow of Crommyon is explicitly invoked (an example cited by Gryllus): her defence of her young is used to refine the distinction between conscious and deliberate acts of courage (human) and unconscious fearlessness, experienced by 'animals and other creatures which have no fear of dangers because they are devoid of understanding'. The speaker likens them to children.

At the beginning of Plutarch's dialogue, Circe announces she is withdrawing, so that it will not appear that Gryllus is influenced by her presence or a desire to please her. Nevertheless, one theme that emerges from his praise of animals concerns the particular superiority of females, especially mythical creatures and hybrid monsters: the sow of Crommyon, the Pythoness, the Sphinx, and the vixen of Teumessus, who also terrorized the countryside near Thebes. As Gryllus expands on the rational and selfless courage of beasts, he asserts the superiority of animals to humans by citing the moral and physical strength of the female of many species. Not only do females defend their brood with warrior fierceness, they do not couple after they have conceived. He also mentions Aethe, the superb racing mare given to Agamemnon at Troy in exchange for a soldier who was reluctant to fight: how much more valuable this brave mare than a cowardly man!

Does this bear on the character of Circe and her spells? Such a view upturns the conventional scale of values, according to which the female of the species is inferior—'a defect in nature' in Aristotle's phrase. It also seems to me revealing that Gryllus fails to observe taxonomic distinctions between creatures domestic and wild, and that he furthermore includes mythical monsters associated with female wisdom and prophecy: the Sphinx with her riddle and puzzles, and 'the Pythoness who fought with Apollo for the oracle at Delphi'. Both could be called avatars of Circe herself, intermediate figures in the pantheon, divine but not Olympians, of neither the underworld nor the empyrean, neither good nor bad, but supernaturally adept, powerful and dangerous. They exercise their wisdom through understanding secret languages, deciphering hidden codes.

Swine, hog, porker, pig are words of abuse in English: the associations of Gryllus, the grunting animal's namesake, persist in spite of the Plutarchian character's cunning tongue. The related adjectives—in English—figuratively denote beastliness more strongly than words associated with other animals: hoggish, swinish, piggish; verbs describing the activities of pigs pass as metaphors of baseness, instincts and low status: to grunt, to wallow, to swill. The suitors in the *Odyssey* are referred to as swine, consuming the goods of Odysseus in his absence. Horace works up the metaphor with mordant moral vehemence:

You know about Circe's drink, and the siren voices:
Had Ulysses let himself go and drunk what he wanted,
He'd have lost his true shape and from then on lived like a nitwit
At the mercy of a sleazy mistress, lived like a hog
Settling down cosily in the mud, lived like a dog.
In comparison with him, the rest of us look rather weak:
As they put it in Greek, we simply don't COUNT. We CONSUME . . .

The hog and the dog, taken at their most negative, the one gluttonous, the other ravenous like Scylla, become emblematic of the monster and of insatiable hunger; as such they act as fantastical lenses, magnifying those human drives that cause profound moral anxiety. Dante does not identify the chief glutton in hell, a compatriot whom he knew, but dubs him simply in death as in life *Ciacco* (Hog). In medieval symbolic schemes of morality, pigs often accompany the vices of *Luxuria*, Lust and *Gula*, Gluttony: Lust looks at herself in the mirror of Venus in the background of Sassetta's *Ecstasy of St. Francis*, painted in 1437; and Gluttony, mounted on a hog, guzzles a meat pie in a sixteenth-century sculpture in the cloisters of Chartres cathedral. *Animal Farm* (1945), George Orwell's famous modern fable, significantly subtitled *A Fairy Story*, relies on some of the pig's brutal reputation to depict the corruption of power. The vernacular keeps another aspect of the tradition alive: high on the hog, happy as a pig in shit. And the latest evolutionary speculations, positing a pre-Jurassic pig as *homo sapiens*' ultimate ancestor, suggest that swine might even convey human primitiveness more accurately than monkeys.

Gryllus' defiance recuperates these instincts—and pleasures—on moral grounds, by discriminating between degrees of greed and brutishness; his clever logic-chopping opens the possibilities of an ethics of pleasure. He explicitly disavows human love of luxury, saying, ' "as Zeus is my witness, there's nothing I would more gladly lie down on and relax on when my stomach's full than deep, soft mud." '

But the point of the 'Gryllus' lies more with mocking human vainglory and hypocrisy than with defending sins of the flesh. Erasmus refers to the dialogue in the dedicatory preface to *In Praise of Folly*, where, in the voice of Folly herself, he lists the frivolous and absurd topics that Homer and Virgil and Apuleius explored when they most wanted to be serious: 'for how unjust is it, if when we allow different recreations to each particular course of life, we afford no diversion to studies; especially when trifles may be a whet to more serious thoughts . . .' Erasmus knew that Gryllus was more than just a noble representative of his fellow pigs; he had become emblematic of a certain kind of refusal, of the laughter that mocks self-righteousness, pride, portentousness and pomp: his *Folly* judges happier and wiser the swine Gryllus than the man Ulysses.

More bitter misanthropes than Erasmus seize upon the Gryllus episode to attack human pretensions to virtue. Machiavelli's *porcelotto grasso* (fat porker) scathingly declares:

> Viver con voi io non voglio, e rifiuto . . .
> Tanto v'inganna il proprio vostro amore,
> che altro ben non credete che sia
> fuor del'umana essenza e del valore . . .

> (I do not want to live with you; I refuse to . . . /Your own self-love so deceives you/That you do not believe there exists another good /Beyond the essence of humanity and its value . . .)

Machiavelli keeps close to Plutarch in his defence of animals, but his assault on humankind is more directly dyspeptic, as one might expect. The enchantment Circe casts on the Odyssean crew excludes them from society, but from that vantage point they expose human shortcomings and follies, clowning in voluntary exile from the human race.

Circe's powers have not, usually, been interpreted in this critical, playful mood. When Edmund Spenser, at the end of the sixteenth century, reintroduced Gryllus into a chivalric English landscape of enchantment in *The Faerie Queene*, he was developing, in the character of Acrasia, a Circean mistress of beasts and beastliness and openly revising Plutarch's character. But he set aside the mocking, tongue-in-cheek grandeur of Plutarch's creation and Gelli's imitation (both of which he knew) in favour of the medieval emblem of vice, and staged a despicable and squalid brute who chooses to be a brute. Spenser shares the uneasiness of his contemporary, Jacques Amyot of Lyon, Plutarch's first modern translator, who included a palinode at the beginning of the dialogue to explain away its mischievous heterodoxy about humankind's inferiority. This 'Summary' was then taken entire into an English translation of 1603 by Philemon Holland. Holland extends an apology along these lines: 'The intention of Plutarch was to show that the intelligence and knowledge of God is the only true privilege and advantage that men have above the beasts . . .' However, as Plutarch could not have known the true God, he is to be excused his lapse: 'This scrap of an argument contains the trial of all heathens and atheists' by showing them that animals are better than they. Circe is crucially at

'Pig-hog, wilt thou be mine?': The nursery rhyme Walter Crane illustrated in
The Baby's Opera, 1877, *makes joyful nonsense of the dangers of Circe's sties.*

issue here: 'the fabulous tale of Circe,' this preface continues, 'by which
allegories the Philosophers and Poets implie and teach thus much, that
worldly pleasure doth make al persons brutish . . .' In conclusion, the
translators hastily pronounce the dialogue unfinished and consequently
unsatisfactory.

Spenser's moral line echoes this: in *The Faerie Queene*, the paragon Sir
Guyon destroys the Bower of Bliss, where Acrasia, one of Circe's sister
enchantresses, rules. Her name means lack of continence, and the wild
beasts who throng her ruined realm are her lovers, changed into 'figures
hideous/according to their minds like monstruous'. In this compressed
manner, Spenser suggests that the men's metamorphoses body forth their
inner natures; they are not degraded to the condition of beasts but exposed

as being beastly within, transformed according to a form of commensurate, Dantesque retribution: when these victims of her lovecraft are changed back into men, 'they stared ghastly, some for inward shame'.

Spenser then names one: 'Grylle by name, [Who] repyned greatly', and reproached his rescuers bitterly for restoring him, 'That had from hoggish forme him brought to naturall.'

The canto's last verse sermonizes without equivocation, as Grylle has his way and is allowed to go back to his grunting state:

> Saide Guyon; 'See the mind of beastly man,
> That hath so soone forgot the excellence
> Of his creation, when he life began,
> That now he chooseth with vile difference,
> To be a beast, and lacke intelligence!'

To which Guyon's guide replies, keeping up the pressure of Christian disapproval:

> The donghill kinde
> Delightes in filth and fowle incontinence:
> Let Gryll be Gryll, and have his hoggish minde . . .

Spenserian and Christian equivalences of beastliness and sin prevail in the English literary tradition, and Grylle or Gryllus becomes a byword for piggery: Puritans and divines and scourgers of folly seem to enjoy delivering themselves of devastating condemnations of his choice, and expatiating on Gryllus' 'lewd immodest beastliness', his 'subtile-smelling swinish snout'. By extension, of course, the enchantments of Circe stand condemned as the dunghill kind: sermons against licence; temperance tracts; denunciations of women, song, carousing, feasting and so forth routinely invoke the dread goddess with the human voice and her lure, of whose irresistible fatality Gryllus was the vivid proof.

In John Milton's masque of 1634, *Comus*, Circe and Bacchus have brought into the world Comus, personification of revelry and wantonness, as we saw. Comus 'excels his mother at her mighty art' and presides over a rout of monstrous changelings, who 'roll with pleasure in a sensual sty.' Through the mouths of the Lady, an allegory of chastity, and Comus, advocating pleasure, Milton struggles with the issue of nature's gifts and their virtuous application within a Puritan idealism. The masque ignores the 'unnatural' hybridization of Comus' victims, to explore the deeper

Circean question about harmonious creation's purpose and its rationale. Comus asks, in a speech of intense lyricism:

> Wherefore did Nature pour her bounties forth,
> With such a full and unwithdrawing hand,
> Covering the earth with odours, fruits, and flocks,
> Thronging the seas with spawn innumerable,
> But all to please and sate the curious taste?

The Lady rejoins with an impassioned encomium to restraint and continence; the narrative naturally gives her the moral victory. Even Comus feels 'a cold shuddering dew' as she speaks. But Milton at this early stage in his writing life expresses throughout his delight in spells of words and music, in beauty, not austerity, in pleasure not utility, in theatre and spectacle. He could not be otherwise than painfully alive to the problems such a masque poses; he stages his own poetic arts as a type of Comus' conjuring, invoking his vaunted 'power to cheat the eye with blear illusion'. *Comus* looks backward to Acrasia's Bower of Bliss and forward to *Paradise Lost* and Milton's dazzling and bold commitment to angels' sexual union and the God-made, innocent sexuality between Adam and Eve before the Fall.

Alongside, or perhaps beneath, the loud chorus of disapproval that greets Circe's realm, another complicated, ironical, complex score interprets the burden of her enchantments. It is not so much what Gryllus says about animals that is right as his robustness in puncturing Odysseus' complacency about humans. In this respect, Plutarch's 'Gryllus' anticipates humanist satires about human folly—Erasmus, More—in its jaundiced but humorous angle of view, and his protagonist inaugurates an invigorating vision of the bestial and the grotesque. Plutarch's inventive polemic opens the path to later developments of entertainment: to the grotesque, that representation of the monstrous, which issues a challenge to the authority of reasonable morality and fixed meanings; and to jesting, merriment and other light modes that adopt instinct and play over deliberation and stability. Gryllus' affinity with beastliness associates him with nonsense rhymes; his hybridity becomes analogous to 'Babel and babble', the defining dynamic of linguistic movement and hence production of new meanings and fresh evaluations.

Circe presides over Gryllus' choice: behind the elective beast, a doubled

OPPOSITE *A fawning victim of the goddess. Bronze, mid-fifth century* B.C.

comic mirror of humanity, stands the feared and even derided witch, herself a figure of art, with her song, her voice, her sway over mutations, combinations and metamorphoses that can challenge thought and make settled values twist and turn.

XIII

'ALL MY BUSINESS IS MY SONG'

When the Muses were born and song came into the world, some of the men of that age were so ravished by its sweetness that in their devotion to singing they took no thought to eat and drink, and actually died before they knew what was happening to them. From them sprang thereafter the race of cicadas, to whom the Muses granted the privilege that they should need no food, but should sing from the moment of birth till death . . . and after that go to the Muses and tell how each of them is honoured on earth.

Socrates, in Plato, Phaedrus

Gryllus the porker is mentioned in one other place in classical literature, in Pliny the Elder's *Natural History*, written around the same time as Plutarch's dialogue. His brief appearance there extends the meanings of the mythical man who made a great refusal of humanity and lays another rich layer of metaphor on Gryllus' comic change of shape. It illuminates further the meaning of his vaunted swinishness, endowing him with characteristics that install him at the heart of the history of comic fable and make him a key to one of the most versatile and durable tactics in the resistance of fear.

In his detailed section on the arts, Pliny lists a number of artists who excel in minor genres, citing a much-prized specialist in low-life subjects, for example, who singled out donkeys and barbershops—both motifs with ample salacious possibilities. Then he comes to a certain Antiphilos, who painted public mythologies of the scabrous variety, among them the orgiastic *Liber Pater*, the totem of a phallic cult. This artist, 'in his comic works', writes Pliny, included 'a character called Gryllus, of a ridiculous appearance . . . after [him] such type of images are called grylli'. It is likely that this 'ridiculous appearance' was pig-like, but the character Gryllus inspired a further, expanded meaning for humanist scholars and influenced the satirical, Erasmian view of human folly: grotesque, absurd, misshapen and hybrid figures from the margins of manuscripts were known as grylli. In Middle English, the expression 'grim and grill' meant fierce and cruel; the terrible, hideous giant whom King Arthur meets in mortal combat is described, in the course of a stream of dazzling, alliterative invective: 'Grees-growen as a galt [pig] full grillich he lookes!' In Dutch, the word *gril* came to mean a caprice, whim or freak, and the whole genus of imaginary creatures began to populate the area of nonsense, where nothing is taken seriously, not even meaning itself.

Pliny refers not openly but only by implication to Plutarch's dialogue; and he does not connect his Gryllus with the legend of Circe. But the association lingers as a scent on the breeze, since monsters of ill-assorted limbs, not only hogs, belonged in the enchantress' tradition. He gives no details of Gryllus' particular absurdities of feature, but the character is clearly not exclusively piggish. After him, the tradition awards the generic name to squat, therianthropic hybrids who, like Circe's mutated victims, have animal heads or limbs, or two or three or even four heads sprouting from their shoulders or, masks on legs, have faces where their bodies should be. These grylli have survived in most numbers as Græco-Roman phantasmagorias on antique gems from Egypt, and the language of museum cataloguers echoes the chimerical quality of these inventions: some are labelled 'cock-headed anguipedes', others 'radiate chnoubis daemons'.

Antique gems carved with ridiculous but magical grilli, including a large cricket. Greco-Roman (?) second century A.D.

Classical cameos are the chief source for these humorous grotesques; they were probably used as amulets and love charms—the Circean sphere of influence. Such engraved stones were credited with manifold powers of magic and witchcraft: a mermaid with a mirror could make the wearer

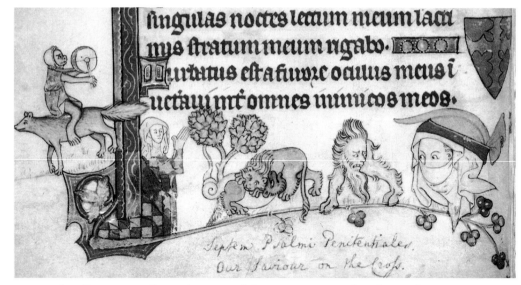

fingulas noctes lectum meum lacri
mis stratum meum rigabo. [X]
turbatus est a furore oculus meus i
uctaui int omnes inimicos meos.

Septem Psalmi Penitentiales.
Our Saviour on the Cross.

This illuminator enlivened a page of the seven penitential psalms with comic marginalia: a striding bearded head, a bright-eyed coquette in a wimple and a monkey riding on a fox backwards. The Grey-Fitzpayn Hours, *English, c. 1300.*

invisible, for example. When people in the ancient world commissioned a curious gem with a strange hybrid creature or a metamorphosed beast-man cut into the stone, they were attaching to themselves the ambiguous powers of protection and fear generated by this source.

The painter of Gryllus, Pliny tells us, was born in Egypt, the word also turns up later, in the fourth century, to denote a certain type of comic actor, a performer in a kind of Egyptian dance; *grullographeu* in Greek meant to draw caricatures. Many terracotta figurines of grotesque subjects of both sexes survive; they represent actors from satyr plays, playing buffoonish slaves or heroes reduced to folly and degradation. Circe herself was the subject of a lost satyr play by Aeschylus, which concluded a tetralogy about Odysseus and Penelope, and she and her lover even look rather gryllus-like, squat and bulbous, in the Bœotian vase painting, mentioned earlier. On one side, Odysseus appears as a pot-bellied, bandy-legged, cock-eyed beggar who is leaping across the sea, his tunic filled by the fat-cheeked winds blowing from each corner; on the other side, Circe appears at her loom, and has been portrayed with a large head and exaggerated African features. The perils—and pleasures—of hybridity and metamorphosis, the idea of human animality and baseness, are inherent in the themes with which the ribald and often Fescennine satyr plays dealt.

The full and exact character of ancient grylli has been lost—there remains only a scant number of references; the form survives most vividly in the drolleries doodled in the margins of medieval manuscripts from the thirteenth century onwards. The grotesque inventions of Hieronymus Bosch were already called '*grilli*' in his own century (Pl. 27). Dutch phantasmagorists, like Arent van Bolton, continued the tradition, and incorporated it into the grotesque. A visual equivalent of the nonsense rhyme, these fabricated monsters are presented not to convey meaning, but to mock it; in this they were sometimes perceived as satanic—as 'juggling fiends . . . That palter with us in a double sense'.

The figure of Gryllus ravels up monstrous beast-men, migrating souls, caricatures, comic players, the mocking of meaning and, by implication, truth; the thread unwinds from a pun, a chief source of dream imagery, fantasy, and the kind of nonsense that shores up anxious spirits with gaiety. Yet Plutarch and Pliny were writing in different languages, and the Latin modifies the Greek profoundly: for *gryllus* or *grillus* is the Latin word for cricket, and Pliny uses it in this sense as well. Pigs and crickets have very little in common, but both were associated with gluttony by the Greeks, who do not seem to have distinguished the cicada family members, confusing locusts, the plague that swarms and lays all in its path to waste, with crickets, who have rather more modest appetites. (Penelope's suitors devour Odysseus' substance like locusts as well as behaving like swine.) Both animals have a domestic character, the pig in its sty more perjoratively than the cricket in the hearth. The nineteenth-century French entomologist Jean-Henri Fabre commented, 'The cricket is extraordinary: of all the insects, he alone has a fixed home.' In terms of Odysseus' unmanned companions, the tameness matches the meaning of their ensnarement by Circe's indoor luxuries.

The surprising associations of the two creatures also prompt another line of speculation, through their characteristic sounds: both make a strongly individual noise. English 'grunt' and 'chirp' distinguish them clearly, but *gril-* catches onomatopoeically the harsh grating of both. This capacity of both creatures to utter—in a manner of speaking—placed them in an ambiguous relation to the human. Aristotle, in his book about the soul, writes: 'Voice is the sound produced by a creature possessing a soul.' He takes this thought further, weaving it into the very nature of consciousness and personal identity: 'Not every sound made by a living creature is a voice (for one can make a sound even with the tongue, or as in coughing), but that which even causes the impact, must have a soul, and use some imagination; for the voice is a sound that means something'. Aristotle notes that many animals 'e.g., those which are bloodless . . . have no

In this most enigmatic engraving, two women lie sleeping in mirror image poses; an apocalyptic sky lowers, naked figures flee a burning citadel and disturbing phallic creatures crawl out of the waters towards the dreamers. Marcantonio Raimondi, The Dream of Raphael, *1508.*

voice'. Later, he classifies mute creatures separately from dumb animals; among the latter, dogs, for example, make sounds expressive of their possible use of imagination, and he singles out insects—specifically ants and bees and grubs—as lacking the imagination necessary for utterance. In his *History of Animals* he clarifies this difference: 'Some are endowed with voice: of these latter some have articulate speech, while others are inarticulate; some are noisy, some are prone to silence; some are musical, and some unmusical; but all animals without exception exercise their power of singing or chattering chiefly in connection with the intercourse of the sexes.' The distinction interestingly shifts crickets, of the bloodless species—and the tongueless sound—into a different position in this aural taxonomy. For the cricket family is an extremely vocal exception to this rule. Elsewhere, Aristotle pauses on the nature of the soul of insects, and comments on the way crickets sing from clearly personal knowledge: 'It is by the friction against the membrane that they make their buzzing, just as boys do through reeds pierced with holes, when they have put a thin membrane over them . . .'

Nevertheless, crickets' stridulation marks them down, among animal species, in an in-between state, near the soulfulness and the play of vocal expression—the sound of boys whistling—yet still exiled from it, and in that song, according to the description of Aristotle, significantly limited to sexuality: a close reflection of hybrid consciousness of the man-beast. Crickets and cicadas were kept in cages, as they still are in China and Japan; one Greek poet wrote an epitaph to his 'songstress'. Longus' pastoral love idyll, *Daphnis and Chloe*, describes Chloe making a pet of a cricket so that its song will soothe her love pangs at night: an insect lullaby. To those who find Mediterranean nights more shrill than tranquil, this ancient application of the crickets' chorus might be surprising. Yet Aristotle himself was sufficiently taken with the noise of the insects to compare them to nightingales, and this is where the figure of Gryllus throws open another world of meaning. The cricket is a bug, but one that escapes the bogey status of other bugs through its quasi-human song.

The insect was famous in fable, of course, from Plato and Aesop on. In the *Phaedrus*, Socrates tells a myth of origin which attaches cicadas by special bonds to the Muses: the insects were once men, men so besotted with song that they forgot to eat and drink. (In their case, the self-forgetfulness of pleasure involved not gluttony, but the opposite.)

The story of the proverbial pleasure-loving insect was chosen by La Fontaine for his first fable, the book opening with the lines that every schoolchild used to know by heart:

> La Cigale, ayant chanté
> > Tout l'été
> Se trouva fort dépourvue
> Quand la bise fut venue.

> (The cricket having sung her song
> > All summer long
> Found—when the winter winds blew free
> Her cupboard bare as bare could be.)

The insect embodies idleness, indulgence, gaiety, heedlessness: the improvident epicurean idler in contrast to the industrious and thrifty ant, who has stored up for the winter.

La Fontaine echoed Aesop when he closed with the ant's rebuke:

Vous chantiez? j'en suis fort aise:
Eh bien! dansez maintenant.

John Newbery, translating for children in the mid-eighteenth century, rendered the famous lines:

Ah, cried the Ant— . . .
As then you sung—you now may dance.
In vain you here for food apply,
I'll feed no idle folks, not I.
You sang your song. How nice, my dear!
Now dance your life away.

But the ironies of these fables are multiple. Hedonism does not stand consistently condemned in La Fontaine's opus, and his biography of Aesop familiarized vernacular readers with the identity of the poet as himself a blithe songster, a cricket. La Fontaine also bowed to Plutarch's Gryllus in a boldly mordant poem, 'Les Compagnons d'Ulysse', in which one after another each of his changed companions, from a lion to a bear to a wolf, insists: 'Je ne veux point changer d'état.' (Not for anything would I change my state.')

The choice of Gryllus here becomes a generic refusal of human responsibility in the name of freedom. La Fontaine relates it with his usual biting sarcasm; indeed, he offers an edifying palinode in conclusion as he dedicates the poem to the king's grandson; but this disapproving moral, 'Ils étaient esclaves d'eux-mêmes' ('They were but slaves to themselves'), autodestructs in midair, with a sly, parodic playfulness worthy of a gryllus lampooning human folly on the stage. As Richard Danner comments in his perceptive study of La Fontaine, 'what really shines in "Les Compagnons d'Ulysse" is *le plaisant* . . . his well-chosen blend of rhetorical strategies exuberantly sings the merits of metamorphosis.' Interestingly, when William Godwin, the radical philosopher, children's publisher and writer, did a version of Aesop, he wrote, without a hint of scolding, 'the grasshopper is the merriest creature in the world; he sings all the summer long . . .'

It is significant that Aesop himself was explicitly identified as a cricket and his satiric fables perceived as cricket's songs in the popular medieval account of the fabulist's life written by the Byzantine scholar Planudes (*c.* 1255 to *c.* 1305), translated in the fifteenth and sixteenth centuries and later circulated in La Fontaine's widely read introduction to his own celebrated fables. Aesop there calls himself a cricket—the eighteenth-century English translation following the female gender of the French *cigale*. 'I never did any one an injury . . .', he goes on. 'All my business is my song. You, great king, have now that innocent creature before you, there is nothing I can pretend to but my voice, which I have ever employed in the service of mankind.'

The creature recurs, quietly but merrily, in fabulists' self-presentation: an illustrator of Hans Christian Andersen in 1900 draws a cricket taking a bow on the title page; L.M. Budgen gave herself (himself?) the pseudonym *Acheta Domestica* (house cricket) for a collection of fanciful natural history tales, and was pictured as the insect on the binding, tooled in gold, with the inscription, 'He filled their listening ears with wondrous things.' Roald Dahl also introduces into James' new band of friends, in *James and the Giant Peach*, a very talkative, suave gentleman grasshopper. (Though these are not the same species, in folklore they are readily mixed up.) The demeanour, costume, and even voice of the cricket have acquired a higher tone—class—since Pliny's Gryllus, a trend that mirrors the general drift towards social betterment in children's stories.

❖   ❖   ❖

Aesop himself was also traditionally portrayed, in literary and visual media, as a dwarfish and misshapen gryllus-like figure: 'They all unite in this opinion,' writes John Newbery in *Fables in Verse* (1757): 'that his person was greatly deformed, that his body was crooked, that he was big-bellied & badger-leg'd, that he had a flat nose, hunch back, blubber lip, a long misshapen head, & that his complexion was so swarthy, that he took his name from it, Aesop & Aethiop, according to their account, signifying the same thing.'

In his legendary biography, the fabulist figures as a brute, a mute and a slave, and the dire extremes of his abject state require heaps of animal metaphors: 'What a monstrosity he is to look at! Is he a frog, or a hedgehog, or a pot-bellied jar, or a captain of monkeys, or a moulded jug, or a cook's gear, or a dog in a basket?' He alarms women with his ugliness: illustrations from Renaissance editions of the biography show him swollen and misshapen and huge, as women, including his employer's wife, flee from him. Later, the goddess Isis takes pity on him and grants him the power of speech. Sold into the household of a philosopher called Xanthus, he begins to excel in witty sallies, some of them ribald. One day Xanthus orders Aesop to prepare the best banquet available. Aesop serves four courses of tongues all differently dressed, whereupon Xanthus falls into 'a most outrageous passion' and belabours Aesop. He responds: 'Sir . . . you

The fabulist Aesop was reputed to be so ugly that when his new master's wife first saw him, she took fright and ran away. Life of Aesop, *Naples, 1485.*

charged me to make the best entertainment I could . . . & if the tongue be the key of knowledge, what cou'd be so proper as a feast of tongues for a philosophical banquet?'

Several such exemplary demonstrations of Aesop's cleverness eventually win him his freedom, his legend turning on his redemption through speech, articulacy, storytelling. In the end, this intimate of the beasts is the victim of far sharper human brutality: he is thrown to his death off a cliff by the citizens of Delphi for refusing to give greater honour to Apollo than to the Muses. An artist as grand as Velázquez portrayed the poet as the nemesis of great men and their pretensions. Locating a passage in the *Vita* in which Aesop's master fusses after defecating that he has voided some of his grey matter as well, the art historian Nicholas Tromans has persuasively identified the vessel and cloth in Velázquez's portrait as a night-soil bucket and washrag, denoting the common baseness of humanity.

Within the fabulous tradition's own account of its origins, the gryllus-cricket's song thus levels the distance between the high and the low, and grounds wisdom in baseness. This kind of monstrosity correspondingly rises up the scale of values during the high Renaissance and Enlightenment, giving a new resonance to Plutarch's clever and satiric entertainment: the name was associated with artists' wayward and original inventiveness, especially in popular or broad expression, as in the pasquinade, or political jest, or in nonsense compilations that deliberately set out to be vulgar. 'The pleasant new work and jests of a common labourer called Grillo, who wanted to become a doctor, in storied rhyme' was published in Venice in 1521 by an allegedly one-eyed con-artist and buffoon, who is portrayed on the title page chasing crickets. 'Grillo' could have been his real name, but it is more likely to have been an adopted sobriquet, considered suitable for such social satire. The cavorting peasants in Dutch art inherited Aesopian and gryllus-like deformity of shape; in the light of the classical tradition well known to the Dutch humanists, these figures have been too easily mis-read as disparaging representations of uncouthness among the lower orders. As Svetlana Alpers has pointed out with regard to Bruegel's paint-ings of feasting, they spring from comic rather than moralizing impulses and share the Erasmian spirit of sceptical sympathy. Bruegel is looking at people singing, dancing, having fun, and his humour helps him tolerate their sport: '[he sees] folly not as something to be scourged,' writes Alpers, 'but as the human condition. Festive comedy starts with the admission that this is how it is, and then goes on to explore the nature and place of such natural letting-go.' In this respect, the sprightly and gambolling progeny of Gryllus are the polar opposites of Goya's spectres, his grinning *bobalicón* and shrouded *coco*.

The cricket's song, emblem of its philosophy, figures forth poetry, light-ness of spirit, refusal to be earnest, rejection of suffering as the locus of identity. The association sprang spontaneously to Keats' mind, when in the last days of 1816 Leigh Hunt challenged him to a friendly joust on the theme of 'the cheerful little grasshopper of the fireside'. Keats' resulting sonnet—far outshining Hunt's—opens with the lines:

> The poetry of earth is never dead:
>   When all the birds are faint with the hot sun,
>   And hide in cooling trees, a voice will run
> From hedge to hedge about the new-mown mead;

> That is the Grasshopper's—he takes the lead
> In summer luxury—he has never done
> With his delights . . .

Song, dance, summer luxury and delights, improvidence have all been traditionally ascribed to the Circean temptress' empire of the senses.

Carlo Collodi knowingly introduced *il Grillo Parlante* (the Talking Cricket) into *Pinocchio*, but his moral fable of 1883 runs explicitly against the grain of the insect's usual carefree character, as if Collodi were extending his moral compass to rewrite the Aesopian tradition. Pinocchio defies the *Grillo Parlante*'s urgings to go to school, telling him he wants to lead 'the life of Riley'; when the cricket admonishes him, the puppet picks up a wooden mallet and in a fit of temper crushes him against the wall. Thereafter, the cricket makes occasional re-entries into the text as the Voice of Conscience or Good Sense.

There are no antecedents for *Pinocchio's* didactic cricket, but as Collodi was a reformer, educationalist and radical, he is perhaps laying a claim to the improving character of fable itself by recasting the emblematic songster as a kindly but preachy counsellor, revising by implication the idea of the comic and pleasurable functions of diverting stories: they can be fun, life can be fun, but both can also be virtuous. Walt Disney, who was profoundly influenced by animal fables, similarly uses the entertainment medium of film to amuse children while instructing them; Jiminy Cricket, who plays a more sustained part in his *Pinocchio* (1940), tries to use Aesopian tricks to persuade the puppet to listen to the voice of conscience and turn against a wasted life of truancy and crime.

When Gryllus opts to become one of Circe's party, against all the conventions and values of his peers, his choice of an animal state not only refers to porcine greed and brutishness but may also have implied, to an audience with a Latin ear, allegiance to those aspects of Circe's enchantments that define the human condition but have been buried all too quickly by the derogatory tradition: the interdependent existence of pleasure and art, of song and language, of dance and expressiveness, of laughter and human survival. These fall under the Muses' sway, as Socrates describes in his original myth about early men who were so enchanted with song that they were turned into crickets. Idleness, pleasure and the arts of language—these disparaged aspects of human existence that are embodied in the ambiguous personae of Circe, Gryllus, and her transformed beastly company, subtly rise in the legend of Gryllus and its tributaries to reclaim value for themselves and the qualities they stand for. Above all, the wanton cricket represents the possibility of accepting common humanity in littleness, paltriness and ugliness.

The gryllus figure acts not only as the imaginary mouthpiece of the fantastic and merry world of fable and fairy tale; it also populates its brighter side. In this respect the gryllus is a close relation of the beast in all animal fables, that long-enduring vehicle of satirical thought. The meanings that deformity of face and figure carries, and the invitation to complex, mixed feelings such images issue, have not been sufficiently explored, for their malign history has obscured consideration of their profound appeal.

In this respect, the phantasmagoria of Hieronymous Bosch, an early exponent of the grotesque at its most curious, is strong evidence of the appeal of monstrous fabrication, for his delicate concoctions have never suffered from changes in aesthetic fashion: they fascinate viewers at a directly popular level of entertainment.

Circean transmogrification dominates his iconography. The metamorphic hells—and paradises—he envisions teem with dwarfish bodies that hug the ground and outsized walking heads wearing hats and shoes. Such monsters accompany the demons that torment St. Anthony, as they do in Bruegel's treatments of the subject, but they are not identical with them; rather they are nonsense made manifest, hatched or spawned in the unholy and disorderly universe of unlikely and fantastic combinations. His visions of bird- and fruit- and mollusc- and crustacean- and fish- and egg-hybrids have invited profuse speculation, and their meanings cannot be pinned down, indeed they depend on their enigmatic polyvalence and impenetrability for their wondrously peculiar uncanny atmosphere. Michel de Certeau has commented, on Bosch's *Garden of Earthly Delights,* 'The painting organizes, aesthetically, a loss of meaning.' He then makes the crucial point that this expression of fantasy, split from all stable referents, relates it to mystical aspirations: 'This metamorphosis is frequent among the mystics: the criterion of the beautiful replaces that of the true. It carries the sign from one space to another, and it produces the new space. It is by this metamorphosis that a chart of knowledge is transformed into a garden of delights.'

Certeau's insight into the pleasure that Bosch's other worlds bring to the spectator bears on the role of monstrous figures in later fantasy materials, for contemporary dwarfs and elves and even hobgoblins often share the caricatural and monstrous appearance of Bosch's inventions, though they are not the selfsame species. While giants seldom confer benefits directly during their lives but bequeath their magic and riches after their deaths, the comical deformed creatures of fairy tale can bear magical gifts to those who recognize their worth. The evil characteristics of dwarfs in northern mythology have significantly diminished in some twentieth-century inter-pretations. Snow White's seven magic helpers, for example, have none of the malignity of Wagner's *Nibelungen* or even Tolkien's fell cosmology. In Charles Perrault's *conte* of 1697, 'Riquet à la houppe', the hero is ridicu-lous in outer shape, small and ugly, so that 'even his mother's heart could not warm to him at all'. But he is witty and bright, and he can confer power and wisdom with his love. Even more interestingly, the eloquent illustrator of *The History of Mother Twaddle* (1807) set the scene when Jack buys the magic bean in a contemporary marketplace, with young girls in bonnets smirking and an old beldame knitting on the ground beside her basket of fowls for sale. In the centre of the engraving, Jack is making his purchase:

> 'Come buy,' cried a Jew, 'dis rare bean for a fairing,
> It possesses such virtues dat sure as a Gun,
> To morrow vill grow near as high as de Sun.'

The 'Jew' is portrayed as squat, tiny, with a huge head, full beard and large nose: conventional anti-Semitic traits, which the transcribed heavy accent emphasizes. However, his role in the story could not be more benign: his promise is borne out, he changes Jack and his mother's fortune, and he occupies the place that a fairy godmother or other benefactor takes in most tellings of the story. This early nineteenth-century rendering unconsciously taps into the equivalence between gryllus-like peculiarity of form and the transforming energy of fantasy. It also suggests an origin for the bean, in contrast to any other fast-growing seed, such as a sunflower: beans lie at the heart of Pythagorean cult, for it was forbidden to eat them. Pythagoreanism was the pagan religion that believed in metempsychosis, the migration of souls from one body to another; Ovid's *Metamorphoses* concludes with a long invocation of Pythagorean principles. The writer and illustrator of *Mother Twaddle* possibly designated a 'Jew' as the ven-dor of the magic bean because such a figure could stand in generically for pagan magic; the bean itself might have been transmitted as an intrinsic element in the story on account of its central role in a magical belief system that adhered above all to a vision of natural phenomena as constantly changing from one thing into another—a belief system that governs the realm of fairy tale, as in the case of Jack. 'All things change, but nothing dies,' writes Ovid at the close of his poem. 'The spirit wanders hither and thither, taking possession of what limbs it pleases, passing from beasts into human bodies, or again our human spirit passes into beasts, but never at any time does it perish . . .'

Lewis Carroll plays with the magic of metamorphosis throughout *Alice in Wonderland*, and he even turns his heroine into just such a gryllus when she nibbles a bit of the mushroom: 'the next moment she felt a violent blow on her chin: it had struck her foot!' In the manuscript draft, he illustrated the passage with a drawing of Alice as a huge walking head on the ground. But Tenniel did not reproduce the image in the published version: Carroll was ahead of his time. Both the *Alice* books, playing with identity through

Dwarfs, goblins, imps, elves share the magical feature of diminutive size: here the simpleton Jack parts with his mother's goose for a single bean. But it will grow into the beanstalk. The History of Mother Twaddle, *London, 1807.*

*When Alice eats the magic mushroom, she grows long
and thin, small and squat: Lewis Carroll's original drawing imagined her like a medieval drollery, a head on feet
such as Bosch might have dreamed.*

distortions of the body and peopled with a fantastic cast of talking beasts
like the Gryphon and the Mock Turtle, work inside the nonsense tradition
of the animal fable. As comic, metamorphic, magic, occasionally
grotesque, savagely critical of adult follies and devoted to treacle and other
treats, Carroll's creations are the most eloquent modern exponent of
Circean sporting with nature and the pleasures that beasts and monsters
can inspire.

Dwarfing characters, adding bumps and lumps that deviate from ordinary human anatomy, has become, in the late twentieth century, a highly
common form of magic charm. Crook-backs are considered lucky in some
parts of the world: in Italy, until recently, rubbing the hump was commonplace. Bes, the Egyptian god of portals, who makes rude grimaces to give
protection to his votaries, was depicted as a dwarf. Some of this ancient
superstition still permeates the totem world of toys. The proportions of the
medieval gryllus haunt characters like Tolkien's Hobbits, the Smurfs
(highly popular in the 1980s) and, the greatest charmer of them all, the
benevolent E.T. of Steven Spielberg's huge success. The Disney Corporation felt confident enough about the gryllus as winning culture hero to
remake Victor Hugo's dark fantasy of medieval Paris and Charles

A contemporary lucky charm: the mascot of the Pittsburgh Steelers, football team. Pittsburgh, 1990s.

Laughton's pitiless Gothic love story, turning it into a jolly family film, with Quasimodo as a cuddly and lucky mojo in their animated version of *The Hunchback of Notre Dame*.

Quasimodo was issued as a figurine; many other squat trolls with pudgy faces and big heads teem on the shelves of toy shops, are collected as lucky totems by individual children or adopted as mascots by American football teams, such as the Pittsburgh Steelers. The stumpiness of many a soft toy or teddy bear appeals to this same comic grotesque sensibility. Santa ornaments for Christmas rarely portray him as tall—but rather as dumpy and paunchy and very short, with again the large head of the gryllus type. The twentieth-century approach to medieval drollery generally cutifies and infantilizes it: garden gnomes, teddy bears, Smurfs, E.T. and Snow White's Dozy or Dopey dwarfs are neotenic, that is, they have retained in maturity bodily characteristics of children. The ogre and the gryllus share a fantastic childishness, but ogres instil the repression of instincts, whereas hobgoblins, dwarfs, elves, little folk have come gradually to inspire stronger and stronger attachment and identification. The Teletubbies, lolloping, babbling toddlers in bright Babygros, represent the apotheosis of the trend elevating and cherishing babyishness. Soft toys are by no means always thrown out as childish things by adults.

Metamorphosis can bring about many kinds of redemption, change foul to fair, fell to kind, ugly to lovely. The sentimental domestication of the gryllus represents a twentieth-century popular strategy to accept, as the original 'porker' wryly accepted, the base creatureliness of the human, to overcome—even repress—the hostility that physical claims, on the part of babies for example, can often excite.

The cricket's song, the emblem of its philosophy, figures forth poetry, defiance, hedonism. Song, dance, pleasure, improvidence have all been traditionally ascribed to the Circean domain, where the senses are not seen as the opposite of reason or necessarily the enemy of knowledge and wisdom. On account of its connections to fable, the creature becomes, as we shall see, the presiding familiar of fairy tale in the seventeenth and eighteenth centuries. Fantastic nonsense, featuring fairies, ogres, monsters, hybrids (as well as talking animals) was told in the Aesopian spirit of play by numerous writers, accompanied by a frothily sugared dose of morality and ironic commentary on human nature. Giambattista Basile introduces the tone of caustic levity about evil enchantments and other calamities that will sound again in literature and other media confronting the fear of the unknown, the fear of the dark. However the protagonists of such tales achieve their triumphs against adversity—by guile or force, by Odyssean trickery or Herculean giant-killing, or by other means altogether—they continue to laugh. Or rather, the authors and their audiences consider the comic register the most apt to their purposes of rallying, consoling, amusing, enthralling.

But, as a final envoi on the topic of crickets, it is worth mentioning that the famous fable profoundly slanders the insect: far from wanton crickets begging from worthy ants, it turns out that, in nature, it is ants that take advantage of crickets. The latter feed by piercing juicy stems of grasses and sucking on the sap; other little insects take the opportunity to follow crickets around, to eat the sap that then oozes from the plant—and ants often drive crickets away from the food supply the crickets have provided. This signal example of animal commensalism, or one-sided help between species, has been overlooked by the legendary defamation of the idle songster, Gryllus' namesake.

So do we discover the fallibility of ancient wisdom: maybe it is time to re-evaluate the reputed dangers of Circe and her phantasmagorias, too.

OPPOSITE *On this Victorian book binding, the light-hearted cricket is paired with the plotting spider—both of them storytellers, but of different kinds.* L.M.Budgen, Episodes of Insect Life, 1849–51.

"He filled their listening ears with wondrous things"

XIV

'FEE FIE FO FUM'

If 'tis wrote against any thing,—'tis wrote, an' please your worships, against the spleen; in order, by a more frequent and more convulsive elevation and depression of the diaphragm, and the sucussations of the intercostal and abdominal muscles in laughter, to drive the *gall* and other *bitter juices* from the gall-bladder, liver, and sweet-bread of his majesty's subjects, with all the inimicitious passions which belong to them, down into their duodenums.

Laurence Sterne, *Tristram Shandy*

 In the fairy tale *L'Oranger et l'abeille*' ('The Orange Tree and its Beloved Bee'), the ogres Ravagio and Tourmentine ('tall as giants and their skin was pistol-proof') are discussing a foundling, Aimée; the author, Marie-Catherine d'Aulnoy, an effervescent spinner of worldly, witty and jewelled stories, has great fun with the wordplay:

'Tiens, Ravagio, voici de la chair fraîche, bien grassette, bien douillette, mais par mon chef tu n'en croquera que d'une dent; c'est une belle petite fille; je veux la nourrir, nous la marierons avec notre ogrelet, ils feront des ogrichons d'une figure extraordinaire; cela nous réjouira dans notre vieillesse.

(See Ravagio, here's some fresh meat, nice and plump, nice and fat and tender, but I swear that you won't have the tiniest nibble; it's a lovely little girl; I want to feed her up, we'll marry her to our ogre cub, they'll make us some ogrillons of a remarkable appearance; they'll be the joy of our old age.)

When breakfast was over he said to the giant "Now I will shew you a fine trick, I can cure all wounds with a touch; I could cut off my head one minute, and the next put it sound again on my shoulders: you shall see an example. He then took hold of a knife, ripped up the leathern bag, and all the hasty pudding tumbled out on the floor." Ods splutter hur nails "cried the Welsh giant. who was

Crafty Jack outwits a giant in a gargantuan contest over hasty pudding. The History of Jack and the Giants, *illustrated by Richard Doyle, 1842.*

'The Orange Tree . . .' was first published in Mme. d'Aulnoy's early collection at the end of the seventeenth century in Paris, but it was also included in her many, highly successful eighteenth-century English editions, and it was through such translations that the word 'ogre' was introduced into English. Fully invested with classical and Christian

An amorous ogre is baulked when the princess' champion conjures a magic field of razorblades. Giambattista Basile, 'The Flea', from Il Pentamerone, *illustrated George Cruikshank, London, 1893.*

anthropophagic and hellish traits, the ogres of fairy tales, successors to the burlesqued villains like Herod in the mystery plays, become roundly comic, and their downfall is contemplated with ebullient optimism. Whatever their might and their magic, they meet their match in the stories' hero (sometimes heroine) and fail to assuage their ravenous hunger. There is humour and gratification, it turns out, in imagining ogres, in contemplating the outrageous scope of their desires, as well as watching the spectacle of their ultimate defeat.

The word 'ogre' was imported into French from Italian, from *Il Pentamerone*, or *Lo Cunto de li Cunti* by the Neapolitan courtier, historian and bellelettrist Giambattista Basile, whose cycle of fifty stories can lay claim to being the foundation stone of the modern literary fairy tale. Published in Naples in 1633–36 soon after the author's death, it contains the first written versions of 'Cinderella' ('La Gatta Cenerentola') and 'The Sleeping Beauty' ('Sole, Luna e Talia'), for example. Marie-Jeanne L'Héritier, a contemporary and relative of Charles Perrault, and pioneer writer of *contes*, also found her models in Basile. D'Aulnoy, whose writings were fashionable and much reprinted in England as well as France, furthermore adopted Basile's stylistics, in her extended lists and relish for metaphorical description, as well as fashioning her own mocking and worldly mordancy from echoes of his cynicism. But L'Héritier and d'Aulnoy were latterday *précieuses* in their Parisian contacts, and they polished and prettified the tales to remove Basile's jocular crudity.

The Neapolitan's tone throughout pays homage to Rabelais, in its comic extravagance and its insistent insouciant bawdy; this may come as a surprise to the twentieth-century reader who no longer expects salaciousness or ribaldry to dominate the fairy-tale genre. Basile's tales are told by old women, and the seamy comedies they offer are inextricably connected to their imagined voices, as well as arising (as it were, naturally) from the 'delicate' matters the fairy tales deal with—erotic, transgressive, personal, intimate. Interestingly, they often take the Circean point of view: the bestial, the lowly, the disfigured are redeemed when the heroine—or hero—arrives at a fresh understanding of an ogre's true, inward nature. Metamorphosis in Basile's stories takes place internally; sometimes there then follows an outer change, from the feared shape of some kind of beast into the human; sometimes, the outer appearance endures but is no longer perceived as vile. This is the redemptive core of 'Beauty and the Beast' stories, which Basile rekindles again and again. These comic stories are 'consolatory fables', a true embodiment of that function of romance and fairy tale to face up to the dark in order to lighten its shadows.

Basile probably collected the tales in Venice and Crete as well as Naples; and by claiming to report women's stories, he continues the tradition of the male author as mouthpiece for a cycle of tales, as in Boccaccio's *Il Decamerone*, and Straparola's *Le Piacevoli notti*. But he takes this literary imposture a step further because he specifically chooses to ventriloquize in the voice of old wives, each one more grotesquely ugly than the next—female Aesops, storytelling grylli, despised beldames and crones, hook-nosed, hunchbacked, boss-eyed, splay-footed, dribbling, crippled.

Many of the stories tellingly go on to unmask false conceptions of such disregarded and brutalized figures; surprisingly, Basile's offhand vulgarity, his lubricious tongue and his Rabelaisian and baroque flourishes of language, diction and fantasy operate humanely, to turn away scorn from predictable targets and soften prejudice. His enterprise confronts fear by emptying it of its rationale, not by vanquishing it in a duel of wits or weapons, as later fairy tales tend more and more to do. Basile's ogres and ogresses can turn out to be sweethearts to the core. This current in his collection runs counter to the predominant dualism of the fairy-tale witch or ogre figure so familiar from the later Grimms' tales. Basile's stories reveal their own knowingness about the prevailing drift of prejudice: they are not Ur-versions, but challenges and reversals—reinscriptions—of the originals, turning the tables on the expectations of listener or reader and teaching a kind of alertness and compassion. Of course, they do so with unalleviated jocularity, so that part of the comedy consists in the material itself: in the very absurdity of a kindly ogre, in the ugliness and folly of a good witch. The irony of this maintains the light, laughing mockery of Basile's dominant tone, but does not altogether undo the wonderful transformations of beasts he achieves.

Ogres are used as stock in his stories: the word *orco* or *orca* designates a character in the same fairy-tale shorthand as 'king' or 'princess' or 'prince'. As with a chesspiece, the naming prescribes a certain position on the narrative board, and narrows the possible moves. Ogres can be properly ogreish in Basile—one, for example, is murdered by the enterprising heroine who renders down his blubber to make a salve for the wounds of her stricken beloved. But Basile also regularly overturns the assumptions of wickedness in the ogre kind. The opening story places the issue of transformation—ogre into benefactor—firmly in first position, when the dumbling hero, lazy, spoiled and good-for-nothing, driven out of house and home by his exasperated mother, meets: 'un Orco, o mamma mia quanto era brutto!' ('An ogre—Oh my God how ugly he was!') The tale then expatiates colourfully on the depths and richness of this ugliness:

> Era costui un nanerottolo, uno sterpo da fascina, aveva la testa più grossa di una zucca d'India, la fronte bitorzoluta, le soprac-ciglia unite, gli occhi storti, il naso ammaccato con due froge che sembravano due chiaviche maestre, una bocca quanto un pal-mento, dalla quale uscivano due zanne che gli arrivavano fino ai malleoli; il petto peloso, le braccia setolose, le gambe ricurve, i piedi piatti a papera: insomma pareva un diavolo, un parasacco, un brutto pezzente e una malombra spiccicata che avrebbe fatto impaurire un Orlando . . .

> (This was a terrible little dwarf, a sprog of the evil eye; his head was bigger than a yam, his forehead warty, his eyebrows meeting in the middle, squinty-eyed, his nose swollen by two nostrils like gratings on a mains sewer, a mouth like a grain hopper, with two tusks protruding that reached down to his ankles; his chest was hairy, his arms covered in bristles, he had bandy legs, flat feet like a goose: in short, he looked like a devil, a boo-bagger, a walking phantom that would have put the wind up a Childe Roland . . .)

But our hero Antuono, like many simpletons of the genre, is not fazed one whit, and exclaims, 'Good day, Sir, what's happening? How are you? Is there anything you want?' And then, with the nonsense twister that will clinch their relationship, he asks, 'How far is it from here to where I have to go?' At which the ogre laughs, and offers to attach him to his service.

So the hero is a kind of Jack: the ogre commands riches and magic powers just as the master of the beanstalk does, but in this version the ogre loves the youth and regales him with boons—first a donkey that shits gold, then a tablecloth that produces banquets—and then, when the heroic fool has been cheated out of both by a rascally innkeeper, the ogre gives him a magic club that rains blows on all and sundry. He gives it to him with a telling phrase: 'L'opera lode il maestro; le parole sono femmine e i fatti sono maschi, staremo a vedere . . .' (The work glorifies the master; words are female and deeds are male, as we shall see.)

The hero returns to the tavern and the magic stick does its worst, until the innkeeper, crying mercy, restores all the stolen gold, the magic donkey and the enchanted cloth. The youth returns home, buys dowries for his six sisters (we are told they are six spinsters as dried up as beanpoles); he also makes his mother rich. And so it ends: 'Pazzi e bambini Dio li aiuta' (God helps mad folk and children).

The benevolent ogre inspires several more raunchy and inventive tales. As Ruggero Guarini has observed in the introduction to his recent, lucid and highly readable translation into modern Italian of the *Pentamerone*, none is quite so entertaining as the ogre in the tale called 'Viola'. The heroine, an abused younger sister, suffers from the malignant jealousy of her two elders. As one ruse in a whole series of attempts to rid themselves of her, they drop their weaving into a neighbouring ogre's garden and then lower her down on a rope to fetch it back. The ogre is having a stroll after gorging himself on one of his great blowouts, and lets go a fart—another diabolical sign. When he turns round, he finds the lovely young girl standing there, and:

> remembering that he had heard once from certain students that Spanish horses are impregnated by the wind, he thought that the flow of his fart had made some tree pregnant, and given birth to that light-footed creature; therefore, embracing her with great love, he said, 'Daughter, daughter mine, part of this body, breath of my spirit, who could have ever said that I would give form with a bout of wind to such a lovely face?

The ogre takes her in and coddles his new protégée—eventually helping her marry the prince of her choice.

Even more unexpectedly, Basile's humour mitigates the malignancy of witches and crones. They act, of course, as the *Doppelgänger* of his imaginary narrators. 'Le Tre corone' (The Three Crowns) contains elements of the French Bluebeard, the German Mother Holle and the Russian Baba

Yaga, and other later fairy-tale staple figures, but again its ripe and blithe humour includes sparing the usual suspects. It is told by a certain Tolla who, in the introductory list describing the horrible old women, is given the geriatric epithet *bavosa*—dribbling. Tolla's preamble takes up the proverbial moral that truth will out: it scents the air like oil, she says, and lies are a fire that cannot remain concealed.

Her tale then opens with a king who has no children and prays to be granted an heir: he is given the choice between a daughter who will flee him or a son who will destroy him. He chooses the girl, because—and here occurs one of the book's recurrent worldly-wise observations—a king should consider the common good, and a runaway daughter, while she may besmirch the honour of her parental home, is herself of great social benefit to others. The girl, Marchetta, is duly born: her father shuts her up in a tower, gives her a good education under lock and key, marries her off to a prince of his own choosing, and then sends her away. But *en route* she is carried off by the wind to the house of an ogress. There she meets the ogress' servant—yet another ancient hag—who laments the young girl's destiny, but proceeds to give her excellent advice on how to handle her ordeal. If she keeps house well—on the servant's behalf—fortune will smile on her. So the old woman and the young strike a bargain, a *quid pro quo*: her experience of the ogress' ways will protect the young heroine from harm at her hands, while the young heroine's vigorous labours will save the servant's old bones. There follows a long description of the crone's physical weakness and ills. The old woman then promises Marchetta that she will be fully rewarded.

So it turns out. Marchetta cleans and sweeps and polishes and does the laundry for the ogress with delicate perfection; the ogress, a clear embodiment of harsh employers, is so overcome by the splendours of the fragrant soup that Marchetta prepares that she swears by all manner of things that she will give the cook all she desires:

> 'io giuro per . . . i tre testimoni che fanno impiccare un uomo, per i tre palmi di fune che fanno fuori l'impiccato; per le tre cose che scacciano l'uomo dalla casa: fetore, fumo e femmina malvagia; per le tre cose che consumano la casa: zeppole, pane caldo e maccheroni . . .'

> (I swear by . . . the three witnesses whose words hang a man, by the three handspans of rope that swing a hanged man; by the three things that drive a man from home—stench, smoke, and a

25 OVERLEAF
In Guido Reni's
The Massacre of
the Innocents,
1611–13, the
women scream as
they try to save
their children
from Herod's
henchmen.

26 LEFT *After*
Joseph was
warned by an
angel in a dream,
the Holy Family
escaped the
slaughter into a
haven of calm,
evoked as a
musical interlude
by Caravaggio in
The Rest on the
Flight into Egypt,
1595–6.

27 *In* The Temptation of St Anthony by *Hieronymus Bosch, 1490, the holy hermit is kept company by a pig, symbol of gluttony, idleness and lust, sins he resisted. His other assailants are embodied as grotesque grylli: combining fish and fowl, metal and fur, nature and artifice, they represent heterogenous mischief-making – devilry.*

28 *The Homeric enchantress Circe*
turned Odysseus' companions into
swine when she lured them into her
bower of bliss. In Dosso Dossi's
sumptuous painting, she displays her
seductive nakedness as she casts spells
from a book of magic at her feet and the
tablet in her hands. In Renaissance
tradition, Circe turned her human
victims into a whole menagerie of
different species. Circe and Her Lovers
in a Landscape *(detail), c.1518–25.*

29, 30, 31 & 32 *Albert Eckhout portrayed an indigenous Brazilian* LEFT *against a colonial plantation; a baby at her breast, a heaped basket on her head, she figures forth the region's riches, which include bananas, seen beside her.* Tupi Woman, *1641–3.*
Maria Sibylla Merian pioneered analytic botanical illustrations of tropical flora and fauna, as with her banana flower and butterflies, published 1705 ABOVE LEFT; *fantasies of the tropical paradise, its bounty and ease, mystery and sensuality, filled Western fantasies, as in Henri Rousseau's* The Dream, *1910* TOP. *By contrast, the nineteenth-century Mexican artist José Agustin Arrieta depicted local fruits as scanty and hardwon* ABOVE RIGHT.

33 Over the corpse of the woman who blasphemously sold a consecrated host, two devils struggle with angels for possession of her soul; their bodies have been scored and their faces scratched out in an iconoclast's attempt to neutralize their power. Paolo Uccello, The Miracle of the Profaned Host, 1467–8.

spiteful woman; by the three things that consume the household: doughnuts, hot bread, and macaroni . . .')

This sequence of baroque swirls and flourishes and curlicues, in Basile's inimitable accumulative style, captures on the page the traditional story-teller's technique of listing and repetition and enumeration, drawing on images both high and low, serious and absurd, poetic and obscene, sublime and earthy. But Marchetta has been warned that her mistress will gobble her up as a tasty morsel, just as she has devoured all her predecessors, unless she hears her swear on the three crowns. This will be the formula of her magic reprieve.

When the ogress eventually invokes the long-awaited crowns, March-etta comes out of hiding; the enthralled ogress gives her the keys to her house and all its contents but forbids her to enter one room. The Bluebeard plot demands, of course, that Marchetta disobey; but, unlike her later, ter-rified counterparts, she is so indignant at what she finds in the forbidden chamber, and so furious at the ogress' demands, that she insists on leaving her employ then and there. Far from preventing or cursing her, the ogress gives Marchetta a magic ring, to call on if ever she finds herself in danger.

Marchetta, disguised as a boy, offers herself for service in a nearby king's household, but the queen falls in love with the youth—another echo of a familiar plot from *Phaedra*, Potiphar's wife and fairy tale—for when the cross-dressed heroine rejects the queen, she is denounced as attempting to rape her. Marchetta remembers the ring; she calls on the ogress, and a voice rings out in her defence from the countryside around: 'Lasciatela andare, che è femmina!' ('Let her go, for she is a woman!')

So through the ogress' kindly magic, Marchetta is recognized and vindicated. The king asks to hear her story, whereupon, in an ending that combines pithy local detail with the cruel insouciance of the genre, he orders that his wicked wife be thrown into the sea tied to the weights of a tunny-fish net, and he marries Marchetta (Basile blithely overlooking her earlier marriage).

The mildness of Basile's villains possesses an intrinsic absurdity that buoys his comic enterprise of sharpening our wits and cheering us up. His joyous dénouements always conclude with a moral that cheekily thumbs its nose at the idea of morality: he is trifling with fables' improving purpose. Basile makes nonsense not merely by deploying bizarre impossi-bilities in character and setting but in the outcome of the plot itself. Yet, for all his jaunty amoralism and rapscallion twists and turns, the casual violence he describes and the self-seeking motives he parades, Basile's storytellers stick to a soft message, which can have the effect of disabling the horror; defanged and declawed, the benevolent ogresses and ogres hardly bring about the suspense or thrills that their far more diabolical counterparts inspire later, in 'Hansel and Gretel', for example. The popularity of his ogres' cruel and grisly epigones in the Grimms, Perrault, and even D'Aulnoy eclipsed Basile's broad and merciful comic manner.

Thus the tone of tongue-pulling rebellion and humorous complicity of later fantasy and nonsense practitioners, of the great tradition of the French fairy-tale writers and the English nursery storytellers, like Lewis Carroll, finds an unlikely ancestor in the urbanely witty and self-mocking Neapolitan writer. Basile's storytellers confront horror to welcome it and sweeten it, to show it up as a fallacy, and even make it homely. He ventriloquizes 'female laughter' in his confrontation with the monstrous. The note of comedy continues to mark Italian storytelling: Italo Calvino, collecting Italian folk tales in the 1950s, noticed the special liveliness of women's voices and humour in the sources he was combing.

❖   ❖   ❖

In Charles Perrault's famous *Contes du temps passé* (1697), ogres' cannibal appetites liven up 'Puss in Boots', 'Hop o' My Thumb' and, through the wolf-grandmother rather than an ogre or giant, 'Little Red Riding Hood'. In 'The Sleeping Beauty in the Wood', Perrault pauses to explain that the wicked queen *était de race Ogresse* ('was of the Ogre race'), an early use of the word in French. Italian players, travelling to England and other places in Europe at the time, were also staging comedies featuring preposterous ogres who try to feed princesses steaks from the bodies of their lovers and who own seven-league boots and magnets of such power that one ogre attracts an iron tower with a princess captive inside it. Perrault and his contemporary women writers keep a light touch throughout, even when they delight in producing shivers and thrills. But in the Grimm Brothers' later, seminal anthology, the tally of blood-drinking, child-stealing, omophagous assailants cannot be made, and the mood turns sinister. Besides the familiar stories 'The Juniper Tree' and 'Hansel and Gretel', many more introduce ravening ogres and flesh-eating witches; only occasionally will a Mother Holle perform an act of kindness.

Needless to say, these writers' collections are the foundation stones of nursery stories in the West, the most popular and accepted material for children's entertainment. Ogres appear more regularly than fairies. In some modern favourites—'The Three Billy Goats Gruff' or 'The Three Little Pigs'—the victims or potential victims of the troll or the wolf are animals, who overcome the huge and horrible threat against all the odds. Roald Dahl grasped the essential when in *The BFG*, he named the cannibal crew of ogres the Fleshlumpeatter, the Bonecruncher, the Childchewer, the Gizzardgulper, the Maidmasher, and the Bloodbottler, among others. Iona and Peter Opie, pioneering collectors of children's materials, remark that this kind of story is sometimes termed 'a swallow tale' because of the amount of devouring that takes place in it.

With the literal-mindedness which is a feature of much fantasy material, death—extreme death in another's jaws—is the most obvious meaning that the ogre conveys. But the precise nature and status of that material or spiritual death changes, and fairy-tale cannibals refract different motives in the story, as and when it is told and as it is received. The plots carry different warnings depending on the sex of the protagonist, which often reflects the target audience. The cannibal is a subject in a gendered plot in which 'cunning and high spirits' win the day, and the boy's own variety has eclipsed the girl's in such stories' transmission since the seventeenth century. Tales of the 'Beauty and the Beast' cycle menace their heroines with death by engulfment, and this obliteration, where a woman's body is in question, often means sex, or childbirth. Psyche's sisters explicitly warn that her mysterious bridegroom is probably a monster who wants to eat her, especially if she becomes pregnant, as such tender meat delights beasts. (I have proposed elsewhere that 'Bluebeard' conceals women's fears of dying in childbirth: again, the threatened annihilation arises from sexual congress, or union.) By contrast, in tales starring male heroes, the ogre's appetite tests their strength and cunning in survival. With his inevitable final victory, the boy hero becomes rich and powerful and gains control of the ogre's magic—of his hen that lays the golden eggs, his golden harp that plays by itself, his seven-league boots, his cap of darkness, his sword of sharpness. These are predominantly tales of social betterment, not of psychosexual anxieties, and humour holds out the promise of a different kind of conversion. In Basile, the ogres may turn out to be benefactors; in giant-killing tales, the hero often becomes a rich prince by supplanting the ogre. Ridicule in Basile encloses everyone in its embrace: hero, ogre, reader. But when the stories are written to encourage children, the protagonists escape ridicule: they form comic successors to the tales of victory over Kronos and other paternal figures.

Ogres' key features in nursery stories have been inherited from the epics of the classical corpus, which are hardly comic and star the first giant-killers and dragon-slayers, often founders of their people, their nation. Polyphemus, the cannibal Cyclops from the *Odyssey*, provides two of the fairy-tale ogre's chief traits: hulking scale and rank stupidity. In early modern fairy tales, ogres are giants, all brawn and no brain, sometimes rich and always greedy: the giant at the top of the beanstalk tries to satisfy his perpetual cravings for meat on 'sheep and hogs . . . [which] he would tie . . . round his waste [*sic*] like a bunch of candles'. These villains do not bestride the world like a colossus. Indeed the grand, imposing end of the lexicon of size does not even apply; they are not colossal or titanic or majestic or even simply tall, but rather made monstrous by gargantuan, humungous exaggerations of height and weight. In the eighteenth-century home and the Victorian nursery, the heroes' assailants are given ludicrous grandiose names like Brandamour and Bombomachides, Grumbo, Blunderbore and Thundel, and their two or three heads apiece do little to improve their wits.

The Brobdingnagians among whom Gulliver lives during his second voyage differ from the fairy-tale kind in their gentleness, but the scale of the pores in their skin 'so coarse and uneven . . . with a Mole here and there as broad as a Trencher, and Hairs hanging from it thicker than Packthreads' fills Gulliver with no 'other Motions than those of Horror and Disgust'. Likewise, ogres of Brobdingnagian proportions in fairy tales are revolting and, at the same time, abject in their ugliness. Some further mark of difference and/or excess disfigures them and sets them apart from the human race: the *oni* of Japan have fangs, the Cyclops have only one eye in the middle of their forehead, the Hundred-Handers are just so endowed; Blunderbore and Thundel of the nursery giant-killing tales have oversized heads in proportion to their bodies, as in the case of dwarfs, who are their inverted reflection.

Ogres are fated to be outwitted by tricks played on them by heroes much smaller than themselves. They prey on children, but the pint-sized youngest and weakest child, like *le petit Poucet* (Hop o' My Thumb) in Perrault's *conte*, Finette in 'The Subtle Princess', or the small and cunning cat, like Puss-in-Boots, challenges and defeats them.

Fairy tales deepen giants' ignominy. In 'Hop o' My Thumb', the hero is abandoned with his six brothers in the forest by his starving family, and takes shelter in the house of 'an ogre who eats babies', laments his grieving wife. But Hop o' My Thumb is undaunted; he notices that the ogre's baby daughters sleep with gold crowns on their heads, and so he switches them for the caps of his brothers. The ogre comes fumbling in their bed for a night-time snack:

'Why, what a nasty trick I have almost played on myself!' he says, when he finds the crowns. He changes direction, looking for the caps, and 'With that, he slit the throats of his seven daughters.' In the morning, when his

The ogre's seven daughters 'showed signs of great promise and had already taken to biting babies in order to suck their blood . . .' But Hop o' My Thumb tricks the ogre into cutting their throats. Charles Perrault, 'Le petit Poucet', illustrated by Gustave Doré, 1862.

wife goes to the children's room, she finds her 'seven daughters, with their throats cut, swimming in blood'.

'She responded with a fainting fit,' writes Perrault. 'Most women faint in similar circumstances.' (This is typical Perrault: dry, mocking, world-weary, and manipulative with his sophisticated ironical clichés.)

'Le petit Poucet' was first translated into English in 1724 for a chap-book; a related series of stories borrows the character and introduces the famous bloodthirsty refrain, not found in the French, which rings out in the castle as the giant comes sniffing for his prey:

> 'Fee Fie Fo Fum
> I smell the blood of an Englishman . . .
> Be he alive or be he dead
> I'll grind his bones to make my bread.'

A second group of sprightly giant-killing tales centres on the tiny hero Tom Thumb, a cousin in puniness to Hop o' My Thumb and star of several impish pranks that neither Jack nor the Perrault hero enjoys. Tom Thumb is born, as a gift of the fairies, to a childless couple, and his mother summons the fairies' further help to clothe him, in articles of dress from the miniature world of Queen Mab:

> His shirt it was by spiders spun;
> With doublet wove of thistles down . . .
> His stocking, of apple rind, they tie
> With eyelash pluck'd from his mother's eye,
> His shoes were made of a mouse's skin,
> Nicely tann'd with the hair within.

Tom Thumb finds himself pitted against dreadful perils: the giant is only one foe in a whole absurd sequence of adversaries with whom the diminutive hero must do battle, using a 'needle for a sword, a helmet of a Hazel Nutshell and a Coat of Mail of a Mouse's Ear'. His assailants include a raven, a bumblebee, and the mess of milk porridge destined for Giant Grumbo, into which Tom falls. 'Old Grumbo the giant . . . swallowed Tom like a pill, clothes and all.' The further escapades of Tom Thumb involve him in many more swallowings: Grumbo vomits him into the sea; there he is gulped by a fish, which is served up on King Arthur's table. Tom Thumb is found inside, a mini Jonah, safe and sound. Tom then jumps down the throat of a miller but jumps out again when the miller yawns; next, he encounters a salmon, and so it goes on—dizzy, larky nonsense in which lurks the dark theme of devourer and devoured, survivor or victim. Unusually, the story of Tom Thumb's adventures ends with his funeral. This may seem to break the rules of heroic fairy tales, but it chimes with the macabre comic pleasures of many traditional nursery rhymes, like 'Ding dong bell,/Pussy's in the well . . .'

English entertainments also feature the stock English hero, Jack. He first appears in early chapbooks, then achieves renown in early nineteenth-century children's thesauri, like Benjamin Tabart's *Collection of Popular Stories for the Nursery*, published in 1804. Sometimes these tales strike a chivalric, Arthurian note straight from medieval romance, as Jack performs acts of knight errantry, rescuing damsels and dispatching one ogre after another. One of these is so huge that 'we shall scarcely fill one of his hollow teeth', complains Jack's companion-at-arms. A writing blank of 1810 illustrates the abduction of Jack's swooning sister by the giant; but our hero, kitted out with 'the Sword of Sharpness, Cap of Knowledge, Shoes of Swiftness and invisible Cloak', 'breaks the Enchantment and relieves his Sister'. (The shoes of swiftness later turn into seven-league boots.) Jack sometimes marries a damsel at the end, and the ogre's wife is rewarded for her compunction by becoming the 'Duchess of Draggletail'.

An even more popular set of variations on this theme, the famous 'Jack and the Beanstalk', features a hero who is no knight errant but, rather, a wastrel, one of the dumblings or simpletons who make good in so many consoling stories. This Jack goes to market with his widowed mother's last item of worldly goods, and instead of buying a goose or something useful for them to eat, he accepts from a hawker a handful of beans—or even a single bean—which, as everyone knows, then grows into a beanstalk and leads him up to the sky. There he finds the bloodthirsty ogre's castle. He escapes the giant through cunning, by putting a dummy in his bed and hiding behind a curtain or under the bed when the giant comes after him to club him to death, or by digging a pit into which the huge bulk of the ogre topples. This material has inspired many pantomimes since the eighteenth century, and it provided the frame story of Stephen Sondheim's highly successful musical *Into the Woods* (1988).

Equally high spirits but less gore are to be found in the tale of Tommy Trip's exploits, published and possibly written by John Newbery in 1767; with the help of his dog Jouler, whom he rides astride, crying 'Tatinvivy' (*sic*), little Tommy lays low the might and pride of 'Woglog the Great Giant'. The introduction sets out the glorious tale: 'how he [Woglog] was conquered by little Tom Trip, who beat him, notwithstanding his amazing bulk, & reduced him, (who was before wild & outrageous) to such a sense of himself that he afterwards became a very good man . . . employed his

The miller has swallowed Tom Thumb, but when he yawns, the hero escapes. Popular Fairy Tales, *c. 1820.*

time chiefly in relieving those who were in distress, and correcting those who were turbulent & unruly'.

The tongue-in-cheek story goes on to deny the more extreme acts of terrorism perpetrated by Woglog before his trouncing (that he stamped on and sank the pier of Westbridge is a 'false and invidious' story, proclaims the author). Nevertheless, Woglog is the genuine article, and his merits ring with the patriotic pride of the Englishman: 'we cannot give those who have never seen Mr Woglog a better idea of his prodigious bulk & size than by comparing him with what they call the giant of the *Netherlands*'.

But it turns out that 'this giant . . . is only made of basket-work, clothed and carried on four men's shoulders, who are concealed; the boy that looks out of his pocket & cries "Papa Papa" is indeed natural, is a real urchin like you or I, and ty'd there only to carry on the deceit, & to amuse the populace; but our *Woglog* is *Woglog* whatever the world may think or say to the contrary'. After his reform, Woglog carries men and women to their destination, a latter-day St. Christopher; he thwacks gamblers over the head and sends them home resolved to reform, saves horses from the whip, and 'As Aesop visited 7 wise men, Woglog goes to 7 wise women . . . [and] found them all silent.' So do paragons comfort their hearers with prejudices. At the end, with glad self-reflexivity, Woglog is identified 'with his friend John Newberry [*sic*]', that is, the story's probable author. In conclusion, we are told that Woglog leaves 'an Apple, an Orange, or a Plumb-cake for good children indoors at their books'.

Polyphemus captured Odysseus and his men in order to eat them, and they left him helpless and blinded; later stories, developing the figures of the foolish giant and the trickster hero, visit the ogre's sins upon him in starkly neat variations on the biter bit: it is he who wanted to eat, who himself gets eaten. Puss-in-Boots traps the ogre into showing his magical powers—including changing himself into a mouse, whereupon Puss snaps him up. A Tripura tale from the Southern Silk Route describes how a giant who is preying on local cattle is similarly tricked by a clever boy: this hero taunts the ogre into turning himself into a fly, and when he does so, the boy swallows him. In Perrault's *conte*, Puss' ruse puts an end to the mouse; but in 'The Giant and the Orphan' the giant continues to buzz noxiously in the boy's tummy, and refuses to come out and risk swatting. So a shaman is found, who gives the hero a potion to drink that finally douses the fly.

The trick resembles Jack's. In an early English chapbook version, the jesting humour is broader and darker and the imagery even more viscerally explicit. Jack first traps one giant in a pit; he then explores the castle, which is 'strewn with bones and skulls'. 'In the next room,' he finds, 'were

Hearts and Livers . . . the choicest of his diet, for he commonly ate them with Salt and Pepper'. But no sooner has Jack dealt with this ogre than the ogre's brother, Blunderbore, comes sniffing for him. Jack swaddles his own tummy, stuffs it with animal lights and other grotesque foodstuffs, and then slits it open, proclaiming loudly that in this way he can feast on his dinner over and over again. The giant is delighted at this economy, and greedily imitates Jack, slitting open his own belly in emulation: 'and out dropt his Tripes and Trolly-bubs'.

The witch in 'Hansel and Gretel' is cruel and scheming, but she, too, is slow-witted and short-sighted in her small red eyes, and so she also fails to see through Hansel's trickery. When she prods him to see how well he is fattening up, he holds out a scrawny twig instead of his finger through the bars of his cage. Later, Gretel brings the story to a triumphant happy end, when she asks the witch to show her how to get into the oven and is able to shove her in.

Such reversals give fairy tales their characteristic dynamic: the biter bit, the cook cooked, or, as it is expressed in Italian, the *beffatore beffato*. Gretel, Finette and other heroines are also tricksters, though in common perception the category hardly ever includes girls.

Jack and Tom and boy giant-killers make frequent appearances doing doughty battle with dreadful foes in small anthologies with titles like *History of the Giants; or The History of Mother and the Marvellous Atchievments* [sic] *of her son Jack*, which was published in 1807 by John Newbery and illustrated with clear and expressive engravings. The young heroes also inspired jolly plays and pantomimes. In *The Ogre and Little Thumb; or The Seven League Boots*, by William Ware, performed at Covent Garden in 1807, the ogre's name is Anthropophagos, and his two agents, Will o' the Wisp and Jack o' Lantern carouse to a bloodthirsty chorus—the genesis here of Captain Hook and his crew on the pirate ship of *Peter Pan*:

> 'Tis our chief delight, in the gloom of night,
> To some luckless wight to shew our light,
>   He! he! he!—ha! ha! ha!
> Then lead his steps to the Brazen Tower,
> Where plump he falls into the Ogre's power
> Who, at one sup, does eat them up,
> With his Fe fa fum . . .

One of his victims quakes with fear as he approaches the Tower, expecting the giant to loom at any moment:

"And in stalk'd the Giant with a very long stride. . .', but the giant's wife hides Jack. . .

He'd open his mouth with a horrible grin;
He'd show his long teeth, and think it no sin
To crack every bone, every bone in our skin
Crunch, crunch, munch, munch, crunch, crunch,
Crunch, crunch, munch, munch, crunch, crunch,
To crack every bone in our skin.

So in these stories born of the Enlightenment's new interest in children, diabolical hunger dominates the passions of both ogres and ogresses, but they fail to satisfy it and are mocked in the attempt.

❖   ❖   ❖

In 1805 the radical philosopher William Godwin set up shop in Hanway Street, London, not far from the British Museum, selling children's books; he is perhaps the earliest exponent of what has come to be called political correctness in literature for the young. The flaming atheist and revolutionary shows himself a mild, amiable, humane, and slightly dull schoolteacher, but his selections and revisions can throw light on how an alert pedagogue did not scorn fantastic tales in favour of improving works of entomology and other sober fact-finding, as Jean-Jacques Rousseau had advocated in his tract on education, *Emile* (1762). Instead, Godwin seized on the latent political thrust of the stories, and attempted to deal with the prejudice, horror and cruelty they so often evinced.

Several of the new titles that Godwin published in the Juvenile Library were also written by him. As 'Edward Baldwin', he retold traditional

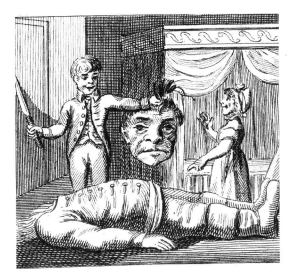

. . . and helps him cut off his head. The History of Mother Twaddle, *London, 1807.*

classical fables by Aesop and others, did easy and lively digests of Greek and Roman history and produced quantities of instructive grammars, glossaries and other manuals. The shop sold wonderfully illustrated companion volumes of fairy tales, retelling the standards in bright new versions and introducing some novelties. Tabart's *Collection of Popular Stories for the Nursery*, in three volumes, included 'Jack the Giant Killer', 'Tom Thumb' and 'Jack and the Beanstalk'; these versions are crucial seeds of English hero stories in all their various later transmutations on stage and in picture books and children's poems. Fairy tales may contain eternal, psychological insights that can cross borders and span historical periods, but they are articulated within economic and social circumstances which modify their messages. The clodhopping character of fairy-tale ogres and giants, their mighty tyranny and equally mighty fall clearly reflect wishful thinking about authority figures from fathers to kings; but their popularity also engages with particular historical conditions at the time the stories were told, and it is interesting to review in this light Godwin's contribution to the British Jack and Tom hero tales. Just as the excesses of the Sun King can be glimpsed in the *mondain* ironies of Perrault and his contemporary *salonnières*, so during the revolutionary turmoil of the late eighteenth century, the downfall of cruel giants can appear to offer dreams of justice restored, tyranny overthrown.

It was long thought that Godwin edited the collection, but careful bibliographical work by Peter Opie and others has established that his second wife, Mary Jane Clairmont, did the work of editing the stories for their friend and associate Benjamin Tabart. But it also seems clear that the

Godwin household was involved all together in the production of the books. Godwin's daughter Mary, whose mother was Mary Wollstonecraft and who, as Mary Shelley, would later write *Frankenstein*, began writing as a child and at the age of ten and a half produced a story in verse, *Mounseer Nongtongpaw*, in which she shows an extremely precocious grip on questions about otherness, flying in the face of English feelings about France in the era of Napoleon.

Godwin needed to hide his identity, as his atheism and republicanism would hardly have won him many customers intent on purchasing improving materials for young minds; he may also have been evading creditors. But in 1807 the anxiety seems to have lessened, as the family moved to a different premises on Skinner Street, and Mrs. Godwin gave her name to the new shop, with a carving outside of Aesop telling his stories to a group of children. The irony of the incendiary Godwin's avuncular success with the young was not lost on some contemporaries, the playwright and reformer Thomas Talfourd remarking on 'the old-fashioned presents to be obtained at the shop by unsuspecting aristocracy'.

Does the Godwin household's low-key but sustained assault on tyranny, intolerance and received ideas, conducted clandestinely from within the pages of light entertainment for children, affect the character of the ogres who make such frequent and vivid appearances in the fairy-tale collections published in the Juvenile Library? Tabart's selection, which takes in French fairy tales already familiar from chapbooks, like 'Cinderella', does seem to lean towards stories in which little boys—and, seldom, but occasionally, little girls—defeat unjust tyrants and authorities; cleverness as well as justice are on their side. Similarly, the dumb giants in chapbooks and early fairy tales embody a tyranny that necessarily collapses through its own hyperbole, its own excessive appetite.

It is easy to read between the lines with hindsight and catch the Godwin household's character and sympathies in the Juvenile Library's publications. Their books advance the Romantics' pleasure in imagination, despite Godwin's interest in Rousseau, who had condemned any materials that stimulated children's over-excitable (in his view) minds. But in many respects the publications of the family represent an Enlightenment project to demystify and to illuminate, to disarm bugbears and demons not simply by defeating them in battles of wits or feats of arms. Understanding, knowledge, broad-mindedness are advocated; one can change an ogre's shape by learning more about him—this liberal lesson in the value of education motivates many of their productions, cutting across the fairy tales' dismissal of any complexities about goodies and baddies.

The Godwin-Tabart variation of 'Jack and the Beanstalk' introduces a long, social exposition to the tale of magic and mayhem: when Jack reaches the top of the beanstalk, the giant's wife tells him that his mother and father have been bitterly wronged by the giant. He used to be the family's neighbour, but took advantage of Jack's father's generosity and ended by defrauding him of all the family goods and by murdering him. The young lad is thus given an honourable motive for killing the giant. At the end, social wrongs are righted, fortunes justly redistributed in a realignment of power along egalitarian lines.

The child Mary Shelley has a lighter touch, as she wittily alters the usual view across the Channel. In her story, John Bull goes to France and marvels at all the sights he sees there; each time inquiring as to who owns the palace, demesne, or even young lady in question, he receives the reply, 'Je vous n' entends pas', which he mistakes for the name of a mighty lord, and marvels all the more at the property and power and display of this 'Mounseer Nongtongpaw'.

The poem expands a comic number written by Charles Dibdin several years earlier for a musical play *The General Election*; the child author introduced a number of extra episodes, including a flight in a balloon. Many of her innovations are inspired by the longing for food experienced by a child in a household where want was familiar. John Bull enters an inn where rich dishes are steaming; he meets a huntsman carrying game and a shepherd 'with his flock . . . The sheep were large and fat'; he also sees a banquet being prepared:

> Then he beheld a train of cooks,
>   Whose heads rich dishes bear;
> With a keen appetite he looks,
>   And longs to have a share.

Mounseer Nongtongpaw is illustrated with large, clear, witty and highly appealing engravings by William Mulready, a friend of the Godwin family, and works as delightful entertainment, its seriality compounding the joke which is then underlined by a refrain that delivers the pleasure of the anticipated inevitable outcome. This sprightly, good-natured attack on English ignorance and insularity, this light-footed satire of xenophobia and specifically Francophobia, this mockery of the English love of aristocracy and awestruck relation to wealth, however gotten or used, was advisedly picked for elaboration by Godwin's daughter. The strongly implied criticism of lack of curiosity, of laziness in learning foreign languages, of sustained ignorance about other peoples and other societies coheres with the Godwin's European connections and background; this was the earliest publication of Mary Shelley, and, in an oblique way, it recalls her mother Mary Wollstonecraft and her expertise in French thought and language. Mary Jane Clairmont, her stepmother, was able to do versions of Perrault for Tabart's volumes from the French; she also rendered Godwin's Aesop into French, and translated *Swiss Family Robinson* for the first time into English for the Juvenile Library in 1814.

Godwin's radicalism animates the arrangement, selection and ways of telling the 'traditional' fables: he begins with Aesop's 'Dog in the Manger', a classic lesson in sharing along communal lines, and he occasionally introduces remarks or anecdotes from his personal experience, which vividly raise some of the live issues of the day. Godwin was writing during the agitation for the abolition of slavery as well as during the turmoil of the French Revolution's aftermath. The story 'The Old Woman and Her Maids' opens with caustic proto-Marxist comments on master-servant power relations. Rich people keep servants for two reasons, this ancient fable informs us: to wash and dress them because they are too idle to do that for themselves, and to make products which are then sold for the master (or mistress)'s advantage. 'Washing the Blackamoor White' (a tenacious Aesopian fable) offers another parable about petty domestic tyranny: 'A very foolish woman once had a black footman,' it opens, whom she had employed after the death of her uncle, for whom he had previously worked. The cautionary fable continues: 'Miss Moggridge . . . looked at Nango. Upon my word said she, I think him a very handsome man.' Then Godwin opens a parenthesis which may strike contemporary ears as achingly embarrassing, clumsy, and overly well-meaning, but in 1805 Godwin felt children should know this: '(That is a thing by no means impossible. The other day I stopped involuntarily to look at a negro I passed in the street . . . he was quite animated and seemed to feel great interest in what he was saying. His features were finely formed. I have seldom seen a more open and manly countenance. His story was a gay one. But there was nothing brutal or insulting in his manner, while he told it.)'

Returning to his story, Godwin then tells how Nango's new mistress decides to wash him white and so puts him in the tub and scrubs him all morning till she gives up. The story condemns her lack of curiosity about anything beyond her nose: 'Of course she had never seen a globe or a map in her life.'

Godwin was preoccupied with this unthinking form of response, and though he did not reflect specifically on the possible unfairness of ogres' representation, and on their role in establishing a prejudiced nationalism, he did pause interestingly on figures of fear:

> in the ordinary Fable book every object, be it a wolf, a stag, a country fir, a Heathen God, or the grim spectre of Death, is introduced without ceremony or explanation: and as few parents, and fewer governesses, are inclined to interrupt their lessons with dialogue, the child is early taught to receive and repeat words which convey no distinct idea to the mind. The author of the present work has endeavoured never to forget, that the book he was writing, was to be the first, or nearly the first, book offered to the child's attention. He has introduced no leading object without a clear and distinct explanation.

So when he comes to telling 'The Faggot-Binder and Death', he stops to explain, in a Rousseauesque spirit of sweet reason, 'I know not what shape Death has.' He is clearly uncomfortable with his role as a scaremongering narrator:

> And I have great doubts whether there is any such a person: no matter; this, you know, is a fable. Death is generally represented by the painters under the figure of a skeleton. You have bones in every one of your joints, and, if the skin and the flesh were gone, these bones would still hang together, and make a figure with legs, and arms, and fingers, and ribs, just as you now have. After a man has been dead some years, his skin and flesh waste away, and all that is left of him is a skeleton.

With this direct (and atheistic in tendency) lesson in elementary biology, Godwin tries to weaken the impact of the *memento mori* of his Gothic fable. But it is doubtful whether his matter-of-factness would lift the spirits of an anxious child. Nevertheless, Godwin is a pioneer in deconstruction. He wanted to teach children to look hard at the bogeyman and find that he is not there at all, or that what you thought was there is very different and not nearly so terrifying.

Godwin's strategy—to use fiction and fantasy to introduce children to ideas and thinking, and to rationalize their fears through application of sweet reason—has proved highly influential and indeed durable. Writers for children often invoke the imaginary, artificial status of a book's contents as proof of the illusory nature of the monsters and terrors conjured in

The things that lurk in the dark are exposed to the light: nothing but pictures in a book turned into bits of paper. Michel Piquemal, The Monster Book of Horrible Horrors, *illustrated by Korky Paul, London, 1995.*

its pages; the story confronts the scary, drawing off its messengers and proponents into the disinfected repository of nightmares: representation.

'Why! You're nothing but a pack of cards!' cries Alice, cross but highly relieved, at the end of the frightening trial scene. She had been trapped in a common nightmare that she was being found guilty of a crime and did not know what it was, as it had not even been named. *The Monster Book of Horrible Horrors* (1995), a large format children's book by Michel Pique-mal, exemplifies the method of dealing with nightmares by giving them extravagant, baroque expression and then declaring them to be only fig-ments. Piquemal's work is a generous, gleeful, wonderfully energetic pic-ture book which dramatizes the primal dream of being snatched away and snaffled up: the whole nightmare crew is mustering for a feast—witches, warlocks, trolls, 'a horrible Ogre (with a horrible face) . . . giants, vam-pires, dwarfs and spooks', and the Yeti and King Kong as well. Their bulges and blemishes, their hairy warts and wens, their toothy jaws, their watering eyes and general physical repulsiveness are illustrated by Korky Paul with terrific panache and in high spirits; their slavering insatiability hyperbolically extreme. The monsters' gnarled and knobbly appearance

OPPOSITE   *The hero at work.* Jack the Giant-Killer, *woodcut, Banbury, c. 1820.*

draws on the diabolical tradition, and the slime and ooze and other effluents of their decaying bodies share the anatomical excesses of the uncontainable grotesque. But unlike Godwin's antagonists, these monsters erupt from a compartmentalized realm of phantasmagoria, and are emphatically disconnected from nature and history and experience.

First the tiny hero, 'Alf the Elf', routs them—with a mouse. But even this proof of their puniness and cowardice will not bring enough comfort, it is thought, to the child reader who is haunted by fear of the dark, for the authors then collapse their own deliriously realized edifice: Alf declares that he will 'turn them [the monsters] into bits of paper!' The illustration shows the book's own pages fluttering, empty, without substance. They are all, the last verses declare, in a final glimpse down the *mise-en-abyme*, 'kept prisoner in this book'. It is the use of comic hyperbole and of grotesque excesses of invention that distances these bogeys and makes it possible to laugh and agree that the ogre today, as the story says, has no counterpart whatsoever in the real world but exists only in the mind.

Or rather, humour relaxes the fear, builds up resistance, but it does not altogether extirpate it. Lewis Carroll's knowing and brilliant tribute to Anglo-Saxon heroics, 'Jabberwocky', parodies monsters like Grendel in a spirit of merriment. The famous first quatrain appeared in *Misch-Masch* (1855), one of Carroll's family scrapbooks, dating from his student days. He entitled it 'Stanza of Anglo-Saxon Poetry' and followed it up with a wonderfully mock-solemn learned disquisition on the meanings of 'this curious fragment'. But when Tenniel realized the poem visually for *Through the Looking Glass*, his illustration of the Jabberwock was considered too frightening to remain the frontispiece, as originally planned, and was replaced by the mild White Knight. Tenniel's bat-winged, rodent-fanged flying dragon, with goggle-eyes and hairy claws like spider's legs and a tail so long that it curls into the depths of the tulgey wood till out of sight, is dressed, oddly enough, in a waistcoat and scaly ankle hose—an anthropomorphizing touch that does not hollow out his terror as do Carroll's dazzling invention and irreverent laughter.

XV

'OF THE PALTRINESS OF THINGS'

'Whatever you do, laugh and laugh and that'll stop him.'
Ingrid Bergman to Ann Todd about Alfred Hitchcock

In the classic German children's picture book *Struwwelpeter*, a story warns Johnny Head-in-Air that if he does not look where he is going, he will come a cropper, and sure enough, he walks straight on and falls into the river. There is nobody standing by to watch his soaking, except the little fishes, who 'enjoy the fun and laughter'. In 1845, when Dr. Heinrich Hoffmann's book was published, it was greeted as comic, and its child readers were expected to laugh—and learn.

Johnny Head-in-Air has a high pedigree: in Plato's *Theaetetus* a similar tale turns up as a metaphor for different ways of living, contemplative and active. Socrates, discussing philosophy's deepest questions—What is Man? And how is he to live a good life?—alludes to Thales, founder of Greek natural philosophy. 'Thales was studying the stars . . .' he says, 'and gazing aloft, when he fell into a well; and a witty and amusing Thracian serving-girl made fun of him because, she said, he was wild to know about what was up in the sky but failed to see what was in front of him and under his feet.' This maidservant from Thrace, however flatteringly Plato/Socrates describes her, soon expands into 'the common herd': 'Whenever he [the philosopher] is obliged . . . to discuss the things that lie at his feet and before his eyes, he causes entertainment not only to Thracian servant-girls but to all the common herd, by tumbling into wells and every sort of difficulty . . . a lack of resource which makes him look very comic.'

The maid, inferior in social position to the philosopher, marginal through geographical origin and subordinate in gender, would not fall down a well, as she has her feet on the ground and looks where she is going. This anonymous woman became, in commentaries on Plato down the centuries, the epitome of barbarian ignorance and of banausic oblivion to the higher things of the mind. Yet her spontaneous merriment at Thales' mishap reverberates with a tonic, liberating irreverence, as Adriana Caverero has commented in an inspired essay: '"Servant" is a possible polite translation for the Greek word for slave. It is not a bad translation . . . The servant, as a female figure of oppression, is nonetheless capable of a desecrating laughter. Her laughter resonates within her confinement to the "sphere of necessities".' 'The Maidservant from Thrace' is a counterpart to the legendary Aesop, using laughter to level inequalities and point out the folly of the great. Her anonymous laughter expresses the reversal of the comparative positions of maid and master, as it often does in the comedy of pratfalls and banana skins. Children reading *Struwwelpeter* were being placed in the position of the maid, invited to laugh at someone who may seem their superior (or has set himself up as such—for Johnny is also sticking his nose in the air) but who can be shown not to be.

Similarly, ogres lose their bite when they are shown up as blundering fools, as we have seen; their rapacious appetites present a manageable, even pleasurable threat when made absurd by exaggeration, nonsense parodies and high spirits, as in the case of the ogres whom Jack gulls or Lewis Carroll's 'Jabberwocky'. Nonsense unsettles the certainties of sense and disturbs conventional ascriptions of meaning; poking fun packs aggressive weapons as well as strong armour. In her celebrated writings 'The Guilty One' and 'The Laugh of the Medusa' (1975), Hélène Cixous roused women to rise up against misogyny, patriarchy, subordination and silencing, not with weapons of war or even words, but with great gusts of laughter. 'All laughter is allied with the monstrous,' she writes. 'Laughter breaks up, breaks out, splashes over; Penthesileia could have laughed; instead she killed and ate Achilles.'

Cixous has the support of much popular, unofficial, and nursery material for her trust in laughter. From the jocularity of the eighteenth-century fairy tales until today's comical *BFG* and his grotesquely bloodthirsty and cannibal relatives, stories have promised that the bogeyman can be floored by merriment at his expense. Basile practises the benign and cunning comic arts of metamorphosis in the *Pentamerone*, but he also addresses the aggression of ridicule: his book opens with an old woman's skidding on a puddle of oil. Flung upsy-daisy, pantomime style, she shows her all; the protagonist, a princess who has never even smiled, finds this spectacle irresistibly funny, bursts out laughing, and is cured of her melancholy. But the old woman is not amused and, unlike Thales, whose reaction to the maid's merriment is not discussed, she takes her revenge on the giddy princess and sets her a series of ordeals which are worked out in the course of the book. Thus the crone's unwitting exhibition of herself and the response it provokes sets up the frame story of Basile's Catherine wheel of tales. The difference between the maidservant who laughs and the princess who laughs is patently one of social station: laughter is the legitimate weapon and defence of the underdog and can be abused by those who already enjoy power and privilege. Basile's jests thus probe the limits of jesting and the proprieties of laughter.

Humour is clearly one of the chief and most successful ways in which popular culture resists fear, and its energy has been advocated since Freud distinguished jokes from humour, commenting, 'The ego refuses to be distressed by the provocations of reality, to let itself be compelled to suffer . . . Humour is not resigned; it is rebellious. It signifies not only the triumph of the ego, but also of the pleasure principle, which is able here to assert itself against the unkindness of real circumstances.' But humour has a history too, intertwined with cultural changes in appropriate responses, in common values and in ethics. The larks played by Florentine humanists, as recounted in comic tales of cozenage and high spirits, can strike the contemporary reader as callous, even wicked: in Antonio Manetti's 'The Fat Woodcarver', a reportedly true incident of merry mischief-making, a band of friends decide to pretend that they no longer recognize the hapless protagonist; when one after another of his circle, including his wife, fails to respond to his greetings, he thinks he has lost his identity and his mind begins to turn. Eventually, he is driven out of Florence. The tricks played on Parolles in *All's Well That Ends Well* or on Malvolio in *Twelfth Night* teeter perilously on the brink of bullying for contemporary audiences, no matter how egregious, pompous, dishonest and stupid these characters have shown themselves. The very disappearance of the verb 'to cozen', meaning to gull or deceive, possibly indicates the depreciation of the term's positive sense.

A theme of this book has been a contradiction at the heart of human responses to fear: the processes by which people seek to undo enemy power simultaneously make it visible. In other words, the drive to define and delimit 'home', to name and circumscribe the abode and the milieu to which one belongs and where one feels safe, leads to naming and defining things—and people—out there beyond the fence, on the other side of the perimeter wire. Humour takes part in this making of likenesses and differences. The perception of the French philosopher Henri Bergson, writing at the beginning of the twentieth century, is blazingly acute: 'Our laughter is always the laughter of a group . . . The comic will come into being, it appears, whenever a group of men concentrate their attention on one of their number . . .'

Humour has been used highly effectively to heal: Brazilian Indians clowned and capered by sick-beds to help the ill to recover, and psychotherapists today are experimenting with laughter as a form of medicine. Obviously, overcoming fears is in itself therapeutic, and humour relaxes the grip of bogeys, real or fantastic. It can also act as an effective restraint on individual behaviour. One of the arguments invoked by moralists to justify coarseness and ribaldry stressed the disarming effect that laughter can have on vice, by shaming the perpetrator in public: 'this [arises] not only from Tragedies,' wrote one Dutch observer in the seventeenth century, 'but even and often much more from comedies and farces: for as in these the foibles and vices are represented in mockery to the entire world, and as the unvirtuous person usually tolerates chastizing much better than being laughed at and mocked, it is no wonder that this will make him watch out.' The American critic William Gass also points out the communal morality of humour: 'Laughter is social . . . unlike self-abuse, and the laugh is a social corrective like a curtsy or the guillotine.'

Through these benefits, some thinkers stress that humour's effects are largely benign, a form of communal catharsis. Mary Douglas, for example, cites jokers acting as ritual purifiers among the Kaguru, the Gogo, the Dogon, and other African tribes:

> A joker enjoys privileges of open speech others are forbidden, and can therefore cleanse the community; his *modus operandi* is different from the straightforward flouting of taboos, however . . . [The joker] has a firm hold on his own position in the structure and the disruptive comments he makes upon it are in a sense the comments of the social group upon itself . . . he lightens for everyone the oppressiveness of social reality, demonstrates its arbitrariness by making light of formality in generality, and expresses the creative possibilities of the situation . . . his jokes expose the inadequacy of realist structurings of experience and so release the pent-up power of the imagination.

Clowning can also draw the teeth of actual threats, not only sweeten their effects. A recent mayor of Bogotá, a city in which there were many incidents of road rage, some of them fatal, dressed the traffic policemen in clown costumes in order to defuse attacks on them; the experiment was successful. In the same way, it becomes rather hard to play the piano or even type a letter if an audience watching you is laughing its head off—even good-naturedly. Some comic representations seek to produce this disarming effect.

This is one kind of humour, which the metamorphoses of nonsense, trifles and pleasure induce. Plutarch's Gryllus and part of the gryllus tradition embody it. The 'play upon form' can be intoxicating and merciful—but not always. Humour's fun can indeed reorganize concerns to make them less distressing, but the concerns are not necessarily well founded or well understood in the first place.

There is a kind of laughter that mocks what is most cherished, and the grip exerted by that most cherished desideratum relaxes only when it is deflected. A clown who points at someone's nose and goes off into gales of laughter is funny, but not if the nose is yours. Most professional comedians today no longer mock their audience in the manner of the Fool in *King Lear* but rather take themselves, or versions of themselves as their chosen comic personae and as their targets. Rowan Atkinson, John Cleese, Rik Mayall, Jo Brand are their own fall guys. A contemporary young British stand-up comic with a rancid turn of humour like Mark Lamarr will still cast about for suitable victims; finding women and Others on the whole off-limits in the climate of the times, he will settle to attack the geriatric, the ill and the physically decaying—they are not likely to be out there in the auditorium. On occasion, however, he may single out a member of the audience for ridicule and chance it that he can carry the rest of the room with him—against a middle-class woman, for example, on the night I saw him perform, who rashly (intrepidly?) chided him for his use of four-letter words. Shared social values permit this choice of target regardless of the comedian's own preferences or inclinations, and it will alight on common fears—of decay, of illness, of dying. Humour is not personal but political in the widest sense: its effect happens through its reception by a community or social group. 'The joke form,' as Mary Douglas has written, 'rarely lies in the utterance alone, but . . . it can be identified in the total social situation.'

Fall guys invite identification, of course, and while laughing at them exempts you from being laughed at, you simultaneously recognize the situations depicted as all too familiar. They are unawares; your awareness, by contrast, grows. Hobbes chided laughter for its nastiness in a famous passage, where he described it as 'sudden glory arising from a dawning belief in some eminency in ourselves, by comparison with the infirmity of others.' Baudelaire aligned laughter with the fruits of the Fall: 'Laughter is satanic, it is therefore profoundly human. It exists in man in consequence of the idea of his own superiority; and, indeed, as laughter is essentially human, it is essentially contradictory, that is to say, that it is at one and the same time the sign of infinite grandeur and infinite paltriness.'

When Baudelaire includes laughter among the penalties of the Fall as an assertion of superiority, as a consequence of pride and the drive to mastery, he does not make the sympathetic point that humans might vaunt themselves in this way out of anxiety about their own situation: roaring at another's misfortunes draws attention to one's own reprieve. Baudelaire was appropriating for his own decadent lexicon the Christian proscription on jokes, the Church Fathers' ascetic ideal having relegated laughter to the status of a bodily spasm or emission, to be controlled by the mind. In *The Name of the Rose* (1981) Umberto Eco takes up the theme with ingenious levity: the plot turns on Aristotle's lost treatise on Comedy, which has in fact been suppressed by the Church because laughter is humanity's chief, magnificent defence against God and religion, its defiance of a moral order built on hierarchy and punishment.

Ogres—their kidnappings and cannibal banquets and other horror stories about them—lend themselves easily to analysis in this light: readers or listeners merrily give way to mirth in relief that the calamities described have not happened to them. (George Cruikshank's frontispiece to Grimms' fairy tales shows the storyteller guffawing helplessly.) Bergson comes to the same point by a different route: for him as well, humour releases the spirit from mechanical, automatic, even explicable responses and lifts it to a higher, spontaneous, vital plane. He took falling over as the locus classicus of humour, writing that the involuntary nature of a fall excites mirth, and that if a man goes on flailing and tumbling, like a clockwork toy whose spring has gone, his mishaps get funnier each time. Again, one feels relief that it is not oneself who is the fall guy, and this relief fuels the laughter.

That release of anxiety is in itself life-affirming for Bergson, just as for Freud humour allows a breakthrough of joy and libido and the expression of the unconscious. Freud acknowledges those joyful feelings of 'superiority' at work but lays stress on the tonic liberation of the reprieve effected. The protective-aggressive uses of laughter can also help the social historian to identify the imagined assailants, just as a gun cupboard or arsenal will reveal the type of warfare, the terrain, and the nature of the target. Humour, in releasing tensions, may lighten the atmosphere and freshen the air, but this is not always the case. As Bergson adds, in a perception that also draws attention to the difficulties of writing about humour at all: 'Laughter . . . also is a froth with a saline base. Like froth, it sparkles. It is gaiety itself. But the philosopher who gathers a handful to taste may find that the substance is scanty, and the after-taste bitter.'

John Limon, in a recent, subtle essay about stand-up comedy, starts with a joke Immanuel Kant tells (humour not being Kant's strong suit, it is hardly a gem): an Englishman opens a bottle of beer which foams out of the neck in a great head of froth. This causes great wonder and exclamations in his companion, who comments when asked to explain his response, '"Oh, but I'm not amazed at its coming out . . . but at how you managed to get it all in."' Limon develops a complex argument about the relation of the sublime to the ridiculous from this starting point, but he does not draw attention to the joke's Indian setting nor to the Indian identity of the witness who marvels at the ejaculating bottle. Limon is concentrating on Longinus' view that 'ridicule is an amplification of the paltriness of things' and, perhaps politely, does not remark on the oppositions drawn by the joke's cast of characters. But he is right that the paltriness of things is of the essence, and humour works to show that some things are lesser than others. It is because the sublime and the ridiculous cohere in human sexuality that, as we shall see, the banana as pure sign of phallic ambivalence can do better service for a clown than a bottle of beer.

The structure of racist insults and jokes is unpleasant to analyse, but in relation to the apparently intrinsic funniness of the banana, two underlying cultural-historical principles are worth picking out here, for the fruit has played a significant part in racial insult and symbolism. As Christie Davies comments in *Ethnic Humor around the World*, some of the most common jokes told in every kind of society contrast the stupid with the canny—usually but not always to the advantage of the teller's group. In

Civilization under threat: the blonde in the monster's grip, the electric city underfoot. Publicity still for King Kong, *1933.*

Mexico, Yucatecos are the butt of 'stupid' jokes while Regiomontanos (from Monterrey) are 'canny'; in England, the Irish are foolish, Scots cunning, and so forth. Through its popular culture, especially film, the United States has disseminated its values globally, and attitudes to its own black population have been and continue to be profoundly influential. It is wiser not to reiterate some jokes of the past, for they belong in unspeakable territory, and echo the extremes of madness in anti-Semitism, racism and bigotry in earnest. Black men, or sometimes white actors in black face, often play the fall guy in early American movies: the silent version of 'The Wizard of Oz' (1925), directed by the slapstick comic Larry Semon, features a farmhand who keeps falling into haystacks, off ladders, and generally tripping up. Even in *Men in Black*, a contemporary film that is highly alert to colour and its symbolism, Will Smith, the black recruit to the secret alien defence team, has on occasion to play the naïf dumbo to Tommy Lee Jones' superior instruction. Black performers have been cast as easy sources for the 'sudden glory' of which Hobbes spoke.

The second principle at work in humour that is worth attending to here directly concerns the bogeyman himself. He has been recognized in various strangers throughout history, as we have seen. The feared marauders of lullabies and fairy tales and Gothic fantasies inhabit a world of shadows: they are things that come in the night, and they approach with fear of the dark. One adventitious effect of this Western symbolic equivalence of black night and the devil has been its coloration of perceptions about Africans and their diasporic descendants. (The words for this racial difference unthinkingly assume this: 'Negro' and 'Moor' derive from adjectives meaning 'black'. But maybe it does not need pointing out that this is hardly a more accurate description of physical flesh tone than is 'white'.) The folklore that jumbled fairy-tale ogres, parental bogeymen, New World cannibal legends and male fears emerges clearly in a comic ballad printed in a black letter broadsheet of around 1830. (Tripping up imaginary enemies takes many forms.) 'The London Ladies and the Ojibbeway Indians' is illustrated with a cut showing a caricature 'blackamoor' (not a Native North American, in spite of the name) dancing a jig. The first verse sets the English climate of anxiety in jocular mood:

> What a fuss there is all up and down
> With the pretty girls in London town,
> The deaf and dumb, blind, lame and gay,
> Are all in love with the Ojibbeways.

The song then reviews the usual fear of obliteration through women's unruly inclinations ('This nation will be peopled with Jim along Joes'), and, in a scatological step, alludes to ogres:

> Said the parson, will you marry this damsel rum,
> Then Strong Wind hollowed out fee fa fum.

The ballad ends, not altogether unexpectedly, with the conventional primal scene of the cannibal feast: food standing in for sex, and consumption for obliteration, as the imagery of hell-fire and of devils roasting sinners returns to the streets of the Victorian city under the British empire:

> Now all you English ladies gay,
> If you fall in love with the Ojjihebeways [*sic*],
> You'll be frizzled to death in a stone potan,
> With a rum tum tiddy iddy, yam tam jam.

In the southern United States, 'boogieman' was slang for blacks; indeed 'boogie-woogie', the jazz piano music invented by Clarence 'Pinetop' Smith in his recording of 1928, is another example of an insult reclaimed, incorporated, and subverted by its target: not only did 'boogie' trail a whole raft of devilish associations, but 'woogie' echoes 'wog', as in 'golli-wog' and 'Woglog', whom we met before, the giant who was defeated by Tommy Trip astride his dog Jouler. Pinetop Smith, in a vivid instance of claiming a negative as a positive, of accepting an insult with pride, claimed you had to sell your soul in order to play boogie-woogie—it was the devil's music.

The word 'Mahomet' was applied to diabolical idols in England and France—voodoo dolls *avant la lettre*, worshipped by portmanteau villains such as Herod in the mystery plays; in French, the word for a grotesque image, *marmouset*, itself slippage around the prophet's name, became further confused with a species of monkey. The devil was called 'the ape of God', by no less an authority than Augustine, because he imitated the divine blasphemously, through inversion and parody. The word *simius*, ape, was related by Isidore of Seville in his fanciful etymologies to *similis*, like, stressing the animal's powers of mimicry. In French, *le singe* was seen as a meaningful anagram of *le signe*, and the animal's copycat powers of signifying inspired pleasure, awe and fear: it did not need Darwin to notice the closeness of humans to apes. Naughty monkeys frolic in the margins of medieval manuscripts, playing tricks and filching from unwary travellers. They were famed, as noted before, for cackling at travellers, apparently participating in that mark of the human, Baudelaire's satanic mirth. The animal's cleverness at imitation made it a symbol of representation, the symbol for art itself, as we saw. In the seventeenth century a fashion for monkey pictures developed in Italy and Holland, showing monkeys dressing up, reading, painting: the chimpanzees' tea party at the London Zoo, which was a feature of children's treats in the city until 1972, is the direct successor of this comic anthropomorphism. It still continues on television in Britain in the advertisement for PG Tips tea.

Once Darwin's views became naturalized, this fugue of associations with devilry of every sort, alongside the Christian symbolism of blackness, contaminated perception. Throughout the nineteenth century, the search was on for the 'missing link' and white palaeontologists and biologists as well as caricaturists and propagandists looked to Other peoples and Other places—Indonesia, Africa, Australasia—to find examples of the intermediate species between *Homo sapiens* and the great apes. *King Kong* (1933), encapsulates these underlying misconceptions: this classic film, still one of the most popular ever made, begins as an ethnographic expedition, to find the 'Eighth Wonder of the World'. Kong is once described as an ape in the film, but he is far more deeply anthropomorphized, as a king who is worshipped as a god by the dancing and drumming savages outside his sanctuary. The moment that he desires Fay Wray, inspecting her in the palm of his hand as she screams, King Kong defined, for generations of viewers, his tragic, transgressive, beast-like male desire. King Kong is a dark, looming, cannibal giant who snatches tiny victims; like the bogeyman of myths, he changes scale phantasmagorically in the course of the film, all the better to penetrate the innermost corners of the mind. Like ogres and giants in fairy tales, he symbolizes a prior time of greater barbarism that threatens to wreck the civilization of the heroes, exercises an irresistible fascination, but cannot in the end prevail against it. In the course of the film, he changes, however, into a symbol of tragic male bondage and is felled by his own overweening desires. The final icon of the film—King Kong on the pinnacle of the Empire State Building snatching at aeroplanes like a cat swatting flies—crystallizes the lure and fascination of the imagined unruly and primitive rampant, the very thrill of the bogey inside us.

King Kong was censored when it was first made: scenes of him chomping on his victims were cut, as was the scene when he sniffs at Fay Wray's petticoat, his nostrils flaring, thanks to Willis O' Brien's pioneering animation. (Steven Spielberg pays homage to this predecessor's effects with shots of human legs twitching as their owner disappears down the monsters' jaws, in both *Jurassic Park* and *The Lost World*.) The association of Kong's distant habitat with this kind of feeding frenzy should also be seen as a cultural preconception. Cannibals, who are ubiquitous in Western folklore, are removed to the periphery at the start of the imperial enterprise and excluded from the record of European fact and fiction (Columbus was expecting to find cannibals as well as gold in the New World.) The identification of anthropophagi itself feeds on the folklore: Black Peter, who accompanies Santa Claus on his annual visits and does his work of chastisement on his behalf offers a perfect example of the slippage that occurs from the seventeenth century onwards between black devils and *l'omo nero*, or bogeyman, of nursery terrors.

The dynamics of humour are available to all, and the target of a joke can borrow his assailant's weapons, turning them back against him in kind. The theme of the trickster monkey in black culture adopts and mocks its cultural, derogatory models, inverting, teasing, pastiching, playing mischievously with their assumptions. Games, songs, jokes and tales of 'the signifying monkey' flourished in black folklore as comic retaliation, aping white fears in order to mock them.

Calypsos are a form of work song, satirical, scabrous, sometimes obscene, which have their origins in slave flyting songs against the plantation bosses. The word 'calypso' derives from an African phrase 'kaa iso!', meaning 'go on', urging the performers to continue, as in 'encore', and in the eastern Caribbean the songs are still called Kaiso. In Trinidad, their most energetic source, the word was recast by Spanish colonists with a humanist background to echo the name of Calypso, the nymph who diverts Odysseus for seven years on her island; within the epic, she doubles the role of Circe as a mistress of dalliance and a distraction from duty (though her character is far less developed). It would be appropriate if this Circean echo were struck in the naming of the local Caribbean song that defies the call of duty and transmutes toil and weariness into music and vitality—and also revels on occasion in self-derision.

'The Mighty Sparrow', a Calypso King, born Francisco Slinger in Grenada, moved to Trinidad as a child and wrote political songs for the annual Carnival throughout the 1950s and 1960s. Many of his targets were national, but he also responded scabrously to the U.S. presence in Trinidad during the war and the power of the 'Yankee dollar'. Sparrow, like other Carnival songwriters, fell foul of the censorship laws. His song 'Congo Man' goes far beyond the borders of the permitted anywhere else but Carnival time in Port of Spain; it epitomizes ideas about humour's relation to the unruly, subversive unconscious as well as to the traditional themes of stories about fear. The words play up with outrageous relish the deepest racist anxiety about black sexuality, as Sparrow takes on the mytheme of the cannibal preying on women. His lyrics closely echo popular colonial prejudices in a masterpiece of avenging salaciousness; they take the insults and turn them into a means of defiance—this is the essence of fooling, to show up the folly of the powerful. The song reproduces the structure of the banana skin joke: the fruit is consumed but does not disappear, its residue trips up the unwary, its trace is slippery (the mocker mocked, the biter bit).

'This is a story, ladies and gentlemen,' Sparrow begins, in voice-over recitative, 'about two lovely white women travelling all the way from Africa . . . [they] found themselves deep in the heart of the Balooba, in the heart of the Congo, in the hands of my big brother . . .'

The backing picks up, and Sparrow then launches into the calypso tune:

> Two white women travelling through Africa
> Find themselves in the hands of a cannibal headhunter.
> He cook one up and he eat one raw
> But they so good he wanted more.

Much lip-smacking, throat-gurgling, slurping and trilling follows, as Sparrow conjures up his 'big brother' and exults in the complete primal cannibal scene:

> [He] tie them up and he put them to lay them on the ground,
> Light up the fire and he started dancin' round and round.
> One of the women started to beg
> He bite she chest and then he catch she by she leg.
> . . . He eat she raw.
> The next one started screamin' with all the voice she got.
> He lift she up and he put she inside a big, big pot.
> The water was warm, she started to wiggle,
> The Congo started to laugh and giggle . . .

In the chorus, the ogre's appetite threatens his victims with rather more than gastronomic consumption:

> Oh, I envy de Congo Man
> I wish it was me, I wanna shake he hand
> He eat until he stomach upset
> And I—I never eat white meat yet.
> What about you? I never eat a white meat yet.

This outrageous example of Carnival bawdy seizes hold of the cannibal

OPPOSITE *A devil with a monkey's tail, up to his tricks. William Hone,* Ancient Mysteries Described, *London, 1823.*

trope, though it must be admitted that, in the typical calypso manner, women's fears in particular are played upon, mocked and exploited. The *double entendres* in the chorus attack the convention in the high offensive of the carnivalesque by striking at the core of the fear: not of being eaten, but of being raped. The song was banned in Trinidad in its original version; but was eventually released in the doctored (!) version above.

'A joke is seen and allowed when it offers a symbolic pattern of a social pattern occurring at the same time,' writes Mary Douglas. As we cannot live in radical isolation or subjectivity without contingency, or shape ourselves as subjects without points of reference, the history of laughter's role in a group's narrative becomes interestingly connected with the trajectory of prejudice and distrust, even hatred, as well as loyalty and affection and common fellow feeling. But it would be a Casaubon's task to cover all the permutations of humour's uses in self-definition, and it is possible to disclose its workings as a defensive manœuvre by concentrating on the changing significance of one familiar automatic comic trigger: the banana.

REFLECTION

ALBERT ECKHOUT: EIGHT BRAZILIAN PORTRAITS

 The portrait of a free Tarairiu Indian woman, painted in 1641–43, contains notorious 'evidence' of New World cannibalism: a severed foot protruding from her basket, slung on her back, and a severed hand that she holds with apparent insouciance, while her alert expression, looking straight out, quizzes the viewer with the boldness of a harlot in contemporaneous Dutch art, as if challenging this imagined audience to regain its powers of speech after being dumbfounded. Meanwhile, a hunt (a man-hunt?) is represented in full cry in the background, positioned so that it is taking place between her legs, just above the toothed jaws of her hound as it laps at water. Eckhout treats the scene with observant, musing detachment, as if this method of food provision was just another curiosity, another process in the rich variety of the country.

Cannibalism, however, packed a dark and frightening menace in circulating stories that began to be printed in fairy-tale and other genres from the later seventeenth century onwards. Perrault was a generation younger than Eckhout, and his gruesome tales of ogres and cannibals in the contes *were published in Paris and Amsterdam at the end of the seventeenth century and the beginning of the eighteenth; they were being read in Europe just as the imagery of New World cannibals was spreading from sources like Eckhout. The hard reality of the fantasy was taken for granted, as can be seen from Eckhout's supposed portraits, where it emerges without comment as a natural part of a seeming documentary story about indigenous Americans. It formed a ghostly matte backdrop to the theme of the banana joke, as we shall see.*

Albert Eckhout, who was born around 1607 and died in 1665, travelled to Brazil for the Dutch governor of the huge colony, Prince Mauritz of Nassau, to document the flora and fauna—and the peoples; he was thus working in the New World during the second phase of European colonization. All unconsciously, his resulting corpus sets the tone for the spectacle of Orientalism, in which the banana—tree and fruit—becomes a crucial background index of natura naturans, *of the bounty of the tropical paradise and its aptitude for cultivation.*

Eckhout's full-length, lifesize portraits of Brazilians constitute, along with John White's drawings and watercolours of Virginia a hundred years earlier, the first visual records of the native peoples of the Americas. But they are portraits only in a manner of speaking, for the desire of the patron, who was characteristic of his time in his avid collecting of curiosities and his enthusiasm for encyclopaedic archiving, focused the artist's attention necessarily on documenting the differences and particularities of his subjects as specimens of nature's wonders. Eckhout's 'portraits' do not document men and women of the New World as individual personalities with attention to character through physiognomy, as works by his contemporaries Rembrandt or Jan Steen might do. They hyphenate at least two, if not three kinds of painting: the genre scene, capturing typical

The Tarairiu or 'Tapuya' woman LEFT: a foot protrudes from her basket and she carries a dangling hand. The male Tarairiu BELOW also takes up a commanding position in the wild landscape, and is richly armed. Albert Eckhout, 1641–3.

A Tupi woman LEFT *appears next to a banana plant against an orderly, peaceful plantation, with a baby on her hip and emblems of manufacture and industry in her basket. A Tupi man* RIGHT *displays the tools of his trade, demonstrating his cultivated relation to the land. Albert Eckhout, 1641–3.*

pursuits and activities of a social group; the company portrait, attending to the uniform, accoutrements and characteristic context of a trade or rank; and the painting of curiosities, like shells and toads and knobbly gourds, which Eckhout himself also produced for Prince Mauritz.

Many of Eckhout's Brazilian studies are still lifes, dramatically arranged against turbid grey skies on high stone ledges, dislocating scale in a manner that emphasizes the wild grandeur of their native habitat, and avoiding purposefully the usual domestic intimacy of Dutch interiors with arrangements of fruit and flowers. These compositions make manifest the prodigal bounty of the New World's products, especially the families of large cucurbitae *(melons, gourds and cucumbers), of yams, bread-fruit, mangoes—novelties to be marvelled at. He deliberately avoids metonymies of corruption and pollution so common in the Dutch* vanitas *tradition: the colonies are crammed with natural wonders and monsters, his work seems to say, and move to a healthy cycle of life—and death.*

The eight standing portraits have recently been rehung frame to frame,

A Brazilian woman of African descent LEFT *in a magnificent hat trimmed with peacock and parrot feathers, holds up a basket laden with fruit; a pipe is stuck in her sash. At the feet of her male counterpart* RIGHT *lies an elephant tusk, symbol of exotic riches, on which Albert Eckhout signed his name.*

in the manner of a Dutch cabinet, in the National Museum of Denmark, but this cramped display does not do them justice. Still, they make a unique and impressive show, in spite of the worn paint surface which has allowed the primer to discolour the flesh tones. The series reached Copenhagen early on in its history, as a gift from Prince Mauritz to his cousin Frederick III, king of Denmark, in 1654. Some of Eckhout's still lifes are grouped with them, and it is helpful to bear them in mind when looking at the portraits, as Eckhout assembles items of flora and fauna around his subjects and in the background with a similar accumulative appetite, disregarding seasonal rhythms or nature's own antipathies, so that a land-crab might appear in the same clearing as a castor oil plant, a bird spider and a dead boa constrictor beside wild strawberries. This type of scientific spectacle, in which the life cycle of a plant is given on a single plate, or the metamorphoses of a creature over its life cycle in the same taxidermist's vitrine, also accounts for the apparel of Eckhout's subjects, who carry paraphernalia that inventory for the viewer the region's artefacts.

Setting his still life of tropical fruit and vegetables against a cloudscape, Albert Eckhout enhanced the spectacular tropical effects of size, lushness and prodigality. Dutch, seventeenth century.

The portraits are also organized in a taxonomy of racial types, based on skin colour and matched in couples; the kind of graduated system that obtained in the slave plantations and colonial and match-making society of Brazil. The mestizo has a magnificent jaguar-spotted sword-belt, for example, which picks up the pattern in the bark of the prodigious hermaphroditic papaya tree rendered precisely beside him. His female counterpart, in contemporaneous designation a 'Mameluca', has been painted as a variation on the goddess Flora, and she stands under a cashew tree, with nuts at different stages of development growing on it, as in a botanical illustration. Heliconias bloom behind her; passion fruit appear prominently in her fine-woven simple basket; she is wearing a loose white shift over her own full-bodied ripeness, her breasts and pose offering herself as much as the fruits of her country. Both of these subjects have rather doughy faces, recognizable from any number of Dutch portraits of the time, so although they may have been sat for by models, the paintings themselves do not convince us that the models were Brazilians, painted from life by Eckhout when he was there. He could have made notes on the flora, fauna, clothes, and so forth, like an ethnographer, and then assembled the figures later in his studio.

The next pair at first glance look more convincingly indigenous, as portraits of Tupi or Tupinamba Indians, but on closer scrutiny, the same couple may well have posed, for their features are very similar. They would then have been coloured in with the equivalent in russet hue of annatto powder, which was used as a cosmetic. The woman is carrying a magnificent example of basketry on her head, heaped with a hammock, a calabash, and a bundle—again, examples of local handiwork. Another splendid calabash hangs from her arm at her waist, while, to her left behind her, a banana tree is rendered with scrupulous attention to its different phases of production: the slashed root stock of its predecessor, the quill-like new leaf, the flower 'like a calf's heart', the bunch of ripening fruit (Pl. 29).

In the far background, the plantation house itself appears: a double row of lemon trees planted to form an allée *up to the front door, date palms, some sheep and cattle, a cow being milked. This is an ideal picture of nature governed by industrious husbandry, in which a slave's baby at the breast becomes part of the admirable fertility that the productive cycle processes. Again, breast and nature's fruits form a visual rhyme; she looks out at the viewer, as does the baby, intensifying the effect of her presence. Her male counterpart similarly links two aspects of nature's gifts but faces the other way, towards the jungle, for he stands with his hunting and fishing gear (again, much collected for cabinets of curiosities) against a background of a rushing stream; behind him, a man-made clearing in which crabs can be seen; at his feet, another gigantic root vegetable, a manioc (on a prize-winning scale, such as used to be wheeled to village fêtes after the war in a barrow).*

Eckhout, clearly fascinated by the abundance of Brazilian produce, finds a metonymic equivalent in size: there are doubtless smaller, or even simply small, calabashes and cutlasses, baskets and manioc roots than the ones he selected for representation; but the items he singles out for attention slip from diversity and plenty into a generalized gigantism that enhances their fascination and power. The relation of the figures to the backgrounds also gives them physical stature: they appear to be life size, but Eckhout gives no familiar markers to gauge their height. For him, the earth burgeons and blooms; the human elements are upstanding, even giant, specimens of creation's rich diversity and, by implication, of the colonial enterprise's virtuous ordering.

This is a characteristic of European perspective. Though there are no known examples by a Latin American artist from Eckhout's time, a mid-nineteenth-century painting by the Mexican artist José Agustin Arrieta, showing a market vendor with her meagre produce arrayed on a mat before her, discloses that the bounty of the rain forest can be scanty, its products puny, and husbandry not entirely effortless (Pl. 32).

Another pair, of Africans, may have been observed from life, as Eckhout does seem to realize that black children when young are paler in complexion than their parents; these are the most successful paintings in the series, though the same acquisitive ethnographical axioms inspire the display of the child's pet parakeet and sweet-corn snack, as well as the mother's sumptuously woven and ornamental hat, tufted with peacock and parrot feathers, that she is modelling for our delectation. The banana makes its second appearance in the series of portraits, among the fruits piled improbably high in her equally richly decorated container.

❖   ❖   ❖

Where Albert Eckhout perceives a well-calibrated system of plenty and production, Maria Sybilla Merian, who travelled to the subcontinent half a century later, presents a more sinister process of decay. Merian made the earliest botanical illustrations of the banana, its flower, and its fruit, from direct observation of the plant in the Dutch colony of Surinam (Pl. 31).

Maria Merian was born in Germany, where her father Matthias was a prolific publisher and printer of engravings, but she left her native country for Holland, where she worked as an exceptionally industrious and skilled scientific illustrator. She also led an adventurous life for an artist of her time: she spent nearly twenty years in a Labadist convent in Frisia with her mother and her own two daughters. It was an experimental utopian community, somewhat akin to a hippie commune of the 1960s, that lived by the pantheistic and near antinomian teachings of a charismatic Protestant theologian, Jean de Labadie. In 1699 she broke with the Labadists, however, and travelled to the 'New World'. She stayed in Surinam there nearly three years, undertaking a wide-ranging record of the region's flora and insect life. Unlike Eckhout, and unusually not only for her sex but also for the times, she embarked for South America under her own auspices, was not working to a commission and did not enjoy a patron's support. Her elder daughter, Dorothea, did the hand-colouring of the magnificent prints Merian produced for several folio volumes; these provide, at one level, highly reliable, dazzlingly detailed representations of natural phenomena that are still little known in Europe.

Merian studied the prodigious fruits of the region with unsurpassed intensity; she isolates them as single items of interest, thereby dissolving the viewer's ability to assess their size accurately, except by reference to examples already known: her pineapple, crawling with caterpillars and feeding two or perhaps three varieties of butterfly might have looked huge to a contemporary eye, less informed than we are as to the normal dimensions of tropical phenomena. In the case of the banana, her fervent—and religious—imagination quickened the petals and sepals and stems with wayward rhythm and vivid colour, staging a drama of consumption in which reptiles, arthropods, caterpillars and butterflies are taking part simultaneously. The human hand leaves its mark, too, not only in the artist's decisive arrangement and selection, but in the cut made in one of the fruits, to display the section.

At another level, Merian's botanical plates tell a more than scientific tale: they provide a metaphorical narrative—an allegory, even—about colonization and colonists and their relation to the abundance and variety of flora and fauna in the Americas. According to Labadie, God's handiwork, visible in nature, was unspotted; 'plants and insects . . . were examples of the "innocent self": they were beings that had not changed since the moment God had created them, that were still united to him, doing what God wanted of them. If there was any stain in plants and insects, it was in the use that sinful humans made of them.'

Like Eckhout, Merian follows the tradition of the botanical plate when she compresses into a single image the processes of time and nature, but in spite of her commitment to the Labadist belief in creation's goodness, she does not represent a well-calibrated cyclical process, with its connotations of paradisiacal unchangingness, as Eckhout's noble savages imply. She gives evidence of parasitism, putrefaction, nature self-consuming and consumed: a violent cycle of metamorphosis and mutual devouring that her religious beliefs perhaps allowed her to see as harmonious and unblemished. Portraying nature's operations in this way does not issue a condemnation, or even an apology, for the implied similarity with colonial usufruct; rather the contrary: her dark vision of nature's processes of damage and self-interest can be taken as a fatalistic acceptance of the colonial enterprise itself.

There are no people in Merian's images, but she does refer here and there to informants and helpers, some of whom identify the plants and their properties (one Indian woman tells her the 'peacock flower'—Flos pavonis—is used to induce childbirth, and sometimes also as an abortifacient). Merian's magnificent, cankered vision of nature inaugurates the expulsion from Eden of the tropical paradise itself. In her botanical studies there begin to stir doubts and guilt about the colonies, which were to instigate much fantasy and fear about their inhabitants.

XVI

GOING BANANAS

'It is a banana, madam,' said the rogue . . .

'Such a thing never grew in Paradise,' I said.

'Indeed it did, madam,' says he, all puffed up like a poison adder. 'This fruit is from the island of Bermuda, which is closer to Paradise than you will ever be . . . THIS IS NOT SOME UNFORTUNATE'S RAKE. IT IS THE FRUIT OF A TREE. IT IS TO BE PEELED AND EATEN.'

Jeanette Winterson, Sexing the Cherry

'Incipe, puer parvo, risu cognoscere matrem,' Virgil wrote: 'Learn, little boy, to know your mother through laughter'. Did he mean the child's laughter? Or the mother's? Or, by omitting the possessive, did he want his readers to understand that recognition and laughter happen together at the very start of understanding, identity, and life itself? Georges Bataille writes, 'Laughter is reducible, in general, to the laugh of recognition in the child . . . A mother provokes a child's laughter by making faces at it, leading to the disequilibrium of sensations. She brings her face suddenly near her child, engages in games of startling expressions or makes funny, little cries.'

Laughing is a means to knowledge and a way of communication, and the humour that buoys it involves familiarity. Learning what to be afraid of and what not to be afraid of enters imagination and thought with the earliest exchanges; these tropes play with fears in order to allay them, but they can also identify enemies and culprits with random evils that strike, and consequently can shape prejudices, terrors and hate. Beyond these intimate negotiations of early language, fantasies quiver through culture and shape societies and their history. Then laughter can fail to soothe or bring relief; it can raise the very devils that it imagined needed holding at bay.

One of the cast of characters in the popular comic Viz, Tommy Johnson *is named after the seventeenth-century botanist who displayed in his apothecary shop the first banana seen in England.* The Big Hard One, *London, mid-1980s.*

The mere look of a banana and the sound of the word are funny—or so it seems now. But it was not always so. The banana is also pure sign, a sign that can be peeled to reveal a history of a certain historically specific fear. Beyond its immediately cheerful colour and suggestive shape, it has a story to tell, peculiar to the West. It can be scried, like coffee grains or the flight of geese, to reveal history at work on a symbol. It is one of the more vibrant examples of the imagination's versatility in play with social, economic and cultural forces; its comedy tells a funny story (funny ha-ha and funny-peculiar) about modern desires and fears.

The phrase 'going bananas', meaning going crazy, is recorded by the *OED* in 1935 but really gained widespread currency in the 1960s; its connotations are zany, in the tradition of the *commedia dell'arte*, from which that word derives: the *zanni* were the stage tricksters, who clowned and fell about. Going bananas implies the zaniness of losing control, as when a clown's legs whirl and he teeters; it is a state precariously poised on the edge where pleasure yields to distress. The phrase refers to monkeys, as in the related slang of 'going ape shit', and the fruit's comic character does arise from its multiple connections to the wild and to Baudelaire's 'nature'—which humour sets at a distance, as we shall see. The banana is a twentieth-century emblem not simply because the history of trading and nutrition domesticated an exotic natural product with unusual features far beyond its native habitat. It is vividly packed with both post-Darwinian and post-Freudian meanings. It makes clear our closeness to animals, particularly to apes, who are the only other creatures who use their hands to eat, and can peel bananas. It is one of the signs of the human to be able to close finger and thumb on an object, so this simian skill points up monkeys' likeness to ourselves. Toy gorillas, in plush or plastic, often brandish the fruit, half eaten, in one hand. A computer game features King Kong-style gorillas fighting on skyscrapers with exploding bananas. The humour such toys appeal to gives expression to a known truth about what we are, and children are expected to be happy with that, because they are considered nearer the animal state anyway.

Transformation through reconciling laughter and the acceptance of baseness, weakness, limits, even monstrosity, governs the comedy of the gryllus genre of nonsense and fable. The grotesque in all its variations, including its Circean bestiality, presents one form of self-protective humour, the iron in its flavour being a metaphor for its steeliness rather than its tongue-burning, wormwood bitterness. But disarming targets by tripping them up, as in the banana family of jokes, constitutes another mode of humour, which addresses and confronts—and also cancels—some of the same threats: the fear of being robbed of humanity, of being obliterated.

Because slipping on a banana skin seems one of the oldest jokes in the world, it is a challenge to draw up its biography. After a moment's reflection, it is clear that it cannot be very ancient. The banana skin slipped into the old comic tradition of folly, embarrassment, egg-on-your-face; it was added to the prop cupboard alongside the custard pie and the flour bag and the inkpot or chimney soot (in one of the farces by the nun Hroswitha, written and performed in the tenth century, the foolish villains are blackened when a spell makes them mistake filthy saucepans for beautiful hoydens, whom they fervently embrace). The banana skin is a newcomer to jokes compared to the venerable slapstick itself, for example, which was wielded by clowns of the *commedia dell'arte* to punctuate a pratfall or add some pedal to a spot of laughter. After all, the banana became known in the Old World, evidence suggests, in the fifteenth century at the earliest, and the fruit became common in Europe only after its importation from the Caribbean began around 1900. An exclusively élite delicacy would not have inspired popular bottoms-up funny business.

The fruit entered the comic bloodstream with the music hall. 'Have a banana' was already a comic catchphrase in routines of the early part of the century, and most schoolchildren in the 1940s and 1950s knew the funny answer: 'What did you say? I can't hear you, 'cos I've got a banana in my ear.' Marie Lloyd, famous for her repartee, is often credited with the fruit's début as stock innuendo, when she picked up a banana skin from the stage, and remarked, 'If the man who threw this wants to get his skin back, he can come to my dressing room afterwards.'

By the early 1920s the banana-skin joke was already so hackneyed that it was mocked, with understated skill, by Buster Keaton in his twenty-minute short *The High Sign* (1921), a film in which gags fall pell-mell: first Keaton, standing by a fruit barrow near a cop, pickpockets the gun out of the oblivious cop's holster and replaces it with a banana—an early instance of the now commonplace phallic pun. Several scenes later, the hulking villain, lugubrious gang leader of 'The Blinking Buzzards', is spotted acting suspiciously by the same policeman, who draws. He then finds that he is threatening the villain with a banana. There is a close-up; the villain looks at the fruit, takes it, peels it, and wolfs it, ogreishly eyeing the cop all the while with such sinister intent that this unfortunate takes to his heels. The Blinking Buzzards' chief then drops the skin on the ground, setting up Buster Keaton, who comes round the corner in the next sequence. Just as Keaton is sauntering towards the banana skin, he catches the runaway cop's eye, and it is his turn to make a dash for it. The joke is that he looks as if he is going to step right on the banana peel and come a cropper, but he frustrates our expectations: he skips it, walks straight on by, then gives us in the audience 'the high sign' of the title, the waggling thumbs and hands of the Blinking Buzzards' secret code, as if conscious that he has cheated our anticipation of his downfall.

The High Sign enchains a whole series of gins and booby traps, all of which catch their prey—usually Keaton. It is a film in which all the plants bear fruit—exploding cigars, trapdoors, panels—but one single achingly promised pratfall does not take place: in order to be funny, the joke needs the banana skin to fail.

But why the banana at all? Most of us know that autumn leaves, icy pavements, even loose scree, as well as the peel or pith of almost any fruit much more familiar to our forebears, like strawberries or pears or cherries, are much more likely booby traps. One answer is obvious: the banana's shape, and that shape's associations, which Marie Lloyd and music-hall bawdy songs were already playing on.

One circulating story, collected as far afield as Perthshire and Arkansas, began to be told after the Second World War. Two little girls on a train are

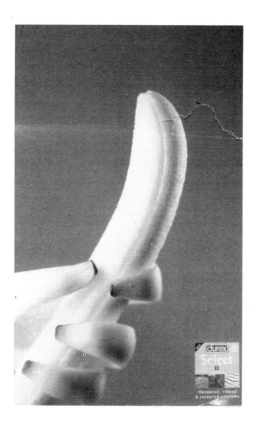

Some things can best be communicated in banana form. Advertisement for condoms, 1990s.

sitting in the compartment with a soldier, just demobbed, who offers each of them a banana. The older girl accepts and begins to eat it; at that moment, the train enters a tunnel. She asks the younger girl, 'Have you started your banana yet?' 'No.' 'Well don't,' she warns her. 'It makes you go blind.'

The explicit sexualizing of the fruit took happily and readily in popular perception of it, famously conveyed by Andy Warhol's cover for the Velvet Underground & Nico's 1967 release, and echoed in the famous marketing slogan in the UK: 'Unzip a banana'. *Viz*, the raucous, outrageously filthy and highly popular comic, features Tommy 'Banana' Johnson ('He's got a big banana') alongside 'Felix and his Amazing Underpants'. By the mid-1990s, the equivalence of banana and penis had been so thoroughly internalized that British schoolchildren were given instructions about condoms using bananas (and, admittedly, cucumbers) for classroom demonstrations; Durex used the banana in an advertisement around the same time. The relationship between what is precious and what is threatened is, of course, very close, and humour struggles to defend these areas, often in the most contradictory, topsy-turvy fashion. 'In those circumstances in which the essential humanity of the human has been called into question,' writes William Gass, 'in just those very circumstances, the height of humor has been scaled.' That a man's most precious part should be—like a sausage, or a piece of pipe, like a banana . . .

Unexpectedly, the originator of the first sight gag on film that releases sexual anxiety through comic antics with the banana was a woman, Alice Guy-Blaché, in her tiny masterpiece, *Madame a des envies* (The Missus has cravings), made in 1906. As we shall see, and as Marie Lloyd's repartee shows, it is not unusual for women to handle this kind of humour: from a female point of view the subject offers a particular ambiguous image of power. As Mary Douglas has commented, 'The message of a standard rite is that the ordained patterns of social life are inescapable. The message of a joke is that they are escapable. A joke is by nature an anti-rite.'

The short, comic film opens with Madame, played by a six-foot cross-dressed titan, waddling—she is in the last stage of pregnancy, padded out with deliberate fakery—as she takes the air in a park. Her eyes catch sight of a boy eating a lollipop; the craving rises; she snatches the lollipop from his hand and makes off with it. We see her in close-up, voluptuously sucking. Next, it is the turn of a one-legged beggar, who is about to eat a banana; Madame pounces. Next, she snatches a pipe and draws on it with furious appetite, while the robbed smoker gets into a brawl with her husband; in the tussle, she falls upside down into a flowerbed. Each time she seizes another object of her craving, we see her in close-up—some of the earliest shots of this kind in the genre—grimacing, rolling her eyes and munching deliriously; when her husband bends over to rescue her from the flowerbed, it turns out to be a cabbage patch, and he finds a fine new baby sitting in one of the cabbages.

The final sequence shows Madame, the stuffing pillow shed, slim once again, with the baby in a pram behind her, pushed by her dwarfed husband, while she proudly strides ahead, looking for . . . her next prey. The quickfire gags draw on variety show stock characters: the tiny put-upon husband, the woman of gigantic and predatory appetite, the lewd accidental morphology of the sausage, the pipe, and so forth. Other Guy-Blaché short films also relish old joke material: hosepipes, glue pots, runaway donkeys, collapsing beds; but she may well have given the banana its cinematic début as phallic icon.

In the early part of the century, bananas were also finding a place as a conventional sign of male gender at a less popular level than Guy-Blaché's comedies. Several of the famous, riddling, 'metaphysical' still lifes of Giorgio de Chirico include the fruit: *The Uncertainty of the Poet* (1913), for example, shows an ambiguous headless sculpture/ woman standing in one of the artist's empty urban spaces beside a large bunch of bananas, its many fruits bristling in rhythmic counterpoint to the torso's pronounced belly and buttocks. One of the fruits lies apart from and behind the parent bunch, compositionally aligned to the smoke streaming from the engine on the horizon. De Chirico thus staged modernity as dreamlike with ejaculatory overtones, and imbued its signs with lumbering solemnity. The Surrealist vision of everyday objects renders them unfamiliar, incongruous, and the work's coolly bizarre antinomies (nobility of ancient Rome, awful bathos of bananas) produce a confusion of tone that matches the title; but the overall 'metaphysical' effect is lugubrious to the point of comedy. *The Uncertainty of the Poet* exemplifies humour's 'tendency to oscillate between the uncanny and the ridiculous', in Ernst Gombrich's words; it plays with expected categories, consistent registers and due order according to the principles of comic representation, and of existential, modern absurdism and its shaky catharsis. The painting shows the female body maimed in a familiar aesthetic fashion, and ruefully conveys the crippling and crippled condition of male sexuality through the outlandish many-limbed trunk of the bunch of bananas.

(It is perhaps appropriate to De Chirico's morose view that in an early twentieth-century manual of dream interpretation, the writer warns, 'To dream of bananas foretells that you will be mated to an uninteresting and an unloved companion.')

The bathetic relationship of the fruit with the penis informs much of the comic associations attached to it since the turn of the century. Linda Nochlin made this point with sharp wit when she mimicked a *belle époque* soft porn postcard of a young woman, proffering apples for sale on a dish in such a way that the fruit rhymed with her naked breasts, as in the Eckhout portrait. Nochlin posed a male friend in the same style, naked except for his socks, and substituted the phallic rhyme of bananas on his proferred dish. The resulting photograph could not strike anyone as erotic: it reveals cultural differences in response to male and female nudity, as Nochlin intended, but it makes riotous mock of male anatomy, too.

Pop culture carried banana lore in its mocking baggage of happy *double entendres* and childlike play. The word with its internal rhymes and its sequence of consonants fortuitously combines both the b-stem and the n-stem associated with nursery nonsense and consequently lent itself to endless comic appropriation, even in Japan, where the successful young novelist Banana Yashimoto changed her first name to make a punkishly defiant anti-traditional point. Bananaman still features in the *Dandy*

The irresistible double entendre: *Ritchie Adams and Mark Barkan's 1968*
Tra-La-La Song *for a children's television programme was recorded by The*
Dickies the following year.

comic, alongside other personalities like Desperate Dan, Beryl the Peril, Growing Paynes and Korky the Kat; Bananaman is a perennial big, lumbering, hopeless and helpless fall guy, an anti-Superman hulk who always tries to go to the rescue and always messes up, sabotaging the efforts of various comic (and sometimes racialized) opponents such as 'Taw Mass the Tank Injun and his Injun braves' who are camping out on the 'central reservation of the M1'. 'Top banana' is American slang for the top-billing comic in a variety show. In the late 1960s, a band called the Dickies printed its name over a bright yellow bruised fruit and issued a crazily souped-up protopunk take on 'The Tra La La Song', the theme tune of *The Banana Splits' Adventure Hour,* a wholesome American television programme for kids. Fun-loving was never going to get away with innocence, especially where bananas were concerned, and this occasion was no exception. The *Banana Splits* song has the distinction of not merely associating bananas with monkeys, but singing about their identical appearance:

> Two banana, four banana, one banana, three,
> Swingin' like a bunch of monkeys, hangin' from a tree
> Hey there ev'rybody, won't you come along and see
> How much like Banana Splits ev'ryone can be.

❖   ❖   ❖

The banana's associations with male sexuality, with its absurdity and its pathos, and at the same time with the jungle and monkeys and exotic parts have turned its biography into a troubled tangle of modern dilemmas, one that interestingly and often accurately takes the temperature of racial prejudice. Members of some football crowds in England have made monkey noises and gestures at black players; they have even been known to throw bananas onto the pitch in abusive mockery. Nick Hornby gave a passionate and ferocious account of the Arsenal–Liverpool match in August 1987:

> We could see quite clearly, as the teams warmed up before the kick-off, that banana after banana was being hurled from the away supporters' enclosure. The bananas were designed to announce, for the benefit of those unversed in codified terrace abuse, that there was a monkey on the pitch . . .
>
> Those who have seen John Barnes, this beautiful, elegant man, play football, or give an interview, or even simply walk out onto a pitch, and have also stood next to the grunting, over-weight orangutans who do things like throw bananas and make monkey noises, will appreciate the dazzling irony of this.

The Liverpool supporters were mocking their own player; this pseudo-hilarious use of racial abuse serves to define an outsider and exclude him. John Barnes himself has commented 'I remember being eighteen and playing at West Ham, and bananas came on the pitch left, right and centre—and that happens down there all the time.' In contrast, he dismissed his Liverpool supporters' actions: 'I thought, well' (and he shrugged), 'a couple of bananas. So what? West Ham, it's much worse down there . . .' But, as the revulsion of a fan like Hornby shows, the comic manœuvre hardly shakes ignorance or prejudice. Comedians, humorists and party raconteurs work with the shared values of the group they address. As Mary Douglas emphasizes, 'The joke works only when it mirrors social forms; it exists by virtue of its congruence with the social structure.'

The banana has served to shape a certain perception of the bogeyman, and its skin has served to trip him up, while the fruit—and its freight of meanings—has stayed around, to be used in retaliation. Just as it leaves a residue that extends the comedy of its shape, so its symbolism connects to unfinished business that lingers on in the mind as anxiety, as envy, even as remorse. The banana skin, which remains after the fruit has been consumed, presents, in metonymy, an image of the return of the repressed. Issues of sex and power are wondrously compacted in this funny fruit; historical guilt, loss of authority, the search for identity, female ambivalence about male power, male dreams of adequacy and fears of inadequacy are all raised by its yellow curve. The theme that will emerge follows a cultural emphasis even more highly marked during the last decades: the submerging of narrative beneath spectacle, the weakening of discursive intelligence in favour of visual stimulus, the leaching of history by image.

The banana is a mythical fruit in the prime sense argued by Roland Barthes in *Mythologies*: it presents as natural, universal and timeless a compact of meanings that have been laid down over the centuries. It enters the repertory of humour at a defined moment of imperial expansion, carrying a socio-economic cargo that is still changing in meaning.

The banana's seemingly natural link to sex has focused the fruit's modern Western meaning around issues of male performance and potency; fears in these areas have led, skipping sideways along lines of anxiety, to race—partly on account of the banana plantations' siting. 'Banana republic', dating from 1935 in the *OED*, describes a corrupt and hopeless puppet dictatorship, but the term disparages the local people, for submitting to (collaborating with) their paymasters, invariably international or American fruit companies operating cartels in Central America. Woody Allen called one of his less successfully zany comedies *Bananas* (1971) and recklessly—or perhaps, heedlessly—guyed Fidel Castro and a guerrilla revolution on a Caribbean island. The move, from masculine anxiety (a perennial Allen theme) to racist stereotyping, arises from more than geography. Others, especially blacks, have been ascribed sexual ease and prowess, greater command of pleasure, and a general familiarity with the Circean world in its desirable as well as its bestial aspects, according to cultural phenomena of the twentieth century as diverse as the delusions of the Ku Klux Klan and the perversely aestheticized phallic icons of Robert Mapplethorpe.

This large, and largely unspeakable, ground of white desire and fear opens the possibility of analysing further the uses of laughter. What appear to be the intrinsically comic connotations of the banana are the product of twentieth-century anxieties ranging from a new emphasis on male virility to male unemployment and redundancy, its humour a defence against fears which remain nameless because the jokes themselves act as screens and veils. The history of bananas throws light on basic human fears, which humour confronts and tries, often successfully, to deal with. But its effectiveness as a remedy does not entail that it should elude diagnosis.

Even the phallic identification, which seems so natural, has been acquired within the North American and European tradition only recently: in Africa and in India, the banana supplies so many comforts and necessities—food from the bud and the leaves, shade, shelter, building materials, wrappings for food and other goods, and even shrouds—that it is not only thought of exclusively in terms of the single fruit, but also belongs in rituals centred on fertility and women's guardianship of life: it is planted in sacred precincts in India and features prominently, for example, in women's rituals in Uganda, where it is the staple crop. An Indonesian legend, from the Central Celebes, gives the banana a crucial role at the beginning of human society: the Creator one day let down a stone on the end of a rope, as is his way with his gifts to his creatures, but the first man and woman scorned the stone and asked for something else. 'The Creator complied,' the story continues, 'and hauled away at the rope; the stone mounted up and up till it vanished from sight. Presently, the rope was seen coming down from heaven again, and this time there was a banana at the end of it . . .'

The first parents in the mythology of the Celebes are delighted, but they hear the divine patriarch's voice boom out above: 'Because ye have chosen the banana, your life shall be like its life. When the banana tree has off-spring, the parent stem dies; so shall ye die and your children shall step into your place. Had ye chosen the stone, your life would have been like the life of stone, changeless and immortal.' The plant here figures as the whole cycle of growth, and symbolizes human life, process, transformation, ripeness and procreation, all aspects of the knowledge of good and evil, as opposed to immortal, unchanging stasis. It embodies the lesson in time and death that Kronos is forced to learn when Zeus overcomes him and he has to relinquish his power to the future generation. 'Were they in fact so fool-ish to choose,' asks the Sanskrit scholar Wendy Doniger O'Flaherty, 'instead of the sterility of an eternity of stone, the luscious phallic banana of death? Did they really make the "wrong" choice?'

The banana's history in the West begins with the banana as a principal candidate for the identity of the forbidden fruit itself in the Garden of Eden. In the seventeenth century, when savants were equally keen on gardening and the Bible, the general opinion of herbalists and botanists and connoisseurs of simples was that the banana, not the apple, was the most likely tree of the knowledge of good and evil. (The palm was preferred for the tree of life.) Such books are not always reliable guides—the vegetable lamb, also known as the borometz, which grew on a stalk in Scythia, also makes an appearance in such books as part of God's flora. The learned apothecary Thomas Johnson described it with enthusiasm in his *Herbal* (1636) under the title 'Of Adams Apple tree . . .' He reported that 'The Grecians and Christians which inhabit Syria, and the Jewes also, suppose it to be that tree of whose fruit Adam did taste; which others thinke it to be a rediculous [sic] fable . . .', but he paused to pass on the belief that 'if it be cut . . . may be seene the shape and forme of a crosse, with a man fastned thereto.' He said he could not see the crucified saviour himself, however.

Though nobody argued wholeheartedly that the banana was the fruit whereof Adam did eat, Linnaeus believed in the story sufficiently to give the plant the name *Musa paradisiaca*. A sister species, the plantain, he called *Musa sapientum*, on account of another legend: that the gymnosophists, or Wise Men of the East, whom Alexander the Great encountered, sat in the shade of such a tree and occasionally ate a banana.

The frond of the banana has straight seams, and it is easy to tear along them and make squares of bright luminous green, nature's own shot silk, which is what Adam and Eve probably did when they made shift with 'aprons' to hide their shame from God in the garden. In countries where French, Spanish, and Portuguese are spoken—which means the original export markets of the fruit, such as the Canaries, parts of Africa and the Caribbean, as well as Latin America—the word 'fig' is used in Creole for banana. Only the savoury variety, the plantain, is called *banane*. In 1750, the Revd. Griffith Hughes, in his account of Barbados, declared, 'And as the fruit of the Banana-tree is often by the most ancient Authors called a Fig, I may, I hope without Presumption . . . look upon the Fig-tree in Paradise to be no other than the Banana-tree.' This may be another example of those inspired linguistic slips across cultures that result in widespread conventional misapprehensions. The fig leaf may have the appropriate trefoil shape, but that it is hard to attach to the body every child confronted with a Renaissance statue has noticed. Banana leaves, on the other hand, can be draped and threaded—like cloth.

The botanical link to the symbolic forbidden fruit and, by implication, to carnal knowledge arose from those bounteous features of the banana which make Westerners giggle or laugh aloud at the mere mention of it. The semi-mystical concept of 'signature', developed by Renaissance Neoplatonists, gave the connection a serious foundation. The form of a natural phenomenon was believed to mimic the function for which it was created. Thus the rounded leaves of sow-bread or cyclamen were seen to imitate the vessel of the womb, and the plant was recommended for 'women in their extreme travell with childe . . .'

When the banana was first harvested in the New World, it epitomized the natural plenitude of the tropics, the earthly paradise where everything fruits and flowers in glorious abundance the year round. The banana is not, however, indigenous to the Americas with which it has become so closely identified; the word is West African, noted for the first time in works like García de Orta's travel chronicle of 1563 and Filippo Pigafetta's

A Report of the Kingdom of Congo in 1597. It is likely that the banana travelled to Africa from China and India, where it is recorded far earlier than in the New World. Was it transported in the same long-distance canoes in which Javanese sailors brought rice to Madagascar two thousand years ago? Perhaps. Then Arab traders carried it across the continent to Guinea on the west coast, where Portuguese navigators found it; they took the root stocks (known as bull heads, from their appearance) to the Canary Islands, where (Spanish) bananas are still grown—within the frontiers of the European Community. A Spanish friar, one Thomas de Berlanga, may have been responsible for the fruit's subsequent journey to the Americas, for he planted it in San Domingo in 1516; the English, those comparative latecomers to the New World, saw the plant's obliging nature and took many banana stocks from the Spanish-dominated islands to their doomed pioneer colony of Roanoke in Virginia. A Spanish prisoner observed them making drawings of many plants they carried away with them. Again, we see the convergence among Elizabethans of gardens and the promised land.

The single flower which grows on each banana plant and produces the bunch was described by the mercenary and ethnographer J. G. Stedman as 'something like a calf's heart': it has a huge bud shape, with a blueish purple bloom on fleshy red petals and a soft whey-like scent, and it hangs down and then pokes out from the end of a bizarrely corrugated thick stem in a manner that is definitely lewd. Wallace Stevens vividly captured this raunchiness in a poem:

> Fibrous and dangling down
> Oozing cantankerous gum
> Out of their purple maws,
> Darting out of their purple craws
> Their musky and tingling tongues.

When Thomas Johnson hung up a stem of bananas, brought from Bermuda, to ripen in his shop in Holborn in 1633, it was the first time its wonders were displayed to the public in London.

Bananas thereafter emerge as a motif in Western dreams of the tropics, saturated with promise of plenitude, with *luxe, calme et volupté*. They were first imported into Britain at the end of the nineteenth century—the shipping company Fyffes,which still carries the Caribbean harvests, gives 1888 as the first year—and the annual consumption of the fruit has now reached five billion bananas in the United Kingdom alone. At the end of the 1980s and of the Cold War, the fruit embodied Western access to cheap luxuries and pleasures and plenty for the former Eastern bloc; in the aftermath of 1989, East Germans coveted appliances and bananas, polar expressions of capitalism's consumer liberality. The fruit's history continues, as the stake in a bitter economic war between small countries and the superpower of the United States: American fruit companies insist on forcing down the price of bananas and effectively cutting out the producers from island states like Jamaica, Dominica and St. Lucia. Meanwhile, its nutritional virtues continue to be promoted, for it is rich in potassium and other essential trace elements, including serotonin, a natural antidepressant and the chief ingredient in Prozac. Athletes use the fruit as almost magical power food: 800 bananas were eaten every day by players at the Wimbledon tennis tournament in 1997. In just over a hundred years, it has become a staple, a prime source of natural nourishment which we expect to consume plentifully and cheaply. This dependence on the fruit's availability has added to its potency as a symbol.

Early representations of the tropical paradise and its typical fruits, like the banana, continue to reverberate, but the tone changes. The decline from stunned wonder at its marvels to laughter maps with almost appalling accuracy Western fantasies about and relations with the inhabitants of those natural regions. Banana jokes include banana-skin jokes when they target shared objects of desire, the desire often camouflaged as derision, and the derision often masking fear as well. In the twentieth century, both began to gather around issues of race, the old tropical trope turning into rollicking farce. This trend offers a depressingly neat graph of labour, of empire, of economic competition and, in countries like England and the United States, of immigration and internal migration.

As Albert Eckhout's paintings reveal, the banana becomes an unconscious marker of the tropical paradise. An equestrian portrait drawing of the revolutionary leader Toussaint L'Ouverture shows the liberator of Haiti in Napoleonic mode, in a direct echo of the grandiloquent homage by Jacques-Louis David to the emperor's Italian campaign. Toussaint L'Ouverture, born in slavery in Saint Domingue (as Haiti was then called), led revolutionary forces in the wake of the abolition of slavery by the French and won several decisive victories in the colonial wars that convulsed the Caribbean at the end of the eighteenth century; for a while he then ruled in Haiti. Denis Volozon, the artist, sets the scene of his heroism by including behind the traditional flowing mane of his stallion (a famous

On his rearing white
stallion, mane and tail
flying, mantle swirling,
Napoleon points towards
Italy; the Alps rise up
mightily behind him.
Jacques-Louis David,
Bonaparte Crossing the
Alps, c. 1800–1.

mount called Bel Argent), a luxuriantly fruiting—and improbably tall—banana tree. Napoleon has the lofty peaks of the Alps; Toussaint the mighty protuberance of bananas.

This equivalence continues to animate the vision of difference: colour, distance, prodigiousness and strangeness are compressed into the banana; as the wheel is to St. Catherine, the hourglass to the figure of Death, or the bridle to the virtue of temperance, so the banana becomes the characterizing attribute of the colonized world in its seductive aspect as a place of refuge, a beckoning Eden.

The metonymy seeps from overdetermined observation of natural phenomena into the symbolic order, without contact or reference to an original witness: the painter Douanier Rousseau, who never left France, scattered the banana through his tropical dreamlands as nearly pure sign as possible—yellow spikes in close multiple bundles appearing simultaneously as flowers and fruits. Rousseau's visions teem with an untamed fruitfulness and fertility, where dusky women luxuriate and offer themselves, where lions and other wild beasts roam alongside Indian braves (*Repast of the Lion*; *The Jungle: Tiger Attacking a Buffalo*), and are often joined in primordial combat, in the implacable but thrilling cycle of unrestrained *natura devorans*. The reclining nude on the deep velvet maroon couch in *The Dream* (1910, Pl. 31), one of Rousseau's most famous paintings,

On his rearing white stallion, mane and tail flowing, Toussaint L'Ouverture, revolutionary fighter against slavery, raises his sword; a banana tree in fruit denotes his field of operations. Denis Volozon, c. 1840.

points, wide-awake, to a greeny-black piper, who, accompanied by round-eyed lion-esses, stands among luxuriant blooms and birds and foliage—including bananas—in his striped skirt like the feathered apparel of Latin American natives. A black Orpheus, he is charming the living creatures around him, like the nude, like the gold-red snake gliding out of the picture on the right.

Such heady fantasies invited the mockery of a singer, performer and artiste with inside knowledge of popular entertainment and its Oriental-ism. In the Paris of Douanier Rousseau a generation later, Josephine Baker shamelessly guyed the banana's sensual and exotic associations for her pre-dominantly white audience when she stripped down to her notorious banana costume in the *Revue Nègre* of 1926. Like the maidservant from Thrace, she laughed joyously at their folly. Unlike her Thracian precursor, however, she satirized their position by enacting its preconceptions, by col-luding with their fantasies. Performed at the Folies Bergères, the *Revue Nègre* was part of the variety show that capitalized on—and crowned—the capital's new mania for 'négritude'. The scenario called for Rousseau's Jardin des Plantes scenery: Josephine Baker entered a stage jungle, by dusk (of course), and crawled along the trunk of a fallen tree on all fours; there, to the beat of native drums, she came across the sleeping body of a young white man, for whom she launched into her dance.

It was at once a Charleston, a music-hall knees-up, a bump and grind, and a Mama Dinks' chicken routine. Various fairy godfathers and -mothers have been proposed for the costume, a scanty parody of a Hawaiian hula skirt made of hanging bananas, but Josephine Baker is reported to have said, 'It is Cocteau who gave me the idea for the banana belt. He said, "On you, it will look very dressy." ' A film survives of her dance, from Berlin in 1927. In the censored American version of 1935, not only was Baker persuaded to wear a showgirl bra, but the frolicsome fruit were changed into curious spikes, more rebarbative than jaunty.

The numbers in the *Revue Nègre* were multilayered in their aims and their effects: in a later number of the show, the actor known as Benglia was made up in Josephine Baker style, wearing nothing but a grass skirt, and danced with the male clown, Dorville—consciously driving the comedy home, as if Baker's self-parody might not make the point. But the inflamed reception of the carnival of negritude clearly expressed a serious excitement, stirred at the same time as laughter: this response expressed cathartic relief that the animality was just a show, the sexual vigour just a lark. But it was a response mixed with an erotic recognition of the show's pull, its seductive attraction. It thus constitutes one of the most precise historical moments when the Other becomes trapped in the definition it is mocking, knowingly, with all the flighty joy of the comic.

Josephine Baker had performed straightforward masturbatory fantasy scenes for a white audience in the first tour of the *Revue* the year before, in a number with Joe Alex, in which she writhed naked around his near-naked body in the 'Danse du Sauvage'. She had also inaugurated her clown persona then, with an acrobatic, rubber-legged rendition of 'Yes, Sir, That's My Baby'—for which she blacked herself up. But the comic entertainment Baker so vivaciously developed in the notorious banana dance engages in battle with forces on both the audience's side and the performers'; 1926 marks the second phase of popular banana lore. In the famous 'Yes, We Have No Bananas', the racist banter that unfortunately underlies the frothy nonsense of the single lyric shows in the cover sheet of the song in its 1923 American publication,where the caricatured, rubber-lipped faces are highlighted in garish green and crimson.

Josephine Baker would not have been unaware of this: she was brought up in a town where the laundries advertised that they washed only for whites. Yet she pretended to be what Rousseau dreamed of: the spirit of the jungle. She bounced her bananas, showed herself off, to the rapture of the night crowds of sophisticates and fans: she embodied the untamed, unfettered libido, yet she also spoofed the expectation of it, she knew different.

Josephine Baker in her banana costume for the Revue Nègre, Paris, 1926.

Raising a triumphal arch of bananas: the tropical beach romp choreographed by Busby Berkeley for The Gang's All Here, *1943.*

She inhabited the fools' double consciousness, the ironic cynicism that turns all appearances unstable. She perhaps achieved a new synthesis: the comic erotic. In the footage and the stills that survive, her jubilation lights up her eyes, sets the pulse beating with her feet. But as spectacle, she—and her bananas—cannot resist sufficiently the lapse into alienation and commodification: her wit, her energy, her mischief, her resplendent self-fabrication meet that stone wall of mass media culture, its feeding on stereotype, and her joy freezes in the gaze of racial ascriptions.

Carmen Miranda, another incandescent stage performer in her own country (Brazil), also clowned for her public, also found herself enmeshed in the complicated humour arising from 'nigger-loving' and its complex beckonings and disavowals. She was born in Portugal and emigrated as a child with her parents, and in her early career as a singer she adopted the ornaments and head-dresses and bangles and jewels and braids and belts of the women of Bahia, traditional street vendors descended from the African slaves brought to Brazil during the centuries of colonial development. The character she invented eventually inspired the logo of Chiquita, one of the largest banana companies in the world: the famous totem who pops up in turban and Spanish flounces and used to deliver, in a Carmen Miranda accent, an advertising jingle to which every child in America in the 1950s could sing along.

Carmen Miranda adopted the persona of a Bahiana advisedly: the hierarchy of skin colours that had obtained in Brazil ever since the colonial taxonomies, as encoded in Albert Eckhout's paintings, allotted Bahiana women a degraded status. Yet these African street vendors were independent businesswomen who worked in public and enjoyed a different independence from their bourgeois superiors on the social scale. They thus embody a historical and social counterpart of the imaginary free spirit that Josephine Baker, an urban American, also conjured for her fans, mocking its mystique and their own fascination. In Carmen Miranda's case, she repudiated her own white-Catholic convent formation in favour of a magnified, African-Latino personality, with its insistent primitive message and its necessary cargo of fruity signifiers.

Carmen Miranda was born in 1909, only three years after Josephine Baker, but because the most familiar stage of her film career coincides with Hollywood Technicolor, she gives the impression of belonging to another, later era. She invented her African *alter ego* in a spirit of joyous primitivism analogous to Baker's, in a film made in Brazil, called *Banana da Terra* (1939), but with its translation to Hollywood, its impact changed.

The Gang's All Here (1943), a comic spectacular directed by Busby Berkeley, opens with the song 'Brazil', lusciously crooned in Portuguese by a cabaret MC, plunged into deep chiaroscuro. Half-black and half-white, he gives the only hint of the colour or race themes to come; the film then cuts to a shot of the docks, where a steamer called S.S. *Brazil* is landing sugar and coffee, soon followed by a gargantuan basket of tropical fruit swung over the side. This turns out to be nothing less than Carmen Miranda's hat.

She breaks into a samba as she steps out onto American soil and there follows a huge number, a most extraordinary and hyperbolic showstopper, starring Carmen Miranda as 'The Lady in the Tutti Frutti Hat'. The scene on the dock shifts seamlessly, according to dream logic, into a Broadway nightclub decorated as a banana grove, with barrel organ players galore, performing monkeys, and an infinite chorus line of banana-waving showgirls; Carmen Miranda arrives on a fruit wagon to the sound of monkey chatter and cries; the chorus then lever giant bananas and strawberries in prolonged routines with bawdy overtones. They manipulate the bananas erect, make Mexican waves and kaleidoscopic patterns by opening and closing their legs, and assemble a banana xylophone for Carmen Miranda to play, while all the while she is sparkling and trilling the come-hither lyrics. The various elements of this camp, hilarious fantasia eventually climax in an explosion of bananas from Carmen Miranda's head.

Carmen Miranda, the 'Lady in the Tutti-Frutti Hat', successfully imported to Hollywood her manic, effervescent, glitzy variation on the traditional Brazilian street vendor's costume. She became the trademark of Chiquita, one of the largest banana importers.

In 1939, Carmen Miranda was imported from Rio, where she was a national figurehead of the liberal régime and one of the country's beloved stars, as part of Hollywood's propaganda efforts on behalf of Roosevelt's Good Neighbor policy with Latin America. She subsequently became one of the highest-paid performers in Hollywood, with films like *Down Argentine Way* (1940), *That Night in Rio* (1941) and *The Gang's All Here*. But her career went into a decline in the 1950s, when politics no longer needed positive Latin American representations. The United States was closing in on itself. Then Miranda became too foreign, too sexy, too strange with her flashing eyes, exuberant eroticism, busy hands, uncrushable high spirits.

The temptation for both Josephine Baker and Carmen Miranda lay in the power accorded to them by the perception of their sexuality. This is the inextricable conundrum for the performer who belongs by allegiance to any less than mainstream social group—whether to harness the energy that fear and prejudice generate. But to ignore its potential to capture and

Between the earthly paradise and the banana plantation, then and now, lies a certain distance: a British colonial official, Harry Johnston, photographed women workers in the Caribbean in 1908–9.

enthral an audience means working outside a familiar code, and because comedy is, as we have seen Bergson write about the joke, essentially a group activity, this can be self-defeating: 'Laughter appears to stand in need of an echo . . . our laughter is always the laughter of a group.'

Pirandello makes a distinction between the humorous and the comic, arguing that the comic defines what he calls the opposite, and elaborates a group perception of what it is not. By contrast, in Pirandello's thesis, humour sympathizes with its objects and encompasses a 'sentiment of the opposite, or other', and this is the kind of laughter that can open up the possibility of transgression, can act as social criticism. While we may feel that we are likely to slip on the banana skin and become the butt of the group that thereby excludes us, it is likely, in most of the comedy of this kind of embarrassment, that we are being invited to distance ourselves from the victim: clowns are mostly not-us. And for this reason, as Umberto Eco comments in his essay on Carnival, dictators allow jesters of this kind,

Peace brings plenty, and plenty means bananas: after World War II, Britain's Prime Minister Clement Attlee supervises the distribution of the fruit ration.

even favour them, whereas they censor satirists and parodists, those performers of the humour that invites the audience to identify with and to belong to the groups it targets.

❖   ❖   ❖

The banana has endured astonishingly undiminished as a sign of an ease-ful existence that envelops others, elsewhere: it provides the ultimate dream of the indigent sharecroppers in William Faulkner's *As I Lay Dying*, published in 1930, as they transport their mother's body to the big city. In Britain, during the Second World War, when a population that had grown accustomed to the fruit's arrival on the banana boats from the Caribbean was deprived of it, the banana gained in allure, becoming a symbol of the *douceur de vivre* that was lost and risked being lost forever. A naval officer who took part in the D-Day landings recalled a scene that expresses poignantly the meaning of the fruit: as the troops crossed the Channel, they passed the débris of a banana boat that had been torpedoed. The cargo was floating, far below the deck of their battleship, a glowing tropi-cal yellow against the greenish grey dun of northern waters. None of the soldiers had seen the fruit since the beginning of the war, and they did everything they could to fish some out of the sea as they passed through this tantalizing flotsam; but they had no lines, no nets, no harpoons, and no means to raise them. So they sailed past, helpless.

The new Socialist government, elected after victory, almost immediately organized a distribution of bananas to children. The precious fruit became the emblem of the nutritive bounty of Britain's dominions, now restored to peacetime governance, wise and benevolent. This was taking place at the same time as the active recruitment of man- and woman-power from the Caribbean: the first boat, crowded with West Indians solicited as workers in the services of the nation's reconstruction, arrived in 1948. Others followed throughout the 1950s.

Auberon Waugh remembered this time of post-war hope at the family table, when the banana ration was distributed: 'the great day arrived when my mother came home with three bananas'. But before the eyes of his three children, who had only heard of the deliciousness of the banana but had never had one, his father, Evelyn Waugh, took the fruit, peeled it and cut it, poured on cream and sugar, and 'ate all three. It would be absurd to say that I never forgave him. But he was permanently marked down in my estimation from that moment, in ways which no amount of sexual transgression would have achieved . . . From that moment, I never treated anything he had to say on faith or morals very seriously.' Truly the paternal ogre in the bosom of the family.

The intensity of the desire for the fruit must have inspired the rococo opening of *Gravity's Rainbow* (1973), Thomas Pynchon's huge Second World War novel. He sets the beginning in London, in a most improbable rooftop grove, which the hero, Pirate Prentice, has grown under glass to make up for wartime deprivation. Gathered together there is a cartoon crew of spies, combatants, and buddies, endowed with a Rabelaisian appetite for bananas in every imaginable form, from night-time cocktails to his hero's famous Banana Breakfasts of mush or fritters.

Attitudes have profoundly altered since then, when the banana symbolized Britain's return to normal authority over the seas and the Prime Minister Clement Attlee could be shown on newsreels offering a banana to a schoolgirl. Only think of a *Private Eye* cover with such a photograph; or indeed, think of Tony Blair, let alone Bill Clinton, attempting something similar. The banana was not innocent of *double entendres*, as we have seen abundantly, but the general public could be counted on not to laugh, as the fruit's desirability overrode, in that era of rationing, all its other significations. The passion for bananas that took over the former German

Democratic Republic after 1989 simply focused the desire to consume, Western-style, this fruit, with its raft of meanings: sun, fun, sex, laughter, plenty, irresponsibility. Nothing else could do the job quite so satisfyingly: not a peach or an orange or a pineapple or a mango. (Watermelons, however, have some of the same function in their connection to happy, smilin', laughin' God's chillun on the slave plantations of the American South.)

The banana becomes funny when it does not have scarcity value, when it comes into surplus, when it is cheap and can be used as an emblem of cheapness, as it was in a 1996 British Telecom advertisement for off-peak telephoning. The labour that farms the fruit and transports it correspondingly falls in value too, literally (low wages, appalling conditions on the fruit companies' huge plantations, barely survival income for the independent growers in the Caribbean) and symbolically. In places where the banana is a staple crop, an essential means of livelihood and hard work, the inhabitants do not tell banana jokes or slip up on banana peel—not surprisingly, perhaps. Claude McKay's classic, lyric novel about a young Jamaican woman rediscovering the value of the island's rural culture is called *Banana Bottom* (1933) after the name of the village she learns to prize. Missing from Western representations of the fruit is any suggestion of toil: everything in the earthly paradise of blooming ripeness is effortless. By contrast, the famous calypso, 'The Banana Boat Song' (also called 'Day-O'), written by Harry Belafonte *et al.*, describes the small holder's vigil as he waits till daybreak for the shipping agent to come and count up the crop. Surprisingly, though the song's lyrics communicate the exhaustion of the farm labourers in Jamaica, Belafonte, the Tarriers group and Shirley Bassey had international successes with different recordings. At that time Jamaican farmers were valiantly presenting their labour as heroic, not exotic or comic. In the heyday of the Caribbean export trade, 'bananamen' were rendered as social-realist Herculeses in sculptures and wall frescos, hauling the massive candelabra of the green fruit like stevedores: a single stem might carry ten or more round clusters of at least twenty bananas each—the weight in fruit of a person ripened from a single flower. Such works attempted to retrieve dignity for men who were low paid and contaminated by association with a paltry, comical fruit in countries where their produce was consumed. One of the photographs taken by Harry Johnston in the Caribbean in 1908–9 reveals the acute difference between heady Orientalist romancing of tropical allure and the conditions that

OPPOSITE *The porn queen's staple: poster for La Cicciolina in* Banane al Cioccolato, *1986.*

obtained on the ground; yet for this colonial officer the resolute, serious-faced woman worker with a metal basin securely balanced on her headcloth still epitomized a kind of dream of harmony: 'the woman who is leading a life close to primitive nature'.

The tropical setting still promises, even in post-imperial times, *luxe, calme et volupté*; the funniness of bananas conveys the fruit's fulfilment of many desires at the literal level of food and the symbolic level of sexual sign; the laughter it inspires reverberates around its paradoxical potency and defends against the threatening associations that it sets stirring.

EPILOGUE:

'SNIP! SNAP! SNIP!'

 A copy of the German children's classic, *Struwwelpeter*, that I found last year had been vigorously defaced: scribbles scratched out the face of Tall Agrippa in his sinister robe and long beard where he stands by the giant inkwell, and a criss-cross of colouring pencil marks scored his upraised scolding finger. The book's title page was missing and so was Struwwelpeter himself—Shock-Headed Peter—with his hag nails and his blond Afro; later pages were hanging off the mesh binding. Here and there, clumsy scissor cuts had slashed into the pages, where the blades, too heavy in the child's hand, had closed crookedly, under their own momentum. Was she, was he, cutting out a figure that was too frightening to allow to remain there, that might have gone on living and speaking from inside the book, even after it had been closed tight shut? On the final endpapers, though, there was the survivor's mocking cry: 'Ho Hah!' boldly scrawled across the pages.

Vandals go for the eyes and mouths of public images. Actors on film posters are sometimes blinded by passengers waiting on the platform for the tube, or blobs of chewing gum stop their grins. Once I saw a tuft of hair stuck into a gob, as if one passenger had snipped another's and stuck it there on an ad, as a scalp, a trophy. One or two paintings in national collections still bear the scars of old iconoclast attacks: there are not many examples of these left, because the works are usually restored. The continuing sight of the damage is painful, even unbearable, as if something living had truly been attacked and left bleeding. But one such survival is a predella panel from Paolo Uccello's story sequence, *The Miracle of the Profaned Host*, painted in 1467–68 (Pl. 33). Its subject adds to the body of spooky lore encrusting the Eucharist and the feast of Corpus Christi.

Two devils at the foot of a bier are haggling with two angels over the corpse of the dead woman who lies there; one of the devils is blue and has

The Tailor swoops in with his scissors to punish Little Suck-a-Thumb. Heinrich Hoffmann, Struwwelpeter, *1845.*

magnificently deployed sooty bat's wings, the other, in front of him, with a clawed foot proprietorially placed on the bier's platform, was once scarlet; he has been deeply scratched, over and over, by someone with a sharp instrument, until almost all his features have gone with the lost paint, turning him into an empty thing, a shade, a ghost. Both devils have also had their eyes obliterated.

The devils' presence is indeed diminished by the vandalism; they have literally been made to vanish by the scraping away of the pigment to the gesso underneath. Even though they are still tugging at the body of the dead woman, they no longer seem so real. The damage exposes the illusion of the image, reveals that the red devil is only as deep as that layer of paint. But even if that were not entirely the case, he certainly cannot lift his head from his task, turn, and look out, and trap you in his glance.

The predella is the last of six images in one of those ugly stories arising from Christian anti-Semitism. It does not issue the blood libel, and depict the accusation of child-stealing and murder that led to the deaths of Jews in England (Lincoln, 1255), in Italy (Portobuffouolà, 1480), and in the Holy Roman Empire and Germany (Landshut, 1440; Trent, 1475) and elsewhere. Uccello's painting tells of a woman who sold a host in order to redeem her gambling husband's coat from the pawnbroker. In the first panel of the sequence, we see her visiting his shop. In the last but one, we see her hanged from a tree for the crime while the money-lender is shown putting the host in a pan to cook it—like Lycaon. It begins to bleed, as it did in the hands of the doubting priest at Bolsena. Soldiers arrive to rescue the host from further desecration, and restore it with full solemnities to the church. The woman's Christian soul has some chance of being saved— hence the struggle between angels and devils at her bier. The sequence comes to an end not with her fate, but with the executions of the Jewish merchant and his whole family, burned at the stake.

Such inflammatory tales were sometimes passed on by nurses, as in the case dramatized by Maria Edgeworth in her novel *Harrington*. But the story Uccello's paintings tell is a rank example of intolerant savagery and records a historical outbreak of persecution in Paris in 1290. Sacred dramas had then reproduced the story, and it had been revived again, possibly in Uccello's presence: St. Antoninus alluded to it during his protracted sermons in Florence against Jewish money-lenders. The paintings were commissioned by a confraternity in Urbino, dedicated to the cult of the Corpus Domini: Uccello's cycle thus clearly dramatizes the obsessive Catholic preoccupation with the true presence of Jesus in flesh and blood in the Eucharist.

As Michael Camille has perceptively written, Jews were scapegoated partly because Christians felt guilty about the new 'profit economy'. It is hardly incidental that the Company of Corpus Domini, the pictures' commissioners, ran the Monte di Pietà—the official pawnshop and money-lenders licensed in Italian cities, which in some cases replaced expelled Jewish businesses. But Camille also draws attention to Christian anxiety 'about adapting to an expanding economy of images, which allowed greater access by more segments of the Christian community to a whole gamut of representations, private, public, and cult'. Neither Jews nor Muslims allow religious images, and their observance of the second commandment unsettled Catholics, with their intense cult of icons and statues. Camille astutely argues that the fantasies of profanity and iconoclasm on the part of 'unbelievers' reflect Christians' own beset feelings about their belief in miraculous representations; that furthermore they enclose repressed doubts about the efficacy of the images themselves. As several visionaries even saw Christ himself, as an infant, in the host, the stories of it bleeding and so forth may also reflect disturbances occasioned by the central principle involved in the mystery of the Eucharist.

Scapegoating functions to expel from a community the profound terrors it experiences about its own members' behaviour. Analogously, the lynch victims of the plantation system and its aftermath were often accused of sleeping with white women: the exact reversal of what was more frequently the case. Bogeymen make us look at the features of our own strangeness. Joyce Carol Oates has made this point, in her essay on contemporary forms of the grotesque: 'I take as the most profound mystery of our human experience the fact that, though we each exist subjectively . . . this "subjectivity" is inaccessible, thus unreal, and mysterious, to *others*. And the obverse—all *others* are, in the deepest sense, *strangers*.' To show the emptiness of fear, to identify its pernicious workings and prevent them, must be part of any system of education and justice. Yet the problem remains that the impulse to find a culprit, however innocent, lies deeply rooted in human psychology and culture.

In the vandalized predella by Uccello, the painted devils are treated as incarnate and living by their attacker. Such acts are not uncommon: the eyes of the demons in the fresco of the Last Judgment in the cathedral of Albi in southern France have also been put out—by cigarettes, in some cases. The iconoclast conceals an iconodule, an adorer of images: belief in the power of the image underlies the attempt at destruction. There is an analogy between the real presence of subjects in religious images and the central article of the Catholic faith that bread becomes flesh when it is consecrated, that it is altogether changed in its substance and nature even though nothing changes in its species or outward sensory character.

The story Uccello paints explores the mysterious and deep ambiguities of semblance in such a doctrine. The hypostatic principle that inanimate stuff, like bread, can become living personal tissue underlies the enterprise of Christian picturing, and any number of icons, statues and devotional images, large and small (let alone relics), have dropped blood, sweat, and tears; they have moved, spoken, cried out, nodded, some have even grown hair, like the fourteenth-century crucified Christ in S. Maria del Carmine in Naples. These miraculous outbreaks do not reverse Christianity's rules of creation; they may be 'signs and wonders', manifesting divine energy and presence, but they also arise logically from the doctrine of the incarnation, its commemoration in the Mass, and its central act of sacrifice. 'They break through the miraculous surface of illusion to a representation of the substance that lies behind the unchanged appearance.'

When that nameless and forgotten viewer took a sharp instrument and stabbed at the devils' faces and eyes in the image to stop them looking, one exercise in penetrating beyond outer appearance inspires a representation that itself is seen as more than mere picturing. Ritual alters semblances, can magick them into living appearances; by analogy, images have a relationship to phenomena that is more than illusion, and will provoke a different response from the actual phenomena they represent.

With the global profusion of images via film, television, satellite, cable and the Internet, Protestant scepticism about the power of pictures has been weakening for a long time, and the Enlightenment climate of verifiable phenomena and verbal privilege has changed; we have re-entered the ancient, magical, image-worshipping terrain of Catholic imagination and practice. A New Age of confusion between image and reality has been establishing its reign for a while, probably since the start of television. It is the dominant instrument defining the sacred—and the profane. The success of *Hello!* and *O.K.* magazines, the flash-in-the-pan dominion of Oasis and the Spice Girls, global audiences for Princess Diana's funeral and for murder trials by television (O.J. Simpson, Louise Woodward) belong to the realm of semblance, where appearance is all, and a flickering flux of mirages bewitches the senses into the expected responses, into trust, faith, belief. The death of Princess Diana revealed the intimacy as well as intensity of people's emotions for her, while the profusion of flowers, letters, prayers, soft toys and other offerings laid in wayside shrines in London and elsewhere (on the Internet, too) expressed grief and shock in an improvised, sacred ritual, its features annexed from expiatory sacrifices as well as mourning conventions. The sudden, violent death of someone so mythically wrapped in a seeming eternity of glamour and fame, wealth and beauty brought home the mortality of us all. The communal desire to do something, to mark the event, sprang from the desire to propitiate such assaults of fate—and to avert them.

Serious iconoclastic incidents against images also accord them influence far beyond their inanimate and manufactured substance. Such sporadic expressions of outrage and anger spring from personal variations on the passions that drove the religious breaking of the idols under the Protestant Reformation in England, for example. The monks who destroyed the Scylla sculpture at Sperlonga; the suffragette who slashed the *Rokeby Venus* by Velázquez; Laszlo Toth, who in 1972 took a hammer to Michelangelo's *Pietà* in St. Peter's are expressing how unbearable they find the power that images exercise. The portrait of the serial child murderer Myra Hindley by Marcus Harvey, included in the show 'Sensation' at the Royal Academy, London, in 1997, was attacked in separate incidents by members of the public; demonstrators also gathered outside demanding that the painting be removed. The artist used a four-year-old child's handprints to reconstitute Hindley's notorious 1966 mugshot, taken at the time of the Moors Murders she committed with her partner, Ian Brady. By

Tall Agrippa, an Orientalized giant, puts his victims down the inkwell. 'The Inky Boys', Heinrich Hoffmann, Struwwelpeter, *1845.*

literally branding her face with her victims' touch, as it were, the painter was making a classic example of a *pittura infamante*, an image intended to defame (in the sixteenth century, Arcimboldo pieced together a profile of Herod from the naked bodies of the holy innocents). For the indignant viewers, however, the *Myra* summoned her presence and, in continuing to make her visible at all, seemed to celebrate her crimes. Hindley herself joined in the protest: she felt the image incriminated her with a past self, that now lies behind her. If the Royal Academy had yielded to the demonstrators, it would have done as she wanted, too.

Many of us learn to live peaceably with this power of images to conjure realities. But our restraint does not mean that we are not enthralled, that fantastic pictures in the mind, triggered by verbal description or materialized in visual media, do not stamp out experience on their die. Before I found the defaced copy of *Struwwelpeter*, I had noticed that old copies of children's books often bore traces of their owners' feelings, in the colouring-in, the scrawls, the thumbing and dirt, the torn pages, the splodges. When I was a child, *Struwwelpeter* terrified me. I did not find it funny because I sucked my thumb and I was truly afraid that the Tailor, drawn like a leaping pair of scissors, would come to get me and cut off my thumbs, as he does to little Suck-a-Thumb, who stands at the end of the rhyme with his stumps stuck out and his feet turned in:

> Snip! Snap! Snip! the scissors go;
> And Conrad cries out Oh! Oh! Oh!
> Snip! Snap! Snip! They go so fast,
> That both his thumbs are off at last.

I must have been around seven when I read *Struwwelpeter*, and it took such possession of me that I kept going back and looking at the scissor-man, who comes flying through the door, his feet pointed in dancing slippers, his hair streaming back, his top hat suspended behind him on the wake of his thrust, his whole profile a vision of determination and his scissors longer and bigger than the whole of Conrad's body, until I could not bear the terror any more and took the book to my father when he was gardening and asked him to burn it on the bonfire.

My father was a bookseller and a great reader, and, besides, his previous bookshop, in Cairo, had been torched in the anti-British riots of 1952, and so, although he said he would burn *Struwwelpeter* for me, he had no intention of doing so. I found the book again when I was looking for something else to read from the bookshelves in the sitting room. It was tucked behind the row, and the fear of the scissor-man returned, in a flush and a creeping over my skin, for I had still not stopped sucking my thumb.

The author, Heinrich Hoffmann, appears with the handle 'Dr.' on old copies—on the one I found, for example—but not on current reprintings. He was a psychiatrist in Frankfurt, or, rather, he was what was called, in the mid-nineteenth century, an alienist, and the story goes that he wrote the verses for his son after he had tried to buy him a book at Christmas, but could only find long, dreary, preachy, goody-goody tales. *Struwwelpeter* thus began as a robust spoof-making mock of these pious tomes. In 1845, Dr. Hoffmann was parodying disciplinarians and their frightening methods more than fifty years before Hilaire Belloc did, in his series of comic verses (*A Bad Child's Book of Beasts*, 1896; *Bad Verse for Worse Children*, 1897; *Cautionary Tales*, 1908) and Harry Graham with *Ruthless Rhymes for Heartless Homes* (1899). But Hoffmann's pastiches were not stable in their ironies and tended to flip into an extreme version of the texts he was guying. An American edition of 1969 even carries a foreword that declares: 'This famous book most certainly will bring a healthy and hearty response from its American readers. Teachers, parents, and children themselves may find it a refreshing change in these permissive days.'

'Children themselves'? Is acquiring a taste for punishment part of the refreshing change from permissiveness? Or has this editor, in pedagogical zeal, muddled up a dream of children's budding morality with the profound fascination of fear and the desire to meet it face to face? *Struwwelpeter*'s litany of retributions, satirical or not, provokes mixed feelings. For every American editor rejoicing in a healthy rebuttal of permissiveness, a well-meaning teacher is busily explaining away, telling the class that Conrad has not really had his thumbs cut off but, in clear contradiction of both verse and pictures, is just hiding them behind his fingers and that that is why he is looking so sheepish.

Dr. Hoffmann may have meant his high-spirited parody sincerely, and his creation has enjoyed a huge success, in dozens of languages and hundreds of editions, even if copies have been defaced or (nearly) burned. With the Tailor and Tall Agrippa, he invented vivid, even immortal bogeys, as much flesh and blood as semblance can achieve. They are the very first such that I remember. This book explores the reasons for their vitality and their terror, and turns over some of the ways people have invented for dealing with them and their like.

The make-believe of images, games and stories remains make-believe; they are performances of fantasies or, sometimes, of memories, but their relationship to actual events or inner experiences is symbolic: they enact, rather than act. Yet this precious distinction, easy to make in words, is hard to maintain in practice. A mother who took to heart urgings that adults should always treat children's imaginings with respect responded seriously to her daughter's worries one night that there was something under her bed: she looked under it, then made believe she found an intruder, hauled him out, hustled him down the stairs, opened the front door, threw him out, slammed the door, and came back up again, dusting off her hands and saying, 'Well, that's well and truly got rid of him', only to find her little girl whey-faced in the bed, asking, 'Mummy, was there *really* someone under the bed?'

The incidence of vandalism and iconoclasm and this—touching—anecdote about a mother's over-eager game of Let's Pretend illustrate the same point: the magic of make-believe is a game sometimes, but it can also make some participants believe, make such a convincing semblance of actuality that it supplants real life. The stories and other materials summoning the bogeyman in one guise or another not only give existing fears a face and a form, but can also excite them and shape them in the first place.

And fantasies not only shape individual consciousness but constitute society's character as well. The tidal shore where fantasy laps at actuality changes the contours of them both: they move in a permanent, restless, symbiotic relation and vary as the weather changes, and we are living in a time of a cultural El Niño.

❖   ❖   ❖

Fatalism, so intertwined with superstition, is generally despised in the voluntarist, humanist West. So the guilty must be found, and this can lead to more superstition, to uncovering the agents of evil, the devil and his servants, to fingering guilty parties. To point to the fallaciousness of this move is not tantamount to exposing some extreme relativist position and denying the reality of evil doing and evil persons; it is just that the material of terror focuses only blurringly on understanding harm; instead, it mostly confuses calamity with malignant agency—or rather, makes the damage more bearable by perceiving it as intentional rather than random.

One of the chief moral problems revealed by the fantasies of fear is that they search for a guilty party. Apprehension of dangers—real or imaginary—converts into diagnosis of moral evil. Dreading harm, parents imagine assailants who look human but have somehow been claimed by the spirit world: witches, gypsies, barbarians, phantoms in the past, aliens now, nannies, baby-sitters. In Ireland in 1895, a young woman, Bridget Cleary, agreed with her husband, Michael Cleary, that she was behaving strangely because she had been 'taken by the fairies'. With the help of family and friends, he rolled her in the fire to undo the spell; she died of her burns. Michael Cleary was sentenced for her murder. This was a tragic case of latter-day witchcraft belief; today, the 'Hallowe'en sadist', who conceals pins and razor blades in candy or poisons apples with drugs, has become a new, urban myth, terrifying parents into keeping children indoors. Yet a survey conducted in four cities in the United States found not a single verifiable case in twenty-six years' reporting such incidents.

While fears—and their embodiment, the bogeyman—do not in themselves clarify moral issues, they do give us clues to understanding the engineering of hatred. Historically, the bogeyman has often expressed, in an enlarged, distorting glass, a given society's sorest lesions: just as the 'blood libel' against the Jews reflected profound Christian anxieties about the Eucharist and image-worship, so did the charges of cannibalism and satanism brought against witches. In these cases of scapegoating, the accused were innocent of the child murders imputed to them. But fairy tales and old wives' tales about ogres and bloodsuckers, about giant-killing and dragon-slaying, can also function as vehicles for well-grounded anxieties and griefs. It would be foolish to deny the reality of the bogey-man altogether or, rather, to dismiss the threat that he—sometimes she—represents. Press-gangs nabbing recruits, policemen making overzealous arrests, kidnappers grabbing children for ransom were the historical coun-terpart of the bogeyman of legend; they used to cast his long shadow.

Manmade monsters and devastating scientific experiments that go wrong teem in the art of the late twentieth century, alongside stalkers, rapists and sex killers, and continue to catalyse any number of works that meditate on the human condition. The uncanny theme of the *Doppel-gänger*, so powerful in the folklore of the supernatural, has been given fresh energy by the advent of Dolly, cloned from a cell of a sheep's udder and consequently named by her waggish progenitor after Dolly Parton; the possibility of human clones materializes a fear of doubles that haunts fic-tion from R.L. Stevenson's *The Strange Case of Dr. Jekyll and Mr. Hyde* (1886) to Philip K. Dick's *Do Androids Dream of Electric Sheep?* (1968), which became the cult film *Blade Runner*. The 'replicants' of this dystopic future resemble humans in every respect except that they are fabricated, and have had their minds filled with invented, false memories.

At the weird end of contemporary scariness, aliens who prey for ambiguous motives on human beings also communicate profoundly char-acteristic modern fears and reflect back our own sense of estrangement from ourselves. Aliens not only abduct their quarry, as did the fairies, but they often perform surgical operations, obstetrical in character, thus mim-icking in phantasmagoric fashion the bewildering range of ethical issues raised by reproductive technologies and the new biogenetics. They also excite, as classic bogeymen do, the tendency to confuse fabricated stories with real events, and populate repetitious newspaper reports and talk show confessions. The themes of surrogate pregnancy, *in vitro* fertilization, prolonging female fertility, freezing semen for posthumous insemination, genetic decoding and manipulation of embryos reverberate in vivid contemporary horror entertainment, from literature aimed at juvenile readers to the complex series of *Alien* films. An episode of the *X-Files*, for example, combined these dilemmas with another, even more acute contemporary issue: our failed stewardship of the earth. In a zoo where the animals always fail to bring a birth to term, officers Mulder and Scully dis-covered that aliens were abducting the pregnant animals and 'scooping' the foetuses in order to preserve the species on their planet. Thus, animals that were under threat of extinction on earth were to survive in outer space.

The literary critic and historian Franco Moretti, discussing the nineteenth century's 'literature of terror', emphasized that it truthfully expressed the social climate. Frankenstein's creature has become more malevolent in representations, from the classic film of 1931 to children's Hallowe'en masks today, and one of his most appalling crimes is killing a child. The scene of the murder was censored in the 1931 film. Dracula is also more than ever with us, and has begotten a prolific brood of fanged avatars, comic and in earnest. Moretti concluded: 'The more a work frightens, the more it edifies. The more it humiliates, the more it uplifts. The more it hides, the more it gives the illusion of revealing. It is a fear one *needs*: the price one pays for coming contentedly to terms with a social body based on irrationality and menace. Who says it is escapist?'

But above all other current manifestations of the bogeyman, the threat posed by serial killers and paedophiles today can put the phantasmagorias of the past into perspective. It is impossible to judge how deep the danger is: the cases of known child molesters and the reported high incidence of assaults on children, including infants, have inspired a climate of suspicion that now keeps children behind doors more firmly than at any time in history. A single Myra Hindley, Ian Brady, Gary Gilmore, Frederick West, Rosemary West, Jeffrey Dahmer or Marc Dutroux sends rings of fear far and wide through a society. In conformity with the prevalent sexualization of understanding and interpretation today, the bogeyman no longer always brings death as such, but deals in the new coinage of psychological death: child abuse. While the older stories of the guardian god Bes and the she-devil Lilith and the Judgement of Solomon cast women who place children at risk as women whose maternal drive has been frustrated, and who are consequently still acting in character as biological women, the new female demons of crimes against children have disqualified themselves from the ranks of mothers, from the category of women altogether. A woman like Myra Hindley betrayed every notion of maternal nurture or womanly gentleness, but she has also come to embody a violent sexuality that is more appropriate to the male than the female. Similarly, the stalker, rapist, serial killer of women, inspires widespread fear of travelling alone, of city streets at night, all over the Western world. These are not empty fears.

Yet babies and children are in greatest danger not from strangers, but from their own families. In terms of quantifiable risk, cars pose a greater danger of death or mutilation. But—with the exception of Jean-Luc Godard's film *Weekend* (1968), J. G. Ballard's novel *Crash* (1973) and the film of the book (1996)—cars have largely escaped demonization.

Fears tell us what we value as well as what we dread to lose: the bogeys of today—child-snatchers, child-killers, sexual violators of the young—horrify us at some deeper, personal level than even the atrocities of recent civil wars. Adam Phillips, in *The Beast in the Nursery* (1998), discusses the current pervasiveness of the myth that all our childhoods were a corner of paradise, now lost—but regained through children themselves. We want children to be happy on our behalf, we want them to guarantee the possibility of innocence and goodness, not only in their own conduct and desires but also, crucially, in the desires and responses they inspire in others. So children's physicality, their seductiveness, their appetite and curiosity have become one of the most painful and recurrent issues of the times, with denials of erotic feelings accompanied by ever accentuated, sexualized representations of children's beauty, appetites and even economic power (in fashion, car ads, and charity pleas). Paedophiles have become paramount bogeys of our time because their practices condense a wider cultural pederasty that sanctifies the child and the condition of childhood and the state of childlikeness and infantilizes all of us in pursuit of ideal humanity, at the very same time as society fails to look after children's interests.

The canting word for a sex offender in jail is 'nonce'. 'Nonce' means nothing; noncification turns someone into nothing. The lawyer Helena Kennedy, in her valiant book *Eve Was Framed*, tells of hearing a story from a woman client about another inmate at her prison, a foster parent who had killed babies in her care, cut them up into pieces, and sent the pieces in the post to their natural mothers. Because many female prisoners have been severed, sometimes for ever, from their children, this murderer had been ostracized—or worse. She had been 'noncified', had retreated to her cell and hung a sign on the door saying she had only killed one child. Helena Kennedy had some difficulty identifying her: when she traced the case, it turned out that, like Myra Hindley, like Rosemary West, this woman had collaborated with a man (her husband), had sexually assaulted young girls and boys, and had killed a ten-year-old girl. She was sentenced to twenty years, which she has served, since the trial took place in 1970.

The measures being taken to control paedophiles make them exceptional under the law: in a number of countries, including the United States and the United Kingdom, a register of their names and whereabouts is now kept after they have served their sentences and been released; they are not being restored freedom of movement or universal access to public places, unlike other kinds of vicious criminal, once they are let out of gaol. There are also plans to review the sentence of sex offenders retrospectively and, in some cases, commit them under Mental Health Acts instead. Helena Kennedy writes about the law's attitude to sex crimes that the public wishes to see justice done, even though the general feeling makes these criminals appear to be beyond justice: 'There is a conflict between seeking an explanation for the inexplicable and an unwillingness to allow madness to become an excuse.' Their cases place under increasing strain our continuing adherence to the accepted, underlying principle of justice that imprisonment does not only punish but also redeems the crime and rehabilitates the criminal. In the case of 'nonces', this principle has come under increasing pressure: this variety of crime appears irredeemable, irreparable, its perpetrators psychologically destined to repeat their offence.

Discriminating between types and degree of such crimes seems callous towards their victims: yet the present broadness of the term 'paedophile' aggravates the problem, and forecloses possible pathways to remedies. The word itself is gravely misleading, offering perpetrators the excuse that they act out of love of children. The many different acts of abduction and seduction, the complexities of same-sex and other relationships both within and outside families, and across age groups, the pathology of the various conditions, all need close thinking, in order for noncification—that annulment of both persons and thought—to come to an end.

Imputations of evil reveal more about the accusers than the accused, and, like other ogres in the cultural past, child abusers throw into relief the deepest anxiety of our time: the way we have reified children as objects of desire across the whole spectrum of material culture. They 'love children', in some ghastly masquerade of the way so much of the rest of society also 'loves children': by stimulating their desires, by exploiting their vulnerability and suggestibility, by finding them irresistibly cute, by staging, in any number of advertisements, films and infant beauty pageants, the performance of their seduction. Yet, at the same time, material measures taken to improve children's lives—their play, their care, their education, their health, their nutrition, their prospects—remain paper promises, often made to kindle a warm moral glow for the speaker. Politicians no longer simply kiss babies; they drag them round with them when they canvass, as mascots of their own virtuousness.

Bogeys make present what we dread, and these fantasies include what we know we are capable of perpetrating ourselves. Paedophiles are our late millennial ogres, and they bring the bogeyman very much closer to home than aliens or medieval devils. This is more deeply unsettling, Adam Phillips argues, than fantasies of the sandman or the giant: the farther

OPPOSITE *Flyer, posted in Oxford, 1996.*

away fantasies situate the source of danger, the greater the sense of security at home, even though it is within the home and the family that the most damaging conflicts and hurts arise.

Owning up to widespread, homegrown paedophilia does not, however, probe the reason for such evildoing any more than arguing that all men are violent and all sex is rape does anything to clarify serial killing. It banalizes the harm and the crimes and thus empties them of meaning—and of our responsibility to confront them in all their exceptional aspects and help prevent them, as we attempt imperfectly to do in the case of totalitarian atrocities and civil war. It is easier to follow the Hannah Arendt line and give up analysing such acts by saying that, given a certain set of circumstances, anyone might do it, or even, anyone would do it. Slavoj Žižek is compelling when he argues against the Arendt view, writing that, in the case of 'Hitler's willing executioners', we have to understand that they experienced 'their deeds as a kind of "transgressive" activity . . . which accounted for the "surplus-enjoyment" [of] torturing the victims'. Holding a child-killer at bay as ineluctably Other does not meet the question he or she poses. Yet acknowledging that such a person might be our own darkest face does not suffice either. There are certain individual acts of evil, but no single devil or forces of evil embodied by any group can be blamed. The crucial task is to confront the particular features of the story that makes such conduct yield rewards for anyone at all.

Fears trace a map of a society's values; we need fear to know who we are and what we do not want to be. The strategies of the imagination—scaring, lulling, making mock—cannot wholly soothe or exorcize us; but the long and shifting history of inventive self-defence they reveal can help us understand the power of fantasy: its dangers as well as its rewards.

WATCH OUT

HAVE YOU LOCKED YOUR DOOR

NOTES

Prologue

p.1 **a soft wad from a fleece** For the story of Zagreus, see Nonnus of Panopolis, *Les Dionysiaques*, Canto VI, lines 155–229, trans. and ed. Pierre Chuvin (Paris, 1992) pp. 51–4, 148–57; Otto Kern, *Orphicorum Fragmenta* (Berlin, 1922), pp. 110–11, 230–5, 244–5; Marcel Detienne, *Dionysos Slain*, trans. Mireille Muellner and Leonard Muellner (Baltimore and London, 1979), pp. 68–94; M.L. West, *The Orphic Poems* (Oxford, 1983); Neil Hopkinson, 'Nonnus and Homer', in Neil Hopkinson (ed.), *Studies in the Dionysiaca of Nonnus* (Cambridge, 1994), pp. 9–42; Robert Graves, *The Greek Myths*, 2 vols [1955] (Harmondsworth, 1966), Vol. 1, pp. 118–20.

2 **It moves, it breathes** The goddess of wisdom acquires her title Pallas from this act, from the rescue of the baby's palpitating heart (*pallesthai* in Greek); see West, *The Orphic Poems*, p. 162.

3 **twice born of his own father** Zagreus could also be the son of Hades, Aeschylus hints, born after Persephone's rape and her reign began in the underworld for half the year. West, *Orphic Poems*, pp. 152–4.

Introduction

General note: Jean Delumeau, *La Peur en Occident (XIVe-XVIIIe siècles) Une cité assiégié* (Paris, 1978) is one of the few full-length, historical studies of the theme; see also Yi-Fu Tuan's brisk overview, *The Landscapes of Fear* (Oxford, 1979); Carol J. Clover, *Men, Women and Chainsaws: Gender in the Modern Horror Film* (London, 1992) puts a provocative case for the defence of violence in cinema; Frank Furedi, *Culture of Fear: Risk-Taking and the Morality of Low Expectation* (London, 1997) takes the temperature of current malaise and argues passionately against panic.

6 **'Inborn in all of us . . .'** Aristotle, *On the Art of Poetry*, in Aristotle, Horace, Longinus, *Classical Literary Criticism*, trans. T.S. Dorsch (Harmondsworth, 1965), p. 35.

7 **'. . . terror, disgust and laughter'** Susie Tharu and K. Lalita, 'Introduction', in *Women Writing in India, 600 BC to the Present*, 2 vols (New York, 1991), Vol. 1, p. 2; Anandavardhana, *The Dhvanyāloka of Ānandavardhana with the Locana of Abhinavagupta*, trans. Daniel H.H. Ingalls, J. Moussaieff Masson and M.V. Patwardhan (Cambridge, Mass. and London, 1990), pp. 15–22, 110–13, 506–9; also B.K. Thakkar, *On the Structuring of Sanskrit Drama: Structure of Drama in Bharata and Aristotle* (Ahmedabad, 1984), p. 33. I am most grateful to Wendy Doniger O'Flaherty for help with these references.

taste buds on the tongue Andrew Derrington, 'That's So Revolting', *Financial Times*, October 25–6 1997, p. 11. Fear triggers a region of the brain called the amygdala, whereas disgust activates the anterior insular cortex. See also Julia Kristeva, *Powers of Horror. An Essay on Abjection*, trans. Leon S. Roudiez (New York, 1982) which discusses the feelings excited by the sight or condition of abjection, as epitomized by Holbein's tragic painting of the dead Christ.

8 **'Awful', by contrast** 'The awful glory of God', for example, is a phrase that used to make us giggle in chapel when I was a child.

9 **'No passion . . .'** Edmund Burke, *A Philosophical Inquiry into the Origin of our Ideas of the Sublime and the Beautiful*, ed. Adam Phillips (Oxford, 1990), p. 53. See Morton Paley, *The Apocalyptic Sublime* (New Haven and London, 1986), p. 7.

moment of *sensibilité* See Margaret Anne Doody, *The True History of the Novel* (New Haven, 1996).

10   **intergenerational rivalry** Adam Phillips, *On Kissing, Tickling and Being Bored: Psychoanalytic Essays on the Unexamined Life* (London, 1993), p. 103.

11   **'widely distributed nursery goblin . . .'** John Widdowson, *'If you don't be good': Verbal Social Control in Newfoundland* (St. John's, Newfoundland, 1977); Katharine M. Briggs, *The Fairies in Tradition and Literature* [1967] (London, 1978), pp. 213–31; see also Cecily Peele, *The Encyclopaedia of British Bogies* (Oxford, 1978).

12   **female witches** See, for example, two recent rich and perceptive studies: Robin Briggs, *Witches and Neighbours: The Social and Cultural Context of European Witchcraft* (London, 1996) and Diane Purkiss, *The Witch in History: Early Modern and Twentieth-Century Representations* (London, 1996).

13   **vampires and undead progeny** See Nina Auerbach, *Our Vampires, Ourselves* (Chicago, 1996).

14   **Festivals, carnivals, secular rituals** See Ronald Hutton, *The Stations of the Sun. A History of the Ritual Year in Britain* (Oxford, 1996); and Scott Cutler Shershow, *Puppets and 'Popular' Culture* (Ithaca, NY, 1996).

16   **As Rudolf Dekker points out** Rudolf Dekker, *Childhood, Memory and Autobiography from the Golden Age to Romanticism*, forthcoming, Part III, Chapter 1.
      peals and squeals of the audience Carol Ann Duffy, *Grimm Tales* (London, 1996), adapted for stage by Tim Supple, performed at the Young Vic, 1994. (The published version does not include stage directions for these *Carrie*-like irrepressible returns of the witch.)

CHAPTER 1: 'HERE COMES THE BOGEYMAN!'

23   **'You sweet child . . .'**
                          'Du liebes Kind, komm, geh mit mir!
                          Gar schöne Spiele spiel' ich mit dir:
                          Manch' bunte Blumen sind an dem Strand,
                          Meine Mutter hat manch' gülden Gewand.'
      Goethe, *Selected Verse* (Harmondsworth, 1964), p. 80.

24   **Herder misunderstood** See Theodor Fontane, *Ellernknippen*, trans. Denise Modigliani (Paris, 1995), p. 15.

25   **discovers . . . the body of his own child** Belinda Whitworth, *Gothick Devon* (Princes Risborough, 1993), p. 29.
      'He is the tender butcher . . .' Angela Carter, *The Bloody Chamber* (London, 1975), p. 87.
      alternative phrase for a bogey or hobgoblin See under 'bugge', defined as 'bogy, hobgoblin, black-man; scarecrow', *c.* 1395, in *Middle English Dictionary*, ed. Hans Kurath (Ann Arbor, 1952), p. 2121. I am grateful to Malcolm Jones for this reference.
      sweet furry dorks Peter Wiseman, 'The Gods of the Lupercal', *Journal of Roman Studies* 85 (1995), pp. 1–22. Helena Nyblom, 'Borbytingarna', in John Baners, *Bästa Ett urval Sagor ur Bland Tomtar och Troll Aren 1907–1915* (Stockholm, 1931), pp. 12–31.

26   **Baba Yaga sleeps at night** See 'Baba Yaga and the Brave Youth', in Aleksandr Afanas'ev (ed.), *Russian Fairy Tales*, trans. Norbert Guterman [1945] (New York, 1970), pp. 76–9.
      a Russian word for eating Joanna Hubbs, *Mother Russia: The Feminine Myth in Russian Culture* (Bloomington, 1988), p. 40.
      like the jealous queen in 'Snow White' See John Widdowson, 'The Bogeyman: Some Preliminary Observations on Frightening Figures', *Folklore*, 82 (1971), pp. 99–115.

27   **Joan of Arc, for example** Marina Warner, *Joan of Arc: The Image of Female Heroism* (London, 1981), pp. 90, 91.

parental pain of bereavement Jacqueline Simpson, 'The Folklore of Infant Deaths: Burials, Ghosts and Changelings', in Gillian Avery and Kimberley Reynolds (eds), *Representations of Childhood Deaths* (London, forthcoming); see also Rudolf Dekker, *Childhood, Memory and Autobiography from the Golden Age to Romanticism* (forthcoming), Chapter 6.

In Ireland ... In Scottish ballads See various versions in F.J. Child (ed.), *English and Scottish Popular Ballads*, 5 vols (London, 1882–98), pp. 320–41.

28   disguise of 'Once upon a time' Valérie Dayre, *L'Ogresse en pleurs*, illustrated by Wolf Erlbruch (Paris, 1996). I am most grateful to Lissa Paul for bringing this book to my attention, and to Claas Kazzer for his most helpful background information.

the popular dwarf god Bes See Dimitri Meeks, 'Le nom du dieu Bes et ses implications mythologiques', in *The Intellectual Heritage of Egypt*, ed. U. Luft (Budapest, 1992), pp. 423–36.

a justification for neglecting babies See Judith Devlin, *The Superstitious Mind: French Peasants and the Supernatural in the Nineteenth Century* (New Haven and London, 1987), p. 86.

30   Thomas Adès responded Thomas Adès, *Life Story*, Op. 6 (1992), EMI Classics 5 69699 2, 1997.

private book of hours of 1533 *Heures d'Antoine le Bon, Duke of Lorraine*, Paris BNF Ms NAL 302 f. 29, reproduced in Pierre Riché and Danièle Alexandre-Bidon, *L'Enfance au moyen âge* (Paris, 1994), pp. 30–1.

31   a pioneering journal Dekker, *Childhood*, Chapter 2.

'the man with the long coat ...' Herman Roodenburg, 'The Autobiography of Isabella de Moerloose: Sex, Childbearing and Popular Belief in Seventeenth Century Holland', *Journal of Social History*, Vol. 18, no. 4 (1985), pp. 517–40, p. 522.

discounted her parents' warnings Roodenburg, *Isabella de Moerloose*. See also Dekker, *Childhood*.

32   'The Sandman comes ...' Leslie Daiken, *The Lullaby Book* (London, 1959), p. 47.

Hoffmann's ... fairy tale (1817) 'The Sand-Man', in E.T.A. Hoffmann, *The Best Tales of Hoffmann* (New York, 1967), ed. E.F. Bleiler, pp. 183–214, p. 185.

'Close your little eyes ...' 'Tu die Auglein zu, mein Kind,/denn draussen weht ein arger Wind./Will das Kind nicht schlafen ein,/bläst er in das Bett hinein,/blast uns all Federn raus,/blast endlich noch die Augen aus?' Hans Magnus Enzensberger (ed.), *Allerleirauh viele schöne Kinderreime*, (Frankfurt, 1961), p. 43, trans. Helena Ivins.

33   'Ninne ninne sause' From the 'Wiegenlieder' section of Enzensberger, *Kinderreime*, p. 43.

In an English chapbook *The Famous History of Tom Thumb*, (London *c*. 1750) and later in 'The Sleeping Beauty' (London, 1796).

Le Grand Lustucru I am very grateful to Anne Kearney for giving me a tape on which 'Le Grand Lustucru' is sung.

They were much reproduced See, for example, a lithograph, Metz, Musée des arts et traditions populaires; 'Father Flog and Madam Flog', translation of nineteenth-century *image d'Epinal*, Kansas City, *c*. 1930.

34   'Next month ...' Alexandre Desrousseaux, 'L'Canchon dormoire', 1853, kindly transcribed and translated by Françoise Vreek and her class at the University of Lille, September 10, 1996.

In Holland and Germany Reginald Nettel, *Santa Claus* (Bedford, 1957), pp. 28–9.

36   'Among his prisoners ...' Ted Hughes, *Tales from Ovid* (London, 1997), p. 17.

not dirt in the wrong place See Mary Douglas, *Purity and Danger: An Analysis of Concepts of Pollution and Taboo* (London, 1966).

37   'Hello, Grandmother ...' Paul Delarue, 'The Story of Grandmother', in Alan Dundes

(ed.), *Little Red Riding Hood: A Casebook* (Wisconsin, 1989), pp. 13–20, 15–19.

the Bourgeois de Paris *Journal d'un bourgeois de Paris*, ed. A. Tuétey (Paris, 1881); *A Parisian Journal*, trans. J. Shirley (Oxford, 1977).

'Children, especially pretty . . .' Charles Perrault, *The Fairy Tales of Charles Perrault*, trans. Angela Carter (New York, 1977), p. 28.

38 **bring [the children] to order** See Juliet Wilson Bareau, *Goya: La Década de 'Los Caprichos': Dibujos y Aguafuertes* (Madrid, 1992), pp. 74–7.

39 **'Duermete lucero . . .'** I am very grateful indeed to Helena Ivins and her mother, Purita Ivins, who made the connection with the lullaby for me.

Meanwhile, gigantic ghouls' heads Interestingly, 'Boggle-bo' in English is defined, in the *Oxford English Dictionary (OED)* under 'bogle', as 'an ugly wide-mouthed picture carried about with May games'. I am indebted to Malcolm Jones for spotting this connection.

in the Basque town of Logroño See Gustav Henningsen, *The Witches' Advocate: Basque Witchcraft and the Spanish Inquisition (1609–1614)*, (Reno, 1980), pp. 181 ff.

40 **a drawing inscribed '*Mala muger*'** *The Drawings of Goya: the Complete Albums*, ed. Pierre Gassier, trans. Robert Allen and James Emmons (London, 1973), p. 163. Nigel Glendinning, however, argues that Gassier has confused this drawing with a painting.

41 **early ballad collections** See for examples of the British tradition, Thomas Percy, *Reliques of Ancient English Poetry*, ed. Nick Groom, 3 vols (London, 1997) and Child, *Ballads*.

42 **A music-hall song . . . Colonel Bogey** Another song, a 'novelty Foxtrot' of 1932, plays with the piquant *double entendres* that the figure inspires: 'Hush! Hush! Hush! Here comes the Bogey man, Don't let him come too close to you, he'll catch you if he can . . .' Katharine Briggs, *A Dictionary of Fairies: Hobgoblins, Brownies, Bogies and Other Supernatural Creatures* (London, 1976), p. 33.

The anthropologist . . . pioneering study John Widdowson, *'If you don't be good'*, p. 157.

43 **'God created the world . . .'** John Firth, *The Tongues of Men: and Speech* [1930, 1937] (Oxford, 1971), quoted by Widdowson, *'If you don't be good'*, p. 108.

the bilabial plosive Widdowson, *'If you don't be good'*, p. 109.

nineteenth-century reading primers The film *Celia*, directed by Ann Turner, opens with the story read aloud to a class of eight-year-olds. See Marina Warner, 'The Uses of Enchantment', in Duncan Petrie (ed.), *Cinema and Realms of Enchantment* (London, 1993), p. 21.

Aboriginal Dreamtime *The Oxford Companion to Australian Children's Literature*, 2 vols, ed. Stella Lees and Pam MacIntyre (Oxford, 1993), pp. 74–5.

45 **aliens . . . talked-about monsters** See Elaine Showalter, *Hystories, Hysterical Epidemics and Modern Culture* (New York and London, 1997), pp. 189–201.

devices evolved in nature Carl C. Lindroth, 'Disappearance as a Protective Factor', *Entomologica Scandinavica*, 2 (1971), pp. 41–8.

'The Brobinyak' John Ciardi, *Blabberhead, Bobble Bud & Soade: Selected Poems of John Ciardi*, ed. Anna M. Aschkenes (North Brunswick, 1988), no page numbers.

46 **lateness of the word 'bogeyman'** The film, *The Bogeyman*, for instance, a hokum horror thriller, written, directed and produced by Ulli Lommel, was made in 1980. The title character is stabbed to death by a child whom he abuses, but he returns to haunt the child and his sister—and commit more occult murders.

REFLECTION: GOYA: *SATURN DEVOURING HIS CHILD*

48 **the sequence of *Black Paintings*** Nigel Glendinning, 'Goya's Country House in Madrid: The Quinta del Sordo', *Apollo*, 123 (1986), pp. 102–9; and 'The Strange

Translation of Goya's "Black Paintings"', *The Burlington Magazine*, 117 (1975), pp. 465–79.

49 **The Colossus** See Nigel Glendinning, 'Goya and Arriaza's Profecia del Pirenio', *Journal of the Warburg and Courtauld Institutes*, Vol. 26 (1963), pp. 363–6.
The present titles were assigned by the painter Antonio Brugada in the 1820s and again by Charles Yriarte in 1867. Janis Tomlinson, *Francisco de Goya y Lucientes* (London, 1994), p. 239.

50 **photographs taken before the restoration** Maria del Carmen Torrecillas Fernández, 'Nueva documentación fotográfica sobre las pinturas de la Quinta del Sordo de Goya', *Boletín del Museo del Prado*, 4, no. 17 (1985), pp. 87–96; Tomlinson, *Goya*, p. 239.

51 **'it is not right . . .'** See Marina Warner, *Monuments and Maidens* (London, 1985), pp. 165–6.
In this he shadows his counterpart I have written about the relation of cannibalism and incest before, and will not rehearse my argument again here. See 'Cannibal Tales: The Hunger for Conquest', in *Managing Monsters: Six Myths of our Time* (London, 1994).

CHAPTER 2: 'MY FATHER HE ATE ME . . .'

53 **'Into his belly, fool!'** Hesiod, *Theogony*, in *Hesiod and Theognis*, trans. Dorothea Wender (Harmondsworth, 1973), p. 39.

54 **reborn whole from their father's belly** See Neil Forsyth, *The Old Enemy: Satan and the Combat Myth* (Princeton, 1987), pp. 76–85; Hans Gustav Guterbock, 'The Hittite Version of the Hurrian Kumarbi Myths: Oriental Forerunners of Hesiod', *American Journal of Archaeology*, 52 (1948), pp. 123–34.
Images of Kronos See F. Saxl and I. Panofsky's magisterial work, *Saturn and Melancholy*, ed. R. Klibansky (London, 1964).
Cyclops dragging . . . to the pot P.P. Bober and Ruth Rubinstein, *Renaissance Artists and Antique Sculpture: A Handbook of Sources* (Oxford, 1986), p. 157, Plates 124, 143a.

56 **looking . . . very perky again** 'Lambspring', (Frankfurt, 1625), cited in Gareth Roberts, *The Mirror of Alchemy* (London, 1994), pp. 86–7, and *The Languages of Alchemy* (London, 1997), pp. 19–20.
The Bloody Banquet Julia Gasper, 'Introduction', in Thomas Dekker and Thomas Middleton, *The Bloody Banquet*, ed. Julia Gasper (Oxford, forthcoming).

57 **'Great Heaven came . . .'** Hesiod, *Theogony*, pp. 28–9, lines 155–82.

58 **Kronos here appears** See *La Bible des poètes. Métamorphoses* (Paris, *c.* 1485), frontispiece, hand-coloured; different edition, with woodcuts (Paris, Antoine Verard, *c.* 1507), frontispiece. The black and white engraving to the edition of 1507 focuses on the theme as well as the story with some minor differences that emphasize an allegory of time's passing: astronomical symbols of the months have been added, for instance.

60 **In Shakespeare's play** William Shakespeare, *Titus Andronicus*, ed. Jonathan Bate (London, 1995); see also Jacques Berthoud's forthcoming edition (London).
The maid without hands See Warner, *From the Beast to the Blonde* (London, 1994), pp. 396–8.

61 **'I cut their Throats . . .'** 'The Lamentable and Tragical History of Titus Andronicus' (London, 1660), reprinted as 'Titus Andronicus's Complaint', in Percy, *Reliques*, ed. Groom, Vol. 1, pp. 203–9.

62 **'The Young Queen was twenty . . .'** Perrault, *Fairy Tales*, trans. Carter, p. 69.
'This is a French sauce' 'The Sleeping Beauty' in *The Famous History of Tom Thumb. Wherein is declared his Marvellous Acts of Manhood Full of Wonder and Merriment* (London, *c.* 1750), p. 18.

62–5 **'The Juniper Tree'** *The Complete Grimms' Fairy Tales*, anon. trans. (London, 1975), pp. 220–9; for a contemporary translation, see *The Complete Fairy Tales of the Brothers Grimm*, ed. and trans. Jack Zipes (New York, 1987), p. 175.

65   **... at the head of the table, and ate** *The Juniper Tree*, with libretto by Patricia Debney, performed at the Almeida Theatre, London, July 1997.

66   **In Runge's portrait** *The Artist's Parents*, 1806, in the Museum in Hamburg; reproduced in Robert Rosenblum, *The Romantic Child from Runge to Sendak* (New York and London, 1988), p. 38.

      'Aristocracy ... man to society.' Thomas Paine, *The Rights of Man* [1791–2], cited in Chris Baldick, *In Frankenstein's Shadow: Myth, Monstrosity and Nineteenth-century Writing* (Oxford, 1987), pp. 20–1.

67   **'Genre, genus and genitals ...'** Geoffrey Galt Harpham, *On the Grotesque: Strategies of Contradiction in Art and Literature* (Princeton, 1982), p. 5.

68   **Freud's Oedipal plot** Jerry Phillips made this point in discussion, at the Essex University symposium on cannibalism, May 1995; see his essay, 'Cannibalism qua Capitalism: The Metaphorics of Accumulation in Marx, Conrad, Shakespeare and Marlowe', in Francis Barker, Peter Hulme and Margaret Iversen (eds), *Cannibalism and the Colonial World* (Cambridge, 1998).

69   **'The obscure information ...'** Sigmund Freud, *The Interpretation of Dreams* [1900], in Standard Edition, trans. and ed. James Strachey, with Alan Tyson (Harmondsworth, 1980), Vol. 4, p. 357.

      an early instance of road rage See George Devereux, 'Why Oedipus Killed Laius: a Note on the Complementary Oedipus Complex in Greek Drama', *International Journal of Psycho-Analysis*, 34 (1953), pp. 132–41.

      'One thing you must not forget ...' Sigmund Freud, *The Psychopathology of Everyday Life* [1902] (Harmondsworth, 1980), Vol. 5, p. 279.

70   **'Is there not a possible religion ...'** Paul Ricoeur, *Freud and Philosophy: An Essay on Interpretation*, trans. Denis Savage (New Haven, 1970), p. 535.

71   **'He reached out ...'** Leon Garfield and Edward Blishen, *The God Beneath the Sea* [1970] (Harmondsworth, 1992), pp. 9–12.

      'Through the course of history ...' George Devereux, 'The Cannibalistic Impulses of Parents', *The Psychoanalytic Forum*, no. 1 (1966), pp. 114–24.

72   **'Un coup c'était Cafougnette ...'** Claude Gaignebet, *Le Folklore obscène des enfants* (Paris, 1974), pp. 186–7.

      In another spin A joke told today picks up this theme: A man goes to pee but finds there are no urinals, only holes in the wall; he sticks his penis in one of them, whereupon a child on the other side says, 'Give me a pound or I'll cut it off.' So the man gives the boy a pound. When he goes out, he meets the young tricksters, and asks them how they've been doing. The first says, 'Very well thank you, I've made £12.' Or some such sum; the next says he hasn't been very successful and has only made about half that amount; the third says he hasn't made any money at all. He adds, brightly, 'But I've got a bucketful of willies!'

      another tale of sausages Gaignebet, *Folklore obscène*, p. 191.

73   **'We came to recognize ... drink of water.'** Melanie Klein, 'The Importance of Symbol Formation in the Development of the Ego' (1930), in *The Selected Melanie Klein*, ed. Juliet Mitchell (Harmondsworth, 1986), p. 104, cited in Mignon Nixon, 'Bad Enough Mother', *October*, 71 (Winter 1995), pp. 70–92, especially p. 71.

      Jacques Lacan explores Jacques Lacan, 'Discourse Analysis and Ego Analysis: Anna Freud or Melanie Klein' and 'The Topic of the Imaginary', in *The Seminar of Jacques Lacan, Book 1: Freud's Papers on Technique 1953–54*, ed. Jacques-Alain Miller, trans. John Forrester (New York, 1991), pp. 68–70, 86–8.

74   **Mme de Murat's fairy tale** 'Peau d'ours' ('Bearskin'), trans. Terence Cave, in *Wonder*

Tales, ed. Marina Warner (London, 1994); this aspect of the beast's appetite has been discussed in my earlier study, *From the Beast to the Blonde*, pp. 259–71.

return visits to the Dracula legend Judith E. Johnson, 'Women and Vampires: Nightmare or Utopia?', *Kenyon Review, New Series* 15, no. 1 (Winter, 1993), pp. 72–80.

orality in writing See for example, Angela Carter, *The Bloody Chamber* (London, 1975) and *Shaking a Leg: Journalism and Writings*, ed. Jenny Uglow (London, 1997), pp. 79–104; Lucy Ellmann, *Sweet Desserts* (London, 1988); Michèle Roberts, *In the Red Kitchen* (London, 1990) and *Flesh and Blood* (London, 1995).

75　'**The children grabbed him . . . loves the most.**' Louise Bourgeois, *Destruction of the Father, Reconstruction of the Father: Writings and Interviews 1923–1997*, ed. Marie-Laure Bernadac and Hans-Ulrich Obrist (London, 1998), pp. 115–16.

REFLECTION: *The Nymphaeum of the Emperor Tiberius*

78　**They smashed the sculptures** See Bernard Andreae, 'L'immagine di Ulisse nell'arte antica'; Baldassare Conticello, 'Il gruppo di Scilla e della nave'; Bernard Andreae and Silvano Bertolin; 'Scilla: schede tecniche'; and Bernard Andreae, 'I gruppi di Polifemo e di Scilla a villa Adriana', pp. 42–71, pp. 286–315, pp. 298–315 and pp. 342–57 in *Ulisse: Mito e memoria* (Rome, 1996).

Polyphemus' massive frame Andreae, 'I Gruppi . . .', pp. 358–61; see also John Boardman, *The Oxford History of Classical Art* (Oxford, 1993), pp. 200–1.

Polyphemus . . . partially restored Conticello, 'Il gruppo di Scilla', pp. 280–315.

80　**The muscly and scaly double tail** For Scylla, see Homer, the *Odyssey*, trans. E.V. Rieu (Harmondsworth, 1982), Books X, XII; Ovid, *Metamorphoses*, trans. Mary M. Innes (Harmondsworth, 1955), Book XIII, pp. 304–5; Graves, *Greek Myths*, Vol. 1, pp. 308–10; Diana Buitron-Oliver and Beth Cohen, 'Between Skylla and Charybdis: Female Characters of the Odyssey in Archaic and Classical Greek Art', and Jenifer Neils, 'Les Femmes Fatales: Skylla and the Sirens in Greek Art', in Beth Cohen (ed.), *The Distaff Side: Representing the Female in Homer's Odyssey* (Oxford, 1995), pp. 29–58, 175–84.

sculpture of Scylla Geoffrey B. Waywell, 'Scilla nell'arte antica', in *Ulisse*, pp. 108–19.

CHAPTER 3: The Polyp and the Cyclops

The translations of the *Odyssey* in this chapter are taken from *The Works of George Chapman; Homer's Iliad* and *Odyssey*, ed. Richard Herne Shepherd (London, 1875).

82　'**There grew out of him . . .**' Francis Celoria (ed. and trans.), *The Metamorphoses of Antoninus Liberalis* (London, 1992), p. 87; see also his admirable notes on Typhon, pp. 178–85.

83　'**. . . rapine feeds . . .**' *Odyssey,* trans. Chapman, Book 12, p. 412.

84　'**. . . so full of miseries**' *Ibid.* p. 415.

poisonous herbs . . . deformed her Graves, *Greek Myths*, Vol. 1, p. 59.

a litter of puppies Ovid, *The Art of Love*, quoted Graves, *Greek Myths*, Vol. 1, p. 310.

86　'**But even then . . . the friends I fear'd**' *Odyssey*, trans. Chapman, Book 12, p. 415.

87　'**Hung all along upon it . . .**' Chapman, *ibid*., p. 411.

88　'**. . . entrails made his meat**' Homer, *Odyssey*, Book 9, trans. Chapman, ibid., p. 381.

'**Nobody's treachery . . .**' Homer, *Odyssey*, Book 9, trans. E.V. Rieu, p. 150.

90　'"**Serpent!" screamed the Pigeon**' Lewis Carroll, *Alice's Adventures under Ground, the Facsimile*, ed. Russell Ash [1985] (London, 1995).

92　'**. . . With Lapland witches**' John Milton, *Paradise Lost*, ed. Alastair Fowler (London, 1991), Book II, pp. 120–1, lines 650–65, 659–61, 662–5.

H.R. Giger, the Swiss artist H.R. Giger *Arh+* [A Rhesus Positive] (Berlin, 1991).

CHAPTER 4: THE DEVIL'S BANQUET

96   '. . . a hundred lions' Dante Alighieri, *The Divine Comedy*, Vol. 1: *Inferno*, trans. John D. Sinclair (London, 1958), Canto XXXI, line 118; see pp. 384–9.

'huge, shaggy beings . . .' Thomas Carlyle, 'The Hero as Divinity', in *On Heroes, Hero-Worship, and The Heroic in History* (London, 1894), p. 197.

'In the giants . . .' Jakob Grimm, *Teutonic Mythology*, 4 vols, trans. James Steven Stallybrass (London, 1880), Vol. 2, p. 528.

Albion who is . . . remembered Susan Stewart, *On Longing: Narratives of the Miniature, the Gigantic, the Souvenir, the Collection* (Durham, North Carolina and London, 1993), pp. 81–4.

97   'Giants survive . . .' Mark A. Hall, *The Yeti, Bigfoot & True Giants* (Minneapolis, 1994), p. 90.

98   '. . . long time fought with God' *Beowulf and the Finnesburg Fragment*, ed. C. L. Wrenn, trans. John R. Clark Hall [1911] (London, 1980), Chapter 11, lines 740–5, p. 58; Chapter 11, line 714, p. 57; Chapter 23, lines 1636–8; Chapter 24, lines 1692–3, p. 106; Chapter 1, lines 110-13, p. 25.

99   '. . . a heathen wild and grim' *Menologium of Saint Basil II* (AD 984), quoted in William Smith and Henry Wall (eds), *Dictionary of Christian Biography* (London, 1877), pp. 495–7; see also David Williams, *Deformed Discourse: The Function of the Monster in Mediaeval Thought and Literature* (Exeter, 1996), pp. 286–97.

Barking . . . Patagonia Antonio Pigafetta, *Magellan's Voyage: A Narrative Account of the First Circumnavigation*, trans. and ed. R.A. Skelton (New York, 1994), pp. 45–9.

the Cerne Giant Rodney Castleden, *The Cerne Giant* (Tiverton, 1997); *Cerne Giant*, Archaeology in the National Trust, Dorset, leaflet, *c.* 1996; Paul Newman, *Gods and Graven Images: The Chalk-Hill Figures of Britain* (London, 1987), pp. 72–101; for Hellequin, see Jean-Claude Schmitt, *Ghosts in the Middle Ages*, trans. Teresa Lavender Fagan (Chicago and London, 1998), pp. 93–121.

100   within the precincts of the giant's body *The Independent*, June 22, 1996.

101   devoured by beasts . . . and others? See Caroline Walker Bynum, 'Material Continuity, Personal Survival and the Resurrection of the Body: A Scholastic Discussion in Its Medieval and Modern Contexts', in Bynum, *Fragmentation and Redemption: Essays on Gender and the Human Body in Medieval Religion* (New York, 1991), pp. 239–297; also Bynum, *The Resurrection of the Body in Western Christianity 200–1336* (New York, 1995).

103   'con sei occhi . . .' Dante, *Inferno*, Canto XXXIII, lines 52–60, p. 422.

104   annihilation of the damned Maggie Kilgour, *From Communion to Cannibalism: An Anatomy of Metaphors of Incorporation* (Princeton, 1990), pp. 65 ff.

106   'designed not to engender . . .' Paul Binski, *Medieval Death: Ritual and Representation* (London, 1996), p. 138.

'When I am gone . . .' Thomas Randolph, 'Ode to Mr Anthony Stafford', in *Specimens of the Early English Poets*, 3 vols, ed. George Ellis (London, 1811), Vol. 3, p. 213.

107   'never the fiend . . .' Percy, *Reliques*, ed. Groom, Vol. 3, pp. 380–5. 'Cock Lorrel's Treat' was printed in Thomas Percy's first edition of *Reliques of Ancient English Poetry*, but it was removed by the book's learned (and Anglican) editor after the Duchess of Northumberland became his patron and he assumed it might offend her. The title refers to a satire that Wynkyn de Worde printed, called 'Cock Lorrel's Bote', and its style parodies courtly praise-song, since it concludes with a blessing on His Majesty. 'Cooke Laurell' was reprinted in the original spelling, in Frederick J. Furnivall (ed.), *Loose and Humorous Songs from Bishop Percy's Folio Manuscript* (Hatboro, Penn., and London, 1963), pp. 37–44.

109   Hogarth's dismissive view David Bindman, *Hogarth and his Times* (London, 1997),

pp. 124–5; Jenny Uglow, *William Hogarth: A Life and a World* (London, 1997), pp. 500–6.

111 **'Guy ultimately fell . . .'** Letter to the author, November 6, 1996.

During Easter week in Spain These are inheritors of sacrificial rituals, such as Julius Caesar observed for example, regarding the Wicker Men of the Celtic tribes: 'figures of vast size, formed of osiers, they fill with living men; which, being set on fire, the men perish enveloped in flames.' Quoted in Newman, *Gods and Graven Images*, p. 147. Cf. the film *The Wicker Man*, 1973, written by Anthony Shaffer, directed by Robin Hardy, which imagines such a rite taking place today on a remote Scottish isle.

112 **Cristina García Rodero** Cristina García Rodero, *España oculta*, introduction by Julio Caro Baroja (Barcelona and London, 1989); Cristina García Rodero, *Festivals and Rituals in Spain*, notes by J. Caballero Bonald (New York, 1992), pl. 151, p. 285; pl. 114, p. 282; pl. 121, p. 283. William Christian Jr. kindly let me see his notes to the archive of Rodero photographs in the Getty Center, Brentwood, California.

114 **the *Tarasque*** Marie-France Gueusquin, *Le Mois des dragons* (Paris, 1981), pp. 82–3.

He . . . secures health and happiness Rodero, *Festivals and Rituals*, pl. 114.

REFLECTION: *THE FEAST OF CORPUS CHRISTI 1996: THE PATUM OF BERGA, CATALONIA*
General note: see Dorothy Pettit Noyes, 'The Mules and the Giants: Struggling for the Body Social in a Catalan Corpus Christi Festival', PhD dissertation, University of Pennsylvania, Ann Arbor, Michigan, 1992; Joseph Armengou, *La Patum de Berga* (Berga, 1994); Josep Noguera i Canal, *Visio Historica del Patum de Berga* (Barcelona, 1992).

118 **a 'true ritual moment'** Bill Christian to the author, Berga, June 1996.

119 **anal birth of new souls** Piero Camporesi, *The Land of Hunger*, trans. Tania Croft-Murray, Claire Foley and Shayne Mitchell (Oxford, 1996), pp. 15–34.

121 **'The music begins . . . end of generation'** Noyes, 'Mules and the Giants', pp. 385–6.

124 **'the plaza after the Patum'** Mossen Armengou, *op. cit.*, p. 431.

'a living civil religion . . .' Noyes, *op. cit.*, p. 430.

'The individual's vertigo . . .' Ibid., p. 212.

CHAPTER 5: 'HOC EST CORPUS'

126 **Zagreus' death** See Graves, *Greek Myths*, Vol. 1, pp. 118–20; M.L. West, The Orphic Poems; Detienne, *Dionysos Slain*, pp. 68–94.

129 **Easter and Corpus Christi declare** See Sarah Beckwith, *Christ's Body: Identity, Culture and Society in Late Medieval Writings* (London, 1993), for a rich study of the Corpus Christi feast; also Louis Marin, *La Parole mangée et autres essais théologico-politiques* (Paris, 1986), Maggie Kilgour, *From Communion to Cannibalism: An Anatomy of Metaphors of Incorporation* (Princeton, 1990), for fascinating and illuminating studies of the imagery of the Eucharist and its historical significance.

Jesus was present . . . ubiquitous Piero Camporesi, 'The Consecrated Host: A Wondrous Excess', in *Fragments for a History of the Human Body*, ed. Michel Feher, Ramona Naddaff and Nadia Tazi (New York, 1989), 3 vols., 1, pp. 220–37.

'Verbum caro . . .' St. Thomas Aquinas, 'Pange, lingua, gloriosi', in *The Penguin Book of Latin Verse*, ed. and trans. Frederick Brittain (Harmondsworth, 1962), pp. 254–5.

130 **An incident . . . in 1750 in Paris** Arlette Farge and Jacques Revel, *The Rules of Rebellion: Child Abductions in Paris in 1750*, trans. Claudia Miéville (Oxford, 1991), esp. pp. 104–13.

131 **playing cards . . . the Four of Spades** British Museum Catalogue 1560, reproduced in Michael Duffy, *The English Satirical Print 1600–1832: The Englishman and the Foreigner* (Cambridge, 1986), p. 22.

Similar stories of a 'blood carriage' Roodenburg, 'Isabella de Moerloose', p. 522.

'. . . at the waxing of the moon' Marsilio Ficino, *Della Religione Christiana Insieme con due libri del medesimo del mantenere la sanità e prolungare la vita per le persone letterate* (Florence, 1568), p. 59, quoted in Piero Camporesi, *The Juice of Life: The Symbolic and Magic Significance of Blood*, trans. Robert R. Barr (New York, 1995), originally *Il Sugo della Vita*, 1988, pp. 36–7.

132 '[like] any jar of jelly . . .' F. Sirena, *L'arte dello spetiale* (Pavia, 1679), p. 30, quoted in Camporesi, *Juice of Life*, pp. 21 ff.

'an oilcloth hat . . . unceasing work' Rumy Hillowala, *et al.*, *The Anatomical Waxes of La Specola*, trans. and ed. Joseph Renahan, Julianne Hillowala and Rumy Hillowala (Florence, 1995), p. 51; Martin Kemp, 'Hidden Dimensions', *Tate: The Art Magazine*, 13 (Winter 1997), pp. 40–5.

133 Hogarth engraved . . . *The Four Stages of Cruelty* Bindman, *Hogarth and his Times*, p. 146; Uglow, *Hogarth*, p. 504.

135 the bloodsucker of street rumours Farge and Revel, *Rules of Rebellion*, pp. 104–13.

CHAPTER 6: 'NOW . . . WE CAN BEGIN TO FEED'

136 'The child builds puddings . . .' Anon., 'The Literature of the Nursery', *The London Magazine*, 2 (November 1820), pp. 477–83.

137 the menu offered Ruth K. McClure, *Coram's Children: The London Foundling Hospital in the Eighteenth Century* (London, 1981), p. 270.

138 'The question is no longer . . .' '"Eating Well," or the Calculation of the Subject: An Interview with Jacques Derrida', in Eduardo Cadava, Peter Connor and Jean-Luc Nancy (eds), *Who Comes after the Subject?* (London, 1991), pp. 96–119, pp. 114–15.

139 the right kind of meats William Wells Newell, *Games and Songs of American Children* [1883] (New York, 1963), pp. 215–21.

140 'If . . . kissing could be described . . .' Phillips, *Kissing*, p. 103.

141 'He seized upon this precious pair . . .' Wilhelm Busch, *Max und Moritz, eine Bubengeschichte in sieben Streichen* (Munich, 1925) (A Boy's Story in Seven Tricks); *Max and Maurice. A Moral Tale in Seven Parts*, trans. Anthea Bell (London, 1975).

142 'pinafores, treacle and innocence' Lewis Carroll, 'Wilhelm von Schmitz', *The Whitby Gazette*, 1854. I am most grateful to Michael Bakewell for this reference.

'"I know *something* interesting . . ."' Lewis Carroll, *Alice's Adventures in Wonderland*, ed. and introduction by Hugh Haughton [1865] (London, 1998), p. 32.

'mashed potatoe' Lewis Carroll, *The Rectory Umbrella and Mischmasch* (London, 1932), pp. 76–7.

'Now if you're ready . . .' Carroll, *Alice's Adventures through the Looking Glass* [1871], ed. and introduction by Hugh Haughton (London, 1998), p. 162.

144 'When we play monsters . . .' Quoted in Phillips, *Kissing*, p. 3.

Butterfly swinging Many thanks to Elaine Jordan for reminding me of this game and naming it.

'I knew—and it always happened . . .' Kate O'Brien, *Presentation Parlour* (London, 1963), pp. 14–15.

145 differentiating oneself within them Gregory Bateson argues that 'play and its paradoxes are necessary for the survival of organisms, since adaptation occurs by loosening up the rules for communication. Play and other types of reframing [thus] prevent the organism from being trapped within one set of interpretive procedures . . . Without these paradoxes the evolution of communication would be at an end. Life would then be an endless interchange of stylized messages, a game with rigid rules, unrelieved by change or humour.' Bateson, *Steps to an Ecology of Mind* (New York, 1972), p. 193; Susan Stewart, *Nonsense: Aspects of Intertextuality in Folklore and Literature* (Baltimore, 1989), p. 31.

the wicked stepmother . . . rival for authority For this argument, see Warner, *Beast*, pp. 218–19.

147   **'. . . the child's cannibalistic rage'** Eric Charles White, *Kaironomia, On the Will-To-Invent* (Ithaca, NY and London, 1987), p. 148.

the child as cannibal There is a large literature on cannibalism as a historical phenomenon, but see especially Claude Rawson's article, 'A Primitive Purity, Cannibalism, Utopias and the Invitation to Disbelief in Early Travel Narratives', *Times Literary Supplement*, July 26, 1996, pp. 3–4.

150   **David McKee's . . . picture book** David McKee, *Not Now, Bernard* [1980] (London, 1990).

152   **'Sausage' . . . increasingly popular** Brian Viner, 'When Uncle Harry Met Sausage', *Hampstead and Highgate Express*, September 26, 1997, p. 64. This father also calls his child 'pigeon' and 'chicken'.

'Sweet Niblet' James R. Kincaid, *Erotic Innocence: The Culture of Child Molesting* (Durham, NC, 1998), p. 103.

. . . they can't run away' Told to the author in Hermione Lee's garden, York, July 10, 1997.

153   **'And she began thinking . . .'** Carroll, *Wonderland*, p. 56.

'Nurse, who peppered . . .' Harry Graham, *Ruthless Rhymes for Heartless Homes* (London, 1899), p. 8.

The plum pudding then arrives Carroll, *Wonderland*, p. 56.

154   **'Mankind's place . . .'** Joyce Carol Oates, 'Reflections on the Grotesque', in *Gothic Transmutations of Horror in Late Twentieth Century Art* (Boston, 1997), p. 35.

155   **poised with carving knife to eat** Butcher's shop, Okehampton, Devon. The writer Iain Sinclair photographed a fish, similarly clothed and equipped with knife and fork, seated at a table dining off fish in the window of a fishmonger's, in the East End of London. 'Pedagogical Explorations', Jago Gallery, London, 1998.

'The butcher that killed this ram . . .' *Gammer Gurton's Garland; or, The Nursery Parnassus* [1783] (London, 1866), p. 8.

Babe (1995) *Babe*, directed by Chris Noonan, based on Dick King-Smith *The Sheep Pig* (London, 1983).

156   **'the whole gigantic fruit . . .'** Roald Dahl, *James and the Giant Peach: A Children's Story* [1961] (London, 1996), p. 123.

critical biography of Dahl Jeremy Treglown, *Roald Dahl* (London, 1994); see figs 21 and 22, pp. 220–3.

157   **the artist-writer's political sympathies** See Raymond Briggs, *When the Wind Blows* (London, 1982) and *The Tin-pot Foreign General and the Old Iron Woman* (London, 1984).

158   **for failing to correspond to the fantasy ideal** See Warner, *Managing Monsters*, pp. 33–48.

Chapter 7: 'Terrors Properly Applied'

162   **'Fai la nanna . . .'** Alessandro Falassi, *Folklore by the Fireside: Text and Context of the Tuscan Veglia* (London, 1980), pp. 97, 275–6.

'Duerme, duerme, negrito . . .' Kindly remembered and sung and subsequently transcribed for me by Pepa Christian, who knows it from her family in the Canary Islands: June 24, 1996—many thanks to her.

163   **Christian anti-Semitism** See Ruth Mellinkoff, *Outcasts: Signs of Otherness in Northern European Art of the Late Middle Ages*, 2 vols (Berkeley and Los Angeles, 1993).

Isabella de Moerloose Roodenburg, *Isabella de Moerloose*, pp. 517–40, p. 522.

Edgeworth . . . anti-Semitism Michael Ragussis, *Figures of Conversion*, 'The Jewish

Question' and English National Identity (Durham, NC and London, 1995), pp. 57–76, 66. I am most grateful to Jonathan Arac for bringing this to my attention.

The blood libel of cradle-snatching See R. Po-chia Hsia, *Trent 1475: Stories of a Ritual Murder Trial* (New Haven, 1992); Caryl Phillips, *The Nature of Blood* (London, 1997); also Jonathan Frankel, *The Damascus Affair: 'Ritual Murder', The Politics and the Jews in 1840* (Cambridge, 1997) for a modern outbreak and its grave, twentieth-century repercussions.

164 **'Do not undervalue an Enemy . . .'** John Selden, *Table Talk*, ed. Frederick Pollock (London, 1927), p. 136.

Tilting targets Carrousel heads, Moesgaard Museum, Aarhus, Denmark.

'Guy of Warwick' Percy, *Reliques*, ed. Groom, (London, 1997), Vol. 1, p. 49.

Turks survived Some 'Crockery smashers' extant in the 1940s set up Tax Inspectors and Policemen instead.

165 **'It is a common custome . . .'** Loys Lavater, *Of Ghostes and Spirites Walking by Night*, ed. J. Dover Wilson and M. Yardley [1572] (Oxford, 1929), p. 21, quoted in Roodenburg, *Isabella de Moerloose*, p. 523.

165–6 **Gulliver reported** Jonathan Swift, *Gulliver's Travels*, ed. Christopher Fox (Boston, 1995). Part One, 'A Voyage to Lilliput', pp. 74–5.

167 **'terrors, properly applied . . .'** 'The Nurse and Cross Child', in *The Famous History of Tom Thumb. Wherein is declared, his marvellous acts of manhood, full of wonder and merriment* (London, *c.* 1760), pp. 24–5.

168 **The artist Susan Hiller** Susan Hiller, *An Entertainment* (Matt's Gallery, London, 1990).

'Dance, baby, diddy' Harrison Birtwhistle, *Punch & Judy* (1968), CD Etcetera KTC 2014, 1989.

169 **. . . pretending to be an ogre** See L.R. Goldman, *Child's Play: Myth, Mimesis and Make-Believe* (Oxford, 1998), pp. 89, 91, 174ff. for Melanesian examples. This fascinating study was published too late for its arguments to be discussed here.

170 **'Half a century since . . .'** 'The Ogree's Coop', in Newell, *Games and Songs*, p. 221.

171 **'There was once a man . . .'** Tale Type 366, in A.A. Aarne and Stith Thompson, *The Types of the Folk Tale* (Helsinki, 1964). See M.R. James, *The Collected Ghost Stories of M.R. James* [1931] (London, 1970), p. 609, quoted in Jacqueline Simpson, '"The Rules of Folklore" in the Ghost Stories of M.R. James', *Folklore*, 108 (1997), pp. 9–18.

172 **A board book for babies** Stephen Cartwright, *That's Funny!* (London, 1989).

173 **Romantic and Victorian painters** See *Victorian Fairy Painting*, Catalogue, Royal Academy, London, November 13, 1997–8; also Nicola Bown, 'Introduction to the Exhibition *Victorian Fairy Painting*' (London, 1997) and '"A case of such familiars at home": Natural and Supernatural in the work of John Anster Fitzgerald', forthcoming. I am grateful to the author for letting me see this essay. A.S. Byatt's short story, 'Morpho Eugenia', in *Angels & Insects* (London, 1992) vividly dramatizes the connection between entomology and sinister erotic fantasy in the Victorian era.

'Orcs and goblins . . . on the rampage' Warhammer Catalogues, 1996, 1997, *passim*; see Denis Duclos, *America's Fascination with Violence*, trans. Amanda Pingree (Oxford and New York, 1998) for a powerful study of contemporary American dystopic and monstrous fantasies.

175 **costumes and stratagems of power** Cornelia Hesse-Honegger, *The Future's Mirror*, Catalogue (Newcastle, 1996), has given this theme a new twist, by collecting insects near nuclear power stations and documenting in entomological illustrations the effect on insects of radiation.

176 **shivery techno-horror hybrids** See Isaac Asimov and Karen A. Frenkel, *Robots: Machines in Man's Image* (New York, 1985).

One of the earliest films Tom Dewe Mathews, *Censored* (London, 1994), p. 7.

grubs and crickets . . . nutritive value Steven Pinker, *How the Mind Works* (New York and London, 1997).

178 **South American plant hopper** Peter Parks 'Colour in Nature', in *Colour: Art & Science*, ed. Trevor Lamb and Janine Bourriau (Cambridge, 1995), p. 167. My thanks to Steve Jones for lending me this book.

'it is possible to see . . .' Parks, *Colour in Nature*, p. 167.

The yellow and black bands John Burton, *The Oxford Book of Insects* (Oxford, 1968), pp. 130–1.

179 **'If a model is lethal'** Robert Davidson, interview, April 1997.

the insects' cunning crypsis Parks gives as an example the heliconiid butterfly, that imitates 'very distasteful "ithomiid" counterparts': 'In general, if you are distasteful, the last thing you want is for a predator to learn on you. Much better if it learns on another species that you resemble. By the time it comes to you, with luck it will have learnt not even to peck at you.' Parks, *Colour in Nature*, p. 167.

180 **cultural history modifies** See John Gage, *Colour and Culture: Practice and Meaning from Antiquity to Abstraction* (London, 1993).

'basic warning colours . . .' Parks, *Colour in Nature*, p. 167.

poster of the Prodigy The Prodigy, *The Fat of the Land*, 1997, XLI21. An advertising company Blattner and Brunner, from Pittsburgh, proclaimed themselves the 'Killer Bees' and graphically proclaimed their powers of persuasion with a poster showing a hand-grenade, striped black and yellow like the insect.

181 **Lacan . . . comments, ironically** Jacques Lacan, *The Four Fundamental Principles of Psychoanalysis*, trans. Alan Sheridan (Harmondsworth, 1994), p. 73.

'the underside of consciousness' *Ibid.*, p. 83.

REFLECTION: CARAVAGGIO: *THE REST ON THE FLIGHT INTO EGYPT*

188 **The score that Joseph is holding** H. Colin Slim, 'Music In and Out of Egypt: A Little Studied Iconographic Tradition', *Musica Disciplina*, 37 (1983), American Institute of Musicology, Neuhausen, Stuttgart, pp. 303–11; Franca Trinchieri Camiz and Agostino Ziino, 'Caravaggio: Aspetti musicali e committenza', *Studi musicali*, 12, no. 6, Academia Nazionale di S. Cecilia, Roma, pp. 67–83.

189 **'How fair and how pleasant . . .'** I am very grateful to Franca Camiz and Agostino Ziino for playing me the latter's performance of the piece, and to Helen Langdon for introducing me to their work.

190 **the stripes of Christ's cross** Caravaggio's reputation of *stravagantismo* has inspired a lubricious reading of the painting, that the angel's scantily draped genitals are in Joseph's direct line of vision and he is crossing his big toes to control his sexual excitement, while the donkey, that famed embodiment of priapism, registers the effect.

The Allegory . . . by Hans Holbein the Elder In the National Gallery of Scotland, Edinburgh.

CHAPTER 8: 'SING NOW MOTHER . . . WHAT ME SHALL BEFALL . . .'

193 **'whose labour made our world'** Angela Carter, 'Introduction', in *The Virago Book of Fairy Tales*, ed. Angela Carter (London, 1990), p. ix.

194 **A lullaby is weak domestic magic** The artist Susan Hiller catches this melancholy meagreness movingly in her accompanying voice-over to her video sculpture *Belshazzar's Feast/The Writing on Your Wall*, Tate Gallery, London, 1983–9.

195 **Saint Anne** See Warner, *Beast*, pp. 86–7.

Neapolitan humanist Also known as Gioviano Pontano (1422–1503): see Falassi, *Folklore by the Fireside*, p. 104.

'Piss a Bed . . .' Gloria T. Delamar, *Mother Goose from Nursery to Literature* (Jefferson, NC and London, 1987), p. 5.

innocuous and gentle *berceuses* See *A Little Pretty Pocket-Book* of 1765 and *Mother Goose's Melody* of around the same time.

The earliest . . . collection Delamar, *Mother Goose*, pp. 282–3.

The volume reappeared . . . in Boston See *Mother Goose's Melodies*, ed. E.F. Bleiler (facsimile edition of the Munroe & Francis 'Copyright 1833' version), (New York, 1970), pp. v–xxiii, 12, 60, 99–116.

196   **The minor third dominates** See Maurice J.E. Brown, 'Lullaby', in *The New Grove Dictionary of Music and Musicians*, ed. Stanley Sadie (London, 1980) Vol. 2, pp. 313–14. I am very grateful to John Woolrich, the composer, for playing me Igor Stravinsky, 'Four Cat's Cradle Songs', and discussing them and other lullabies with me.

Authored variants of the lullaby Blake caught the intimate poignancy of this exchange between mother and child in his 'Cradle Song' from *Songs of Innocence*, which epitomizes the lullaby as blessing for five gentle stanzas and then turns into a meditation on the child as image of the Saviour: 'Sweet babe, in thy face,/Holy image I can trace.' William Blake, *Songs of Innocence and of Experience*, ed. Geoffrey Keynes (Oxford, 1977), pp. 16–17.

'a beautiful Andalusian . . .' Federico García Lorca, 'Las Nanas infantiles', in *Obras Completas* (Madrid, 1977), pp. 1073–91, p. 1075.

'Yo: Voy en busca de magos . . .'
Federico García Lorca, 'Balada de la placeta', in *Lorca*, selected and trans. J. J. Gili (Harmondsworth, 1960), pp. 1–4.

197   **'Rock-a-bye baby . . .'** Anon., *Gammer Gurton's Garland* [1784], (1866), p. 8.

198   **'Golden Slumbers . . .'** *The Faber Book of Nursery Songs*, selected by Donald Mitchell, arranged by Carey Blyton (London, n.d.), pp. 34–5.

'Summertime . . .' Lyrics by Dubose Heyward and Ira Gershwin; see Edward Jablonski, *Gershwin* (New York, 1988), pp. 262 ff.

'In one example, from a commonplace book' 'Dialogue between the Blessed Virgin and her Child', Advocates Lib. 18.7.21. From a commonplace book (1372), in Carleton Brown (ed.), *Religious Lyrics of the Fourteenth Century* (Oxford, 1952), pp. 70–5.

laments and threnodies for Passion Week Brown, *Religious Lyrics*, see nos 58, 64 and 65, pp. 78–9, 82–3.

199   **'Lullay, lullay . . .'** *Ibid.*, no. 56, pp. 70–5.

War and Peace **(1967)** My thanks to Eleni Cubitt for reminding me of this powerful sequence.

'Her dreams of hope . . .' 'Muttertraum', from *Fünf Lieder aus dem Danischen und Neugriechischen*, op. 40. Interestingly this song was one of several Hans Christian Andersen poems translated by Adelbert von Chamisso, himself a writer of sinister tales. Performed by Olaf Bar and Helmut Deutsch, *Schumann: Lieder, Romanzen und Balladen*, EMI Classics 7243 5 5619921, 1997.

200   **'The first to display images . . .'** Kaja Silverman, *The Acoustic Mirror: The Female Voice in Psychoanalysis and Cinema* (Bloomington, 1988), pp. 76–8; Michel Chion, *La Voix au cinéma* (Paris, 1982), p. 76.

'. . . name the dreams of a child?' Lorca, *'Las Nanas'*, p. 1077.

Mayflower **Pilgrim Father** Iona and Peter Opie, *The Oxford Dictionary of Nursery Rhymes* (Oxford, 1977), pp. 61–2.

201   **Walter Benjamin . . . pointed out** Walter Benjamin, 'The Storyteller: Reflections on the Work of Nicolai Leskov', in *Illuminations*, trans. Harry Zohn (London, 1969), p. 101.

'are diffused with . . . brooding' Daiken, *Lullaby Book*, p. 13.

202   'Dinogad's smock, pied, pied . . .' 'Dinogad's Smock (A cradle song)', in Aneirin, *Y Gododdin: Britain's Oldest Heroic Poem*, trans. and ed. A.O.H. Jarman, (Dyfed, 1988), pp. 68–9.

'Babbo tornate . . .' My thanks to John Woolrich for playing me this example, sung by Caterina Anigucci, from Garignano, 1966.

204   'Now we are at home . . .' Gilles Deleuze and Félix Guattari, '1837: Of the Refrain', in *A Thousand Plateaus: Capitalism & Schizophrenia*, trans. Brian Massumi (London, 1988), p. 311.

'The common compliment . . .' Holt White, note to *Titus Andronicus*, ed. Dr. Johnson, in *The Plays of William Shakespeare*, 14 vols (London, 1793), Vol. 13, p. 287.

'Come on, close your eyes . . .' Desrousseaux, 'L'Canchon dormoire' ('Dors mon p'tit quinquin').

205   'Go to sleep . . .' 'Fate la nanna coscine di pollo/la vostra mamma v'ha fatto i' gonnello,/ve l'ha cucito torno torno,/fate la nanna coscine di pollo./Fate la nanna possiate dormire/il letto vi sia fatto di viole,/il materasso di piume gentile,/il capezzale di penne di pavone/e le lenzuola di tela d'Olanda;/fate la ninna e poi fate la nanna!'/Falassi, *Folklore by the Fireside*, pp. 94, 274.

'These are sleeping songs . . .' *Ride a Cock Horse*, chosen by Sarah Williams, illus. Ian Beck (Oxford, 1986), p. 39.

206   'So lulla lulla lulla lullaby bye . . .' It was only during the research for a programme, made for BBC Radio 3 by Beaty Rubens, that I came across Paul Robeson's 1932 recording of this lullaby and realized it is the famous 'Ma Curly-Headed Baby', by George Howard Clutsam.

'All the Pretty Little Horses' Sung with deep, tragic grandeur by Odetta, who changes the more usual 'peckin' to 'pickin' on *At the Gate of Horn*, TLP 1025, *c.* 1962. Softened versions give 'The bees and the butterflies *buzzing* round its eyes . . .' or 'fluttering', as in Peter, Paul and Mary's 1960s recording. See *Golden Slumbers: A Selection of Lullabies from Near and Far* (Caedmon Soundbook CBI), introduction by Harriet Herbst, *c.* 1965, p. 10.

CHAPTER 9: 'HEROD THE KING IN HIS RAGING . . .'

208   'cradling Adolf's or Benito's tons . . .' Tony Harrison, *The Kaisers of Carnuntum* in *Plays Three* (London, 1996), cited in Oliver Taplin, 'The Chorus of Mams', in *Tony Harrison: Loiner*, ed. Sandie Byrne (Oxford, 1997), pp. 171–225.

a *ninna-nanna*, or Italian lullaby Remembered by Emilia Warner, née Terzulli, October 1997, learned in Molfetta, Puglia, Italy.

210   observing and relating . . . from the sidelines Eugene Field, *Cradle Lullabies* (Chicago, 1909) includes both a 'Corsican Lullaby' and a 'Jewish Lullaby' in English verse, in which the dire sorrows of the past are lifted by the advent of the child, pp. 17, 23.

the *Ludus Coventriae* See Martin Stevens, *Four Middle English Mystery Cycles: Textual, Contextual and Critical Interpretations* (Princeton, 1987), pp. 181–2.

211   'the mightiest conqueror . . .' 'The Shearmen and Tailors' Play', in *English Mystery Plays: A Selection*, ed. Peter Happe (Harmondsworth, 1975), pp. 362–79 [transliterated into modern spelling]; see also Hardin Craig (ed.), *Two Coventry Corpus Christi Plays* (London and Oxford, 1957), pp. 17–32.

'I stamp I stare!' Happe, *English Mystery Plays*, p. 374.

Villains of the mystery plays Michael Camille, *Master of Death: The Lifeless Art of Pierre Remiet Illuminator* (New Haven and London, 1996), pp. 131–2, 158.

212   '. . . the idea of travestied authority' Hugh Haughton, *The Chatto Book of Nonsense Poetry* (London, 1988), p. 14.

'O sisters too . . .' Craig, *Two Coventry Corpus Christi Plays*, pp. 32, 377.

Holy Family . . . to Israel William L. Smoldon, *The Music of Medieval Church Drama* (Oxford, 1980), pp. 212–13, 218.

213 'Chorus of Mams' Tony Harrison, *The Big H*, in *Dramatic Verse 1973–1985* (Newcastle, 1998), quoted in Taplin, *Tony Harrison: Loiner*, p. 183.

215 Poussin's interpretation Elizabeth Cropper and Charles Dempsey, *Nicholas Poussin* (Princeton, 1996), pp. 253–78.

216 '. . . regrouping of forces' Deleuze and Guattari, 'Of the Refrain' in *A Thousand Plateaus*, p. 320.

a rhapsodic *tour de force* John Ruskin, *Modern Painters II* (1846), Part III, Section II, Chapter 3, para. 21: 'Their [mothers'] shrieks ring in our ears till the marble seems rending around us, but far back, at the bottom of the stairs, there is something in the shadow like a heap of clothes. It is a woman, sitting quiet,—quite quite,—still as any stone; she looks down steadfastly on her dead child, laid along the floor before her, and her hand is pressed softly upon her brow.'

217 shot by . . . the baby's own father Jean de La Fontaine, 'Le Loup, la mère et l'enfant', *Oeuvres complètes*, Vol. 1 (Paris, 1991), p. 163.

'The first world we find . . .' Adam Phillips, 'First Hates: Phobias in Theory', *Kissing*, p. 19.

218 'A Cossack Lullaby' *Lermontov, Major Poetical Works*, trans. Anatoly Liberman (London and Canberra, 1983), pp. 186–9.

'Baby, baby, naughty baby . . .' Iona and Peter Opie, *The Oxford Dictionary of Nursery Rhymes* (Oxford, 1977), p. 59.

219 'Entendez-vous . . .' Daiken, *Lullaby Book*, p. 26, recorded on *Berceuses du monde entier*, K 294.

alarming section of grim lullabies 'Wiegenlieder' section in Enzensberger (ed.), *Viele Schöne Kinderreime*, p. 52, trans. Helena Ivins.

'Susse putinchen . . .' *Ibid.*, p. 52, trans. Helena Ivins.

maternal ambivalence Roszika Parker, *Torn in Two: The Experience of Maternal Ambivalence* (London, 1995).

220 'O Can Ye Sew Cushions?' Daiken, *Lullaby Book*, p. 41.

221 'Mony o I hae little . . .' *Golden Slumbers: A Selection of Lullabies from Near and Far* (Caedmon Soundbook CB1), p. 24.

The woe the mother expresses In *Menaphon*, Robert Greene gives Sephestia a song which Benjamin Britten later set: 'Mother's wag, pretty boy,/Father's sorrow, father's joy;/When thy father first did see/Such a boy by him and me,/He was glad, I was woe;/Fortune changed made him so,/When he left his pretty boy,/Last his sorrow, first his joy . . ./Weep not, my wanton,/Smile upon my knee;/When thou art old/There's grief enough for thee . . .'

Lorca was gleeful Lorca, 'Las Nanas infantiles', *Obras Completas*, pp. 1088–9. The familiar male suspicion turns up in lullaby dress in the work of Paul Hiebert, Canadian humorist (he makes no claim to have *heard* it): 'Sleep, my darling, sleep away,/Daddy's gone to town with hay,/And at four o'clock will come/The man who sells aluminum;/Mother's sold on kitchenware/Sleep she wants to do her hair . . .' Paul Hiebert, *Sarah Binks* (Oxford, 1947). My thanks to Liz Derbecker and Leslie McGrath for this reference.

'Heidschi bumbeidschi . . .' Austrian, collected in Berlin from Karjane Neubert, student.

222 'Pig and Pepper' episode Carroll, *Wonderland*, ed. Haughton, p. 54.

'Sleep, you black-eyed pig . . .' W.H. Auden and Louis MacNeice, *Letters from Iceland* [1937] (New York, 1965), p. 143.

'Ah Bo Bu . . .' Personal communication from Maeve Casey, after the Kate o'Brien

Memorial Lecture, Limerick, Ireland, February 1997.

223　**This decoy technique** Walter Burkert, *Creation of the Sacred: Tracks of Biology in Early Religions* (Cambridge, Mass., 1996), p. 25.

CHAPTER 10: 'AND THOU, OH NIGHTENGALE . . .'

224　**Penelope . . . compares herself** Homer, the *Odyssey*, trans. E.V. Rieu [1946] (Harmondsworth, 1982), Book XIX lines 518–29; see Francis Celoria (ed.), *Metamorphoses of Antoninus Liberalis* (London, 1992), pp. 62–3, 135–42.

225　**'. . . he caught her tongue . . .'** Ted Hughes, 'Tereus', in *Tales from Ovid* (London, 1997), p. 23.

　　　glosses on Antoninus Liberalis Celoria, *Antoninus Liberalis*, pp. 62–3, 135–9.

226　**'The moon on thy window . . .'** Poetical Commonplace Book of Charlotte Hester Burney, Harvard MS Eng. 926.

　　　'Hush ye winds!' Houghton Library, Harvard, Harvard bMS Eng. 893 (224).

227　**'Chew chew chee chew chee . . .'** Margaret Grainger, *The Natural History Prose Writings of John Clare* (Oxford, 1983), p. 312, quoted by Nick Groom, reviewing *John Clare in Context*, ed. Hugh Haughton, Adam Phillips and Geoffrey Summerfield (Cambridge, 1994). *Times Higher Education Supplement*, 21 April 1995, p. 18.

228　**the lullaby . . . language acquisition** Crucial work in this field is being done by Sandra E. Trehub, the psychologist. See Sandra E. Trehub and Laurel Trainor, 'Singing to Infants: Lullabies and Play Songs', in *Advances in Infancy Research*, forthcoming. I am most grateful to Dr. Trehub for sending me this paper before publication. See also Sandra E. Trehub, Laurel J. Trainor and Ann M. Unyk, 'Music and Speech Processing in the First Year of Life', *Advances in Child Development and Behavior*, 24 (1993), pp. 1–35.

　　　a comparison with birds Marcia Barinaga, 'Baby Sparrows Thrive on Word Salad', *Science*, 270 (December 1, 1995), p. 1437.

　　　exceptions are the fly-catchers John Terborgh, 'Cracking the Bird Code,' *The New York Review of Books*, January 11, 1996, pp. 40–4.

　　　'borrow bits and pieces . . .' J.M.D., 'Bird Vocalization', under 'Imitation', in *Oxford Companion to Animal Behaviour*, ed. David McFarland (Oxford, 1981), pp. 301–3.

229　**Phonetic and prosodic patterns** 'These results suggest that maternal prosody is finely tuned to infant affect, and that mothers use pitch differentially to regulate infant arousal. In speech to infants, several prosodic features known to convey emotional information are exaggerated well beyond the range of normal adult speech, providing prominent affective vocal cues for the infant . . . These findings suggest that the relationship of prosodic form to communicative function is highly salient in the melodies of mothers' speech, and that these characteristic intonation patterns are potentially meaningful to the preverbal infant. Anne Fernald *et al.*, 'A Cross Language Study of Prosodic Modifications in Mothers' and Fathers' Speech to Preverbal Infants', *Journal of Child Language*, 16 (1989), pp. 477–501. See also Henry Benett-Clark, 'Song', in McFarland (ed.), *Animal Behaviour*, pp. 527–36.

　　　'may facilitate . . .' Fernald *et al.* "A Cross Language Study', pp. 477–501.

　　　typical sound clusters Daiken, *Lullaby Book*, p. 9. Leslie Daiken quotes the table drawn up by Hana Fukuda of the characteristic repeated sounds in various languages, showing the concentration of *ninna-nanna* in the Mediterranean basin, for example, from France to Tunisia.

　　　Coleridge . . . rebelliously acclaimed S.T. Coleridge, 'The Nightingale: A Conversational Poem', in *Lyrical Ballads: Wordsworth and Coleridge*, ed. R.L. Brett and A.R. Jones (London, 1968), pp. 40–4.

　　　Research shows that birdsong C.K. Catchpole and P.J.B. Slater, *Bird Song, Biological*

Themes and Variations (Cambridge, 1995), pp. 100–6.

robins . . . sing *Ibid.*, p. 102.

Among familiar species *Ibid.*, p. 60.

North American redwings Terborgh, 'Bird Code', p. 43.

females give signals G. Ritchison, 'The Function of Singing in Female Black-headed Grosbeaks (*Pheuctitus melanocephalus*): Family Group Maintenance', *Auk*, 100 (1983), pp. 105–16.

230 **vervet monkeys** See Jean Aitchison, *The Language Web: The Power and the Problems of Words* (Cambridge, 1996); James Gould and Carol Gould, 'Language', also 'Vocalization', in McFarland (ed.), *Animal Behaviour*, pp. 332–6, 593–5.

New research . . . parents' speech 'In the second year . . . fundamental frequency patterns in parental speech may serve increasingly specific linguistic functions, drawing the child's attention to stressed words within the stream of speech. This progression is seen as continuous and cumulative: the ability of the older child to use intonation and to parse language builds on the child's early and enduring attentional and affective responsiveness to frequency patterns in parental speech.' Fernald et al., 'A Cross Language Study', pp. 477–501; see also Brenda Shute and Kevin Wheldall, 'Pitch Alterations in British Motherese: Some Preliminary Acoustic Data', *Journal of Child Language*, 16 (1989), pp. 503–12.

the role . . . patter and nonsense Trehub et al., 'Music and Speech Processing'. See Kornei Chukovsky, 'The Sense of Nonsense Verse', in *From Two to Five*, trans. and ed. Miriam Morton (Berkeley, 1963), pp. 89–113, for a pioneering and spirited defence of fantasy in child education.

231 **devices that . . . imprint language** Fernald *et al.*, 'A Cross Language Study', pp. 477–501; Shute and Wheldall, 'Pitch Alterations', pp. 503–12; Alan Cruttenden, 'Phonetic and Prosodic Aspects of Baby Talk', in *Input and Interaction in Language Acquisition*, ed. Claire Gallaway and Brian J. Richards (Cambridge, 1994), pp. 135–52.

Walter Benjamin was scornful Walter Benjamin, 'Spielzeug und Spielen', in *Über Kinder, Jugend und Erziehung* (Frankfurt, 1969), p. 68 quoted in Jeffrey Mehlman, (ed.), *Walter Benjamin for Children: An Essay on His Radio Years* (Chicago, 1993), p. 4.

'Mothers reassure . . .' J. Sieratzki and B. Woll, 'Why Do Mothers Cradle Babies on Their Left?' *The Lancet*, 347 (June 22, 1996) pp. 1746–8.

huge . . . scholarly literature Trehub et al., 'Music and Speech Processing', pp. 1–35; W.P. Fifer and C.M. Moon, 'The Role of the Mother's Voice in the Organization of Brain Function in the Newborn', *Acta Paediatrica*, Supplement 397 (1994), pp. 86–93.

'A Cradle Hymn' Isaac Watts, *Divine Songs for the Use of Children*, 25th edn (London, 1761).

232 **A recent medical study** P. De Chateau, and Y. Andersson, 'Left Side Preference for Holding and Carrying Newborn Infants II: Doll-holding and Carrying from 2 to 16 Years', *Dev. Med. Child Neurology*, 18 (1976), pp. 738–44; P. De Chateau, 'Left-side Preference in Holding and Carrying Newborn Infants', *Acta Psychiatrica Scandinavica*, 75 (1987), pp. 283–6.

bilateral division of function in the brain Sieratzki and Woll, 'Why Do Mothers', pp. 1746.

233 **'the left hemisphere . . .'** Sieratzki and Woll, citing J.B. Hellige, *Hemispheric Asymmetry: What's Right and What's Left* (Cambridge, 1993); E.D. Ross, 'Non-verbal Aspects of Language', *Neurological Clinics*, 2, no 1 (February 1993), pp. 9–23.

A baby's brain, as it grows Jean Aitchison, *The Articulate Mammal: An Introduction to Linguistics* (London, 1989), pp. 52–61.

this fresh line of inquiry The research concludes: 'Along the right hemisphere affect-communication vector, left-side cradling facilitates the flow of auditory and visual communication between mother and infant and channels somato-affective feedback and infant sound to the mother's right hemisphere, which in turn tunes the melody of the mother's voice—the lullaby will not sound the same, and will not feel the same with the baby on the other side.' Sieratzi and Woll, 'Why Do Mothers', p. 1748.

'The Child in the Sheepfold' Jon Arnason, *Icelandic Folktales and Legends*, trans. Jacqueline Simpson (London, 1972). Selected from Jon Arnason, *Islendzkar thjodsogur og aefintyri* (Leipzig, 1862–4), pp. 105–6. Sung under the title 'Ghost Song' on *Engel Lund: Icelandic Folksongs*, arranged by F. Rauter, CPMA 4.

Carolyne Larrington Personal communication, for which I am very grateful, November 21, 1996.

234 **'the articulation . . .'** Richard Handler, 'An Anatomist of Culture', *Times Literary Supplement*, August 24–30, 1990, p. 891, reviewing Regna Darnell, *Edward Sapir: Linguist, Anthropologist, Humanist* (Berkeley, 1990).

French Symbolist poet Stéphane Mallarmé Stéphane Mallarmé, *Recueil de 'Nursery Rhymes'*, ed. Carl Paul Barbier (Paris, 1964), pp. 32–3, 70–1, 13–4.

235 **meaning of 'shibboleth'** I've used the translation of the Jerusalem Bible, as it is clearer than the Authorized Version. To the Gileadites, *shibboleth* meant either 'ear of corn' or 'a stream in flood' (*OED*), the latter now being preferred as the massacre took place by the Jordan.

the word Scheveningen I am very grateful to Mariët Westermann for this information, in a letter of June 3, 1997.

the case of 'Lillibulero' The musical setting has been attributed to Henry Purcell. See Laurence Sterne, *The Life and Opinions of Tristram Shandy*, ed. Graham Petrie (Harmondsworth, 1986), p. 622.

236 **'. . . so great an effect'** Percy, *Reliques*, ed. Groom, Vol. 2, pp. 358–61.

'my uncle Toby' Sterne, *Tristram Shandy*, p. 92, for example.

'one opens the circle . . .' Deleuze and Guattari, 'Of the Refrain', in *A Thousand Plateaus*, p. 311.

237 **Virginia Woolf . . . 'pixerina-witcherina'** Hermione Lee, *Virginia Woolf: A Working Life* (London, 1996), pp. 547–8. This kind of secret family language is related to the nonsense rhymes of Lewis Carroll and Edward Lear. Garbling language seems to have been a particular enthusiasm among Victorian and Edwardian families, both as a parlour game and as a way of creating a private world. Pippa Lewis recalls that when she was a child, her aunts used to put 'arp' in front of every syllable, so that 'How are you?' became 'Harpow harpare yarpou?' Her relations pattered in this manner very rapidly. Personal communication, January 6, 1998.

Reflection: Louis Desprez: *The Chimera*

240 **Medusa and Kali . . . household protection** See John Boardman, 'The Diffusion of Classical Art', in Boardman, *Classical Art*, pp. 345–78.

The *sheela-na-gig* See Eamonn P. Kelly, *Sheela-na-gigs: Origins and Functions* (Dublin, 1996). Jack Roberts *The Sheela-na-gigs of Britain and Ireland: an Illustrated Guide* (Limerick, 1995). I am grateful to Cáit ni Cheallacháin for giving me these manuals.

'Such beasts . . . forbidden places' Jean-Pierre Vernant, *La Mort dans les yeux* (Paris, 1985), Chapter 5.

simian grimace Desmond Morris, *The Naked Ape: A Zoologist's Study of the Human Animal* (London, 1994), pp. 109–10.

242 **'. . . who breathed awful fire . . .'** Hesiod, *Theogony*, trans. Dorothea Wender, lines 320–3, p.3; cf. Homer, *Iliad*, Book VI, trans. E.V. Rieu (Harmondsworth, 1950), p. 122.

243 **Bellerophon's later career** Ginevra Bompiani, 'The Chimera Herself', in Michel Feher, Ramona Nadaff and Nadia Tazi (eds.), *Fragments for a History of the Human Body* (New York, 1989), Vol. 1, p. 380.

'the creature of language . . .' Ibid., pp. 364–409; 377.

Borges . . . bestiary Jorge Luis Borges (with Margarita Guerrero), *The Book of Imaginary Beings* (London, 1974), trans. Norman Thomas di Giovanni, pp. 41–2.

244 **Desprez's Chimaera** Ragnar von Holten, 'Desprez, Graveur original', and Régis Michel, 'Le Fantasme de la Chimère', in *La Chimère de Monsieur Desprez*, Catalogue, Pavillon de Flore, 10 Février–2 Mai (Paris, 1994), pp. 180, 53–6.

CHAPTER 11: 'IN THE GENRE OF THE MONSTROUS'

General note: see Wilson Yates, 'An Introduction to the Grotesque: Theoretical and Theological Considerations', in James Luther Adams and Wilson Yates (eds.), *The Grotesque in Art and Literature* (Grand Rapids and Cambridge, 1997), pp. 1–68 for a useful survey of the literature. I have found most helpful André Chastel, *La Grottesque* (Paris, 1988), Geoffrey Galt Harpham, *On the Grotesque: Strategies of Contradiction in Art and Literature* (Princeton, 1982); Peter Stallybrass and Allon White, *The Politics and Poetics of Transgression* (London, 1986) and Michael Camille, *Image on the Edge: the Margins of Medieval Art* (London, 1992). Other important works on the topic include an early study, Wolfgang Kayser, *The Grotesque in Art and Literature*, trans. Ulrich Weisstein (Bloomington, 1963) and the famous work by Mikhail Bakhtin, *The World of Rabelais*, trans. Helene Iswolsky (Cambridge, Mass., 1968). See also two fascinating studies of earlier forms of grotesque: Andy Orchard, *Pride and Prodigies: Studies in the Monsters of the Beowulf-Manuscript* (Cambridge, 1995) and David Williams, *Deformed Discourse: The Function of the Monster in Mediaeval Thought and Literature* (Exeter, 1996).

246 **'The monstrous figure . . .'** See Mark Dorrian, 'Monstrosity Today', *Artifice*, 5 (1996), pp. 48–59 for a thoughtful piece about contemporary photography's roots in the grotesque tradition. I am also grateful to the writer for giving me another draft chapter, 'On the Monstrous and the Grotesque' from his forthcoming book.

247 *terribilità . . . capriccio* Chastel, *De la Grottesque*, p. 31.

The poet Horace Horace, *On the Art of Poetry*, in Aristotle, Horace, Longinus, *Classical Literary Criticism* (Harmondsworth, 1965), p. 79

248 **'The language of the devil . . .'** Dorrian, 'Monstrosity Today'

the style spread northwards See Monique Riccardi-Cubitt, 'Grotesque', in *The Grove Dictionary of Art* (London, 1996), pp. 699–702; Chastel, *La Grottesque*, pp. 19–35.

Dürer: . . . 'all things together' E. H. Gombrich, *A Sense of Order* (London, 1994) [1979], p. 251; see also Jean-Michel Massing, 'Dürer's Dreams', *Journal of the Warburg and Courtauld Institutes*, 49, 1986, pp. 238–40.

249 **'Painters and poets . . . figures of men and animals.'** Francisco de Olanda, *Diálogos*, trans. L. Rouaud (Paris, 1911), pp. 109 ff., quoted Chastel, *La Grottesque*, p. 35. This conversation's historical authenticity has been questioned, but Chastel endorses it.

253 **'Here's Ralph with his Raree-show . . .'** *The Alphabet of Goody Two Shoes* (London, 1765), quoted in Leonard de Vries, *A Treasury of Illustrated Children's Books. Early Nineteenth Century Classics from the Osborne Collection* (New York, 1989), p. 187.

Francis Bacon had described Harpham, *On the Grotesque*, p. 181.

nature's prodigies . . . on display See Elizabeth Allen, *A Guide to the Hunterian Museum* (London, 1993), p. 26; Jan Bondeson, *A Cabinet of Medical Curiosities* (London, 1997), extract published in *Udolpho*, 31 (Winter 1997), pp. 12–16, 32; Gaby Wood 'The Macabre Case of the Sicilian Dwarf', *London Review of Books*, 19, no. 24 (December 11, 1997).

254   **'the solid testimony of truth'** Written on the preparatory drawing for the frontispiece to *Los Caprichos*, Prado, Madrid.

255   **one of the owls . . . grasps the artist's chalk holder** See Juliet Wilson Bareau, *Goya. La Década de 'Los Caprichos' Dibujos-y aguafuertes* (Madrid, 1992), pp. 9–13.

256   **'I'm not afraid of witches . . .'** Goya to Martin Zapater, February 1784, in Francisco Goya, *Letters of Love and Friendship in Translation*, trans. Jacqueline Hara (Lewiston, Queenston and Lampeter, 1997), p. 650.

257   **For Baudelaire** Charles Baudelaire, 'Quelques caricaturistes étrangers', *Oeuvres complètes* (Paris, 1968), p. 388.

    such scenes . . . turned into pure spectacle Roger Malbert, 'Introduction', *The Disparates*, Catalogue, South Bank Touring Exhibition (London, 1997), pp. 6–11. The *Disparates* have had a difficult history: they were hidden away when Goya left Spain for France in 1824 and were not arranged and edited by the artist, only inscribed in fourteen instances on the proofs by his hand. Eighteen of the prints were not published until 1864, under the misleading rubric, *Los Proverbios. Merry Folly* echoes an early tapestry cartoon for 'Blind Man's Buff', and the painting, *El Pelele* (The Straw Mannequin) of 1791–2; Cristina García Rodero has photographed a similar game, being played today in Spain. It is related to 'Bumps', the ambiguous celebration visited on birthday girls and boys at school in England, or winners of races or other athletic events.

    terms for new, inner fantasies See Jean Starobinski, 'En Guise de conclusion', in *PhantasiaImaginatio, Atti del V Colloquio internazionale del lessico intellettuale europeo*, ed. M. Fattori and M. Bianchi (Rome, 1986), pp. 565–85.

258   **'the historic Enlightenment . . .'** Terry Castle, *The Female Thermometer: Eighteenth-Century Culture and the Invention of the Uncanny* (Oxford, 1995), p. 17.

    'Besides, it should be noted . . .' Jean-Pierre Cèbe, *La Caricature et la parodie dans le monde antique* (Paris, 1966), p. 354.

259   **'Radiates, vegetables . . . they were men!'** H.P. Lovecraft, 'At the Mountains of Madness', in *Tales of H. P. Lovecraft*, ed. Joyce Carol Oates (Hopewell, New Jersey, 1997), pp. 137–221, quoted by Victoria Nelson in 'H.P. Lovecraft and the Great Heresies', *Raritan*, Winter, 1996, pp. 92–121.

261   **'A crucial distinction . . . today's chimaerae'** For the idea of the Counter-Enlightenment, see Isaiah Berlin, 'The Counter-Enlightenment', and 'Vico and the Ideal of Enlightenment', in *Against the Current: Essays in the History of Ideas*, ed. Henry Hardy (Oxford, 1991), pp. 1–24, 120–9.

CHAPTER 12: CIRCE'S SWINE: 'WIZARD AND BRUTE'

264   **From St. Augustine to James Joyce** St. Augustine, *City of God*, Book XVIII, p. xvii, ed. David Knowles, trans. Henry Bettenson (Harmondsworth 1972); James Joyce, *Ulysses* [1922], ed. H.W. Gabler *et al.* (London, 1984), pp. 350–497; see Merritt Y. Hughes, 'Spenser's Acrasia and the Circe of the Renaissance', *Journal of the History of Ideas*, 4 (1943), pp. 381–99; see also Judith Yarnall, *Transformations of Circe: The History of an Enchantress* (Urbana and Chicago, 1994) and Gareth Roberts, 'The Descendants of Circe: Witches and Renaissance Fictions', in Jonathan Barry, Marianne Hester and Gareth Roberts (eds.), *Witchcraft in Early Modern Europe* (Cambridge, 1996), pp. 183–206.

265   **'. . . O such deformities!'** John Keats, *Endymion*, Book III, lines 500–4, in John Keats, *Poetical Works*, ed. H.W. Garrod (Oxford, 1982), p. 118.

    Machiavelli . . . Giambattista Gelli Niccolò Machiavelli, 'L'Asino', in *Tutte le opere* (Florence, 1971), p. 971; John Baptist Gelli, *Circe* [1548], trans. H. Layng (London, 1744); first French translation by Denis Sauvage (1550), English translation by Henry

Iden (1557). See Emmanuel Hatzantonis, 'I Geniali rimaneggiamenti dell'episodio Omerico di Circe in Apollonio Rodio e Plutarco', *Revue belge de philologie et d'histoire*, 54, no. 1 (1976), pp. 5–24.

266   **'No doubt . . . journey to Hades'** Richard Brilliant, 'Kirke's Men: Swine and Sweethearts', in Cohen (ed.), *The Distaff Side*, pp. 165–74.

pens and sties . . . 'swine' There follows a crux in the text, which some translators take as specifying '[swine] of nine years old'—that is, no longer sucking pigs, but ready for the table? (Though nine years sounds on the old, tough side.)

Forbes-Irving . . . excellent study P.M.C. Forbes-Irving, *Metamorphosis in Greek Myths* (Oxford, 1990), pp. 176–7.

267   **In Homer, Circe** See Apollonius of Rhodes, *The Voyage of Argo*, trans. and ed. E.V. Rieu (Harmondsworth, 1971).

268   **'a lady full of wantonness . . .'** Christine de Pizan, *The Epistle of Othea to Hector, or the Boke of Knighthode*, trans. Stephen Scrope, ed. George F. Warner (London, 1904), pp. 111–12.

'In like wise the flesh . . .' *The English Works of Sir Thomas More* (London, 1931), Vol. 1, pp. 10–11, quoted in Hughes, 'Spenser's Acrasia', p. 388.

The Dutch engraver Joost van den Vondel, *De Vernieuwde Gulden Winckel der kunstlievenden Nederlanders* (The Golden Shop of Art-loving Netherlanders, Revised), (Amsterdam, 1622).

supping together . . . more dangerous Brilliant, 'Kirke's Men', pp. 165–74, 167; Roberts, 'Descendants of Circe', pp. 198–201.

269   **Modern translators** Brilliant, for example, gives 'the dread goddess who talks with mortals . . .' 'Kirke's Men', p. 165. Homer, *Odyssey*, trans. Robert Fagles (New York, 1996), p. 234.

270   **'And now, as easily . . .'** Homer, *Odyssey*, trans. E.V. Rieu, Book XXI, lines 406–11.

271   **'I denti più che d'avorio . . .'** Machiavelli, 'L'Asino', in *Tutte le opere*, p. 964.

272   **She is captured . . . in the manner of a sibyl** Dosso may be picturing Melissa at the moment in *Orlando Furioso* when she undoes the spells of Alcina and frees the transformed knights from their enchanted shapes. Another Dossi, of around 1520, in the Galleria Borghese in Rome, has been traditionally called after Homer's *maga*, but has now been reidentified as one of Ariosto's enchantresses, either the good fairy Melissa, or the wicked Alcina. Both are in many ways avatars of Circe, but they also possessed the power to turn people into plants; several of these arboreal metamorphoses are taking place on the upper left. The figure in this case is richly apparelled and turbaned, again in the manner of a sibyl, with a torch of knowledge lit at a significant lamp. See Felton Gibbons, *Dosso and Battista Dossi: Court Painters at Ferrara* (Princeton, 1968), pp. 198–216.

273   **Knowledge of female monstrosity** I am grateful to Adriana Cavarero, and her talk 'Ondine Goes Away', delivered at Warwick University on November 4, 1996, for her thoughts about sirens' and monsters' relation to speech.

Circe gives him a brew Graves, *Greek Myths*, Vol. 1, pp. 299–300.

274   **abbé Fénelon** Fénelon, 'Ulysse et Gryllus', from *L'Education des filles: dialogues des morts*, ed. Emile Faguet (Paris, 1933), pp. 157–63; see Stephen T. Newmyer, 'Of Pigs and People: Plutarch and the French Beast Fable', *Ploutarchos*, 13, no. 1 (December 1996), pp. 15–22.

He defends his companions See Plutarch, 'On the Use of Reason by "Irrational" Animals', in *Essays*, trans. Robin Waterfield, ed. I. Kidd (Harmondsworth, 1992), pp. 375–99; see also Plutarch, 'Beasts are rational', in *Plutarch's Moralia*, trans. Harold Cherniss and William C. Helmbald (Cambridge, Mass., 1976), Vol. XII, pp. 489–533.

a 1930s study of 'theriophily' George Boas, *The Happy Beast in French Thought of the*

Seventeenth Century (Baltimore, 1933); also, George Boas, 'Theriophily', in *Dictionary of the History of Ideas*, ed. Philip P. Wiener (New York, 1973), pp. 384–9.

Foucault's comment   Michel Foucault, *Madness and Civilization: A History of Insanity in the Age of Reason*, trans. Richard Howard (New York, 1965), p. 20.

275   '"Who was he when he was human?"'   Plutarch, *Essays*, p. 384.

276   'the animal mind . . .'   Ibid., pp. 386–7.

In all these points   See Richard Sorabji, *Animal Minds and Human Morals* (London, 1993), pp. 119–21.

'This is just the case . . .'   Gelli, *Circe*, p. 50.

one of Plato's *Dialogues*   Plato, *Laches*, 197b, in *The Dialogues of Plato*, trans. R.E. Allen (New Haven and London, 1996), Vol. 3, p. 80.

278   '**You know about Circe's drink . . .**'   Horace, *Epistles*, I.2 'To Lollius Maximus', lines 23–9, quoted in Brilliant, 'Kirke's Men', p. 170.

Dante does not identify   Dante, *Inferno*, Canto VI, line 52, p. 88. I am grateful to Ann Lawson Lucas for bringing this use of pig imagery in Dante to my notice.

the latest evolutionary speculations   The lystrosaur, a most horrible- (and greedy-) looking beast, was recreated with animatronics by the zoologist Peter Ward for the Channel 4 programme *Equinox* on British television, in November 1997. Despite its fierce appearance, the primordial boar was placid.

Erasmus knew   Desiderius Erasmus, *In Praise of Folly* [1915] (London, 1951), pp. xix, 70.

279   '**Viver con voi . . .**'   Machiavelli, 'L'Asino', pp. 973–6.

Spenser . . . reintroduced Gryllus   Hughes, 'Spenser's Acrasia', pp. 381–99; see also Roberts, 'Descendants of Circe', pp. 200–3; Gareth Roberts, 'Circe' and Supriya Chaudhuri, 'Grill', in A.C. Hamilton et al. (eds), *The Spenser Encylopaedia* (Toronto, Buffalo and London, 1990), pp. 165–7, 342.

Amyot of Lyon . . . Philemon Holland   Plutarch, *Les Oeuvres morales de Plutarque*, trans. J. Amyot, 2 vols (Lyon, 1588), Vol. 1, p. 969; Plutarch, *The Philosophie commonlie called The Morals*, trans. Philemon Holland of Coventry (London, 1603), p. 562.

280   **Spenser's moral line . . . 'hoggish mind'**   Spenser, *The Faerie Queene*, Book II, Canto XII, verses 86–7, ed. J.W. Hales (London, 1910), 2 vols., vol. 1, p. 334.

281   '**lewd immodest beastliness . . .**'   John Marston, 'Reactio', in *The Poems of John Marston*, ed. Arnold Davenport (Liverpool, 1961), line 30, p. 821; cf. John Davies, 'Epigram against Grillus, his Greedy Gluttony', in *The Scourge of Folly* (London, 1611), and, in a lighter vein, George Alexander Stevens, 'The Birthday of Folly', in *Songs Comicall and Satyrical* (London, 1788): 'Circe was a precious piece—/A plague upon the gypsey!/She dol'd out drink somewhere in Greece/And made her tenants tipsy.'

282   '**Wherefore did Nature . . .**'   John Milton, *Comus*, ed. A.W. Verity (Cambridge, 1913), 77, 710–14, p. 29.

Chapter 13: 'All My Business Is My Song'

284   '**. . . such . . . images are called grylli**'   'Idem iocosis nomine Gryllum derediculi habitus pinxit, unde id genus picturae grylli vocantur' (Pliny the Elder, *Historia Naturalis*, Book 35, ed. A. Ernout, Paris, 1962, pp. 84–5.

285   **phantasmagorias on antique gems**   Jurgis Baltrusaitis, *Le Moyen Age fantastique: antiquités et exotisme dans l'art gothique* (Paris, 1955) pp. 11–13; Michael Camille, *Image on the Edge: the Margins of Medieval Art* (London, 1992), pp. 37–8; A. Furtwangler, *Die antiken Gemmen*, 3 vols, Vol. 3: *Geschichte der Steinschneidekunst* (Leipzig and Berlin, 1900), see Vol. 1, plate XIVI, examples 33–9, Vol. 3, pp. 113 ff.;

Roy Kotansky, 'The Chnoubis Gem from Tel Dor', *The Israel Exploration Journal* 47, 1997, pp. 257–60.

'. . . **full grillich he lookes!**' *Alliterative Morte Arthure* in *King's Arthur's Death: The Middle English Stanzaic Morte Arthur* and *Alliterative Morte Arthure*, ed. Larry D. Benson (Exeter, 1986), p. 147.

286   **Many terracotta figurines** See Jean Starobinski, *Portrait de l'artiste en saltimbanque* (Geneva, 1970), p. 70.

Circe herself was the subject Peter Wiseman, 'Satyrs in Rome', in *Historiography and Imagination* (Exeter, 1994), p. 76; R. Seaford, *Euripides's Cyclops* (Oxford, 1984), pp. 22, 24.

287   **the form survives most vividly** Baltrusaitis, *Le Moyen Age fantastique*, pp. 11–53.

inventions of Hieronymus Bosch Felipe de Guevara, *Comentarios de la Pintura*, c. 1560–63, quoted by Baltrusaitis, ibid., p. 46.

satanic—as 'juggling fiends . . .' See Michel de Certeau, *The Mystic Fable: The Sixteenth and Seventeenth Centuries*, trans. Michael B. Smith (Chicago and London, 1992), Vol. 1, pp. 66–7, 72: 'In the end these "disorderly" combinations rely more on proportion (miniaturizing, hypertrophy) than hybridization (by substitution, inversion, and collage) . . . The aesthetics of the Garden do not consist in generating new lights for intelligibility, but in extinguishing it.'

the Latin word for cricket Pliny, *Historia Naturalis*, Book 29, 39, 140, 143, ed. A. Ernout, pp. 65–8. *Grillos* does not appear in extant ancient or Hellenistic Greek sources meaning cricket, and the Greek word for hog is often spelt with one lambda only. But, intriguingly, while the stem *gril*- does still apply to pigs' grunting and related activity in modern Greek, *grillos* does now mean cricket, as in Italian *grillo*. I am most grateful to Peter Wiseman, Professor of Classics at Exeter University and author of *Remus: A Roman Myth* (Cambridge, 1995), who encouraged me to continue this line of inquiry, maintaining that there exists an irregular verb: 'I hypothesize, you conjecture, s/he speculates.'

Pigs and crickets . . . little in common Malcolm Davies and Jeharaney Kathirithamby, *Greek Insects* (London, 1986), p. 134. An alternative word for crickets—*akris*—may derive from either a word for piping or crying, or from another root, meaning to eat. Both possibilities extend the sympathy between the otherwise odd species of animal, the hog and the cicada (pp. 135–6). Other words for members of the genus—*mantis* and *mastax*—are derived from words for chewing and eating.

'The cricket is extraordinary . . .' Jean Henri Fabre, *Insects*, trans. Alexander Texeira De Mattos and Bernard Maill (London, 1979), p. 36.

Aristotle notes Aristotle, *De Anima* (On the Soul), II, VIII, 420 b, trans. W.S. Hett (Cambridge, Mass., 1995), pp. 114–19; Bart Verschaffel, 'Where There's a Voice, There's a Body', *Theaterschrift* (Theater and Music), (Brussels, Berlin, Dresden, Vienna, 1995), pp. 37–49.

288   **'Some are endowed . . .'** Aristotle, *History of Animals*, Book I, line 31, in *The Complete Works of Aristotle*, ed. Jonathan Barnes (Princeton, 1984), p. 777.

an extremely vocal exception Strictly speaking, the male chirps by rubbing a scraper on one forewing along a row of around 50–250 teeth on the opposite forewing. 'Pierus thinks it is formed in the snout or proboscis: Proclus Dadichus, by rubbing together of their wings [. . .] that is to say, the Grasshopper sings by frequent clapping of its wings together, and so it makes a noise. And the same thinks Hesiod. But that they sing not with their mouth all men know, as neither by the rubbing of their wings together as the Locust doth, but by the reverberation of a little membrane under the *flabells*; (so they call those two coverings behind the hinder thighs clearing to the belly) or as Aristotle describes it in brief. They make this noise by reason of the air striking against the membrane under the midriffe . . . The noise which they make is caused by the rubbing of their wings one against the other, as *Pliny* witnesseth. Jacob Garret an industrious and ingenious apothecary did the same with the wings pluckt off and rubbed together, very cunningly imitated them: insomuch that I wonder at Scaliger, who said it cometh from a kind of I know not what follicle and pipe placed in the hollow part of the belly; and at Sabinus who ascribeth it to the collision or grating together of their teeth, the which Pliny also, but falsely, writeth of the locusts.' (Edward Topsell, *The History of Four-footed Beasts, Serpents, Whereunto is now Added, The Theater of Insects; or, Lesser Living Creatures . . . Collected out of the* Writings of Conrad Gesner *and Other* Authors, London, 1658, pp. 992–5). The way the insects make their chirrup distinguishes grasshoppers and locusts, for unlike crickets, they rub their *hind femur* against their forewings. Davies and Kathirithamby, *Greek Insects*, p. 135.

'It is by the friction . . .' Aristotle, 'Youth, Old Age, Life and Death and Respiration' 15 (9) 475a, 5–21, in Barnes (ed.), *Complete Works of Aristotle*, p. 755.

289   one Greek poet . . . his 'songstress' Leonidas of Tarentum, quoted in Davies and Kathirithamby, *Greek Insects*, pp. 136–7.

Longus' pastoral love idyll Longus, *Daphnis and Chloe* (Cambridge, Mass. and London, 1978) Book 1.14.4, pp. 30–1.

Yet Aristotle himself Aristotle, 'On Things Heard', 804a 23ff.; in Barnes (ed.), *Complete Works of Aristotle*, p. 1235; Davies and Kathirithamby, *Greek Insects*, p. 137.

The insect was famous Aesop, *The Fables*, trans. S.A. Handford [1954] (Harmondsworth, 1964), p. 142.

In the *Phaedrus* Socrates, in Plato, *Phaedrus*, trans. Walter Hamilton (Harmondsworth, 1973), p. 70.

290   'Vous chantiez?' Jean de la Fontaine, *Fables*, Book I in *Œuvres complètes, Vol. 1: Fables, contes et nouvelles*, ed. Jean-Pierre Collinet (Paris, 1991), p. 31.

'Ah, cried the Ant—' Abraham Aesop, *Fables in Verse*, trans. J. Newbery (London, 1757).

La Fontaine also bowed Jean de la Fontaine, 'Les Compagnons d'Ulysse', *Fables*, Book XII, in La Fontaine, *Œuvres complètes*, pp. 451–4.

lampooning human folly See Stephen T. Newmyer, 'Of Pigs and People: Plutarch and the French Beast Fable', *Ploutarchos*, 13, no. 1 (December 1996), p. 20; Richard Danner, *Patterns of Irony in the Fables of La Fontaine* (Athens, Ohio, 1985), pp. 112–27.

'the grasshopper is the merriest creature . . .' Edward Baldwin [William Godwin], *Fables Ancient and Modern* (London, 1805), p. 12.

Budgen . . . *Acheta domestica* L. M. Budgen, *Episodes of Insect Life by Acheta Domestica* (London, 1849–51). In *Illustrated Books, Children's Books and Related Drawings*, Sotheby's Catalogue (London, 1988), pp. 35–6. The cover illustration of a collection of lullabies shows Harlequin riding on a puppet cricket, saddled and bridled. *Berceuses du monde entier*, Harmonia mundi, K 294 CM 546.

291   these are not the same species See John Burton, *The Oxford Book of Insects* (Oxford, 1968), pp. 10–17.

Aesop . . . dwarfish and misshapen 'Life of Aesop', in *Fables in Verse* trans. J. Newbery (London, 1757), p. vii.

Renaissance editions *Aesopus vita et fabulae Latine et Italice* (Naples, 1485), pl. 17.

Sold into the household Nicholas Howe, 'Fabling Beasts: Traces in Memory', *Social Research*, 62, no. 3 (Fall 1995), pp. 641–59. *The Life* survives in a tenth-century MS., Pierpont Morgan MS M.397. See also Jan M. Ziolkowski, *Talking Animals: Medieval Latin Beast Poetry 750–1150* (Philadelphia, 1993).

'a most outrageous passion' Abraham Aesop, trans. Newbery, pp. xiii–xiv.

292   demonstrations of Aesop's cleverness Warner, *Beast*, p. 163.

292   **Velázquez portrayed the poet** Nicholas Tromans, 'The Iconography of Velázquez's Aesop', *Journal of the Warburg and Courtauld Institutes*, 59 (1996), pp. 332–6.

293   **'The pleasant new work and jests . . .'** *Opera nuova piacevole e da ridere de un villano lavoratore nomato Grillo quale volse diventar medico, in rima istoriata* (Venice, 1521); see Irving Lavin, 'Bernini and the Art of Social Satire', in *Drawings by Gianlorenzo Bernini from the Museum der Bildenden Kunste, Leipzig, East Germany* (Princeton, 1981), pp. 39–54.
       Bruegel is looking Svetlana Alpers, 'Bruegel's Festive Peasants', *Simiolus*, 1972–3, pp. 163–76.
       'The poetry of earth . . .' John Keats, 'On the Grasshopper and the Cricket', in *Keats: The Poetical Works*, ed. H.W. Garrod [1956], (Oxford, 1982), p. 40.

294   **Song, dance . . . improvidence** Keats ferociously rejected her blandishments in *Endymion*, where he follows Ovid and depicts 'hell-born Circe' casting vicious spells in jealous spite. Keats' poem contradicts itself, since Glaucus, Circe's victim, also possesses comparable powers of enchantment, and greets the young Endymion as his prophesied saviour; together they then revive 'all lovers, whom fell storms have doom'd to die . . .' Endymion moves through the crowd, and 'all were re-animated'. It is not clear who gives Glaucus the parchment which contains the spell that revives the lovers, but it sounds like Circean magic. John Keats, *Endymion*, lines 477–710, ibid., pp. 117–23.
       Collodi . . . il Grillo Parlante Carlo Collodi, *The Adventures of Pinocchio*, trans. Ann Lawson Lucas (Oxford, 1996), pp. 12–13; see also her article 'Epiphany and Metamorphosis: The Significance of Animal Characters in *Pinocchio* and *Alice*', *Italian Studies*, forthcoming.
       Collodi was a reformer See Lucas, 'Introduction', *Pinocchio*, pp. vii–li.
       as Socrates describes Plato, *Phaedrus*, trans. Walter Hamilton (Harmondsworth, 1973), p. 70.

295   **The meanings that deformity . . . carries** I am much indebted to Mariët Westermann and Margaret Carroll for their insights into this theme in several conversations.
       a garden of delights See Michel de Certeau, *The Mystic Fable*, Vol. 1, pp. 49–72.

296   **Charles Perrault's *conte*** 'Ricky with the Tuft', from Perrault, *Fairy Tales*, trans. Carter, pp. 99–110.
       '"Come buy," cried a Jew . . .' B.A.T., *The History of Mother Twaddle, and the Marvellous Atchievments [sic] of Her Son Jack* (London, 1807).
       'All things change . . .' Ovid, *Metamorphoses*, trans. Innes Book XV, p. 339.

297   **Alice as a huge walking head** Lewis Carroll, *Alice's Adventures under Ground, the Facsimile*, ed. Russell Ash [1985] (London, 1995), no page numbers.

298   **Bes, the Egyptian god of portals** Véronique Dasen, *The Dwarfs in Ancient Egypt and Greece* (Oxford, 1993).

300   **ants . . . take advantage of crickets** Fabre, *Insects*, p. 36.

CHAPTER 14: 'FEE FIE FO FUM'

302   **'Tiens, Ravagio . . .'** Marie-Catherine D'Aulnoy, *Les Contes de fées*, 2 vols., (Paris, 1956) pp. 179–205, p. 180; *The Fairy Tales of Madame d'Aulnoy*, trans. Anne Thackeray Ritchie (London, 1892), p. 145.

303   **'The Orange Tree'** *The Diverting Works of the Countess d'Anois* (London, 1707), and in *Queen Mab: A Select Collection of Tales of the Fairies* (London, 1782).

304   **There is humour and gratification** Maria Tatar, *Off With Their Heads! Fairy Tales and the Culture of Childhood* (Princeton, 1992), pp. 22–50.

304–5 **Basile's tales . . . Circean point of view** See Piera Schiavo, 'G.B. Basile: il riso impossibile nel "Cunto de li Cunti"', *Quarto Quaderno di filologia, lingua e letteratura* *italiana* (Verona, 1992), pp. 105–21.

305 **Basile probably collected** See Nancy L. Canepa, '"*Quanto 'nc'e da ccà a lo luoco dove aggio da ire?*" Giambattista Basile's Quest for the Literary Fairy Tale', in *Out of the Woods: The Origins of the Literary Fairy Tale in Italy and France* (Detroit, 1997), pp. 37–80.

the very absurdity of a kindly ogre See Antonella Ansani, 'Beauty and the Hag: Appearance and Reality in Basile's *Lo Cunto de li cunti*', ibid., pp. 81–98.

male author as mouthpiece See Ruth B. Bottigheimer, 'Straparola's *Piacevoli Notti*: Rags-to-Riches Fairy Tales as Urban Creations', *Merveilles et Contes*, 7 (Dec. 1994), pp. 281–95.

306 **'Era costui un nanerottolo . . .'** Giambattista Basile, *Il Racconto dei racconti*, trans. Ruggero Guarini (Milan, 1994), p. 29.

307 **'remembering that he had heard . . .'** Ibid., pp. 199–200.

The old woman . . . promises Marchetta See Warner, *Beast*, pp. 209–40, where this kind of alliance is explored more fully.

'io giuro per . . . i tre testimoni . . .' Basil, *Racconto*, p. 456.

310 **'female laughter'** Adriana Cavarero, *In Spite of Plato: A Feminist Rewriting of Ancient Philosophy*, trans. Serena Anderlini-D'Onofrio and Áine O'Healy (Oxford, 1995), pp. 31–50.

Calvino . . . Italian folk tales Italo Calvino, 'Introduction', in *Italian Folk Tales*, trans. George Martin (Harmondsworth, 1982), pp. xviii–xxiii.

one ogre attracts an iron tower See Warner, *Beast*, p. 55.

311 **(I have proposed elsewhere . . .)** Ibid., pp. 259–72.

312 **'sheep and hogs . . . candles'** *History of Jack and the Giants* (London, 1775), pp. 5–6.

Brobdingnagians Jonathan Swift, *Gulliver's Travels*, ed. Christopher Fox (Boston, 1995), pp. 120–1.

'Why, what a nasty trick . . .' Perrault, *Fairy Tales*, trans. Carter, pp. 124–5.

314 **giant-killing tales . . . 'Old Grumbo . . .'** See *Popular Fairy Tales; or, a Lilliputian Library, containing twenty-six choice pieces of Fancy and Fiction, by those renowned personages of King Oberon, Queen Mab, Mother Goose, Mother Bunch, Master Puck, and other Distinguished Personages at the Court of the Fairies—Now first collected and revised by Benjamin Tabart* (London, not before 1818), pp. 153–5; see also, *The History of Tom Thumb: a tale for the nursery* (London, 1804) and *The Life and Death of Tom Thumb, the little giant. And Grumbo the great giant, king of the country of eagles* (Edinburgh, 1720) in *Old Chapbooks, Fairy Histories, Romances and Folktales* (Bodleian, Harding A.64; no. 7).

English entertainments *Tabart's Collection of Popular Stories for the Nursery*, Part III (London, 1804). Bodleian Douce S 568; see also, *Popular Fairy Tales—Now first collected and revised by Benjamin Tabart*, p. 142; writing blank, December 31, 1810, John Johnson Collection, Bodleian Library, Oxford; *Popular Fairy Tales*, p. 105.

315 **the famous 'Jack and the Beanstalk'** *The History of Jack and the Beanstalk* (London, 1807).

Tommy Trip's exploits 'The Adventures of Little Tommy Trip & his Dog Jouler', in *Fables in Verse for the Improvement of the Young & the Old by Abraham Aesop, Esq. To which are added, Fables in Verse & Prose, with the Conversation of the Birds & Beasts. At their several Meetings, Routs & Assemblies by WOGLOG the great GIANT. Illustrated with a variety of curious CUTS by the best MASTERS. And an account of the LIVES of the AUTHORS* (London, 1767, pp. xxxi–xxxvi, 50–2.

316 **'this giant . . . made of basket-work . . .'** This passage appears in the 1770 edition, pp. 138–44.

'The Giant and the Orphan' B.K. Borgohain and P.C. Roy Chaudhury, *Folktales of*

Nagaland, Manipur, Mizoram, and Tripura (New Delhi, 1994), pp. 99–100, quoted by Lucien Miller in 'Southern Silk Route Tales: Hospitality, Cannibalism and the Other', *Marvels and Tales*, 9, no. 2 (1995), p. 150.

'strewn with bones and skulls' *Jack the Giant Killer*, 1775.

317 'and out dropt his Tripes . . .' 'The History of Jack and the Giants' (Shrewsbury, *c.* 1711), in Iona and Peter Opie (eds), *The Classic Fairy Tales* (Oxford, 1974), p. 55.

hardly ever includes girls See Marie-Jeanne L'Héritier, 'The Subtle Princess', trans. Gilbert Adair in Warner (ed.), *Wonder Tales*, pp. 65–9. Finette bamboozles the villain-ous seducer, by using one of Jack and Tom Thumb's well-tried tricks—placing a dummy in her bed. By this stratagem she succeeds in defending herself against his advances—and it is significant that both her sisters, who have foolishly believed in his false love, are pregnant by him.

''Tis our chief delight . . .' Farley, *Songs Sung at Covent Garden*, 2 vols (1784, 1803), Vol. 2, pp. 15–16.

320 in 1807 . . . premises on Skinner Street Don Locke, *A Fantasy of Reason: The Life and Thought of William Godwin* (London, 1980), pp. 212–16.

'the old-fashioned presents . . .' *Works of Charles Lamb, Memoir 1865*, cited by Mrs. L.C. Field in *The Child and His Book* [1895] pp. 285–6, noted by Peter Opie in his MS commentary to William Godwin, Bodleian Library, Oxford.

321 At the end, social wrongs are righted One psychoanalyst has commented, however, that the bad giant who kills Jack's father is merely a split-off side of his father and a projection of Jack's own desires. According to this interpretation, the beanstalk takes on less than political connotations: 'frustrated in his dreams [Jack] has an erection—the beanstalk—and climbs over his own penis' (Geza Roheim, *The Gates of the Dream*), (New York, 1952), p. 358).

a shepherd 'with his flock . . .' Mary Wollstonecraft Shelley (Godwin), *Mounseer Nongtongpaw, Or, the Discoveries of John Bull in a Trip to Paris* (London, 1808); see also Emily W. Sunstein, 'A William Godwin Letter, and Young Mary Godwin's Part in "Mounseer Nongtongpaw"', *Keats-Shelley Journal*, 45 (1996), pp. 19–22.

322 'Of course she had never seen a globe . . .' See Jean-Michel Massing, 'From Greek Proverb to Soap Advert: Washing the Ethiopian', *Journal of the Warburg and Courtauld Institutes*, 58 (1995), pp. 180–201.

323 'in the ordinary Fable book . . .' Edward Baldwin (William Godwin), *Fables Ancient and Modern*, 2 vols (London, 1805), 2, endnotes.

'And I have great doubts . . .' Ibid., p. 82.

324 'Why! You're nothing . . .' Carroll, *Wonderland* (London, 1998), p. 108.

The Monster Book Michael Piquemal and Korky Paul, *The Monster Book of Horrible Horrors* (English version by Peter Haswell) (London, 1995).

325 The famous first quatrain Carroll, *The Rectory Umbrella and Mischmasch* (London, 1932), pp. 139–41.

CHAPTER 15: 'OF THE PALTRINESS OF THINGS'

326 fishes . . . 'enjoy the fun and laughter' Heinrich Hoffmann, 'The Story of Johnny Head-in-Air', in *Struwwelpeter* [1845] (Rutland, 1969), no page numbers.

'Thales was studying . . .' Plato, *Theaetetus*, 174 a–d, trans. M.J. Levett, revised Myles Burnyeat (Indianapolis and Cambridge, 1992), pp. 43–4.

'Whenever he . . . is obliged . . .' Ibid., 174c, p. 44.

This anonymous woman Cavarero, *In Spite of Plato* , pp. 31–56.

327 '"Servant" is a possible . . .' Ibid., p. 53.

'All laughter is allied . . .' Hélène Cixous and Catherine Clément, 'The Guilty One', in *The Newly Born Woman*, trans. Betsy Wing (Manchester, 1986), p. 33.

328 'The ego refuses . . .' Sigmund Freud, 'Humour', in *Complete Works* Vol. 21 (1927–31) (London, 1953), pp. 161–6. Besides the writers cited in these notes, see Luigi Pirandello, 'L'Umorismo', in *Saggi*, ed. Manlio Lo Vecchio Musti (Milan, 1939), pp. 12–176; Gershon Legman, *Rationale of the Dirty Joke: An Analysis of Sexual Humour* (London, 1968); Gillian Bennett (ed.), *Spoken in Jest* (Sheffield, 1991). Interest in the subject is growing and the following recent, lively discussions have also informed my argument: Carl Hill, *The Soul of Wit: Joke Theory from Grimm to Freud* (Lincoln, Nebraska and London, 1993); Barry Sanders, *Sudden Glory: Laughter as Subversive History* (Boston, 1995); Peter L. Berger, *Redeeming Laughter: The Comic Dimension of Human Experience* (Berlin and New York, 1997); Lewis Hyde, *Trickster Makes This World: Mischief, Myth and Art* (New York, 1998).

'The Fat Woodcarver' Lauro Martines, *An Italian Renaissance Sextet: Six Tales in Historical Context*, trans. Murtha Baca (New York, 1994), pp. 171–241.

Bergson . . . 'Our laughter . . .' Henri Bergson, *Laughter: An Essay in the Meaning of the Comic*, trans. Cloudesley Brereton and Fred Rothwell (London, 1911), pp. 6–8.

329 psychotherapists today See Robyn Skinner and John Cleese, *Life and How to Survive It* (London, 1994), pp. 71–87.

'this [arises] not only from Tragedies . . .' As formulated by theatre critics of the group Nil Volentibus Arduum in their treatise *Onderwys in de tooneel-poëzy*, ed. A.J.E. Harmsen (Rotterdam, 1989), quoted by Mariët Westermann in *The Amusements of Jan Steen: Comic Painting in the Seventeenth Century* (Zwolle, 1997), p. 129, n.58.

'Laughter is social . . .' William Gass, *Willie Master's Lonesome Wife* (New York, 1971), no page numbers.

'A joker enjoys privileges . . .' Mary Douglas, 'Jokes', in *Implicit Meanings: Essays in Anthropology* (London, 1975), p. 107.

330 Mark Lamarr . . . four-letter words Exeter Festival, July 1997.

'The joke form . . .' Douglas, *Implicit Meanings*, pp. 90–3.

Hobbes . . . 'sudden glory . . .' Thomas Hobbes, quoted in Sanders, *Sudden Glory*; see also Howard Jacobson, *Seriously Funny: From the Ridiculous to the Sublime* (London, 1997).

'Laughter is satanic . . .' Charles Baudelaire, 'De l'Essence du rire: et généralement du comique dans les arts plastiques', in *Œuvres complètes* (Paris, 1968), pp. 370–8, p. 373.

331 'Laughter . . . also, is a froth . . .' Bergson, *Laughter*, p. 200.

332 a joke . . . 'get it all in.' 'Critique of Aesthetic Judgement', 333, in Immanuel Kant, *Critique of Judgement*, trans. Werner S. Pluhar (Indianapolis and Cambridge, 1987), p. 203, cited John Limon, 'Analytic of the Ridiculous: Mike Nichols and Elaine May', *Raritan*, Winter 1997, pp. 102–22.

'ridicule is an amplification . . .' Longinus, *On the Sublime*, ed. W. Rhys Roberts (Cambridge, 1899), Chapter 39, pp. 140–1.

As Christie Davies comments Christie Davies, *Ethnic Humor around the World* (Bloomington, 1990), pp. 10–13.

334 'What a fuss there is . . .' J. Morgan, 'The London Ladies and the Ojibbeway Indians' (London, n.d.), Street Ballads, John Johnson Collection, Bodleian Library, Oxford, no. 75/101. See Warner, *Managing Monsters*, p. 76, for Caliban's voicing of the same threat in *The Tempest*.

335 'boogie-woogie' . . . devil's music Jonathon Green, in *The Cassell Dictionary of Slang* (London, forthcoming), also suggests that the term was borrowed from descriptions of secondary syphilis, and the jerking spasms associated with the disease.

The devil . . . 'the ape of God' J.W. Janson, *Apes and Ape Lore in the Middle Ages and the Renaissance* (London, 1952); Camille, *Images on the Edge*, pp. 12–13.

336   the 'missing link' See Raymond Corbey, 'Introduction: Missing Links, or the Ape's Place in Nature'; Frank Dougherty, 'Missing Link, Chain of Being, Ape and Man in the Enlightenment: the Argument of the Naturalists', pp. 63–70; Piet de Rooy, 'In Search of Perfection: the Creation of a Missing Link', pp. 195–207, *et al.*, in Raymond Corbey and Bert Theunissen (eds) *Ape, Man, Apeman: Changing Views since 1600* (Leiden, 1993), Gillian Beer, *Forging the Missing Link: Interdisciplinary Stories* (Cambridge, 1991), pp. 1–12; Harriet Ritvo, 'Border Trouble: Shifting the Line between People and Other Animals', *Social Research*, 62, no. 3 (Fall 1995), pp. 481–500.
      King Kong (1933) Marina Warner, 'Cannibals and Kings', in Corbey and Theunissen, (eds), *Ape, Man, Apeman*, pp. 355–63.

337   the trickster monkey See Henry Louis Gates, 'The Blackness of Blackness: A Critique on the Sign and the Signifying Monkey', in *Figures in Black: Words, Signs and the 'Racial' Self* (New York and Oxford, 1987), pp. 235–76.
      Calypsos . . . the word derives 'Calypso', in *A Dictionary of Caribbean-English Usage*, ed. Richard Allsop (Oxford, 1996), pp. 131–2: *Kaa iso* comes specifically from the Efik-Ibibio people, who were 'the established middlemen in the slave trade . . .'
      'Congo Man' On *The Mighty Sparrow, Party Classics*, Vol. 2, no. SCR 3247, West Indies Records, Barbados, 1988.

339   'A joke is seen . . .' Douglas, *Implicit Meanings*, p. 98.

REFLECTION: ALBERT ECKHOUT: *EIGHT BRAZILIAN PORTRAITS*
General note: see Thomas Thomsen, *Albert Eckhout: Ein nederlandischen Maler und sein Gonner Moritz der Brazilianen* (Copenhagen, 1938); Peter Mason, 'Portrayal and Betrayal: the Colonial Gaze in Seventeenth-Century Brazil', *Culture and History*, 6 (Copenhagen: Akademisk Forlag, 1989), pp. 37–62; Peter Whitehead, 'Faces of the New World: the Brazilian Paintings of Albert Eckhout', and Zacharias Wagener, 'Customs of the Brazilians', in *FMR*, 9 (1985), pp. 125–40.

342   the New World's products 'A Marrow's a Banana's Father and a . . . It Started Life as a Gherkin, So It Hasn't Done So Bad', in Herbert Rule and Thomas McGhee, *A Marrow's a Banana's Father* [song sheet] (London, 1926).

343   The series reached Copenhagen Mason, *Portrayal and Betrayal*, pp. 37–62. I am very grateful to Peter Hulme for leading me to this article.

345   gigantic root vegetable See Jon Haarberg and Ralf Norrham, *Nature and Language: A Semiotic Study of Cucurbits in Literature* (London, 1980).

346   Maria Sybilla Merian She published three volumes about insects, beginning with *The Wonderful Metamorphosis of Caterpillars* (1679). See David Scrase, *Flower Drawings* (Cambridge, 1997), p. 30.
      Merian studied the . . . fruits of the region Maria Sibylla Merian, *Metamorphosis Insectorum Surinamensium* [Amsterdam, 1705] (London, 1980–1); see Natalie Zemon Davis, *Women on the Margins: Three Seventeenth-Century Lives* (Cambridge, Mass., 1995), pp. 141–216, 295–339.

347   'plants and insects . . .' Jean de Labadie, *Traité du soi et des diverses sortes de soi* (d'Herford, 1672), pp. 8–9, quoted in Davis, *Women on the Margins*, p. 163.
      the 'peacock flower' Davis, *Women on the Margins*, p. 185.

CHAPTER 16: GOING BANANAS
348   'Laughter is reducible . . .' Georges Bataille 'Laughter', in *The Bataille Reader*, ed. Fred Botting and Scott Wilson (Oxford, 1997), pp. 59–63, published in *Le Coupable* (Paris, 1944), pp. 60–1.

350   our closeness to animals See C.W. Andrews and Hugh J.L. Beadnell, *A Preliminary Note on Some New Mammals from the Upper Eocene of Egypt* (Cairo, 1902), pl. IV;

seen at the Apes exhibition, Leiden, July 1993.

351   **'If the man who threw this . . .'** Daniel Farson, *Marie Lloyd and Music Hall* (London, 1972), p. 53.

The High Sign Written by Buster Keaton and Eddie Cline, 21 minutes. In *Killer, the Game of Assassination* (Indiana, 1981), a live role-playing fantasy game by Steve Jackson, there is a section in the rule book called, 'Modern Weapons', which includes 'Bananas (Class A)'. It continues: 'A Banana is the ultimate non-violent weapon. To attack with a banana, you must get within three feet of your victim, draw your banana, and shout "Bang!" Simultaneous attacks are double kills.

'A banana requires no marksmanship. However, a certain amount of skill is required, since a banana is hard to conceal and not truly suitable for a quick-draw attack. If the banana is crushed while in the assassin's pocket, it cannot be used, though it still may be eaten.

'The banana is also the safest pistol from the assassin's point of view. Bystanders are not likely to intervene when one person chases another down the street brandishing a banana. Indeed, they may not believe that they saw it' (p. 19). A 'how-to' illustration follows.

much more likely booby traps I have been given a signed affidavit, however, by Elaine Tobin, a graduate student at the University of Pittsburgh, to the effect that on April 10, 1997, she did slip on a bananaskin, in the basement of the Cathedral of Learning.

the banana's shape For example, A. Frazzini, Paul de Frank and Irving Mills, 'When Banana Skins Are Falling', featured by Geoffrey Gelder and his Kettner's Five (London, 1926), and Ted Waite, 'I've Never Seen a Straight Banana' (London, 1926). My thanks to Max Tyler of the British Music Hall Society for his help with these references, and to John Whitehorn, at Express Prints, for supplying the songsheets.

One circulating story K.M. Briggs (ed.), *A Dictionary of British Folk Tales*, 4 vols. (London, 1971), Vol. 2, pp. 87–8. Briggs collected it herself, in 1944, in RAF Errol, Perthshire, probably, the note tells us, from Mary Studholme, from Cumberland. 'Woman Eats her First Banana', Tale Type 1339B; E.W. Baughman, *Type and Motif Index of the Folktales of England and North America* (Bloomington, 1966), numbers it under 'The Wise and the Foolish' as J22214 (b).

352   **'Unzip a banana'** I am very pleased that Anthony Barnett reminded me of this campaign, the first in his reckoning to use open sexual innuendo.

Tommy 'Banana' Johnson *Viz Comic: The Big Hard One* (London, *c.* 1985), pp. 83, 93.

353   **'. . . the height of humor has been scaled'** William Gass, *Willie Master's Lonesome Wife* (New York, 1971)

Alice Guy-Blaché Born in 1873, Guy became secretary to Léon Gaumont, and the story goes that in the 1890s, when the Lumière brothers and Gaumont were discussing, like proper boys, the minutiae and possibilities of film technology and equipment, and she was taking the minutes, she stopped afterwards to ask her boss if she might be allowed to do something with it all—tell some stories, stage some gags, for example. He allowed her, and from 1902 she made twenty feature-length movies, as well as over a hundred more with synchronized sound. (Her work is gradually being rediscovered on the ends of reels or ghosted within other footage.) Alison McMahan, '*Madame a des envies:* Alice Guy and the Craving for Comedy', during the BFI conference 'The Silent Pioneers: Women in the Early Film Industry', June 10, 1995. *Women Direct*, short film of 1985, in Channel 4's series 'The Eleventh Hour'. My thanks also to Louise Anderson for organizing this event and to Laura Mulvey for her introductory remarks.

'The message of a standard rite . . .' Mary Douglas, *Implicit Meanings*, p. 103.

cinematic début as phallic icon When I viewed the film at the BFI, I was worried that the beggar's lunch might have been a salami—in black and white it is hard to say and she wolfs it sideways, not end up; however Alison McMahan, who introduced me to Alice Guy's films, definitely identifies it as the fruit.

Giorgio de Chirico *The Transformed Dream* is in the St. Louis Art Museum; *The Uncertainty of the Poet* in the Tate Gallery, London.

354 'tendency to oscillate . . .' Ernst Gombrich, *Sense of Order*, p. 272.

'To dream of bananas . . .' Gustavus Hindman Miller, *Ten Thousand Dreams Interpreted*, ed. A.G. Farnell [1901] (New York, 1979), p. 58.

riotous mock of male anatomy Linda Nochlin, *Women, Art, and Power and Other Essays* (London, 1988), p. 142.

355 '**Top banana**' Phil Silvers made a not very funny, but very shouty musical called *Top Banana* (1953) which includes a number that goes 'If you want to be the top banana, you've got to start at the bottom of the branch'.

'**Two banana, four banana . . .**' Words and music by Ritchie Adams and Mark Barkan, London, 1968.

'**We could see quite clearly . . . much worse down there . . .**' Nick Hornby, *Fever Pitch* (London, 1992), pp. 188–9; Pete Davies, *All Played Out: The Full Story of Italia '90* (London, 1991), p. 254.

'**The joke works . . .**' Douglas, *Implicit Meanings*, p. 106.

358 **staple crop** See Giles Foden, *The Last King of Scotland* (London, 1998), pp. 98–9.

'**luscious phallic banana of death? . . .**' My thanks to Wendy Doniger O'Flaherty for passing this story on to me, from *Splitting the Difference: Gender and Myth in Ancient Greece and India* (Chicago and London, forthcoming).

'**Of Adams Apple tree . . .**' Thomas Johnson, (ed.), *The Herball or Generall Historie of Plantes gathered by John Gerarde* (London, 1636), pp. 1514–17; see John Prest, *The Garden of Eden: The Botanic Garden and the Re-Creation of Paradise* (New Haven and London, 1981), pp. 79 ff.

the vegetable lamb . . . God's flora John Parkinson, *Paradisi in sole* (1629) quoted in Prest, *Garden of Eden*, pp. 7, 50–1.

359 **Linnaeus believed** Linnaeus, *Musa Cliffortiana* (Louvain, 1736); see Prest, *Garden of Eden*, pp. 80–1.

gymnosophists . . . ate a banana Anon., *Fruit of the Wisemen*, brochure of Fyffes Group Ltd., n.d.

'**And as the fruit of the Banana-tree . . .**' Reverend Griffith Hughes, *The National History of Barbados* (1750), reprinted London, 1972, p. 176.

inspired linguistic slips I am very grateful to Polly Pattullo for pointing out this slippage to me.

'**extreme travell with childe . . .**' Johnson, *Herball*, pp. 843–6; cf. 'Birthwort' (*Aristolochia clematitis*) which was used to help with births, as its name suggests, and has leaves shaped like a uterus. Ibid., pp. 846–9.

the word is West African Charles de Rochefort (Jacques Amproux), *Histoire naturelle et morale des îles antilles de l'Amérique* (Rotterdam, 1658), p. 91 includes an engraving of the Banana-tree and fruit; it makes an English appearance in the 1729 translation of William Dampier's *Voyages* (1697).

360 '**something like a calf's heart**' John G. Stedman, *Narrative of an Expedition against the Revolted Negroes of Surinam* (London, 1796), pp. 371–3.

'**Fibrous and dangling down . . .**' Wallace Stevens, 'Floral Decoration for Bananas', in *Collected Poems* (London, 1959), pp. 53–4.

361 **American fruit companies insist** See Cynthia McEnloe, *Bananas, Beaches and Bases: Making Feminist Sense of International Politics* (London, 1989).

its nutritional values Rohan Daft, 'Bananas Are the Only Fruit', *GQ/Active*, November 1997, pp. 72–5.

An equestrian portrait drawing The French-born artist Volozon, worked for the American Republic, decorating the Capitol in Philadelphia (1811–20), *Voyage aux îles d'Amerique*, Archives Nationales de France, Paris, April–July 1992, Catalogue, pp. 281–2.

362 **Douanier Rousseau** See for example *Still Life of Tropical Fruit* (1908).

364 **'It is Cocteau . . .'** See Phyllis Rose, *Jazz Cleopatra: Josephine Baker in Her Time* (London, 1989) and Jean-Claude Baker and Chris Chase, *Josephine: The Hungry Heart* (New York, 1993).

367 **Carmen Miranda . . . The Gang's All Here** See Martin Rubin, *Showstoppers: Busby Berkeley and the Tradition of Spectacle* (New York, 1993). My thanks to Matthew Roper, at the University of Pittsburgh Department of History of Art for taping the film for me.
She breaks into a samba Rubin, *Showstoppers*, pp. 159–70.

368 **Miranda became too foreign** See the documentary *Bananas Is My Business* (1994), directed by Helena Solberg and David Meyer; also *Carmen Miranda: The South American Way* (1996), the Discovery Channel biography. My thanks to Maggie Staats Simmons for giving me this video.

369 **'the laughter of a group'** Bergson, *Laughter*, p. 5.
Pirandello's thesis Luigi Pirandello, 'L'Umorismo', in *Saggi*, ed. Manlio Lo Vecchio Musti (Milan, 1939), pp. 13–176.
dictators allow jesters Umberto Eco, 'The Frames of Comic Freedom', in Thomas A. Sebeok and Marcia E. Erickson (eds), *Carnival!* (Berlin and New York, 1984), pp. 1–9.

370 **Faulkner's As I Lay Dying** The closing pages find the family in Jefferson: they have acquired a graphophone, the new Mrs. Bundren has false teeth, and they are all eating bananas. See Susan Willis, 'Learning from the Banana', in *A Primer for Everyday Life* (London, 1991), pp. 42–61.
A naval officer . . . recalled a scene My thanks to Adam Sisman, who remembered his father telling him this story.

371 **Auberon Waugh remembered** Auberon Waugh, *Will This Do?* (London, 1991), quoted in Louise Guinness (ed.), *Fathers: An Anthology* (London, 1996), p. 35.
rococo opening of Gravity's Rainbow Thomas Pynchon, *Gravity's Rainbow* [1973] (London, 1995), pp. 3–10.
Attitudes have . . . altered Nobuyoshi Araki, a Japanese photographer who specializes in erotica, took a photograph of a young girl in her underwear sitting on the floor in the corner of a room, eating a banana; the effect, in the late 1990s, is troublingly pædophiliac, as it is intended to be.
The passion for bananas See *Europe Without Walls: Art, Posters and Revolution 1989–93*, Catalogue (Manchester City Art Galleries, 1993).

373 **'the woman who is leading a life . . .'** Johnston was quoting from Ralph Hall Caine, *The Cruise of 'Port Kingston'* (London, 1908), see Petrine Archer-Straw, *Photos and Phantasms: Harry Johnston's Photographs of the Caribbean*, Catalogue (Royal Geographical Society, London, and National Gallery of Jamaica, 1998), p. 53.

Epilogue: 'Snip! Snap! Snip!'

374 **Struwwelpeter . . . vigorously defaced** June Rogers, 'Struwwelpeter: Changing Attitudes 1845–1979', lecture given at the Osborne Collection, Toronto, February 8, 1979.
Paolo Uccello, The Miracle . . . In the Galleria Nazionale delle Marche (Palazzo Ducale), Urbino. See Franco and Stefano Borsi, *Paolo Uccello*, trans. Elfreda Powell (London, *c.* 1994), pp. 338–40.

375 **Christian anti-Semitism** See Chaucer, 'The Prioress's Tale' in *The Canterbury Tales* for

the legend of 'Little St. Hugh'; Miri Rubin, *Corpus Christi: The Eucharist in Late Medieval Culture* (Cambridge, 1991); R. Po-chia Hsia, *Trent 1475: Stories of a Ritual Murder Trial* (New Haven, 1992), pp. 92–3, 128–9, and Caryl Phillips' fine novel, *The Nature of Blood* (London, 1997), which dramatizes these incidents and their causes.

376 **Jews were scapegoated** Lester K. Little, *Religious Poverty and the Profit Economy in Medieval Europe* (London, 1978), p. 55, quoted by Camille, *The Gothic Idol: Ideology and Image-Making in Medieval Art* (Cambridge, 1989), p. 185.
Christian anxiety, 'about adapting . . .' Camille, *Gothic Idol*, pp. 185–6.
the mystery of the Eucharist *Ibid.*, p. 217.

377 **'I take as the most profound mystery . . .'** Joyce Carol Oates, 'Reflections on the Grotesque', in *Gothic Transmutations of Horror in Late Twentieth Century Art* (Boston, 1997), p. 35.
the impulse to find a culprit See René Girard, *La Violence et le sacré* (Paris, 1972), pp. 105–34 and Walter Burkert, *Creation of the Sacred: Tracks of Biology in Early Religions* (Cambridge, Mass., 1996), pp. 51–3.
the eyes of the demons My thanks to Jean-Michel Massing for this observation.
'They break through the miraculous . . .' Benedicta Ward, *Miracles and the Medieval Mind: Theory, Record and Event 1000–1215* (Philadelphia, 1982), pp. 13–16, quoted in Camille, *Gothic Idol*, p. 219.

378 **The sudden, violent death** See Girard, *Violence*, pp. 9–61, 373–407, and Burkert, *Creation of the Sacred*, pp. 34–55 on the pervasive structure of sacrifice in human society.
the power that images exercise See David Freedberg, *The Power of Images: Studies in the History and Theory of Response* (Chicago and London, 1989) and Dario Gamboni, *The Destruction of Art: Iconoclasm and Vandalism since the French Revolution* (London, 1997), pp. 190–211.

379 **If the Royal Academy had yielded** See Marina Warner, 'Peroxide Mug-Shot', *London Review of Books*, 20, no. 1 January 1, 1998.

380 ***Struwwelpeter . . .* Hoffman's pastiches** See Diane Mason, 'Masturbation, Little Suck-A-Thumb and *Struwwelpeter*', in *Udolpho*, 32 (Spring 1998), pp. 24–9 for an interesting analysis of the book's relation to medical anxieties; Freud interpreted the story of Conrad in the light of the castration complex.
'This famous book . . .' Heinrich Hoffmann, *Slovenly Peter, Or Pretty Stories and Funny Pictures for Little Children* (Rutland, Vermont and Tokyo, 1969).

381 **Conrad has not really . . .** This is how the guide explained the matter in the Hoffmann museum in Frankfurt, which I visited in 1995.
'. . . was there *really* someone under the bed?' I'm very grateful to Charles Glass for this story.

382 **damage . . . intentional rather than random** See Robin Briggs, *Witches and Neighbours: The Social and Cultural Context of Witchcraft* (London, 1996), for a clear and incisive account of this manoeuvre, as well as a most helpful bibliography of the ever-burgeoning literature on witchcraft.
In Ireland in 1895 Hubert Butler, 'The Eggman and the Fairies', in *The Sub-Prefect Should Have Held His Tongue and Other Essays*, ed. R.F. Foster (London, 1990), pp. 102–12.
a survey conducted . . . in the United States See Richard Louv, 'The Bogeyman Syndrome', in *Childhood's Future* (New York, 1997) for a wise analysis of the social and personal costs of scaremongering; also Frank Furedi, *Culture of Fear*, pp. 107–145.

383 **Manmade monsters** See Lee Silver, *Remaking Eden: Cloning and Beyond in a Brave New World* (London, 1998), reviewed by Phillip Kitcher, *London Review of Books*, March 5, 1998, pp. 15–16.
At the weird end See Denis Duclos, *The Werewolf Complex*, trans. Amanda Pingree

(Oxford, 1998); and Elaine Showalter, *Hystories*, pp. 189–201.

384   'The more a work frightens . . .' Franco Moretti, The Dialectic of Fear', *New Left Review*, 136, November–December 1982, pp. 67–85, 85.

Yet babies and children Babies under the age of one form the group most at risk from murder in England and Wales: 44 deaths per million compared to national average of 12 per million; after infants, most casualties occur in the 16–49 age group of men, not among children under the age of 16. Men are more likely to be killed by a stranger (38 per cent) than women (14 per cent). *Criminal Statistics England and Wales* (1996), cited in *The Independent*, November 15, 1997. The Department of Justice in the United States does not corroborate the oft-repeated figure of 4,000 fatal abductions of children by strangers per annum. It assesses the number at around 150. See David Finklehor, co-director of Family Research Laboratory, University of New Hampshire, *National Incidents: Study of Missing Children*, forthcoming, cited in Louv, *Childhood's Future*.

cars pose a greater danger See Mary Douglas and Aaron Wildafsky, *Risk and Culture: An Essay on the Selection of Technical and Environmental Dangers* (Berkeley, 1983).

385   society fails . . . children's interests See James R. Kincaid, *Erotic Innocence*, passim, for a humane and impassioned plea for a change in focus.

a foster parent who had killed babies Her name is given as Carol Hanson; see Helena Kennedy, *Eve Was Framed: Women and British Justice* (London, 1992), pp. 246–7.

measures . . . to control paedophiles See Ray Wyre, 'The Sex Offender in the Community', Gulbenkian Foundation paper (London, 1988), for a sober, careful discussion of the problem and the necessity for calm.

386   'There is a conflict . . .' Kennedy, *Eve Was Framed*, p. 246.

387   'Hitler's willing executioners' See Slavoj Žižek, *The Plague of Fantasies* (London, 1997), p. 57.

ACKNOWLEDGEMENTS

NOTE ON FRONTISPIECES AND MOTIFS

FRONTISPIECE *In Sanzoles del Vino, Zamora, Spain, on the feast of St. Stephen, the day after Christmas, El Zangarrón gives chase to the youths and children of the town; he wears a pig's bladder and carries a bag for offerings. According to local legend, the townspeople stoned the statue of San Esteban for failing to do as they asked and El Zangarrón appeared to defend him. Photographed in 1980 by Cristina García Rodero.*

PART ONE *The Egyptian god Bes (p. 20), with his grotesque grimace and his straddling pose, guarded the bedchambers and lying-in rooms of new mothers.*

PART TWO *The Victorian composer James William Elliott included a soothing lullaby (p. 184) in his anthology* National Nursery Rhymes and Nursery Songs, *London, 1870.*

PART THREE *Gryllus as spear-carrier (p. 238). Arendt van Bolten, engraving, c. 1635.*

Initial grylli from Les Heures de Thérouanne, *Paris, thirteenth century, drawn by hand in* Le Moyen-age fantastique *by Jurgis Baltrusaitis (Paris, 1955).*

LIST OF COLOUR PLATES

The author and publishers are grateful to the following individuals and institutions for permission to reproduce illustrations:

Between pages 116 and 117:
1 *Saturn Devouring His Child* by Francisco Goya, Prado Museum, Madrid
2 *Judith*, 1821–23, by Francisco Goya, Prado Museum, Madrid
3 *The Burial of The Sardine*, c. 1812–19, by Francisco Goya, Prado Museum, Madrid
4 *Celebrations for the feast of Corpus Christi*, anonymous photographer
5 *The Last Judgement*, right wing, c.1480, by Hans Memling, Pomorskie Museum, Gdansk
6, 7 & 8 The climax of the Patum, photographs by Luigi Arxiu (7), John Dewe Matthews (6 & 8)
9 &10 *The Haywain*, left and right wings, early sixteenth century, by Hieronymus Bosch, Prado Museum, Madrid
11 *The Fairy Feller's Master-Stroke*, 1855–64, by Richard Dadd, Tate Gallery, London
12 A moth-hornet *(Sesia apiformis)*, E. and D. Hosking, Frank Lane Picture Agency
13 Cryptic Katydid (probably *Aegimia elongata*), © Brian Rogers, Biofotos
14 *4th Duke of Marlborough and Family*, by Joshua Reynolds, Blenheim Palace, reproduced by kind permission of His Grace the Duke of Marlborough
15 'The Fat of the Land' by the Prodigy, XL Recordings, Konrad Wothe and Frank Lane Picture Agency
16 A larva of a Puss Moth *(Cerura vinula)*, © G.E. Hyde, Frank Lane Picture Agency
17 A Spanish *guita*, anonymous photographer
18 South American butterfly, © Heather Angel
19 A Spanish *cabezudo*, anonymous photographer
20 Radioactive warning sign
21 The Viceroy butterfly *(Basilarchia archippus)*, © Larry West, Frank Lane Picture Agency
22 The Monarch butterfly *(Danaus plexippus)*, © Tom and Pam Gardner, Frank Lane Picture Agency
23 Froghopper in warning livery *(Cercopis vulnerata)*, © Heather Angel
24 Warhammer warrior, © Games Workshop Ltd.

Between pages 308 and 309:
25 *The Massacre of the Innocents*, early seventeenth century, by Guido Reni, Pinacoteca Nazionale, Bologna
26 *The Rest on the Flight into Egypt*, 1595–96, by Caravaggio, Galleria Doria-Pamphili, Rome
27 *The Temptation of St. Anthony*, 1490, by Hieronymous Bosch, Prado Museum, Madrid
28 *Circe and Her Lovers in a Landscape*, c.1518–25, by Dosso Dossi, National Gallery of Art, Washington, DC
29 *Tupi Woman*, 1641–43, by Albert Eckhout, National Museum, Copenhagen

30 *The Dream*, 1910, by Henri Rousseau, Museum of Modern Art, New York
31 Botanical illustrations, by Maria Sibylla Merian, from the author's collection
32 *El Chinaco y la China*, c.1850, by José Agustin Arrieta, private collection
33 *The Miracle of the Profaned Host*, 1467–68, by Paolo Uccello, Palazzo Ducale, Urbino

Black and White Illustrations
Black and white illustrations are reproduced by kind permission of the following:
Allen Memorial Art Museum, Oberlin College, Ohio, 127; © A & M Records Ltd., 355; Ascherburg, Hopwood & Crew Ltd., 203 (bottom); Ashmolean Museum, Oxford, 168, 244 (right); © Bobby Baker, 73; Barnaby's Picture Library, London, 100; B.L. Kearley Ltd., for *The God Beneath The Sea* by Leon Garfield and Edward Blishen, illustrations © Charles Keeping, Gollancz Children's Paperbacks, 70; Bodleian Library, Oxford, 297, 303, 315, 318, 319; The Bodley Head, for *Where The Wild Things Are* by Maurice Sendak, 148, and Editions Milan for *The Monster Book of Horrible Horrors* by Michel Piquemal, illustrations © Korky Paul, 324; Bridgeman Art Library, London, 363; British Film Institute, 47, 270, 366; British Library, 8, for *The Languages of Alchemy* by Gareth Roberts, 56; British Museum, 29, 108, 131, 134, 174, 238, 241, 288; photo © Stephan Buzas, 373; Byzantine Museum, Athens and G. Ballis, 98; Chatto & Windus, for *A Parents' Survival Guide* © Michael Heath, 159; Conway Library, Courtauld Institute of Art, 105; Courtauld Institute of Art, 255, 259; Dover Publications Inc., for *The Picture Book of Devils, Demons and Witchcraft* by Ernst & Johanna Lehner, 183; Fitzwilliam Museum, University of Cambridge, 11, 20, 35, 179 (right), 249, 286; Frankfurter Goethe Museum, 26; Frank Lane Picture Agency, 177 (Martin B. Withers), 178 (Eric and David Hosking); Fratelli Alinari, Florence, 214; © Games Workshop Ltd., 15; Graphics Modern USA, 207; Id Software Inc., 13; Janine Antoni and Luhring Augustine, 76; Koninklijke Bibliotheek, The Hague, 10; Kunsthalle, Hamburg, 52; © LSH, Stockholm, 164; Lambeth Palace Library, photo Bridgeman Art Library, 102; Louvre, Paris, 170; John Dewe Matthews, 119; © Mick Sharp, 244 (centre); Museo di San Marco, Florence, photo Scala, 94; The Museum of The Moving Image, 19; The Music Vault, EMI, 203 (top); National Gallery, London, 193; National Museum, Copenhagen, 341, 342, 343, 344; Osborne Collection, Toronto Public Library, 184, 304; Prado Museum, Madrid 49, 55; Progetti Museali Editore, for *Ulisse: il mito e la memoria*, 85; Random House UK Ltd., for *Not Now, Bernard* by David McKee, 151; © Christina García Rodero, frontispiece, 112, 113, 123; The Ronald Grant Archive, 12, 261, 368; Royal Armouries, 165; Royal Geographical Society, 369; Scala Istituto Fotografico Editoriale, 187, 188, 189; Nigel Sutton, 111; Ulm Museum, 128; University of Missouri Columbia, for *The Dance of Death in Book Illustration*, xii; © Viz Comic/Virgin Books, for *Viz Comic: The Big Hard One*, 349; Warburg Institute, University of London, 292; Wellcome Institute, 93; Witt Library, Courtauld Institute of Art, 22, 41, 103, 133, 209. All other illustrations are from the author's collection.

Text Credits
The author and publishers are grateful for permission to quote the following:
'Futile—the Winds—' by Emily Dickinson by kind permission of the publishers and the Trustees of Amherst College from *The Poems of Emily Dickinson*, Thomas H. Johnson, ed., The Belknap Press of Harvard University Press, Cambridge, Mass., and Faber & Faber, London (Copyright © 1951, 1955, 1979, 1983 by the President and Fellows of Harvard College); 'Sad Cure' by Graham Greene, David Higham Associates, London; extracts from the *Theogony* by Hesiod, translated by Dorothea Wender (Penguin Books, 1973) and from the *Odyssey*, translated by E.V. Rieu, are reproduced by permission of Penguin Books Limited; *Punch and Judy* by Harrison Birtwhistle and Stephen Prusin, © 1968 by Universal Edition (London) Ltd, London, reproduced by permission; *Porgy and Bess* by George Gershwin, and 'The Tra La La Song', Warner / Chappell Music Limited, London W6 8BS, reproduced by permission of International Music Publications Limited; 'Folklore by the Fireside' by Alessandro Falassi, University of Texas Press; Horace poem from 'Kirke's Men' by Richard Brilliant in *The Distaff Side*, Beth Cohen, ed., Oxford University Press, New York; 'The Congo Man' by permission of International Music Network Ltd; extracts from *The Waste Land* by T.S. Eliot, *The Bounty* by Derek Walcott, *Tales from Ovid* by Ted Hughes and *The Kaisers of Carnunton* by Tony Harrison in *Plays Three*, all by permission of Faber & Faber, London.

The publishers and author have made every effort to trace copyright holders and will be happy to correct any mistakes or omissions in future editions.

INDEX